The Collected Essays of
CHRISTOPHER Hill

By the same author:

The Century of Revolution, 1603-1714
Society and Puritanism in Pre-Revolutionary England
Intellectual Origins of the English Revolution
The World Turned Upside Down
Milton and the English Revolution
The Experience of Defeat: Milton and Some Contemporaries
The Collected Essays of Christopher Hill, Volume I:
   Writing and Revolution in 17th Century England
The Collected Essays of Christopher Hill, Volume II:
   Religion and Politics in 17th Century England

The Collected Essays of
CHRISTOPHER
Hill

Volume Three
People and Ideas in
17th Century England

THE UNIVERSITY OF MASSACHUSETTS PRESS

Amherst

First published in the United States of America
in 1986 by the University of Massachusetts Press
Box 429 Amherst Ma 01004

Printed in Great Britain

Library of Congress Cataloging in Publication Data
(Revised for vol. 3)

Hill, Christopher, 1912-
   The collected essays of Christopher Hill.

   Includes bibliographical references and index.
   Contents: 1.   Writing and revolution in 17th-century
England — v.   2.   Religion and politics in seventeenth-
century England.   3.   People and ideas in 17th-century
England.
1.   Great Britain — History — Stuarts, 1604-1714 —
Collected works.   2.   English literature — 17th century —
History and criticism — Collected works.   3.   Literature
and society — Great Britain — Collected works.   I.   Title.
DA375.H54   1986   941.06   84-14446

ISBN 0-87023-467-6 (v. 1)
ISBN 0-87023-503-6 (v. 2)
ISBN 0-87023-550-8 (v. 3)

For Eric Hobsbawm,
who knows about everything, including the seventeenth century

Contents

Preface   ix
Acknowledgments   x
Abbreviations   xi

I   Introduction — Two Fragments on History   1
      1   Partial Historians and Total History   3
      2   Answers and Questions   10

II   The English Revolution   19
      3   Parliament and People in 17th-century England   21
          Postscript   65
      4   Oliver Cromwell   68
      5   A Bourgeois Revolution?   94
          Postscript   123
      6   Braudel and the State   125

III   People   143
      7   The Lisle Letters   145
      8   Radical Pirates?   161
      9   Sex, Marriage and Parish Registers   188
          Postscript   210
      10 Male Homosexuality in 17th-century
          England   226
      11 Karl Marx and Britain   236

IV   Ideas   245
      12 The Poor and the People   247
      13 Science and Magic   274
          Postscript   297
      14 Covenant Theology and the Concept of
          "A Public Person"   300

Index   325

Preface

In preceding volumes of this series I have explained that the contents derive from articles, lectures and reviews written over many years. I have tried to eliminate repetitions and overlaps, and have done a certain amount of rewriting when I found I disagreed with myself, or wanted to elaborate a point. Thus a main reason for reprinting Chapter 8 was to restore a vivid piece of journalism by Marx which was editorially excluded when it first appeared.

As usual I have many debts to acknowledge. I have mentioned in the notes those of which I am most conscious. I am especially grateful to Simon Adams, E.J.I. Allen, Martine Brant, Tim Curtis, John Gillis, Ann Hughes, William Hunt, M.J. Ingram, J.R. Jones, Richard Popkin, Wilfrid Prest, Gary Puckrein, Barry Reay, Judith Richards, Pete Steffens, P.A. Trent and David Zaret for allowing me to read work in advance of publication. I received help and encouragement of various kinds from Alan Bray, Vincent Caretta, Arthur Clegg, Penelope Corfield, Rodney Hilton, Eric Hobsbawm, P.A. Jewell, John Morrill, Marcus Rediker, L.F. Solt, Eileen Spring, David Taylor, Keith Thomas, Edward Thompson and C.M. Williams. None of them is responsible for the errors which stubbornly remain. The staff of Harvester Press were as always patient, skilful and friendly. Bridget inspired me by her example, stimulated me by exchange of ideas and made it impossible for me not to keep at it. She helped especially with chapter 9 and its postscript.

Spelling, capitalization and punctuation have been modernized, except in titles of books. All books quoted were printed in London unless otherwise stated.

Acknowledgments

Earlier versions of the pieces collected in this volume were originally published elsewhere. I am grateful for permission to include them in this collection.

"Partial Historians and Total History" appeared in the *Times Literary Supplement* for 24 November 1972. "Answers and Questions" was an Introduction to *History and Culture*, published by Random House in 1977. "Parliament and People in 17th-century England" appeared in *Past and Present*, No. 92, 1981, and is reprinted with the permission of the Past and Present Society. "Oliver Cromwell" was originally Historical Association Pamphlet No. 58, published in 1958. "A Bourgeois Revolution?" appeared in *Three British Revolutions, 1641, 1688, 1776* (ed. J. G. A. Pocock, Princeton U.P., 1980). "Braudel and the State" is based on reviews published in *History and Theory*, VIII (1969), *New Society*, 26 June 1980, and the *New Statesman*, 20 July 1984. "The Lisle Letters" appeared in the *New York Review of Books*, 11 June 1981. "Radical Pirates?" was published in *The Origins of Anglo-American Radicalism* (ed. M. and J. Jacob, Allen and Unwin, 1984). "Sex, Marriage and Parish Registers" is based on a review in *Economic History Review*, XXXI (1978). "Male Homosexuality in 17th-century England" appeared in *History Workshop Journal*, No. 18, 1984; "Karl Marx and Britain" in the *Guardian*, 12 February 1983. "The Poor and the People" was published in a Festschrift for George Rude, *History from Below: Studies in Popular Protest and Popular Ideology* (ed. F. Krantz, Concordia University, Montreal, 1985). "Science and Magic" appeared in a Festschrift for Eric Hobsbawm, *Culture, Ideology and Politics* (ed. R. Samuel and G. Stedman Jones, Routledge and Kegan Paul, 1983), "The Covenant Theology and the Concept of 'A Public Person'" in a Festschrift for C. B. Macpherson, *Powers, Possessions and Freedom* (ed. A. Kontos, Toronto U.P., 1979).

Abbreviations

The following abbreviations have been used:

Ec. H.R.	*Economic History Review.*
H.M.S.O.	Her Majesty's Stationery Office.
I.O.E.R.	C. Hill, *Intellectual Origins of the English Revolution* (Panther edn., 1972). First published 1965.
M.C.P.W.	Ed. D.M. Wolfe, *Complete Prose Works of John Milton* (Yale U.P., 8 vols., 1953-82).
M.E.R.	C. Hill, *Milton and the English Revolution* (1977); (Penguin edn., 1979).
P. and P.	*Past and Present.*
T.R.H.S.	*Transactions of the Royal Historical Society.*
U.P.	University Press.
W.T.U.D.	C. Hill, *The World Turned Upside Down* (Penguin edn., 1975). First published 1972.

I Introduction –
Two Fragments on History

1. Partial Historians and Total History[1]

"Historians rarely know what they are up to."[*]

The writing of history has always been a battle against the self-styled expert. The history of religion was slowly and painfully taken out of the hands of theologians, constitutional history from the lawyers. But new hydra heads spring up continually. In the past the problem was to make historians of, for example, religion and law aware of the existence of economics. Today the problem is to convince econometric historians of the existence of religion and law, to persuade statisticians that some things in the past are more countable than others, and that there is not much point in counting the uncountable.

Historians of science are divided into those who stress the internal self-sufficient development of scientific ideas and those who stress the effects of society on science. I once heard a distinguished historian of science argue in all seriousness that a knowledge of seventeenth-century history could add nothing to our understanding of Sir Isaac Newton. In the narrowest mathematical sense this may be true; but the Newtonian synthesis is an ideological as well as a mathematical fact. Newton's secretiveness, his silences and suppressions, his passion for alchemy and Biblical prophecy, his strange, twisted personality, can be better understood if we know something of the difficult world in which he lived and was knighted. It is no doubt true that too many historians venture to write about science on the basis of less knowledge than they would think necessary before writing about theology or law, and therefore have been guilty of over-simplifications which need to be corrected. But there is no

---

* E. H. Carr, "Some random reflections on Soviet Industrialization", in *The Rise of Capitalism* (ed. D.S. Landes, New York, 1966), p. 273.

reason to suppose that science is intrinsically any more difficult for historians to understand than theology or law. Charles Webster has recently very correctly criticized those whom he calls "restrictive" historians of science, and argued that their conclusions even about science in the narrowest sense are vitiated by their approach.[2] We must not allow historians of science an autonomy that has rightly been denied to theologians and lawyers, nor permit them to assume that the great thinkers of the past inhabited an ivory-towered vacuum.

Historians of culture suffer from the same apparently inevitable tendency to strive for autonomy. Yet culture is the product of a given society. Any attempt to treat it otherwise means succumbing to what Marx called "the illusion of the epoch", to taking at their face value things which should be evaluated in relation to a larger whole. Thus Peter Laslett described England before the Industrial Revolution as "a one-class society": "the mass of Englishmen cannot be counted as part of England for historical purposes"; "the minority lived for all the rest".[3] A similar error is that of historians who assume that seventeenth-century critics of Oxford and Cambridge were enemies of education and learning. In each case the propaganda of seventeenth-century defenders of privilege has been swallowed whole.

The word "culture" meets with a certain resistance in England. It is all right when used by archaeologists and restricted to material objects; or by anthropologists dealing with relatively unsophisticated societies. But on the whole historians have preferred the word "civilization". "Culture" in its wider usage has a slightly alien flavour — Germanic, Marxist, at best American. There are *Histories of Culture* by the American Preserved Smith and by the English Marxist Jack Lindsay; Arnold Toynbee, Clive Bell and Lord Clark write about civilization and civilizations.

Some of the best cultural history in English has in fact been written by Marxists, or by Marxist-influenced historians. I think of George Thomson on ancient Greece, E. A. Thompson on the barbarian invaders, Edward Thompson and Eric Hobsbawm on eighteenth and nineteenth-century England, Joseph Needham on China, Isaac Deutscher on the Soviet Union, Ernst Meyer and Diana Poulton on English music, Frederick Antal and Eric Mercer on English art. Such unlikely characters as Sir John Hicks in England, Fernand Braudel in France and T. S. Kuhn in the United States have recently written approvingly of some sort of a return to Marx. The advantage that Marxist-influenced historians have is that they think of history as one, take for granted that there are likely to be connections between the culture and the economics of a society, however difficult it may be to analyse them. The vast rumbling Marxist generalizations at least provoke thought, even if only to contradict. Thus Ernst Fischer: "The epic declined with the age of chivalry, and the novel grew up with the bourgeoisie; ... polyphonic music died together with the feudal system, and homophonic music developed together with the bourgeois age" (*The Necessity of Art*). Discuss.

Good cultural history must stimulate ideas about the society which produced the culture. When Eric Gill said "there was not such a thing as portrait painting before about the year 1480", or the Ogdens tell us that English landscape painting is a seventeenth-century creation, it is clear that the explanation of these facts (assuming for the moment that they are facts) must go beyond the range of art history in its narrow technical sense. A historian of ideas like V. Harris, historians of music like Ernst Meyer, G. M. Ruff and D. A. Wilson, a literary historian like A. Harbage, a historian of law like W. R. Prest, all agree in seeing a crisis in English culture around 1615. It does not need any great expertise to relate this to a crisis in English economic and political life. But once the various crises are seen as part of the social whole, they all gain in significance. It may or may not affect our attitude to the art concerned to hear Van Dyck described as "a conscious propagandist of absolutism", or to be told that one of Baroque's most "unequivocal statements" in English painting was made in the inner chambers of Windsor Castle which the papist Antonio Verrio decorated for Charles II. But such considerations cannot but affect our view of the place of Van Dyck, Verrio and, indeed, Baroque in English cultural history, and help us to avoid lazy over-simplifications like "Puritan hostility to art". The hostility of most Puritans was to art of a particular kind.

The great economic historians were great historians of culture — Adam Smith, Karl Marx, Maynard Keynes. Even a generation ago an historian in search of intellectual stimulus would turn to the pages of *Economic History Review*. Now, alas, he is likely to find its pages full of methodological controversies between statisticians who cheer-fully agree that what they are arguing about will not affect our conclusions about the past. One would not need to worry about the mere technologists of economic history if some of them did not attempt cultural generalizations without adequate historical knowledge, or assume that a single key — demography, for instance — will open all doors, when they do not know enough religious and social history even to grasp how unreliable is their basic source, the parish register. Historians should be pluralists. I do not accept what I take to be G. R. Elton's view that political and administrative history is in some sense more significant than social history or the history of culture. The Oxford History of England now seems pretty old-fashioned with its separate chapters on "Education and Science", "The Arts", "Literature", tacked on at the end like a paper tail on to a donkey in the child's game. As in that game, those who did the tacking seem sometimes to have been blindfolded.

No one can be a universal historian these days: all that can be hoped for is modesty in each practitioner, a realization that his specialization gives him only a partial view; and a conscientious attempt, to the best of his ability, to look for connections and inter-relations. Mastery of the techniques — anthropology, computers, is a necessary preliminary. The economic historian, the historian of science or culture, the constitutional historian, like the nineteenth-century antiquarians, will produce raw materials which other historians can use. Modesty, judgment, imagination, a sensitivity to connections: these are what all historians need over and above the special techniques of their particular sub-disciplines, need in order to keep these techniques in their proper place. The attempt to see connections is hazardous and may lead to mistakes. But these can be corrected. Failure to look for connections leads to barrenness, myopia, blinkers.

Economic history is essential to historians of culture because culture is a class phenomenon. L. B. Wright was absolutely correct to isolate *Middle-Class Culture in Elizabethan England* — the culture of the protestant ethic, of the dignity of labour, of love in marriage, plain prose and accurate portraiture — as distinct from the court culture of aristocratic honour, of virtuoso amateurism, of property marriage and a dual sexual ethic, "witty" prose and flattering portraiture. The culture of Van Dyck, Rubens and the court of Louis XIV was very different from the culture of Rembrandt, Bunyan and Milton. Keith Thomas has recently used anthropological techniques to reveal the sub-culture of magic and superstition which existed below both the courtly culture and the middle-class culture. His *Religion and the Decline of Magic* is perhaps the most important contribution to our understanding of English cultural history and indeed English history *tout court*, published in the past generation.

All history should be cultural history, and the best history is. The most significant contribution to the history of religion in seventeenth-century England made during the past decade came in a book called *The Agrarian History of England and Wales, 1500-1640*. Here Joan Thirsk and Alan Everitt distinguish between the culture of the champaign agricultural areas and the culture of the forest and pasture areas: the former stable, docile, controlled, orthodox, the latter mobile, more open, freer, more heretical. Already Professor Everitt is using this as a key to open many doors in the later history of nonconformity. Conversely, one of the most important recent insights into social, political and economic history comes from Patrick Collinson's *The Elizabethan Puritan Movement*, which demonstrates that in the fifteen seventies and fifteen eighties a section of the gentry and peerage, in alliance with town oligarchies, was trying to subordinate the church to its control. This not only throws light on the social basis of Puritanism, it also illuminates the political history of the next century during which this control was fought for, in various guises, and finally won.[4]

Admirable history of English culture in the sixteenth and seventeenth centuries has been written over the past decade by historians of the Warburg Institute. Pride of place must be given to Frances Yates's stimulating books — *Giordano Bruno and the Hermetic Tradition, The Art of Memory*, and *Theatre of the World*, to mention only the most recent. She manages superbly to unite cultural history with total history, to relate her most daringly exotic speculations to the real world in which Bruno, Shakespeare and Robert Fludd lived, to link magic, mathematics and machines, to associate protestant iconoclasm with the evolution of a new philosophic method. Not every historian would accept all that she says, but this is because she bubbles over with ideas which are apt to run away in all directions; but even her errors, if errors they are, are more fertile than most people's truths. D. P. Walker's *The Decline of Hell* similarly deals with intellectual history in a way that is not separated from total history but is an integral part of it. Dr Yates's serious treatment of Hermeticism has been developed by P. M. Rattansi and Charles Webster, who show how this magical ideology of the craftsmen contributed significantly to the scientific revolution.

P. W. Thomas's study of *Sir John Berkenhead, 1617-1679*, suggests that royalist classicism emerged in the defeat and fear of the decade after the civil war. It was the defence mechanism of an insecure élite, their retort to the challenging world of democracy and social insubordination. We may compare the relationship of French classicism to the anxieties and insecurities of the Fronde. There are analogies in other areas of English culture. The restoration brought back bishops, and aimed at restoring traditional certainties against the "enthusiasm" of mechanic preachers and the "atheism" of mechanic philosophers. The propagandists of the Royal Society, some of them a little tarred with the brush of radicalism, took up with gusto the attack on enthusiasm and atheism. Our most religious King, Charles II, was well advised to become patron of the Royal Society as well as head of the Church of England, and to tie both closely to the social hierarchy. It may have been no better for science than it was for religion, but it certainly helped to conserve the newly established order.[5]

In a similar sphere the work of a literary critic like Lionel Trilling gains enormously in depth from his ability to put "literary" questions in a cultural-historical perspective. "Our investigation of sincerity", he says in his recent *Sincerity and Authenticity*, "has no sooner begun than it has led to public and even political considerations." Just because Professor Trilling is intelligently aware of what contemporary historians are up to, he can raise questions of profound interest to those who are not literary specialists — such as the implications of the fact that the word "villain" (on the stage) evolves from the word "villein" at a time of great social mobility, or that the writing of narrative history became old-fashioned simultaneously with the writing of narrative novels.

So I do not think the dearth of formal histories of culture in English is something about which we need worry too much. It is more important that we should not have too narrowly specialized a conception of cultural history, any more than of economic history. Lawrence Stone's majestic *The Crisis of the Aristocracy, 1558-1641*, shows how the best history includes the history of culture: what he has to say about sculpture or about aristocratic patronage of the arts is convincing because he understands the economics of the society. A. L. Rowse, for all his irritating idiosyncrasies, is another historian who sees culture as an integral part of total history, and wrote the better about it because he was a total historian. The history of education, to take another example, is being rewritten with the aid of wills by W. K. Jordan, of statistics by Professor Stone, and with an awareness of the changing social background by Joan Simon and Kenneth Charlton. Since the history of culture exists as a fact, it is perhaps just as well that there are no professors, no departments, no empires, to isolate an autonomous "cultural history" from the rest of history.

NOTES

1. Article in the *Times Literary Supplement*, 24 November 1972. I have left this unchanged: updating would have involved a great deal of rewriting. See especially Peter Burke, *Popular Culture in Early Modern Europe* (1978), ed. Barry Reay, *Popular Culture in Seventeenth-century England* (1985), and David Underdown, *Revel, Riot and Rebellion: Popular Politics and Culture in England, 1603-1660* (1985).
2. Webster, "The Authorship and Significance of *Macaria*", *P. and P.*, 56 (1972).
3. Laslett, *The World We Have Lost* (1965), pp. 19, 52.
4. See p. 214 below.
5. See p. 286 below.

2. *Answers and Questions*[1]

"It is the role of the historian ... to criticize the doctrines accepted in each age as self-evident truths in the light of an experience ampler than, without his assistance, any one of them can command.... Research is a means, not an end, and it is less important to discover new materials than to see the meaning of old."[*]

The word "history" is ambiguous. On the one hand, it means everything that has ever happened in the past; on the other, it refers to what has been written about what is known of the past. History in the first sense is unknowable in its totality. A man living in a small village does not know what is going on behind its hedges; most of what has happened to most of humanity is irrecoverable. We could argue about how much this matters, but the fact is surely indisputable.

History is, therefore, an uncertain discipline. The survival of evidence is often quite haphazard. If we study the distant past, the evidence of archaeology seems random, although it may be true that artifacts like the pyramids and Stonehenge were built to survive and so tell us a good deal about the aspirations of those who planned their erection. But this does not help us to knowledge of those who actually built them, who may or may not have shared the ideological concerns of their social superiors. In later centuries, as we get written or printed evidence, we appear to know more about what life was like. But writing may be used to conceal or distort as well as to reveal; printing has throughout most of the history of most countries been subject to censorship. And again, what happens to survive may give a very lopsided view of the society which produced the writings. Tawney made this point when he said that "the sufferings of the peasantry" were due to the invention of printing.

Historians of the present generation are increasingly conscious of

* R.H. Tawney, "The Study of Economic History", in *History and Society: Essays by R.H. Tawney* (ed. J.M. Winter, 1978, pp. 56, 58).

their ignorance and of the possibility that much of written history is misleading and superficial. The vast bulk of our surviving evidence, until the last few centuries, derives from ruling-class and governmental sources. No sociologist would feel that he could express useful views on what the United States was like today after talking to a Treasury official and a professor of art history. Yet much of the evidence from which we write the history of the last 2500 years is as flimsy as that. Consequently, all historians have to guard very carefully against accepting at face value the self-consoling assumptions of ruling classes and intellectuals in the past. The reason why we think of the Middle Ages in Western Europe as "an age of faith" may be only that those who knew how to write were almost exclusively ecclesiastics.

In our century of the common man we have become embarrassingly aware of how little we know about the lives of ordinary people until relatively recently. About women and children — three quarters of the human race — we are even more ignorant. We can know a few members of the ruling class as individuals in classical Greece or Rome, in Chaucer's or Shakespeare's England. It is virtually impossible to achieve such knowledge about the bottom 80 to 90 per cent of the population until we approach very modern times. So if we are not merely to repeat historical mythology — the self-selected, self-justifying legends of past ruling classes — we are up against great difficulties.

It is not a matter only of ignorance; there is probably a great deal of real distortion in many of our sources. Most of what we know about ancient and medieval heresies and witchcraft, for instance, comes from men so prejudiced against heretics and witches that they were prepared to torture and burn them to death. Most surviving accounts of slave revolts in antiquity and of peasant revolts[2] come from men utterly devoid of sympathy with the rebels' causes. Nor is it only a matter of literary sources, in which the bias is often so obvious that it can be allowed for. Historians of an earlier generation cherished the view that if we could only get behind literary sources into the archives, to government documents, then we should be on firm ground. There is, of course, a sense in which this is true. A tax is a tax: government archives can tell us how much was collected and when. But the more that governmental archives are opened up, the more aware historians become of the truth of William Blake's dictum: "Nothing can be more contemptible than to suppose public records to be true." Their apparent objectivity is frequently spurious. Contemporary civil servants, aware that their archives will soon be opened up to the historian, naturally take steps to remove any evidence that they do not wish posterity to see; anyone who has worked in Whitehall can give examples of this.

But it is not only a matter of deliberate suppression. What is involved is also the unconscious assumptions and prejudices of the administrators, who are no more immune to national and class bias than the authors of "literary sources". Professor G. R. Elton's *Policy and Police: The Enforcement of the Reformation in the Age of Thomas Cromwell* gives a mass of fascinating evidence about what ordinary people thought and said in the fifteen-thirties — but it is ordinary people seen by those trying to govern them. We have little reason to suppose that the lower classes had any more sympathy with the objectives of their governors than the latter had with theirs; the lower we go down the social scale, the less confidence the central government had in its subjects. The events of 1640 to 1660 in England showed how justified this lack of confidence was; but it should make us sceptical of the views of government officials.

A historian has argued recently that, since there is little evidence in ecclesiastical archives that the Scrooby group of Puritans (nucleus of the later Pilgrim Fathers) were persecuted, despite Governor Bradford's later allegation that they were, they must have had some other reason for emigrating.[3] But men and women do not take so decisive a step as emigration without what seem to them good reasons. Only a bias towards the establishment could allow a historian to make such an insinuation. There are stories of atrocities, or alleged atrocities, in the present century where the official version suggests that victims and eye-witnesses grossly exaggerated. We smile at the story of the French general who was discovered amid scenes of catastrophic retreat in March 1918 dictating a dispatch describing his successful advance. When questioned he replied "Mais — c'est pour l'histoire". But suppose his dispatch happened to be the only document that survived? His side won the war, after all, and throughout most of history the defeated leave little evidence. "If we be overcome", Henry of Navarre wrote, "we shall all die condemned heretics". "Rebels and heretics", Adam Smith agreed, "are those unlucky persons who when things have come to a certain degree of violence, have the misfortune to be of the weaker party".[4]

Official documents are no more going to tell us the whole story than diaries, private letters and other unofficial sources. King Alfred exercised a general control over what went into the Anglo-Saxon Chronicle, our main "official" source for his times.[5] Edward I circulated to monasteries his own version of his controversy with Scotland, in order to get it into the chronicles. Official hand-outs about the deposition of Richard II deceived eminent nineteenth-century historians. Under Mary I the records were weeded out in order to eliminate evidence of heresy. Holinshed's *Chronicles*, source of Shakespeare's English history plays, were censored by the Elizabethan government. Almost any official document arising from any government department is engaged in making a case. It therefore omits some facts and arbitrarily emphasizes others. What it leaves out may be well known to contemporary readers, less so to historians. We are not often permitted to glimpse the sort of suppressions and distortions that were revealed in the Ponting case in 1985 and in the Westland farce of 1986.

The historian's job is to piece together the bits of evidence that happen to survive and to make what sense he can of them. He must approach all his sources with a great deal of scepticism: the fact that a document is official does not mean that it is impartial; the fact that a document has remained unpublished for 500 years may simply mean that it was not worth publishing. Superstitious belief in manuscripts, in archives, can be as misleading as naïve acceptance of accounts of historical events written by participants in order to justify themselves in the eyes of posterity.

What I am saying is perhaps less alarming than it may appear. The factual background of most written history is secure enough. No future discovery is likely to shake our belief that a Norman invading army defeated King Harold's troops near Hastings in 1066, that the American colonies declared their independence in 1776, or that Napoleon lost the Battle of Waterloo. But what the Normans were doing there, what the ordinary people thought in 1066, 1776, or 1815 — these are matters on which we are still largely ignorant.

Some progress has been made. Application of anthropological and sociological techniques has enabled the *Annales* school of French historians, and historians like K. V. Thomas and E. P. Thompson in England and Eugene Genovese and Alfred Young in the United States, to cast light on hitherto dark and mysterious areas. We are becoming aware that until the coming of industrialization — and perhaps later — magical beliefs and practices dominated the lives of the population. Religious and other beliefs about which we hear a great deal in traditional sources may in fact have mattered very little to the mass of the people. Historians no longer speak glibly about "ages of faith", are no longer surprised that the bastardy rate was higher in Puritan England than in the Catholic France of the seventeenth century.

Too many historians who believed they were being "objective" were merely ignoring the distorting lenses through which they observed past history. It is easier for a present-day academic to enter into the mode of thought of a bureaucrat in ancient Egypt or eighteenth-century England than it is for him to imagine how ancient Egyptian peasants or eighteenth-century American farmers felt. For this reason there was a short-lived reaction against some of the great trail-blazing writers who opened up the history of ordinary people — R. H. Tawney, G. D. H. Cole, and the Hammonds in England, Carl Becker, L. B. Wright and Vernon Parrington in the United States. The pioneers made mistakes, but these can be corrected. More important, they wrote with imagination and they were sceptical of official attitudes, and this remains of permanent value.

Here we come up against the question of the historian's commitment. He is likely to write better history if he thinks it matters. He may be able to avoid reproducing the illusions of past epochs — mainly ruling-class illusions — if he asks questions that derive from his own society. (He may, of course, introduce the illusions of his own epoch but, since it is very different from most past epochs, the danger, although real, can be avoided.) What is important is that the historian should be aware of what he is doing and make clear to his readers what he is doing. This seems better than thinking one is being objective when one is merely blinkered. The historian must be sceptical of his sources — *all* his sources. He must learn to live imaginatively in the society about which he writes, to participate in it.

History, it has been well said, offers a series of answers to which we do not know the questions. The historian's difficult job is to reconstruct the questions from the recorded answers. This is easier to do when the questions are obviously brash and new — the French Revolution was a question for British radicals; Darwin's *The Origin of Species* was a question for Victorian evangelicals. But historians still argue about the nature of the questions to which the French (or English, or American, or Russian, or Chinese) Revolution was the answer. Most difficult to reconstruct are the questions that were taken for granted by those who answered them or the questions whose novelty is obscured by later events. If a man becomes or stays a Baptist or a Quaker today, for example, the questions include his conviction of the truth of the doctrine of the sect and may include his desire to please or to shock his parents and friends. In the later seventeenth century we should have to add a question about readiness to endure persecution. But it is much more difficult to be certain what questions George Fox and John Bunyan were answering, even though they wrote so much about themselves, for in their case there was no clearly agreed body of doctrine to be taken or left; and, since each of them was the first of his family to be converted to his faith, there was no question of pleasing his family or friends — although there may have been a question about displeasing them. It is hard to reconstruct the questions that faced men in the sixteen-fifties, to which they produced answers deceptively similar to the answers which eighteenth-century Quakers or Baptists gave. But the initial answer, that of Fox and Bunyan, presupposes a very special type of question; the later answers are to different, perhaps simpler questions.

Any serious history, it seems to me, deals with questions. The answers, the narrative, are known. The narrative can be rearranged, but the true originality of the historian lies in identifying questions that seem new to us because they approximate to the questions men and women were originally answering. Historians like Rodney Hilton, Joan Thirsk, A. G. Dickens, Patrick Collinson, Margaret Spufford, Brian Manning, Keith Wrightson, William Hunt, George Rude, Eric Hobsbawm, as well as Keith Thomas and Edward Thompson, identify such new/old questions — to name only the best historians who work on the history of ordinary people in England.

If I am right in so defining the historian's job, this would help to explain why history has to be rewritten in every generation. New bits of experience in the present open our eyes to questions that men had to answer in the past. To deal only with the historiography of the English Revolution: nineteenth-century radicals rediscovered the Levellers, twentieth-century socialists the Diggers. The counter-culture of the later twentieth century helped us to see the significance of Ranters and other drop-out groups. Questions derived from contemporary ecology and feminism helped Carolyn Merchant to write her seminal *The Death of Nature: Women, Ecology and the*

Scientific Revolution.[6] Consider the attention recently given by American historians to the history of blacks, Indians and children, as well as to women and to popular "neutralism" during the American Revolution. Experience in the present helps the historian to sharpen and refine his account of the questions so as to get better answers. If history has any use, it is in deepening our awareness of the process by which society sets questions that men and women, willy-nilly, have to answer. It should make us more aware of the unconscious process of responding to questions which is our daily life.

Today, by contrast with most of the past, the questions are not wholly out of our control. The more we comprehend the question-setting process, the greater the hope of our being able to change the questions, instead of continuing to accept that there is no alternative — as though the questions had been set by some eternal and omnipotent Examiner. For we ourselves participate in setting the questions, even if only passively, by allowing others to set questions for us. We cannot now influence the questions set to Fox and Bunyan but Fox and Bunyan did: they took the whole examining system by the scruff of the neck and worked out new rules. They were not in the long run as successful as they would have wished: their successors could not keep up their pace: they made compromises themselves. Nevertheless, the questions never looked quite the same again once the Society of Friends existed and *The Pilgrim's Progress* had been written.

The English philosopher R. G. Collingwood adjured historians to "think the thoughts of the past". A better, if clumsier, way of expressing it might be to identify the questions that were set to the men and women of past ages. This is less idealistic (in the philosophic sense), for the questions are set by society — or the historical process, if you like. The historian is not primarily interested in the random thoughts of the past; he has to be selective. His concern should be to identify the major questions that men were in fact answering when, for instance, they executed Charles I, established the protectorate of Oliver Cromwell, and then restored Charles II again. The historian is lazily self-indulgent if he or she rethinks any old past thoughts.

The sort of thoughts which some philosophers of history emphasize are those which passed through Caesar's mind when he crossed the Rubicon. Crossing the Rubicon has however become rather an obsession. "Not all facts are important", as Braudel told

Mr Laslett; "only those which have consequences".[7] What matters is not what was actually passing through Caesar's mind at that important historical moment, for that is surely unknowable. He may have been wondering whether his indigestion was due to the cheese he had for lunch.

The important question is the one to which the act of crossing the Rubicon was an answer, the question posed by the political and social set-up of Roman society, which Caesar and his armies were about to recast. This question is vastly complex, and only a historian who knows a great deal about Roman civilization in the first century B.C. can even approximate formulating it correctly. It may be that Caesar never consciously asked himself the question to which crossing the Rubicon was the answer, but his actions answered it nevertheless. "Reasons and opinions concerning acts are not history," Blake observed. "Acts themselves alone are history."

The historian's task, then, is to discover the questions that men and women of a past age were answering and to formulate them in the closest possible approximation to the way in which contemporaries would have formulated them if they had been conscious historians. It would have sounded both boring and pretentious if I had started with that sort of definition of history, but I hope it makes sense now. The good historian must above all be a questioner. He must question the assumptions of the past and of previous historians; he must question his own assumptions and prejudices; and he must force the past to yield up the questions that were being asked, the problems that were being set, as they were experienced by those who lived in the period he is studying. The broader his sympathies, the more he is likely to succeed in this imaginative task.

NOTES

1. Introduction to *History and Culture* (Random House, 1977).
2. Cf. Ranajit Guha, *Elementary Aspects of Peasant Insurgency in Colonial India* (Oxford U.P., 1983), p. 106, who points out that official sources are often not only politically biased but distorted by the fact that they record instantaneous reactions to the event.
3. R. A. Marchant, *The Puritans and the Church Courts in the Diocese of York, 1560-1642* (1960), pp. 160-6.
4. Adam Smith, *Theory of Moral Sentiments* (1871), p. 219.

5. R. H. C. Davis, "Alfred the Great: Propaganda and Truth", *History*, 187
   (1971), pp. 170-82.
6. See p. 298 below.
7. See p. 131 below.

II   *The English Revolution*

3. Parliament and People in 17th-Century England[1]

*"In England in the sixteen-twenties the majority of important events took place outside Parliament."** *

I

All historians of sixteenth- and seventeenth-century England owe an enormous debt to Sir John Neale. I did not know him at all well, and I think there may have been subjects on which we would not have seen eye to eye. But I recall two encounters with him with at least retrospective pleasure. The first was in the mid-thirties, when I applied for a job at University College. Sir John interviewed me, rigorously, and then told me to go away and do some real research before thinking myself fit for a job at a proper university. Our next meeting was nearly twenty years later. I had written a monograph on economic problems of the church which I submitted to a publisher for whom Neale was a reader. He was kind enough to recommend it for publication, which made me feel I had made the grade at last. The book was accepted, though the publishers subsequently withdrew their acceptance, for reasons which were not conveyed to me. But meanwhile Sir John, who had made some very pertinent criticisms, gave me an hour of his time advising me very helpfully on how to meet them. I acknowledged my gratitude in the preface to the book, and am glad to repeat it now.

My original intention was to try to review work done during the past thirty years or so on the relationship of Parliament to people in the early seventeenth century, and of both to the English Revolution. But I have been forestalled by a flurry of articles which have appeared recently, assessing and in many cases attacking what have come to be known as "revisionists". I am thinking of articles by

---

* Conrad Russell, *Parliaments and English Politics, 1621-1629* (Oxford U.P., 1979), p.1.

21

Derek Hirst and J. H. Hexter in the *Journal of Modern History*, and by Clive Holmes in the *Journal of British Studies*; a review article by Hirst in the *Historical Journal* and another by Austin Woolrych in *History*.[2] And I believe there are more to come. I shall therefore make some of my points very briefly, referring to the articles cited for more effective demonstrations than I can make. What I hope to do is to put the issues in a wider context than has so far been done.

The names of S. R. Gardiner and Wallace Notestein figure largely in the current attack of the so-called revisionists, less often the name of Tawney. Yet I believe that to get a proper perspective we should start from the 1950s, when it seemed that consensus was being reached on an interpretation of the causes of the English civil war in terms of the "rise of the gentry". Naturally and rightly, when an orthodoxy seems to be establishing itself, the young react against it: and that is what happened in the nineteen-sixties — though the protagonists are not so young now. The gentry controversy, in which generalizations about an ill-defined social class were tossed backwards and forwards, ended in stalemate; young researchers took to detailed studies of individual counties, initially trying to find a relationship between the gentry and the causes of the civil war, but soon as an end in itself. They discovered, not surprisingly it now seems, that it was difficult to find deep divisions over constitutional matters among the county gentry, and even more difficult to find gentlemen who advocated a take-over of power by Parliament. On the contrary, Professor Everitt[3] and Dr Morrill[4] thought that the gentry were far more interested in local than in national issues; they opposed Ship Money — where they did oppose it — not on high constitutional principle but because taxes fell unfairly on their locality. In most counties the gentry tried to avoid civil war up to the last moment.

Some historians developed a mystique of "the county community", by which they often meant exclusively the gentry of the county, intensely local in their interests, apolitical, neutralist, wanting only to be left alone by the central government. As one critic of Dr Morrill observed, this school came near to proving that the civil war did not happen.[5] At this point a halt had to be called, as Dr Morrill ruefully notes in citing the criticism against himself. He has the endearing characteristic, rare among historians, of being prepared to admit that he has been mistaken. He speaks of himself as guilty of "a certain myopia". And by that time historians had noticed that there were other occupants of counties besides the gentry: Professor Clive Holmes suggested that in East Anglia it was tensions between classes which forced the gentry to take up political positions in 1642.[6] Professor Underdown for Somerset,[7] Dr Blackwood for Lancashire,[8] Dr Fletcher for Sussex,[9] Mr Clark for Kent,[10] Dr Ann Hughes for Warwickshire,[11] Dr S. K. Roberts for Devon,[12] observed that "the county" was not invariably the sole focus of local loyalties: economic regions cut across county borders.

Most of them found the model set forth in Dr Thirsk's volume of the *Agrarian History of England and Wales*[13] relevant, distinguishing between champaign areas where the lower classes were relatively docile, and the forest-fen-pasture areas where lords of manors were fewer and parishes larger, in which the much more mobile population was far less easily controlled. It furnished a supply of hands for the clothing industry and for the new industries which Dr Thirsk's Ford Lectures so vividly described,[14] and so was much more liable to unrest in times of economic depression. Because much less supervised, some of these were areas in which heresies flourished. By a further refinement, Dr Hughes has shown that in the forest areas of Warwickshire the turbulence of the lower classes, encouraged by Lord Brooke, drove most of the gentry there to support the King in 1642; Lord Brooke's gentry supporters came from the champaign areas. Similarly Professor Underdown found (in Berkshire, Hampshire and Sussex) "royalist Clubmen in the downlands, parliamentarian Clubmen in forest and pasture regions".[15] Such facts recall Brian Manning's *The English People and the English Revolution*.[16]

So the continuation of research has left the "county community" historians in some disarray. What threatened to become an orthodoxy has disintegrated before it congealed. So we get Dr Morrill declaring that "the whole of society experienced a much more profound crisis than Professor Everitt has allowed". He is right. And we get the best of the younger county historians, Dr Hughes, dismissing both Everitt and Morrill in a footnote.[17] What remains is a very interesting series of studies of very different counties: generalizations have proved to be premature.

There is a danger of sentimentalizing "the county community" of the gentry: protecting the interests of "the county" often meant protecting the ruling class in its privileges and property. Not all tenants loved their landlords all the time. It is no longer easy to adopt Mr Laslett's picture of a "one-class society",[18] the single class being the gentry. This is indeed how many seventeenth-century gentlemen saw it; but we should always be wary of reproducing "the illusion of the epoch" as though it represented historical truth. The labours of Professors Campbell and Hoskins should have prevented us from forgetting the existence of the yeomanry: Mr Manning has effectively reminded us of the political consequences of lower-class discontent in the bad decades of the sixteen-twenties and sixteen-thirties.[19] The point has recently been rammed home in an excellent book by Dr Buchanan Sharp, *In Contempt of All Authority: Rural Artisans and Riot in the West of England, 1586-1660.*[20]

This is the point at which we return to Parliament, with the help of Derek Hirst and Conrad Russell. Historians — myself included — have often said that the House of Commons in the early seventeenth century represented only the gentry. This was one of the unspoken assumptions of "Tawneyite" orthodoxy, though I suspect that in this respect Tawney was no more a Tawneyite than Marx was a Marxist or Namier a Namierite. Since the work of Derek Hirst this view is no longer tenable. He has abundantly shown that during the first four decades of the century M.P.s had to take more than usual notice of the wishes of their electors. Disputed elections increased three times between 1604 and 1624, and doubled again by 1640. The meaner sort may initially have been drawn into political action by their betters pursuing private feuds; but as the crisis of the 1620s developed they started taking independent initiatives. Troops of apprentices made the Yorkshire county poll of 1625 "more like a rebellion than an election". Wentworth thought the threat was directed "against all the gentlemen".[21]

Dr Hirst has established that gentry and corporation oligarchies had ceased to be the sole force in politics well before 1640. M.P.s were acutely conscious that they must ease the grievances of which their constituents complained; otherwise "we shall hardly be welcome" to our neighbours. The House of Commons was the great inquest of the nation, in which M.P.s were expected to speak out. In their counties J.P.s could not set a bad example to the lower orders by refusing to obey superiors' commands; that made it all the more their duty to raise grievances in Parliament. This was the point of Wentworth's determination "never to contend with the prerogative out of a Parliament".[22] As early as 1604 M.P.s were consulting their constituents about a new law concerning purveyance.[23] Sir Julius Caesar said after the 1610 Parliament that its members "are held among the common people the best patriots that ever were"; most valued for their greatest contempts to the King.[24] The name of courtier was the surest passport to rejection, the Venetian ambassador declared of the 1624 election, no doubt exaggerating;[25] but Chamberlain agreed that there was less regard for letters and recommendations from "great ones" in this election than earlier.[26] The Venetian ambassador repeated his observation for the 1628 elections: those who had refused the forced loan were far more popular than courtiers; the former were everywhere called "good patriots".[27]

Consciousness of a greater potential for government interference in the economy, at a time when rural élites were especially under pressure, may, Dr Hirst suggests, have produced a greater tendency to look to the centre for redress and aid, and increasingly this meant looking to Parliament because of the "apparently uncaring nature of the court".[28] Such men were perhaps less conscious of divisions in the court and Privy Council than M.P.s and later historians were. In 1625 and 1626 constituents took their M.P.s to task for voting supply before grievances had been redressed.[29]

So we come to Conrad Russell. He was perhaps unlucky in reviewing the history of Parliament in the light of the conclusions of the county community historians just when it was becoming clear that those historians were not agreed on what their message was. But Conrad Russell is a very able historian, whose work has made me among many others do a lot of rethinking. I recently revised a book called *The Century of Revolution*, and one change I found necessary to make was to delete the word "the" in the phrase "the opposition" whenever it occurred. I do not know whether "the opposition" encouraged readers to suppose that there was a His Majesty's Opposition ready to take over government in the sixteen-twenties, and I do not think I ever thought so myself. But the phrase is anachronistic and infelicitous; it may lead to misunderstandings. We are much better off without it.[30]

Professor Russell has also emphasized the relative unimportance of the House of Commons, the dependence of M.P.s on patrons in the House of Lords. The Parliamentary crisis of 1626-8 was the result of a decade of war, and unsuccessful war, rather than of any longer-term factors.[31] There was never a revolutionary party in the Commons, no group consciously planning a take-over of power. I am not quite sure whether anyone ever suggested that there was, as it were, a Bolshevik party in the English Revolution. Like the French

Revolution, it took those who had to guide it completely by surprise. I suspect that Professor Russell is hammering at an open door here. Less so perhaps when he argues that there was nothing inevitable about the Revolution: for him it was the result of a series of accidents which happened to coincide in the sixteen-forties.

Professor Russell's meticulous examination of Parliamentary politics has established some of these propositions and made a case for others. Professor Hexter — with whom I always like to agree whenever possible — and Dr Hirst[32] have called some of them in question, and Professor Russell,[33] wise man that he is, has modified his position since the rather strident negativism of his early publications. The pre-civil-war period will never look quite the same again since his work.

So in what follows I shall do no more than indicate the points on which, in my view, the revisionists have not been successful in overthrowing traditional interpretations. Changes in emphasis, yes, and very valuable ones some of them; reversal, no. It is a rash historian who disagrees with Gardiner, as everyone finds out who takes the trouble to read him. Dr Morrill, on rereading Gardiner, "was amazed by [his] moderation and carefulness", and contrasts him with G. M. Trevelyan.[34] Part of the trouble with revisionists — and I have been guilty of this myself in my time — is that one attributes the slipshod (or wild) over-simplifications of epigones to Gardiner, Notestein or Tawney, as the case may be. It is as though one were to blame Conrad Russell for Dr Farnell or Dr Kishlansky.

Some younger scholars have indeed been far more Russellite than Conrad Russell ever was. They were thumped down by Professor Hexter, and finished off by Dr Hirst's rapier.[35] Professor Russell has delicately distanced himself from his more enthusiastic disciples. He properly reminded us, for instance, that we do not know very much about the House of Lords at this period, that peers still had great social prestige, and suggested that what look like protests originating from the Commons may in fact sometimes be expressions of splits in the Privy Council, each group looking for support in the lower House. He goes so far as to speak of "the overwhelming evidence for the Parliamentarians' dependance on aristocratic leadership". Messrs Christianson and Farnell extend this to mean that "early 17th century Parliaments were the instruments of revived aristocratic power". "Retained lawyers like John Selden, and orators of fortune like Sir John Eliot (servant in the Commons first of

Buckingham, then of Pembroke) transmitted directions from the upper to the lower house". "A group of peers organized and led the campaign against Charles I which was victorious on the field of battle during 1644-6".[36]

The idea that the civil war was made by a "revolutionary party in the House of Commons" has, one hoped, gone for ever. But it has been replaced by an even less plausible "reform network" of "Livian revolutionary peers" "transmitting directions" to their stooges in the House of Commons from the sixteen-twenties. They also controlled the City, from merchant princes down to the populace. I quote Dr. Farnell again: "the access which the Earl of Warwick and the young Vane had to the Vice-Admiral's muster-books probably helps to explain the prominence of seamen in the early demonstrations". We can visualize the scene. Warwick and Vane slip off, late at night, to the Admiralty, run through the books and say "Ha: A. B. Seaman Joe Bloggs, 137 Mile End Road. Send one of our client M.P.s along to order him to report for demonstration duty at 7.0 a.m. tomorrow". The seamen were unpaid, their families were starving in a desperate economic crisis for which the government was not unreasonably blamed: but perish the thought that seamen might think for themselves. Rather, for Mr. Farnell, "it was the Machiavellian restatement of classical political practices that further explains much about the role cast for the people by the leaders of the Long Parliament".[37]

It has not been proved that there was a rigid client-patron relationship in the early seventeenth century, of the sort that Namier described in the mid-eighteenth. Half a dozen or so names have been produced, most of which Derek Hirst has shot down.[38] Leading M.P.s were great territorial magnates like Sir Thomas Wentworth, Sir Thomas Barrington, Sir Edwin Sandys, or even Dr. Farnell's "orator of fortune", Sir John Eliot. Such men were richer than many peers, accustomed to running their counties. Farnell's "retained lawyer" John Selden married an earl's widow. We must not mistake the conventional social deference which such men showed to peers for reality.

The one possible dependent "client" among leading M.P.s is John Pym, who had no significant landed estate, no county community, and therefore needed help in finding a borough seat. If anyone was at the mercy of his patron it would be Pym. Yet Conrad Russell, who knows more about Pym than anyone, found no evidence that he ever

accepted a line from the Earl of Bedford, or from his later patron the
Earl of Warwick. Russell gives an example of Pym acting in a way
of which Bedford disapproved.[39] It looks far more like co-operation
to achieve shared political ends than a servile client-patron relationship. Eliot, Buckingham's kept man, in March 1624 opposed a
financial grant sponsored by the Duke; he shifted to Pembroke's
patronage when he rejected Buckingham's policies. In the thirties,
when Pembroke had made his peace with the court, Eliot chose to die
in prison rather than submit. The whole concept of M.Ps. as puppets
whose strings are pulled from above becomes absurd when we have to
face the fact that M.Ps. changed their "patrons".[40] If X can switch to
a new patron as a result of political disagreement, perhaps he could
choose his patron on grounds of political agreement? It is difficult to
avoid the forbidden word "principles" here. The Namier method
seems to me appropriate only to periods in which no serious issues
divided the political nation.

Consider the logic of what we are being asked to believe. Peers
were so important in seventeenth-century society that they could
insert their clients into the House of Commons and retain complete
control over them. A group of six or seven peers caused the civil war.
How did they do it? How did they prevail over the two-thirds of the
upper House who supported the King? What had all those other
peers been doing with their clients meanwhile? The more important
the peerage, the less possible is it for a tiny handful of them to cause a
revolution. However you analyse it, they can do this only by allying
with, or manipulating, a majority of the House of Commons and a
large sector of the population outside Parliament. The only way to
explain why other peers were not taking counteraction through *their*
clients and dependants is to admit that the peers did *not* control
society, that gentlemen and common people had views of their own
and acted independently. The conspiracy theory of the "network of
peers" becomes the opposite of what it set out to be; it demonstrates
the powerlessness of the peers as a social group. But it is also factually
inaccurate. Dr Hirst tells us that aristocratic and court influence
over elections was declining from the sixteen-twenties, as indeed all
the evidence suggests. By 1624 nominees of peers and courtiers were
no longer sure of county seats: they had to take refuge in boroughs
where patronage and pressure were exercised more easily.[41]

II

Commons and crown alike were facing an unprecedented situation. It arose from the combined effects of inflation, rising costs of war and under-assessment of the gentry to taxation. Control of foreign policy, the armed forces and the coinage traditionally fell within the sphere of the prerogative. Consequently, as the Apology of 1604 put it, "the prerogatives of princes may easily and do daily grow" — not only in England. But any extension of the prerogative raised the possibility of a clash with property rights — the point at which the natural rulers dug their heels in. It is of the essence of the situation that no one really understood what was happening. Professor Russell has no difficulty in showing that M.P.s were not revolutionaries: they believed that a satisfactory balance between crown and Parliament had been established centuries ago: all that was needed was to revert to the good old ways.[42] They had no comprehension of how the consensus of the golden days of Elizabeth had been upset: it could only be due to the malevolence of secret enemies, whether papists or the Duke of Buckingham, or a combination of the two. They did not want to establish a different government, or to take over power themselves. All they wanted was to make the system work, as it had worked until very recently.

One useful consequence of Professor Elton's incursion into the early seventeenth century is that he looks at its problems with the eyes of a man for whom the sixteenth-century consensus was normal. Failing to appreciate the underlying socio-economic issues, he usefully reproduces the muddled thinking of the average early seventeenth-century M.P. But to echo the fumbling is not to write the history. With our hindsight knowledge it is easy to perceive that M.Ps. from 1604 to the sixteen-twenties did not think of themselves as on a high road to civil war.[43] But Professor Elton's metaphor perhaps boomerangs. Pioneers starting to make a road across the prairies can have no idea of the cities that will be built at the other end: but they do know that the road will get them away from where they are. Professor Judson thirty years ago produced a powerful case for seeing consistent policies in the House of Commons in defence of property against the prerogative, throughout the first four decades of the century — a defence which was sometimes aggressive, elevating the commonwealth above the King.[44] M.Ps. trod very carefuly in their predecessors' footsteps, noting precedents in their diaries and

commonplace books. And when the press was liberated in 1641 and
hitherto unprintable documents could be published, then it was
revealed that they had been advancing along a road. However
unaware they were at the time of its ultimate destination, they
remembered the milestones.[45]

The Apology of 1604, so written down by Professor Elton, was
quoted by nine M.Ps. in 1621, including John Pym: only four of them
had sat in 1604. Conrad Russell implies that in 1628 M.P.s experienced a sudden traumatic uncertainty as to whether the law did
protect their property;[46] if so they had forgotten similar anxieties in
1610, when the absolute property rights of the subject ("such a
property as may not without their assent be altered") was asserted
"against the King as against any other person". The superiority of the
common law to the prerogative was also as clearly stated as it was to
be in 1628.[47] Sir Robert Phelips in 1628 mentioned Calvin's and
Bate's cases as well as that of the Five Knights in registering alarm at
the law's inadequacy to protect their persons as well as their property:
he cited the 1610 Parliament's refusal to grant supply before grievances were met.[48]

The apparently excessive zeal with which the Commons of James's
first Parliament pounced on Dr. Cowell for a few unfortunate
definitions shows how alert and wary they were to nip in the bud any
possible justification of royal absolutism. In 1626 a M.P. suggested
looking back through all petitions of grievances since 1604, to find
out what had been remedied.[49] The Clerk of the Parliaments kept a
record of significant matters which had occurred during his clerk-
ship: from 1604 onwards confrontations with the crown loomed
large — the cases of Shirley, Goodwin and Cowell, the debates on
impositions. Several copies of the clerk's "books" exist: clearly they
circulated, at least among M.P.s.[50] It was not for nothing that Ralegh
entitled his discourse of 1615 *The Prerogative of Parliaments*. In
1614 Sandys had attacked impositions as a threat to the security of
property and the liberties of Parliament; in 1610 they had been
declared illegal, *nem. con.*[51] Bishop Neile's ill-advised remarks about
Parliament in 1614 led to a hue and cry which anticipated that of
1628.[52]

The evidence for continuity of memory from 1604 to 1640 seems
to me incontrovertible. In 1641 speeches from as long ago as 1610
were published. William Drake in 1632 compiled a commonplace
book of speeches from Parliaments of James and his successor.

Political independence of the crown was continuous in some families — the Herberts, the Sidneys, the Neviles, the Chaloners, and many others.[53] Rather than reading the sixteenth-century consensus forwards into the seventeenth century, it might be instructive to consider more carefully whether the social tensions of the early seventeenth century are not anticipated in the later sixteenth century.[54] We should not think of crown and Commons as regularly in conflict, still less of M.Ps. seeing them in conflict: but equally we should not ignore the permanent, and permanently insoluble, problems which had to be faced. When Conrad Russell came to look at Elizabethan Parliaments he was surprised by their "sense of their own authority".[55]

Since this lecture was first published, Wallace MacCaffrey has cautiously emphasized this point. "The factor of public opinion, as made manifest in the House of Commons, was an element with which Elizabeth had always to reckon". Sometimes it could be used by the government to strengthen its position in foreign negotiations; on other occasions the House of Commons might disobey a royal command, might reject bills sponsored by the government even when explicitly approved by the Queen, might claim the right to determine the succession. In 1586 an attempt was made to tie a financial grant to a reversal of royal foreign policy — an anticipation of 1624.[56] In the last resort the government's power was limited by lack of a standing army and bureaucracy. Taxes could be voted and collected only with the good will of the gentry, the principal taxpayers. So already the Commons had to be informed and cajoled when exceptional expenditure was needed; and "once the Commons was invited to give its advice it would be a short step to offering it unasked." Nor was the necessity of taking account of the opinions of the political nation limited to foreign affairs and taxation: as MacCaffrey stresses, the Elizabethan government's lack of coercive force meant that it had to listen to any grievances which might lead to riot or rebellion if not attended to.[57] It was these spheres — foreign policy, taxation, social order — which were to produce the strains of the sixteen-twenties that led to the breakdown of 1640.

As Dr Hirst pointed out, Conrad Russell made it easier to postulate a descent from consensus to the confrontation of 1629 by starting his discussion in 1621.[58] In that year, owing to a combination of economic crisis, the threatening international situation and the fact that there had been no effective Parliament for eleven years, there was at first a return to the spirit of compromise and pragmatism that had followed the confrontation over election returns in 1604. Nevertheless, in 1621 subsidies were still related to grievances, the King was criticized, and the independence of the House of Commons asserted.[59] Quarrels about the right to imprison, as Professor Russell points out, look forward to the Petition of Right. "This fact is not a significant part of the history of 1621", he comments.[60] Perhaps not: significance is not quantifiable. But fears lest parliaments should be discontinued, already voiced in 1614, were stronger; they were to be voiced in every parliament of the twenties. Both King and Commons knew that an active foreign policy was possible only with co-operation from Parliament: the only conceivable alternative, military absolutism, would involve a profound restructuring of the English state. So both King and Commons proceeded with great caution. Both wanted to make the traditional constitution work.

The crown was caught between upper and nether millstones. It got a series of legal decisions in favour of the prerogative,[61] but in the last resort taxes *could* not be collected without the co-operation of the natural rulers. The Commons were no less trapped, between the crown's demands for financial support and the resentment of their electorate, both gentry and the middling sort of tax-payer; between the wishes of their aristrocratic patrons and their own principles, which were not unrelated to the interests of their constituents. The gentry wanted to co-operate, even to the extent of collecting taxes not voted by Parliament. Their authority as J.Ps. and as landowners necessitated, or so it seemed to them, maintenance of the unquestioned authority of the crown. Yet if the price to be paid was too high, in the form of taxation or failure to protect property, that too could threaten social disorder and loss of gentry control. As poverty grew in the sixteen-twenties, so did the natural rulers' anxiety to do nothing which might unleash the many-headed monster. Considerations of this sort may help to explain acceptance of royal office by Wentworth and Noy, and the relative quiescence with which the dissolution of 1629 was accepted.[62]

Gentlemen had to be seen to enjoy court favour in order to buttress their local power; but their local power was no less based on the approbation of their neighbours. "Let us not palliate with the King", Sir Edwin Sandys had said in 1621, "but with the people".[63] Conrad Russell gives as "one of the most extreme examples of a gentleman's inability to do his job in his country without some favour at court" "the dismissal of Sir Thomas Wentworth from the office of ... chairman of the bench in Yorkshire" in 1626. "Such a disgrace did not make it easy for him to keep his standing in his home county".[64] That indeed is what Wentworth told the Privy Council. But the "disgrace" did not stop him being elected to the next Parliament: it may even have helped, since his rival Sir John Savile had supported the forced loan.[65] It could indeed be argued that Wentworth owed his peerage in 1628 to the fact that he had routed Savile in the election, thus showing his indispensability to the government if Yorkshire was to be controlled. Sir Robert Phelips "was not the creator of opposition" in Somerset, Professor Barnes concluded; "he was its creature".[66]

One source of confusion among historians is a failure to appreciate the conventions of political discourse at this period. M.P.s wanted to maintain in public the dignity and reputation of the King, recognizing the truth of Wentworth's dictum "the authority of a King is the keystone which closeth up the arch of order and government".[67] Yet they could not accept certain aspects of government policy. Sir Dudley Digges put it clearly on 1 May 1628: "I say that the King must not do this, but I do not like to put it in a law, that the King ought not". For laws were printed: anybody might read them. "Let us by no means", Littleton urged, "put it to the question, whether we will trust the King or no. Though we mean well, yet we know not what construction may be made of it". The contortions into which M.P.s got themselves while arguing passionately against abuses of forced loans, arbitrary imprisonment, martial law and billeting, and simultaneously trumpeting their eternal loyalty to the King, shows they were really pushed into a corner. "We are to think", said Sir Nathaniel Rich, "how we may come off not contradicting what the King said yesterday" — but of course not abandoning our position merely because the King disliked it. The Commons' Remonstrance of 14 June explained that "we do verily believe that all or most of those things we shall now present unto your Majesty are either unknown unto you, or else by some of your Majesty's ministers offered under such specious pretences as may hide their own bad intentions".[68] The practice continued even after the outbreak of civil war, as Henry Marten found to his cost in 1643. The same deferential language was used about the King, the same blaming of evil councillors. A point must have been reached at which belief became very strained. Lord Chancellor Ellesmere, not exercising the hindsight of

Whiggish historians, noted that in all Coke's *Reports* "he hath stood so much in phrase upon the King's honour, as in his resolutions he hath no respect for the King's profit".[69]

When all else failed Charles could be criticized, as his father had been criticized, by fulsome praise of "that never-to-be-forgotten excellent Queen Elizabeth".[70] Alternatively, in order to avoid saying directly that the King's promise could not be relied on, one could exude confidence in the present King but worry about the prospect of a less admirable successor.[71] Unless we remember this all the time we shall be needlessly perplexed when we read the private thoughts of, for instance, D'Ewes on James I's "base, cowardly nature", his "self-conceit of his wisdom" and his addiction to the sin of sodomy; or on Prince Charles's "ignorance" and risk of falling into "damned apostacy".[72] Or Selden's "A King is a thing men have made for their own sakes, for quietness' sake. Just as in a family one man is appointed to buy the meat".[73] The myopia of those who see only the gentry in the county community is matched by the deafness of those who hear only the words M.P.s speak in the House, and not the conversations which men confided to their private diaries, or the complaints and uproars coming from beyond the charmed circle of politics.[74] Conrad Russell points out that "diarists frequently skipped divine right imagery, treating it as so much padding".[75] Accounts by outside observers sometimes suggest that words spoken in the House were less decorous than those which diarists wrote down — for example in Pym's speech of November 1621 showing how the King's good qualities were perverted to evil ends.[76] We need not take too seriously a document originating in English Catholic circles which declared that "the Puritan faction" aimed at "changing the monarchy of England into a republic". But it got reported to France.[77]

III

Underlying the disputes between King and Commons was under-assessment to taxation. Sir Walter Ralegh in 1601 had said "our estates that are three or four pounds in the Queen's book, it is not the hundredth part of our wealth".[78] He was not exaggerating grossly: historians take 50 as a reasonable multiplier for converting assessed wealth into real wealth. In 1628 it was proposed that baronets should be assessed at not less than £50, £1000 *per annum* being the minimum landed wealth rendering one eligible for the honour; but this intolerable interference with the liberty of the subject was rejected.[79] By 1628 the subsidy was worth half what it had been at the beginning of Elizabeth's reign, in monetary terms; meanwhile the purchasing power of money had plummeted. The decline was due to gross underassessment and to the establishment of exemptions.[80] It was also due, as Gardiner suggested, to the practice of paying high entry fines and low rents for lands: men were assessed on their rents.[81] Since, as the House of Commons put it in 1621, "the assessing [was] to be as usual by neighbours", there was a rapidly descending spiral. "The more subsidies Parliaments voted, the less money each subsidy yielded".[82] M.Ps. felt aggrieved at having to vote five subsidies where one had satisfied Good Queen Bess: but the underassessment of the gentry meant that a disproportionate share of the burden fell on tax-payers of the middling sort who were assessed much more in accordance with their true wealth. They may have actually been paying five times what their forebears used to pay. "In most parishes", wrote John Rogers in 1629, "the meaner sort bear the chiefest burden, not the richest".[83] "The greater sort as having the law in their own hands will pay what they please", said the anonymous *Considerations Touching Trade* of 1641: the burden fell on "the middling sort".[84]

For this reason, fifteenths, the traditional accompaniment of the subsidy, were abandoned, since their multiplication would have been intolerable for the poorer sort: but this intensified the problem created by declining yields.[85] The system was made workable only by the prosperity of the middling sort which Professor Hoskins discussed, and by the existence of new industries demonstrated by Dr. Thirsk.[86] But the middling sort could not be milked for ever, as their growing wealth gave them increased confidence: and the co-operation of parish élites — constables, churchwardens and the like — was essential if taxes were to be collected. We must relate to this economic background the new interest shown by the middling and lower sort in Parliamentary elections which Dr Hirst has shown, and the determined government campaign "to shut out the meaner sort from municipal politics", as well as the Commons' willingness to extend the franchise.[87]

Hence the insistence of M.Ps. in 1621 that they must have redress of grievances in return for supply, lest they "be made subjects of the people's fury".[88] Hence too the importance in 1624 of establishing Parliamentary control over money voted for the Palatinate. Conrad

Russell denies the significance of this episode, since Parliamentary control was in fact proposed by Buckingham; but the object of his proposal was to satisfy the Commons, and it did this because it gave tangible evidence of the House's concern for the proper spending of money extracted from their constituents.[89] Hence the consultations which Essex and Bedfordshire J.Ps. held in the sixteen-twenties when the localities were faced with demands for a new tax.[90]

As the system slowly ground towards a halt, it became clear that only decisive reorganization or the introduction of totally new taxes could retrieve the situation. The Great Contract of 1610 was one such plan; the compensation which the King was to receive for feudal tenures was not to be based on the subsidy.[91] This may have been one reason why M.Ps. after consulting their constituents lost their enthusiasm for it; another reason was the failure to get impositions abolished as part of the bargain. A third reason was perhaps anxiety lest Parliament should be discontinued if the deal went through.[92] Sir John Holles found "the plebs" even more hostile to the Great Contract than "the better sort".[93] Soon after the dissolution Ellesmere produced a serious programme of financial reform to meet the Commons' criticisms: but it was not adopted.[94] In 1624 the Spanish ambassador reported that schemes for introducing new taxes on the Dutch model were under consideration;[95] but this naturally came to nothing under Buckingham. Coke produced a "carefully thought-out programme" in 1625, and the subject was discussed again in 1626.[96]

Dr Nippel suggested that voting tonnage and poundage for one year only in 1625 — a very provocative act — may have been an attempt to guarantee annual Parliaments.[97] In 1628 Eliot, supported by Pym, Rich and many others, offered a new settlement of the ordinary revenue if Charles would sacrifice Buckingham.[98] Financial reorganization formed part of Pym's and Bedford's programme for 1641;[99] but it took the pressure of the civil war to force it on a reluctant House of Commons. Before that date vested interests at court and the prejudices of the electorate were too strong. Parliament was prepared neither for financial reorganization nor for new taxes without a wholesale change of policies: in this respect its usefulness to government was diminishing. But there was no viable alternative, since without an army *any* tax had to be collected by the gentry and parish élites. For this reason I am dubious about Conrad Russell's repeated suggestion that it would have paid Charles to

dispense with Parliaments altogether. If — like the King of France —
he had had an army and a bureaucracy to collect taxes, yes; without
them he was ultimately at the mercy of those who did the
collecting,[100] as the sixteen-thirties were to show. As Russell himself
points out, Wentworth and Hampden remained in office as Deputy
Lieutenants whilst in prison for refusing to collect the forced loan.[101]
The government could not manufacture local rulers at will.

In 1628 the idea of an excise was floated, but had to be disavowed
in face of virulent opposition in the Commons.[102] Ship Money was
relatively successful largely because it was based on a new assessment
at the parish level: it probably increased the burden on the middle
ranks.[103] Most of the local opposition was initially caused by the
reassessment, with its alleged iniquities as between communities,
rather than by the illegality of the tax. Ironically, the Parliamentary
assessment of the sixteen-forties which financed the civil war was
derived from the Ship Money assessments; and Pym's excise revived
the scheme indignantly rejected in 1628.

So subsidies became increasingly inadequate to pay for the wars of
the sixteen-twenties. But there were wider consequences. Contributions for the militia were based on subsidy assessments. The
problem of reassessment, Mr Hassell-Smith tells us, frustrated all
attempts to provide a new statutory basis for the militia: and so the
government had to fall back on the prerogative, with all the friction
that caused.[104] Lords Lieutenants incurred odium in the sixteen-
twenties by collecting forced loans.[105] Their attempts in the thirties
to bypass Quarter Sessions was regarded as a form of arbitrary
taxation analogous to extra-Parliamentary levies; and all the more
burdensome because in time of peace. As the Earl of Hertford put it,
J.Ps.' opposition attempted to confine the Privy Council's commands "to the rules of the common laws or the statutes to be in
Parliament, whereunto all their assents must be gained".[106]

What we have then is a new financial situation, in that the
government's revenue is totally inadequate to wage war,[107] and a new
social situation, in that many of the middling sort are getting richer
and more self-confident just at the time when M.Ps. need to
demonstrate that they represent the people of England. The Great
Contract's attempt at an overall solution foundered on a combination of the electorate's suspicions of government intentions on the
one hand; on the other, powerful vested interests at court able to
play on the not unfounded claim that the abolition of feudal tenures

would make for "a ready passage to a democracy".[108] As royal
revenue from land and other traditional sources declined, so it
became increasingly necessary to draw on resources from the
expanding commercial sector, whether in trade or agriculture.[109] The
depression which followed the Cokayne Project ended the buoyancy
which had sustained James's extravagance. Tawney thought that "in
the matter of major improvements to the revenue ... the régime had
shot its bolt before Cranfield enlisted in its service".[110] I have seen no
evidence to make me doubt that statement.

Cranfield's attempts at financial reorganization broke down
when Buckingham felt his interests and omnipotence challenged;
and the unprincipled alliance which Buckingham and Charles
struck up with Parliament in 1624 enabled the former to get rid
of Cranfield, the last finance minister who believed in reorganization
in agreement with Parliament.[111] But this alliance could not last.
Tawney rightly pointed out the fantastic *costs* of the Duke's erratic
foreign policy. "The Prince's outlay in Spain and the cost of the
armada mobilized for several months on end to escort the truants
home, together ran to a figure which put the government's German
liabilities in the shade".[112] So at each stage factors beyond the control
of reforming ministers, deriving from divisions within the régime,
frustrated attempts at reform. What Tawney calls 'the admin-
istrator's fallacy" — the belief that "efficient management, combined with public spirit and a logically unanswerable case, can hold
its own against interests and ambitions wielding personal and
political power"[133] — claimed not only Cranfield as a victim but
also some historians.

There were ups and downs — a willingness to give James a fair
chance at the beginning of his reign, a determination by King and
Commons alike to make a success of the 1621 Parliament in face of
previous breakdowns and the threatening international situation;
and the illusory unity of 1624. There was a reduction of tension after
Buckingham's death, which again seemed an opportunity for a fresh
start.[114] Paradoxically, as Gardiner observed, tension may also have
been lowered by Buckingham's foreign policy of simultaneous war
with France and Spain. If neither power could take advantage of that
situation to invade England, there was perhaps less need for alarm
than had been felt in the early twenties. And then, first the Dutch
capture of the Spanish treasure fleet, soon followed by Gustavus
Adolphus's victorious advance into Germany, removed fears of

Habsburg attack,[115] and France was increasingly moving into the "protestant" camp.

But the probem was not merely financial. J.Ps., in Conrad Russell's words, claimed "a favourable subsidy assessment as the reward for their work as unpaid local governors".[116] They would therefore be likely to demand, through Parliament, control over any financial reorganization. Many of the crown's financial expedients affected their local power: monopoly patents threatened to create "a rival system of local government": so did central control over ale-house licensing,[117] which Cranfield said in 1618 was "the disgrace of all the chief gentry".[118] Sir Stephen Proctor was fiercely attacked in 1610 because his job as Collector and Receiver of fines on penal statutes wrested power and profit from J.Ps.[119] Sir Edward Coke seems even to have been alarmed lest the raising of rates by Commissioners of Sewers might let reassessment in by the back door.[120] It was an exceptionally sensitive area.

Conrad Russell speaks of the impotence of Parliament, its dependance on the crown for existence and functioning.[121] In reply Derek Hirst emphasizes the impotence of the government itself.[122] In the sixteen-twenties it could not wage war; in the thirties it was unable to play any significant part in foreign affairs; it collapsed in face of an improvised invasion from Scotland, a third-rate power. Meanwhile it had been unable to pursue any overall policy; concentration on one issue (like Scotland) meant that others (like collecting Ship Money) were pursued with less energy.[123] The impotence of Parliament is part of the impotence of the English state.

Conrad Russell is, I think, too unsympathetic to M.P.s who simultaneously pressed for government action — clearing the seas of pirates, naval war against Spain — while refusing to vote taxes. As Gardiner long ago pointed out, the war of 1625 was not the war for which Parliament voted taxes in 1624. Then, whatever disagreements there might be about strategy, the war was expected to be in defence of the protestant interest. But, as Sir Francis Seymour remarked in 1625, "who knows not that the King is gone against the protestants" in France? It was disingenuous to expect automatic support from Commons or electorate for the wrong war. It was the unpopularity of the war that threatened "the habit of obedience to the county governors".[124] In the nineteen-thirties I was one of many who wished the then government to adopt a firmer line against

Hitler, but I was no enthusiast for rearmament until the government should, in seventeenth-century parlance, have declared its enemy. This attitude was only formally illogical: it made political sense. By 1628, at least, M.P.s had come to fear that billeting and martial law presaged military absolutism, in which arbitrary taxation and arbitrary imprisonment would be the norm, not the exception that ministers proclaimed them to be.

Conrad Russell is right to conclude that war on the scale demanded in the seventeenth century "was not possible without a profound shift in the relations between central and local government".[125] What had to happen before such a war became possible, however, was rather more than a "profound shift in the relations between central and local government"; it was a significant transfer of power. The transfer took place during the English Revolution which Russell — vainly, I think — tries to separate from the Civil War.

But was Parliament after all so impotent? Lord Chancellor Ellesmere, who of course was only a contemporary, thought its strength, and especially that of the Commons, was growing dangerously. Russell points to the Commons' failure to get impositions abolished, despite protests in every Parliament of the two reigns. But on his own premises this is not surprising. A compromise was reached in that the House refused to accept the legality of impositions but the crown did not increase the rates charged. Neither side won, and the Commons had no wish to act in a revolutionary manner by calling for refusal of payment. When a minority in the House did so in 1629, the extremism of their action helped to make the demand ineffective. A similar compromise had been arrived at over elections in 1604. The House of Commons abandoned its immediate demands, but in the long run won its point, that they and not Chancery should control returns.[126] Tacit agreement to differ was also reached over the militia; it functioned for a decade without statutory sanction. As with impositions, law and practice had already diverged long before the breakdown of 1640.[127] This situation could last only as long as mutual confidence had not been eroded.

"Without the safety of numbers which a Parliament provided" Conrad Russell says, "councillors would rarely risk attacks on colleagues who still held the King's favour. ... Courtiers and councillors were finding Parliaments necessary for their own power struggles".[128] Why was this, if Parliament was so impotent? Russell rightly points out that M.Ps.' "greatest ambitions were not for Parliament as a body. Those who wanted to promote policies hoped to do so by converting members of the court".[129] True enough, so long as the court was riven by faction. But public opinion looked to Parliament for a lead. In a pamphlet printed illegally in 1589 John Penry had claimed that the High Court of Parliament was the highest council in the land: Pym made a similar claim in 1629.[130] Beaulieu in 1610 spoke of expectations that Parliament "is like to bring forth very great alteration and reform in the state".[131] Ralegh's *Prerogative of Parliaments* and Gainsford's *Raleghs Ghost* in 1620 both put forward programmes for action to be initiated by Parliament.[132] (And the paradox implied in Ralegh's title is deliberately provocative).

Russell dampingly says that "Parliamentary success in arousing public expectation was equalled only by their failure to satisfy it";[133] but in the long run "public expectation" was what mattered. As Hexter rightly asks, why were so many diaries kept by M.Ps. if what they recorded was so unimportant? At no other period in English history were there so many. Why were M.Ps. arrested if their talk was not dangerous? Why did Gondomar in 1621 say that Spain could not negotiate until Parliament was dissolved?[134] When Charles I in 1628 made the incontrovertible statement that "it is not in the power of the Houses to declare or enact any law without my consent", what "doctrines . . . set on foot at this time" was he finding it necessary to controvert?[135] Why did London watermen in May 1641 claim that "during the Parliament-time they were free from all government" of their gild masters?[136] Why did Charles I in 1643 refer to "that idol of the name of a Parliament"?[137] In all respects here 1628 seems to have marked a turning-point, with Parliament attempting to appeal to a public opinion that had built up outside its own walls, and outside the ranks of what had hitherto been the political nation.[138]

IV

Historians have recently become much better informed of the existence of social tensions at this period. Professor Bowden has told us that the twenties, thirties and forties "were probably among the most terrible years through which the country has ever passed".[139] The population explosion meant that the number of mouths to be fed nearly trebled in the century and a half before 1640, but food production was far indeed from keeping pace. The price of food rose faster than other prices, and the price of the cheap grains on which the poor lived rose fastest of all. More and more families were becoming dependent on wage labour, forced to buy food because they had lost their holdings or were losing their rights in commons, fens and forests. Brian Manning has shown how this situation intensified tensions between rich and poor, town and country, merchants, gentlemen, rich yeomen and artisans on the one hand, the poorer sort on the other.[140]

A mass of evidence substantiates his point that contemporaries were conscious of a threat of popular revolt at least from the depression of the sixteen-twenties onwards. In 1622 Simonds D'Ewes, no radical, spoke of a "hoped-for rebellion", Sherland in 1625 of the danger of a "commotion" among the people. Many observers, foreign and English, thought revolt imminent in 1626-8. These facts seem to me to put the dilemma of M.Ps. into a deeper social context than Conrad Russell has revealed, so making better sense of their actions. We do not need to attribute the breakdown of 1629 (as he does) merely to M.Ps.' frustration and irritation. War accentuated social tensions that were already there.[141] Brian Manning has shown how fear of popular revolt limited M.Ps.' freedom of action in 1640-2. Since the cause was there earlier (if in a less acute form) it is reasonable to suppose that it had similar effects.

In the light of this analysis I want to spend a little time looking at an incident in Parliament in May 1628, which for some reason historians have overlooked — even Russell, who treated the narrative of the period in very great detail.[142] The House of Commons had voted the Petition of Right. The Lords were prepared to accept it but wished to add a clause "to leave entire that sovereign power wherewith your Majesty is trusted".[143] From the Commons' point of view this addition would have destroyed the whole object of the Petition, which was to prevent the law being overruled by appeal to sovereign power or the prerogative. As usual when the two Houses disagreed, a conference followed. After the conference the Lords withdrew their clause and accepted the Petition as the Commons had voted it. Until this date, as far as one can see, there had been a determined minority in the Lords which wanted to go along with the Commons, but never a majority; so something must have been said at the conference which convinced a significant number of waverers. What was it?

Two speeches were made on behalf of the lower House. One, by Glanville, dealt with the "legal part". He rehearsed a series of long-familiar arguments, backed by long-familiar precedents.[144] The only significant new arguments, so far as I can see, came in a speech by Sir Henry Marten, dealing with "the rational part". He started by reminding the Lords "in what passion and distemper many members of the House arrived thither, ... what pockets full of complaints and lamentable grievances, ... brought thither and ... renewed by letters".[145] In these circumstances, the moderation of the Petition was astonishing — but deliberate. The Lords' addition was unreasonable because "the people are discontented", "men's minds are distracted". *We* all know that "sovereign power is a thing always so sacred that to handle it otherwise than tenderly is a kind of sacrilege ... But every vulgar capacity is not so affected ... Sovereign power has not now ... the amiable aspect" it used to have. "Angry men say sovereign power has been abused, and the most moderate wish it had not been so used". "This petition will run through many hands". Men will "fall to arguing and descanting what sovereign power is, ... what is the latitude? whence the original? where the bounds? etc., with many such curious and captious questions .... Sovereign power is then best worth when it is held in tacit veneration, not when it is profaned by vulgar hearings or examinations".

"Our duty and loyalty to his Majesty", Marten continued, makes us reject the Lords' proposal. "We know better than any men ... the apprehensions, fears and jealousies" of "them we serve for". As though the point was not already clear, he underlined it with a sly nudge: "I pray your Lordships to give me leave to use the figure called 'reticentia', that is to insinuate and intimate more than I mean to speak". "We know the humours of the people", and do not wish to be responsible for anything "that may breed wild blood".[146]

His argument must have got across to the stupidest peer. The Petition will be printed. It will be discussed up and down the country, in ale-houses as well as in manor houses.[147] Do your lordships really want sovereign power, its origin and bounds, to be discussed by the vulgar? Their lordships apparently decided that they did not. They must have been convinced that there was a body of opinion outside Parliament which was well-versed in political discussion and was much less moderate than those who had drafted the Petition. We think again of the electorate; we recall that Felton, who assassinated Buckingham a few months later, claimed that the Commons' Remonstrance was the only cause of his action.[149]

It is appropriate to reflect here on the importance of the appeal to public opinion outside Parliament. Wentworth and Hakewill initially argued for proceeding by bill rather than by petition because "acts of Parliament are printed". It was important for the upper House to join in the Petition; otherwise it "may be kept in a study". That too was why the King must give his answer in Parliament.[150] The Houses insisted that the King's second answer should be printed *in English* as well as in French, "for the better satisfaction of the vulgar". Charles ordered the first impression of the Petition of Right to be "made waste paper" and — after the prorogation — substituted one which included both his answers and his speech of 26 June in which he declared that his prerogative remained entire.[151] These were, in Professor Foster's words, "calculated moves to minimize the significance of the Petition". They confirm the existence of an interested public outside Parliament, which no doubt read the speeches of Glanville and Marten when they were printed.[152] The Remonstrance against Buckingham in 1626 had been designed for public circulation, as were the Three Resolutions of 1629. There is evidence of dislike of public affairs being discussed by "the common sort", from the fifteen-nineties onwards. Lord Chancellor Hatton particularly resented "cobblers and tailors" having views about important political matters like the succession.[153] The thinking behind these attitudes is the same as that which led to swords being drawn in the House in November 1641, when it was proposed to print the Grand Remonstrance: it is dangerous to profane the mysteries of state by laying them open to vulgar view. "I did not dream", said Sir Edward Dering à propos the Grand Remonstrance, "that we should remonstrate downward, tell stories to the people".[154]

V

So where are we? Can we arrive at any conclusion, however interim? I believe that the makings of a new synthesis are appearing. Let us agree that the Tawneyites were premature in assuming that all was explained by the rise of the gentry. Let us agree that the county community historians have not proved that there was no civil war, or that it came to each county from outside — though they have taught us a lot about the significance of local opinion which the House of Commons reflected.[155] Let us agree too that there was no revolutionary party in the House of Commons willing the civil war, without postulating that M.P.s were puppets manipulated from the upper House, or that the civil war was caused by the machinations of a handful of peers. But it did happen. I agree with Professor Farnell that "the political struggle in early seventeenth-century England ... was a bitter dispute over the nature of the English state, its goals and the best means of achieving them"; and he stresses the drive towards a dynamic imperial policy.[156] Or to quote Dr Harriss, "the 17th-century crisis marked the death-knell" of the political system which had lasted since the thirteenth century. "If the crown was to be supported by its subjects", two possibilities offered themselves: either absolutism or limited constitutional monarchy. "Shifts in wealth and power in society at large" were among the reasons why the traditional system could not be restored to working order.[157]

Professor Russell reminds us that there had been demands for a Navigation Act as early as 1621. [158] The powerlessness of the state led instead to plans for a private enterprise war in the West Indies: private enterprise was in fact responsible for the colonization of New England and of Providence Island, as earlier of Ireland.[159] Russell also points out the contribution of Buckingham's unpopular wars to the increased religious tensions of the late sixteen-twenties.[160] The New World had been seen from the days of the Hakluyts to the Massachusett Bay Company as a possible refuge when popery should strike. "Ideology", as Derek Hirst puts it, "had meaning for contemporaries as well as for unregenerate Whiggish historians of today".[161] Anti-Laudianism linked the desire of the natural rulers to be left alone to run their localities, alarm about the Habsburg threat to England's independence, the demand for a forward commercial policy and hostility to theorists of royal absolutism.[162]

Such issues were not at the forefront of M.Ps.' minds in the sixteen-twenties and forties. They thought of re-establishing the constitution as they imagined it to have existed under Queen Elizabeth, or perhaps of establishing the kingdom of God on earth. But they did not entirely ignore the significance of economics. The Parliament of 1621 has been called the Business Parliament. The Remonstrance of 1628 was concerned with economic matters. The Navigation Act of 1651 was foreshadowed in the economic thinking of merchants like Thomas Mun in the twenties, the aggressive commercial foreign policy which dates from the Commonwealth and Protectorate by Hakluyt and Ralegh. The abolition of feudal tenures nearly came off in 1610; the question was revived in 1626,

settled in 1646, confirmed in 1656. On 3 May 1660 the first action of
the Commons after accepting the Declaration of Breda was to set up
a committee to prepare a bill confirming the abolition.[163] The battle
for cultivating the forests, fens and commons, which Brian Manning
sees as one of the most important struggles of the century, was lost
by Charles in the sixteen-thirties, and by commoners in the forties
and fifties. The victory of the improvers contributed greatly to
solving England's food problem, at the expense of the yeomanry
which had formed the backbone of Cromwell's army.

Let us then dwell less on the revisionists' error of over-
enthusiasm than on their new insights. But let us relate these insights
to others from non-revisionists like Joan Thirsk, Brian Manning,
Derek Hirst, William Hunt, Keith Wrightson, Carolyn Merchant,
Joyce Appleby, Caroline Hibbard, and David Underdown. Then we
may see a way forward.

Conrad Russell's remark, which I cited as epigraph to this chapter,
can help us here. Discussing the "upper yeomanry", rising tradesmen
and artificers, "most of whom were rising at the expense of
smallholders and the laborious poor", he says "it would be a great
mistake ... to assume that the civil war was not caused by social
change .... Any new social change explanation will have to be based
on the power of these people".[164] It is a fertile suggestion, all the
more so since it comes from the scholar who at one time seemed to
personify the negative "it was all an accident" school of thought.
And the suggestion has been fortified by much recent work pointing
out that parish élites, drawn from precisely the classes to which
Conrad Russell referred, were no less under pressures which they
could not control than were their social superiors.

I refer especially to Wrightson and Levine's *Poverty and Piety in
an Essex Village*, and the independently written book by William
Hunt, *The Puritan Moment*.[165] The two generations before the civil
war saw a great economic divide.[166] The mass of the poor were
getting relatively and absolutely poorer, were becoming a permanent
part of the population, unable to spare the labour of their children to
give them the education which was the necessary condition without
which upward mobility was virtually impossible. The fortunate few
who were conveniently placed to produce for the market, and who
were skilful, industrious or lucky enough to seize their chance, might
prosper by taking advantage of rapidly rising prices. So in villages and
towns new and sharper class divisions were arising — no longer

setting gentry against the rest but gentry, some yeomen, some merchants, some artisans, against the rest. As Dr Morrill points out, this was so new that contemporaries had no word to describe the emerging new rich as a social group:[167] the term parish élites is an invention of historians.

I may say parenthetically that I do not agree with Dr Morrill's conclusion: that it is inappropriate to talk in terms of class in the seventeenth century, because contemporaries had no such word in their vocabulary.[168] There are also those who argue that we should not speak of revolution in seventeenth-century England because the language had no word for it. But people can experience things before they invent a name for them: one might perhaps say that they cannot name them until they have experienced them. Men described and died from T.B. long before the disease was identified. There may of course be good reasons for not applying words like "class" and "revolution" to seventeenth-century England: I am not arguing that now. But it is absurd to suppose that because contemporaries had no word for something, therefore it could not have existed: parish élites, for instance. In fact I think Dr Morrill is wrong to say that there was no contemporary word to embrace Conrad Russell's "upper yeomanry", rising tradesmen and artificers. But the word they used has a meaning so different from that which we give it that we do not recognize it. The seventeenth-century word was "people".[169]

Parish élites increasingly became political as well as economic élites. They supplied the village constables and churchwardens, who controlled wages, administered the poor law, enforced apprenticeship and the statute against cottages. Implementation of the controls necessary to prevent poverty leading to social upheaval devolved, under J.P.s, on them. These controls were accompanied by a crusade against idleness — especially on saints' days — and against the traditional village sports associated with idleness, drunkenness and sexual indulgence which produced bastards to be maintained on the poor rate. Sabbatarianism went naturally with such attitudes. We tend to speak of such manifestations as "Puritan". But a new work ethic was arising in all European countries, accompanied by hostility towards many aspects of traditional popular culture.[170] The necessity of hard and disciplined work, the wickedness of idleness and dissipation, were preached by Catholics and protestants alike. Jesuits no less than Puritans opposed the traditional Sunday sports and the theatre.

Wrightson, Levine and Hunt have shown how in Essex such "Puritan" views appealed to village élites.[171] The decay of trade and consequent unemployment of many thousands in the twenties made the cult of "discipline" the more necessary, especially in clothing counties. "Puritan" social attitudes might be shared by many who did not necessarily accept the theology. They were expressed in Parliament by Sabbatarian legislation, and by M.P.s horrified at Michell and Mompesson's patent for licensing ale-houses which took control of this vital matter out of the hands of the local rulers. Here in 1621 local considerations led to national action, focussing against the royal favourite.

To contrast "local" with "national" politics is to draw a false distinction. Under Mitchell and Mompesson's patent, Dr Hughes tells us, the number of ale-houses in Warwickshire *increased*, at a time when the local authorities were trying to diminish it.[172] In a recent convincing article Mark Kennedy has shown how the royal government made continuous and unscrupulous use of its power and authority to manipulate local institutions in order to force fen drainage schemes upon a reluctant local populace. This became a major issue in both elections of 1640, when there was virtual insurrection in the Fens.[173] Food riots against the removal of corn from a poverty-stricken countryside, riots against drainage and disafforestation by the crown and its favourites, riots against "popish soap" — all these made the simplest people realize that local grievances often stemmed from government policies, from corrupt courtiers, from inefficient or corrupt local administrators.[174] They added up to a national problem. It was *via* such "local" matters that the electorate began to be drawn in to national politics, into "opposition" to the government. The counties could not remain isolated once there was a national economy; nor could the gentry of any county community ignore serious popular grievances.

Conrad Russell refers to monarchy and Parliament as "two declining institutions, both overtaken by the functional breakdown of English administration". M.Ps. "needed to conciliate the King and they needed to conciliate their neighbours, and it was becoming increasingly difficult to do both".[175] But why was it becoming *increasingly* difficult? Professor Barnes argued that in Somerset by 1630 J.Ps. were already working to capacity if they were not to become full-time state servants. In the sixteen-thirties a novel burden was laid on them by the new Book of Orders. And they were given a number of especially distasteful tasks — enforcing composition fines for knighthood, themselves amerced for contempt if they showed lenience. Ship Money, when it clearly became a permanent tax, was the last straw. Meanwhile, J.Ps.' powers of licensing maltsters and brewers — always a sensitive point in controlling their localities — were taken from them.[176] Despite the social prestige attached to the office there was a steady decline in the numbers of J.Ps., by resignation and by purge of the unco-operative; not surprisingly, many of these who remained on the commission tried to avoid the less popular of their functions. Somerset had not been re-rated for Ship Money by 1640; by then the system had collapsed. Phelips, who had relied on the backing of the yeomanry, triumphed over Poulett who relied on the court.[177]

Barnes shows how local governors were affected, from the sixteen-twenties onwards, by opposition to fen drainage and forest enclosures, and by the refusal of yeomen and gentlemen to pay forced loans and Ship Money. Unlike some historians, he saw the Hampden case as all-important in encouraging refusals to pay. Croke's dissenting judgment circulated in manuscript.[178]

Assize judges were responsible for controlling J.P.s, so any appointment of subservient judges by the crown would rouse the apprehensions of the natural rulers.[179] Such fears were in fact raised by the judgments in Bate's, Darnell's and Hampden's cases. The common law indeed was uncertain: that is one reason why Charles forbade the publication of Coke's *Institutes* and why the Long Parliament had them published.[180] But the uncertainty of the law, and disagreements among lawyers, were symptoms, not a cause, of the crisis.

The rise of Arminianism is treated by Conrad Russell and others as almost a personal whim of the King's, which happened to conflict with the inherited prejudices of the Protestant gentry. I always found this unconvincing. Since the Reformation strong links between protestantism and English patriotism had been forged, reinforced by the calculated popularization of Foxe's *Book of Martyrs*, celebration of Guy Fawkes Day, and so on. Laudian theology and ceremonial looked like a throw-back to popery, especially ominous in the light of pro-Spanish government policies at a time when the protestant cause in Europe seemed to be going under in the Thirty Years War. As Dr Hirst shrewdly points out,[181] the presence of a soundly Calvinist archbishop of Canterbury may have been reassuring under James I; it was less so when advancement and protection were being afforded to Arminians in the Church of England and to Roman Catholics outside it. When Abbot was deprived of his jurisdiction for refusing to license Sibthorpe's sermon defending the forced loan, it was the reverse of consoling.[182] Ever since 1610, if not earlier, M.P.s had voiced suspicions of clerical defenders of arbitrary taxation.[183] Such men offered what appeared to be a threat to property, the subjects' absolute right to which the Commons always opposed to the crown's absolute prerogative. Support for Divine Right absolutism by Mainwaring, Montague and others in the twenties came precisely when French Catholic priests were elaborating a theory of royal absolutism in connection with the war against protestant La Rochelle.[184] No wonder Pym, Eliot and many others linked theological with political grievances.

But the analyses of Wrightson, Levine and Hunt suggest an additional dimension.[185] The Book of Sports positively encouraged junkettings harmful to labour discipline and social subordination. In the thirties a new and determined effort was made to snatch the initiative in running the poor law from the localities. Orders in council poured down on local authorities.[186] Laud was trying to restore the long-lost effectiveness of visitations, to increase the effectiveness of church courts, topped by the High Commission. Both would diminish the gentry's control.[187] The gentry, Conrad Russell says, suspected Charles of intending to replace them by increasing use of clergymen as J.Ps.[188] "The beauty of holiness" nearly always involved time-consuming and expensive demands on churchwardens.[189] It was likely to lead to an increase in parish rates. Part of the case against popery had always been its wastefulness of economic resources. The Laudians were enforcing a pattern of life that such men thought obsolete. Parish élites were simultaneously infuriated by the additional administrative burdens placed on them and by taxation which fell especially heavily on their social group. They might also be worried by the threat of social disorder which government policies seemed to be making inevitable. Popery and alehouses and vagabonds were all part of the same menace to control of local government. Parish élites too were between upper and nether millstones.

The rise of Laudianism would strike such men as more than a coincidence. It seemed rather the culmination of long-standing government policies aimed at reducing the hard-won authority of the

new ruling élites. It gave these policies ideological form and co-
herence as well as offering the government in the machinery of the
church the nearest it ever got to a bureaucracy. Hostility to Laudianism strengthened the alliance between J.P.s, the gentry, on the one
hand, and on the other the middling sort, through whom J.P.s *had* to
govern. We are used to tracing the rise of local oligarchy from the
early seventeenth century to its triumph by 1700 (and in the same
period J.P.s take over the moral supervision of their parishes and
shake off control from above); we forget the Laudian attempt to
reverse the trend, forget how vital was the abolition of church courts
in the sixteen-forties and fifties. When they were restored (with no
High Commission) they did not resume activity in these spheres.

Essex of course was exceptional as a clothing and Puritan county,
in the vicinity of London. It remains to be seen how far the
Wrightson-Levine-Hunt pattern applies elsewhere. Dr Hughes and
Dr Roberts found similar phenomena in Warwickshire and Devon;[190]
and the legislation which the parish élites administered was passed by
a national Parliament. But there is scope for further research here.

VI

The crown needs the gentry, the gentry need the crown. The gentry
needs parish élites, they need the gentry. Only the most severe of
strains can break this symbiosis — the sort of strains that came in the
sixteen-twenties and thirties. In 1621 and 1628 M.Ps. again and again
pointed out the disastrous state of the economy, and proposed
remedies — encouragement of the New Draperies, disrupted by
war,[191] would end the clothing depression, and so avert the imminent
danger of revolt by unemployed wage labourers. But encouragement
of the New Draperies meant protection for English merchants in the
Mediterranean: James I's expedition to Sallee was a total failure.
Charles advised English merchants to keep out of the Mediterranean;
more realistic but hardly more popular. English shipping could not
be protected against pirates even in the narrow seas. For a navy
meant taxes, and taxes caught both government and gentry between
the millstones.

The system finally cracked because of the government's inability
to cope with war and invasion: like Russia in 1917. All parties had
been patching up, Micawber-like, for too long. That is the definition
of a revolutionary situation: when the government cannot continue
governing in the traditional way any longer. Nobody willed the

breakdown, but nobody could avert it. In the last stages before total collapse the constitution had become, in Harrington's words, "no other than a wrestling match" between King, nobles and people.[192] Conrad Russell himself uses the phrase "revolutionary situation" to describe 1640-1. The crown had lost control over local government, over collection of taxes, over the army. "The King did not have the physical power to force the major part of his subjects to perform actions that they did not want to perform." He could raise no loans that were not underwritten by a Parliament.[193] "It is certainly true that the Long Parliament owed its opportunity to meet to the refusal of its social inferiors to pay their taxes during the summer of 1640", and to the series of mutinies among the troops which prevented Charles from effectively fighting the Scots. "It is only possible to see the civil war as a social conflict if it is assumed that from the beginning the leadership of the gentry among the Parliamentarians was nominal and the driving force was provided by the radical faction".[194] That seems to me the wrong way of putting the right point. In February 1640 Lord-Keeper Finch felt it necessary to urge assize judges "to break the insolency of the vulgar before it approacheth too near the royal throne".[195] In September 1642 Charles issued his commission of array because he could not trust the loyalty of the trained bands, even in counties which he controlled. The militia was left to Parliament.[196] In 1645 a paper prepared for discussions with the King at Uxbridge described the militia as "the fortress of liberty".[197]

One of the things "revisionists" most dislike is hindsight: they think it Whiggish to consider what happened next. But in discussing men fumbling with problems which their mental apparatus was incapable of solving, it does not help merely to report on their vain efforts to square the circle. In writing the history of the nineteen-thirties it is surely useful to know that one outcome of World War II was the dissolution of the British Empire. It was not what anybody willed in the thirties, and few probably clearly envisaged the prospect; but our hindsight helps to throw light on the otherwise apparently inexplicable behaviour of those who wanted to "stand up to Hitler" but not to rearm without a change of foreign policy, and those who almost welcomed Hitler because they thought Bolshevism the Empire's greatest enemy.

Looking at the seventeenth-century crisis across Europe, we can see that for most countries the outcome was to strengthen absolute monarchy based on a standing army with a bureaucracy to collect the taxes. Conrad Russell is no doubt right to say that the first two Stuarts had no intention of introducing military absolutism. But men's suspicions might be more important than reality. D'Ewes thought that "all [James I's] actions did tend to an absolute monarchy",[198] and Charles was clearly much more positive and determined than his father. Buckingham may have toyed with the idea in 1627, though Gardiner dismissed the suggestion.[199] And even if Russell is right, that is no more final than to say that there were no revolutionaries in the House of Commons. Absolutism was a conclusion to which the logic of events was always pushing: M.Ps. expressed their fear of it in every Parliament of the two reigns. It was precisely what the Petition of Right was intended to avert — arbitrary taxation enforced by arbitrary imprisonment and by a mercenary army out of the control of the natural rulers.

Military absolutism would have deprived these rulers of hegemony in their localities as effectively as social revolution: these were the two poles of impossibility between which they had to manoeuvre. The staunchest supporters of absolutist theories were the Laudians. During the discussions of the Petition of Right the Commons were also dealing with the case of Mainwaring: they at least thought the two connected. An amendment from the Lords proposing to insert the words "upon necessity" about taxation was rejected on 19 May precisely because "these reasons have already been preached by Mainwaring to the King".[200] Apart from Buckingham, the only evil councillors named in the Commons' Protestation of 14 June were Neile and Laud.

We may think that for social reasons military absolutism was an unlikely starter in England. A navy (unlike an army) cannot be used for tax collection or internal repression, and so control was difficult to wrench from the natural rulers. This may help to explain why the government preferred to work through the courts, getting decisions in favour of the prerogative, which Professior Judson described as amounting to "legal absolutism".[201] But military absolutism was always one theoretically possible outcome. Another possible outcome, I think we must conclude, was the revolution that actually happened — subordinating crown and church to an unreformed Parliament, reorganising taxation: both cause and effect of an ambitious commercial foreign policy based on a powerful navy — and a revolution in agrarian relations which ended starvation in years of harvest failure, transformed England from a corn-importing to a corn-exporting country.

The acceptable conclusion that the English Revolution was made by events, not by the conscious wills of men,[202] is no reason for refusing to try to analyse its causes. What events? How did they operate? Were they totally fortuitous? As Dr Hirst puts it, "Certain problems would not go away, and men had reluctantly and hesitantly ... to come to grips with them". Or Hexter: if there was not "*an* opposition" there was opposition, often by the same people, normally on the same issues, from 1604 to 1629.[203] When, in Harrington's words, "the dissolution of this government caused the war",[204] it was no accident that anti-Laudianism linked the disparate oppositions.

In 1639-40 the rank and file of the army — extremely reluctant to fight our brethren of Scotland — seemed happier to rabble popish officers and to pull down altar rails. But they also pulled down enclosures. Selden pointed out that bishops were the universal scapegoat, and asked "When the dog is beat out of the room, where will they lay the stink?"[205] His metaphor is relevant to my argument: the dog was visible, not the stink. But the stink had been there long before Laudians could be blamed for it; it was all-pervasive and very noticeable. Some historians will continue to deny its existence. Others, perhaps with more sensitive noses, will agree that it needs explaining.

NOTES

1. Sir John Neale Memorial Lecture delivered at University College, London, 4 December, 1980. Printed in *P. and P.*, 92 (1981).
2. D. Hirst, "Unanimity in the Commons, Aristocratic Intrigue and the Origins of the English Civil War", and J. H. Hexter, "Power Struggle, Parliament and Liberty in Early Stuart England", both in *Journal of Modern History*, 1 (1978); Clive Holmes, "The 'County Community' in Stuart Historiography", *Journal of British Studies*, 19 (1980); D. Hirst, "Parliament, Law and War in the 1620s", *Historical Journal*, 23 (1980); Austin Woolrych, "Court, Country and City Revisited", *History*, 65 (1980). See now articles by T. K. Rabb and D. Hirst in *P. and P.*, 92 (1981).
3. Alan Everitt, *Suffolk and the Great Rebellion, 1640-1660* (Suffolk Record Society, iii, 1960); *idem*, "The Community of Kent in 1640", *Genealogists' Mag.*, xiv (1963); *idem*, *The Community of*

Kent and the Great Rebellion, 1640-60 (Leicester U.P., 1966); *idem, Change in the Provinces; The Seventeenth Century* (Dept. of English Local History, University of Leicester, Occasional Papers, No. I, Leicester 1969); *idem, New Avenues in English Local History* (Leicester, 1970; *idem,* "Country, County and Town: Patterns of Regional Evolution in England", *T.R.H.S.*, fifth series, xx (1979).

4. J.S. Morrill, *Cheshire, 1630-1660: County Government and Society during the "English Revolution"* (Oxford U.P., 1974); *idem, The Revolt of the Provinces: Conservatives and Radicals in the English Civil War, 1630-1650* (1976).

5. Morrill, *The Revolt of the Provinces*, revised edn. (1980), p. x.

6. C. Holmes, *The Eastern Association in the English Civil War* (Cambridge U.P., 1974), pp. 123-9.

7. David Underdown, *Somerset in the Civil War and Interregum* (1973); *idem,* "Clubmen in the Civil War", *P. and P.*, No. 85 (1979).

8. B.G. Blackwood, "The Marriages of the Lancashire Gentry on the Eve of the Civil War", *Genealogists' Magazine,* 16 (1970); *idem, The Landed Gentry and the Great Rebellion, 1640-60* (Chetham Soc., third series, 25, Manchester, 1978).

9. A. Fletcher, *A County Community in Peace and War: Sussex, 1600-1660* (1975).

10. P. Clark, *English Provincial Society from the Reformation to the Revolution: Religion, Politics and Society in Kent, 1500-1640* (1977).

11. Ann Hughes, "Politics, Society and Civil War in Warwickshire, 1620-1650" (University of Liverpool Ph.D. thesis, 1979).

12. S.K. Roberts, *Recovery and Restoration in an English County: Devon Local Administration, 1646-1670* (Exeter U.P., 1985) pp. 41, 75-6, 214.

13. *The Agrarian History of England and Wales,* iv, *1500-1640* (ed. J. Thirsk, Cambridge U.P., 1967).

14. Joan Thirsk, *Economic Policy and Projects: The Development of a Consumer Society in Early Modern England* (Oxford U.P. 1978).

15. Hughes, *op.cit.;* Underdown, "Clubmen in the Civil War", esp. pp. 36-48.

16. Brian Manning, *The English People and the English Revolution* (1976).

17. Hughes, *op.cit.*, p. 226; Morrill, *The Revolt of the Provinces*, p. 330.

18. Morrill, *op. cit.*, pp. 36-8, 48-9, 113, 120, 151-2, 214; cf. B.G. Blackwood, *The Lancashire Gentry and the Great Rebellion*, p. 27; for Laslett, see p. 4 above.

19. Manning, *op. cit.*, Chapters 2-7; *idem,* "The Nobles, the People and the Constitution", *P. and P.*, No. 9 (1956), *passim; idem,* "The Aristocracy and the Downfall of Charles I" and "Religion and Politics: The Godly People", both in Brian Manning (ed.), *Politics, Religion and the Civil War* (1973), *passim.*

20. Buchanan Sharp, *In Contempt of All Authority: Rural Artisans and Riot in the West of England, 1586-1660* (Berkeley, 1980).

21. D. Hirst, *The Representative of the People?: Voters and Voting in England under the Early Stuarts* (Cambridge 1975), p. 111; J.T. Cliffe, *The Yorkshire Gentry from the Reformation to the Civil War*

(1969), pp. 283-6, 323-5. See now a debate between A. J. Fletcher and myself in *P. and P.*, 98 (1983).

22. Hirst, *op. cit.*, p. 153; Hirst, "Court, Country and Politics", in *Faction and Parliament: Essays on Early Stuart History* (ed. K. Sharpe, Oxford U.P., 1979), p. 131; *Proceedings in Parliament, 1610* (ed. E. R. Foster, Yale U.P., 1966), II, pp. 95, 402.

23. G. R. Elton, "A High Road to Civil War?", in *From the Renaissance to the Counter-Reformation: Essays in Honor of Garrett Mattingly* (ed. C. H. Carter, New York, 1965), p. 334; cf. W. Notestein, *The House of Commons, 1604-1610* (Yale U.P., 1971), pp. 319, 357, 359, 393-4.

24. Foster, *op. cit.*, II, p. 348.

25. S. R. Gardiner, *History of England, 1603-1642* (1883-4), V, p. 182.

26. *Letters of John Chamberlain*, (ed. N. E. McClure, Philadelphia, 1939), II, p. 543.

27. P. Zagorin, *The Court and the Country: The Beginning of the English Revolution of the mid-seventeenth century* (New York, 1970), p. 111; cf. Hirst, *The Representative of the People?*, pp. 144-5, 164-5, and R. E. Schreiber, *The Political Career of Sir Robert Naunton, 1589-1635* (1981), pp. 117-18.

28. Hirst, *The Representative of the People?*, p. 161.

29. *Ibid.*, p. 174.

30. Cf. the caution with which Wallace Notestein approached the word (*The House of Commons, 1604-1610*, Yale U.P., 1971, p. 465.).

31. C. Russell, *Parliaments and English Politics, 1621-1629*, pp. 417-18, 426, 464.

32. Hexter, *op. cit.*; Hirst, "Unanimity in the Commons".

33. Russell, *Parliaments and English Politics, 1621-1629*; C. Russell (ed.), *The Origins of the Civil War* (1973); C. Russell, "The Parliamentary Career of John Pym, 1621-1629", in P. Clark, A. G. T. Smith and N. Tyacke (eds.), *The English Commonwealth, 1547-1640: Essays in Politics and Society Presented to Joel Hurstfield* (Leicester U.P., 1979); C. Russell, "Parliament and the King's Finances", in *The Origins of the English Civil War*.

34. J. S. Morrill, *Seventeenth-Century Britain, 1603-1714* (1980), p. 33.

35. Hirst, "Unanimity in the Commons".

36. Russell, Introduction to *The Origins of the English Civil War*, p. 7; J. E. Farnell, "The Social and Intellectual Basis of London Politics in the English Civil War", *Journal of Modern History*, 49 (1977), pp. 643-4, 659; cf. P. Christianson, "The Peers, the People and Parliamentary Management in the First Six Months of the Long Parliament", *Journal of Modern History* (1977), esp. pp. 575-7, 582.

37. Farnell, *op. cit.*, pp. 643, 651, 654 n.; Christianson, *op. cit.*, pp. 577-8. Hexter has fun with "Livian revolutionaries": Hexter, "Power Struggle, Parliament and Liberty", pp. 22-4. What is especially sad is that Professor Farnell is a very accomplished historian who has written two admirable articles about the City during the interregnum. He rightly sees that these conflict with his present views, but

unfortunately it is his earlier articles which he abandons.

38. Hirst, "Unanimity in the Commons", pp. 53-70. Dr Hirst speaks of "the new *deus ex machina* ...", patronage, for whose efficacy there is as yet little proof": *ibid.*, pp. 60, 62.

39. C. Russell, "The Parliamentary Career of John Pym, 1621-1629", in *The English Commonwealth, 1547-1640*, pp. 148-51; contrast Christianson, *loc. cit.*, pp. 577-8.

40. Hirst, "Unanimity in the Commons", p. 61; K. Sharpe, "The Earl of Arundel", pp. 228-30, 236, 241; *idem, Sir Robert Cotton, 1586-1631: History and Politics in Early Modern England* (Oxford U.P., 1979), p. 160. Hexter, "Power Struggle, Parliament and Liberty", and Woolrych, "Court, Country and City Revisited", have some trenchant words on this subject.

41. Hirst, *The Representative of the People?*, pp. 68-75; *idem,* "Court, Country and Politics before 1629", p. 136; R. E. Ruigh, *The Parliament of 1624; Politics and Foreign Policy* (Harvard U.P., 1971), pp. 95-6; D. H. Willson, *The Privy Councillors in the House of Commons, 1604-1629* (Minneapolis, 1940), pp. 52-5, 68-82, 158, 176-90, 203, 208-13.

42. C. Russell, *Parliaments and English Politics, 1621-1629*, and Introduction to *The Origins of the English Civil War*; M. A. Judson, *The Crisis of the Constitution* (Rutgers U.P., 1949), *passim;* G. H. Harriss, "Medieval Doctrines in the Debates on Supply", in Sharpe (ed.), *op. cit.*, pp. 73-103.

43. Elton, *op. cit.*, pp. 325-7. For some corrections to Professor Elton, see Zagorin, *op. cit.*, p. 78.

44. Judson, *op. cit.*, pp. 221, 228-9, 240, 284, 302, 308, 348, and *passim.* Cf. a useful book by Wilfried Nippel, *Mischverfassungstheorie und Verfassungsrealität in Antike und früher Neuzeit* (Stuttgart, 1980), esp. pp. 166, 191, 223.

45. *Two Diaries of the Long Parliament* (ed. Maija Johnson, Gloucester, 1984), p. xv; Notestein, *op. cit.*, pp. 368, 432-3, 559, 561.

46. Russell, *Parliaments and Politics*, Chapters 6-7. Remarkably, the Apology of 1604 is not printed in J. P. Kenyon's *The Stuart Constitution: Documents and Commentary* (Cambridge U.P., 1966). It can be found in D. W. Prothero, *Statutory and Constitutional Documents, 1558-1625* (Oxford U.P., third edn., 1906), pp. 290-1.

47. Foster, *op. cit.*, II, pp. 157-8, 189, 242, 266, 284; cf. pp. 72, 83, 107-8. *Ibid.*, I, pp. 276-8, and for the outraged reaction of Lord Chancellor Ellesmere, see Knafla, *Law and Politics in Jacobean England: The Tracts of Lord Chancellor Ellesmere* (Cambridge U.P., 1977), pp. 254-62; also Russell, *Parliaments and Politics*, p. 24. Coke in 1624 posed prerogative against property, S. D. White, *Sir Edward Coke and 'The Grievances of the Commonwealth', 1621-1628* (North Carolina U.P., 1979, pp. 99-100). Cf. Hexter, *op. cit.*, pp. 41-2; Hirst, "Unanimity in the Commons", p. 460.

48. *Commons Debates, 1628* (ed. R. C. Johnson and M. J. Cole, Yale U.P., 1977), II, p. 63; IV, pp. 332, 410, 447.

49. Russell, *Parliaments and Politics*, p. 400.
50. Foster, *op. cit.*, I, pp. xxviii-ix. Cf. Notestein's discussion of that extraordinary document, for its time, "Policies in Parliament", *op. cit.*, pp. 434, 577; C. Simms, "'Policies in Parliament': an early seventeenth-century tractate on House of Commons procedure", *Huntington Library Quarterly*, 15 (1951), pp. 45-58.
51. Foster, *op. cit.*, II, pp. 165, 267, 411; T.L. Moir, *The Addled Parliament, 1614* (Oxford U.P., 1958), p. 142.
52. Moir, *op. cit.*, p. 136.
53. *Two Diaries of the Long Parliament*, p. xv; Notestein, *op. cit.*, pp. 368, 432 sq., 559, 561; Blair Wordem, "Classical Republicanism and the Puritan Revolution", in *History and Imagination: Essays in honour of H.R. Trevor-Roper* (ed. H. Lloyd-Jones, V. Pearl and B. Worden, 1981), pp. 188-90.
54. As is argued in a forthcoming book by Tim Curtis.
55. Review by Russell in *History*, 221 (1982), p. 483.
56. W.T. MacCaffrey, *Queen Elizabeth and the Making of Policy, 1572-1588* (Princeton U.P., 1981), pp. 113, 299, 445, 473-6, 489-90, 496.
57. *Ibid.*, pp. 299-300, 466-8, 497.
58. Hirst, "Unanimity in the Commons", pp. 457-8, 460; "Parliament, Law and War in the 1620s", *Historical Journal*, 23 (1980), p. 457.
59. Ed. Notestein, F.H. Relf and H. Simpson, *Commons Debate in 1621*, (Yale U.P., 1935) V, p. 437, VI, pp. 327, 347, 350.
60. Russell, *Parliaments and Politics*, pp. 103, 419.
61. Judson, *op. cit.*, pp. 126-32, 148, 157-8.
62. Cf. Buchanan Sharp, *op. cit.*, pp. 11, 47-50, 64-6, 78-81.
63. *Commons Debates, 1621*, II, p. 416; cf. III, p. 370.
64. Russell, *Parliaments and Politics*, pp. 17-18.
65. J.K. Gruenfelder, "The Electoral Patronage of Sir Thomas Wentworth, Earl of Strafford, 1614-1640", *American Historical Review*, 49 (1977), p. 567.
66. T.G. Barnes, *Somerset, 1625-1640: A County's Government during the 'Personal Rule'* (Oxford U.P., 1961), pp. 294-5.
67. Bodleian Library, Oxford, Tanner MS, lxii, fo. 300, printed in *The Academy*, 5 June 1875, pp. 352-3, and quoted by C.V. Wedgwood, *Strafford* (1935), p. 75.
68. *Commons Debates, 1628*, iii, pp. 193, 272, 278; iv. p. 311.
69. Knafla, *op. cit.*, p. 302. I have pursued this matter further in "Political Discourse in early 17th-century England", in *For Veronica Wedgwood these: Studies in seventeenth-century History* (ed. R. Ollard and Pamela Tudor-Craig, 1986).
70. *Commons Debates, 1628*, iv, p. 62. The speaker is Eliot.
71. F.H. Relf, *The Petition of Right* (Minneapolis 1918), p. 40.
72. *The Diary of Sir Simonds D'Ewes, 1622-1624*, ed. E. Bourchier (Paris, [?1974]), pp. 113, 135, 92-3, 158, 121-3; cf. Notestein, *op. cit.*, p. 282
73. J. Selden, *Table Talk* (1847), p. 97.
74. *The Diary of John Rous*, ed. M.A.E. Green (Camden Society, old series, 66, 1856), pp. 12, 19, 42-3; *The Diary of Walter Yonge*, ed. G. Roberts

(Camden Society, old series, 41 1841), pp. 102-3.
75. Russell, "The Parliamentary Career of John Pym".
76. *Ibid.*, p. 151; *Letters of John Chamberlain*, II, p. 412; Notestein, *op. cit.*, p. 482.
77. Bibliothèque Nationale, Mélanges de Colbert, 11, fo. 453, quoted by Bernard Cottret, "Diplomatie et éthique de l'état: L'Ambassade d'Effiat en Angleterre ... (éte 1624–printemps 1625)", in *L'Etat Baroque: Regards sur la Pensée Politique de la France du premier XVIIe siècle* (ed. Henry Mechoulan, Paris 1985), p. 236.
78. H. Townshend, *Historical Collections* (1680), p. 204.
79. *Commons Debates, 1628*, IV, pp. 17, 222.
80. Russell, *Origins*, p. 96; *Parliaments and Politics*, pp. 49-51, 398.
81. Gardiner, *op. cit.*, V, pp. 200-1; cf. Russell, *Origins*, p. 268; *Parliaments and Politics*, p. 398.
82. Russell, *Parliaments and Politics*, p. 50.
83. John Rogers, *A Treatise of Love* (3rd edn., 1637), quoted by Ann Hughes, Thesis, p. 379; cf. Russell, *Parliaments and Politics*, pp. 257-9.
84. *Op. cit.*, pp. 12-13, quoted by Ann Hughes, Thesis, p. 59.
85. Russell, *Parliaments and Politics*, p. 226.
86. J. Thirsk, *Economic Policy and Projects*, esp. Chapters 4-7.
87. Hirst, *The Representative of the People?*, pp. 49-50; *Commons Debates, 1628*, IV, p. 37.
88. Russell, "Parliamentary History in Perspective, 1604-1629", *History*, 61 (1976), pp. 6-7, 10, 14.
89. Ruigh, *op. cit.*, pp. 199-201, 254; cf S. Adams, "Captain Thomas Gainsford, the 'Vox Spiritus' and the *Vox Populi*", *Bulletin of the Institute of Historical Research*, 39 (1976), p. 171.
90. Hirst, "Court, Country and Politics", pp. 134-5; C. D. Gilmore, "The Papers of Richard Taylor of Clapham", *Bedfordshire Historical Record Society*, 25 (1947-8), pp. 107-8. I owe this reference to Wilfrid Prest.
91. Foster, *op. cit.*, II, pp. 291, 311.
92. A. Hassell Smith, "Militia Rights and Militia Statutes, 1558-1663", in *The English Commonwealth, 1547-1640*, pp. 121-4.
93. Foster, *op. cit.*, II, p. 318; I, p. xix; cf. Notestein, *op. cit.*, pp. 393-4.
94. Knafla, *op. cit.*, pp. 93-104, 263-73.
95. Gardiner, *op. cit.*, V, p. 196.
96. Russell, *Parliaments and Politics*, pp. 244-6; White, *op. cit.*, pp. 209-10.
97. W. Nippel, *op. cit.*, p. 235.
98. Russell, *Parliaments and Politics*, pp. 282-4.
99. Russell, *Origins*, pp. 112-15.
100. Cf. Russell, *Parliaments and Politics*, pp. 336, 397.
101. *Ibid.*, p. 333.
102. *Commons Debates, 1628*, IV, pp. 146, 191, 242, 290.
103. A. Hassell-Smith, *op. cit.*, pp. 107-9; Fletcher, *op. cit.*, pp. 203-5. Giles Randall, preaching in Huntingdonshire in 1636, agreed (R. M. Jones, *Spiritual Reformers in the 16th and 17th centuries*, 1928, p. 254).

Ship Money provoked "a tumultuous assembly of miners" in Derby-shire (J.M. Brentnall, *William Bagshawe, Apostle of the Peak, 1970*, p.3. Cf. Philip Riden, *History of Chesterfield*, Chesterfield, 1984, II, Part 1, p.89).

104. Hassell-Smith, *op. cit.*, pp. 98, 100-1, 104.
105. Russell, *Parliaments and Politics*, pp. 333, 358-9.
106. R. Ashton, *The English Civil War: Conservatism and Revolution, 1603-1649* (1978), pp. 55-9.
107. G.L. Harriss, "Mediaeval Doctrines in the Debates on Supply, 1610-1629", in Sharpe, *op. cit.*, pp. 82-3.
108. R.H. Tawney, *Business and Politics under James I: Lionel Cranfield as Merchant and Minister* (Cambridge U.P., 1958), p. 176.
109. *Ibid.*, pp. 93-4.
110. *Ibid.*, p. 292.
111. *Ibid.*, pp. 285-6, 295.
112. *Ibid.*, pp. 220, 223.
113. *Ibid.*, p. 292.
114. Russell, "Parliamentary History in Perspective", pp. 7-8, 22-4; Hirst, "Court, Country and Politics", p. 133; Hexter, *op. cit.*, p. 44.
115. Gardiner, *op. cit.*, VI, p. 374.
116. Russell, *Parliaments and Politics*, p. 49.
117. *Ibid.*, pp. 101-2, 116, 192; "Parliamentary History in Perspective", p. 14; S.K. Roberts, "Alehouses, Brewing and Government under the early Stuarts", *Southern History*, 2 (1980), pp. 45-71; Hassell-Smith, *op. cit.*, pp. 121-4.
118. M. Prestwich, *Cranfield: Politics and Profits under the Early Stuarts* (Oxford U.P., 1966), p. 252; cf. Tawney, *op. cit.*, p. 293.
119. C. Roberts, *The Growth of Responsible Government in England* (Cambridge U.P. 1966), pp. 11-12, cf. p. 48.
120. Knafla, *op. cit.*, pp. 309-10.
121. Russell, "Parliament and the King's Finances", in *The Origins of the English Civil War, passim; idem, Parliaments and English Politics*, esp. Conclusion.
122. See pp. 37-8 above.
123. Cf. Judson, *op. cit.*, p. 120.
124. Russell, *Parliaments and English Politics*, p. 325; *Debates in the House of Commons in 1625*, ed. S.R. Gardiner (Camden Society, new series, vi, 1873), pp. xii, 78.
125. Russell, *Parliaments and English Politics*, pp. 325-7.
126. Knafla, *op. cit.*, pp. 81, 88, 97, 254-62; Russell, "Parliamentary History in Perspective", pp. 9, 24; Hexter, *op. cit.*, pp. 39-40; Notestein, *op. cit.*, pp. 78, 385, 410.
127. Russell, *Parliaments and English Politics*, p. 76; cf. the many legal problems discussed in Professor F.H. Relf's Introduction to *Notes of the Debates in the House of Lords ... 1621, 1625, 1628* (Camden Society, third series, xlii, 1929), pp. xix-xxx.
128. Russell, *Parliaments and Politics*, p. 15.
129. *Ibid.*, p. 35.

130. J. Penry, *Three Treatises Concerning Wales* (ed. D. Williams, Wales U.P., 1960), pp. 164-5; Sir Thomas Crewe, *Proceedings and Debates in the House of Commons ... in 1628* (1707), p. 22.

131. Notestein, *op. cit.*, p. 260.

132. Ralegh, *Works*, I, pp. 240-2; S. Adams, "Captain Thomas Gainsford, the 'Vox Spiritus' and *Vox Populi*", pp. 141-4; P. Steffens, "Gainsford's *Vox Spiritus or Sir Walter Raleigh's Ghost*", research paper submitted to West Coast Journalism Historians' Conference, 1-2 March 1980.

133. Russell, *Parliaments and Politics*, p. 37.

134. Hexter, *op. cit.*, pp. 26-8, 32; Willson, *op. cit.*, p. 413.

135. *Commons Debates, 1628*, IV, p. 482; cf. White, *Sir Edward Coke and "the Grievances of the Commonwealth"*, p. 251.

136. Christopher O'Riordan, "The Democratic Revolution in the Company of Thames Watermen, 1641-2", *East London Record*, 6 (1983), pp. 18, 20.

137. Quoted by Joyce Malcolm, *Caesar's Due: Loyalty and King Charles, 1642-1646* (1983), p. 190; cf. pp. 88-90.

138. Russell, *Parliaments and Politics*, p. 58.

139. In *The Agrarian History of England and Wales*, IV, *1500-1640*, p. 621.

140. Manning, *The English People and the English Revolution, passim*.

141. Bourcier, *op. cit.*, pp. 58, 64, 122-3; Russell, *Parliaments and English Politics*, pp. 74-5, 252, and cf. pp. 165-6, 339-41; Zagorin, *op. cit.*, p. 111; Rous, *op. cit.*, p. 12. Cf. Maija Johnson, *op. cit.*, p. 4; fear of unpaid soldiers, February 1641.

142. *Commons Debates, 1628*, III, p. 412; cf. Gardiner, *History of England, 1603-42*, VI, pp. 279-85.

143. Dr. J.N. Ball discusses the reasons for the Lords' acceptance of the Petition, but concludes that it was determined by an assurance that the Petition did not limit the royal prerogative: J. N. Ball, "The Petition of Right in the English Parliament of 1628", in *Anciens pays et assemblées d'états* (Etudes publiés par la section belge de la communité internationale pour l'histoire des assemblées d'états, Centre Nationale de Recherches, A.S.B.L., Leuwen, 1964), pp. 58-64.

144. For their familiarity, see *Notes of the Debates in the House of Lords*, ed. Relf, Camden Soc., 42 (1929), p. 187. But see also Judson, *op. cit.*, p. 262, for possible new points in Glanville's speech: that the King might dispense with his own but not his subjects' right and that the object of the Petition was solely to confirm the latter.

145. *Commons Debates, 1628*, II, p. 577. This may be Marten's own contribution to the speech, which had been drafted by the committee. Three weeks earlier he had said "every man has his mouth full of the distance between the King and his people": *ibid.*, III, p. 238. I quote indiscriminately from two versions of Marten's speech printed in *ibid.*

146. *Ibid.*, III, pp. 578-9.

147. *Ibid.*, p. 588; White, *op. cit.*, p. 267.

148. Cf. Wentworth on 22 May; if we accept the Lords' clause, "we shall have no thanks for it when we come home", *Commons Debates, 1628*, III, p. 538.

149. Gardiner, *op. cit.*, VI, p. 352; Russell, *Parliaments and English Politics*, p. 392; E.R. Foster, "Printing the Petition of Right", *Huntington Library Quarterly*, 38 (1974), pp. 81-2.

150. *Commons Debates, 1628*, III, pp. 98, 102, 290, 559 (Wentworth), 627; cf. pp. 111, 212, 273, 279.

151. Russell, *Parliaments and Politics*, p. 21; *Commons Debates, 1628*, IV, p. 204n.

152. Foster, *op. cit.*, p. 83; Russell, *Parliament and Politics*, p. 389.

153. *Change and Continuity in 17th-century England* (1974), p. 192; Marie Axton, *The Queen's Bodies: Drama and the Elizabethan Succession* (1977), p. 90.

154. Rushworth, *Historical Collections* (1659-1701), IV, p. 425.

155. I have been too grudging about these historians in my concern with the superstructure which one or two of them raised on their invaluable factual base. A fairer balance is struck by David Underdown, "Community and Class: Theories of Local Politics", in *After the Reformation*, pp. 147-65.

156. Farnell, *op. cit.*, p. 648. He apparently attributes this policy mainly to "the Providence Company aristocrats".

157. Harriss, in Sharpe, *op. cit.*, pp. 74, 87, 98-100; cf. p. 90.

158. Russell, *Parliaments and Politics*, p. 98.

159. *Ibid.*, pp. 262-3, 293, 299.

160. *Ibid.*, pp. 81-3.

161. Hirst, "Politics, Law and War in the 1620s," *Historical Journal*, 23 (1980), p. 461.

162. Russell, *Parliaments and Politics*, p. 367.

163. [Ed. W. Cobbett], *Parliamentary History of England, 1660-1688* (1808), p. 30.

164. Russell, *Parliaments and English Politics*, p. 1; Russell, *Origins of the English Civil War*, pp. 8-9. The point has been anticipated in lectures which Wallace Notestein gave in Oxford in 1950.

165. K. Wrightson and D. Levine, *Poverty and Piety in an Essex Village: Terling, 1525-1700* (1979); Hunt, *The Puritan Moment: The Coming of Revolution in a English County* (Harvard U.P., 1983). I am grateful to Dr. Hunt for allowing me to read this book in advance of publication. See also my *Puritanism and Revolution* (Panther edn, 1969), p. 229, and *Change and Continuity in 17th-century England*, p. 202.

166. On the polarization of the local community, see for example V. Skipp, *Crisis and Development: An Ecological Study of the Forest of Arden* (Cambridge U.P., 1978), p. 78 and *passim*. See now Wrightson, *English Society, 1580-1680* (1982) and D. Underdown, *Revel, Riot and Rebellion* (1965).

167. Morrill, *Seventeenth-Century Britain*, pp. 108-9.

168. *Ibid.*
169. See Chapter 12 below.
170. See esp. Peter Burke, *Popular Culture in Early Modern Europe* (1978), *passim*; R.C. Walton, "Heinrich Bullinger, Repräsentant der Reichen Bauern und seine Beziehung zur städtischen Oligarchie", in *Reform, Reformation, Revolution* (Festschrift for Max Steinmetz, Leipzig, 1980), pp.138-42; P. Slack, "Poverty and Politics in Salisbury, 1597-1666", in P. Clark and P. Slack (eds.), *Crisis and Order in English Towns, 1500-1700* (1972), pp.181-94.
171. Wrightson and Levine, *op. cit.*, esp. Chapters 6-7; Hunt, *op. cit.*, and now Wrightson, *English Society.*
172. Ann Hughes, Thesis, p.107.
173. M.E. Kennedy, "Charles I and Local Government: The Draining of the East and West Fens", *Albion*, 15 (1983), pp.24-31. Cf. pp.76, 101, 259 below.
174. Buchanan Sharp, "Popular Protest in Seventeenth-Century England", in *Popular Culture in Seventeenth-Century England* (ed. B. Reay, Beckenham 1985), *passim.*
175. Russell, "Parliamentary History in Perspective", pp.17, 26.
176. Barnes, *op. cit.*, pp.97, 169, 194-5, 200, 206, 292-5.
177. *Ibid.*, pp.168, 221, 286, 301-14.
178. *Ibid.*, pp.170-1, 225, 228.
179. *Ibid.*, p.92.
180. Russell, *Parliaments and Politics*, pp.351-8, 363-6. Dr. Prest, unlike Brunton and Pennington, sees a preponderance of common lawyers on the Parliamentarian side in the civil war: see his forthcoming book, *Professors of the Law: A social history of the English bar, 1590-1640.*
181. Personal communication from Derek Hirst.
182. Russell, *Parliaments and English Politics*, pp.28, 421; Gardiner, *op. cit.*, VI, pp.205-6.
183. *Proceedings in Parliament, 1610*, ed. Foster, II, p.328; Notestein, *op. cit.*, p.566; Moir, *op. cit.*, p.130: C. Thompson, "The Divided Leadership of the House of Commons in 1629", in Sharpe (ed.), *Faction and Parliament*, p.253, cf. pp.272, 284.
184. David Parker, *La Rochelle and the French Monarchy: Conflict and Order in Seventeenth-Century France* (1980), Chapter 6, *passim.*
185. See the works cited in notes 165-6 above.
186. See Barnes, *op. cit.*, *passim.*
187. M. Hawkins, "The Government: Its Rule and Its Aims, in *The Origins of the English Civil War*, pp.60-2.
188. Russell, *Parliaments and English Politics*, pp.43, 277, 406.
189. For example, Fletcher, *op. cit.*, pp.82-7.
190. Hughes, "Politics, Sociology and Civil War in Warwickshire, 1620-1650"; Roberts, "Participants and Performance in Devon Local Administration, 1649-1670". Cf. now Underdown, *Revel, Riot and Rebellion* for Somerset, Wiltshire and Dorset.
191. *Commons Debate in 1621*, II, pp.447-57; Buchanan Sharp, *op. cit.*,

p. 30; cf. *Commons Debates, 1628*, IV, pp. 64, 84-5, 316-18.

192. Ed. J.G.A. Pocock, *The Political Works of James Harrington* (Cambridge U.P., 1977), 196; cf. p. 198.

193. Russell, *Origins*, pp. 28, 109-10; cf. Russell, "Why did Charles I call the Long Parliament?", *History*, 227 (1984), p. 375-83.

194. Russell, *Origins*, pp. 26, 10-12.

195. Quoted by Wilfrid Prest in his forthcoming *Professors of the Law*.

196. Joyce Malcolm, "A King in search of soldiers: Charles I in 1642", *Historical Journal*, 21 (1978), p. 267.

197. *Thurloe State Papers*, I, p. 54.

198. Russell, *Origins of the English Civil War*, p. 14; Bourcier, *op. cit.*, p. 59; cf. Notestein, *op. cit.*, p. 259.

199. Gardiner, *op. cit.*, VI, pp. 223-4.

200. *Commons Debates, 1628*, III, pp. 478, 536; cf. pp. 411-12, 416, 624; IV, pp. 102-8, 313.

201. Judson, *op. cit.*, Chapter 4, *passim*.

202. Russell, *Parliaments and English Politics*, pp. 430-3. The point had been anticipated in lectures which Wallace Notestein delivered in Oxford in 1950.

203. Hirst, "Unanimity in the Commons", p. 70; Hexter, "Power, Parliament and Liberty in Early Stuart England", pp. 7-8, 25-8.

204. *The Political Works of James Harrington*, p. 198.

205. Selden, *op. cit.*, p. 22.

POSTSCRIPT

I have added some passages which were omitted, from considerations of space, when this piece was first published. Apart from minor corrections I have left the argument virtually unchanged. It is now a period piece. The nine days wonder of revisionism is over. Its extremer manifestations have failed to convince the more intelligent younger historians, those who matter. Its positive contributions are being assimilated. Professor David Underdown's *Revel, Riot and Rebellion: Popular Politics and Culture in England, 1603-1660* (1985) is a convincing post-revisionist synthesis, starting from the flat statement "I do not regard the English Revolution as a fortuitous accident, unrelated to fundamental political and social processes.... To understand the revolution, we must first try to uncover its causes by paying some attention to the history of the preceding period". This he does by studying three counties, Wiltshire, Somerset and Dorset, in great detail — not just the politics of the gentry but the social, religious, regional and cultural divisions which had long been developing among the inhabitants of the counties, *all* the inhabitants. This opens up quite a new perspective for a total analysis of the "two Englands".[1]

My position is I suppose a modified Tawneyism — seriously modified in the light of work published since the nineteen-fifties. Then Tawney's statistics were called in question; but his case in "The Rise of the Gentry" and "Harrington's Interpretation of his Age" did not rest primarily on statistics. Its greatest strength derived from its reliance on informed contemporary opinion. Dr. Morrill wants us to listen very carefully to the views of "provincial squires".[2] This is a useful thing to do, but I think it is even more profitable to listen to the great thinkers and artists of an age if we want to understand it better than it understood itself. To return to the nineteen-thirties: I think a historian would learn more about society from the poems of Eliot and Auden, the criticism of Orwell and Leavis, than from verbatim accounts of what was said in clubland or from leading articles in the *Daily Mail*.

I have in mind especially a recent contribution from Professor Hexter. He used *Richard II* to illustrate the significance of property issues for Shakespeare and his audience — for the groundlings as well as the gentry.[3] This is rather more Marxist than what most of us have got out of *Richard II*, but Hexter is convincing. It is important for historians not to get fixated on the events of 1640-2, on Parliament and the gentry. Much valuable assistance towards a wider vision has come recently from literary historians like Margot Heinemann, Jonathan Dollimore, Martin Butler, David Norbrook and Simon Shepherd. They help us to see dramatists playing with theories of monarchy, culminating in Lear's acceptance of the possibility of his dethronement — a possibility Charles I never seriously considered; and the contrasting of court and bourgeois standards in Middleton.[4] The Hobbist individualism of Marlowe and some of Tourneur's characters, the conflicts which shoot through metaphysical poetry, the battle of the books between Ancients and Moderns — all these may give us a better understanding of the seventeenth-century social crisis than listening ever so carefully to what provincial squires thought life was about.

Similar help towards grasping the sense of crisis which sensitive men and women felt in the pre-revolutionary decades comes from historians of political ideas, like Quentin Skinner, Robert Eccleshall, Richard Tuck; from historians of religion like Patrick Collinson and Caroline Hibbard, from historians of economic thought like Joyce Appleby; from historians of law, like Wilfred Prest, J. S. Cockburn, Louis Knafla, J. A. Sharpe; from historians of science, like Charles Webster, J. R. and M. C. Jacob, Carolyn Merchant and Brian Easlea; from social historians, like those mentioned on pp. 46-7 above, together with Margaret Spufford and Bernard Capp; and from historians of public opinion like Joyce Malcolm.

All these studies confirm Wallace MacCaffrey's analysis of tensions in the society, at least since the reign of Elizabeth: tensions that were cultural as well as religious, political and regional, and which affected the élite no less than the populace. They contributed both to the breakdown of government in 1640-1 and to the release of apparently new ideas after the collapse of censorship. They increase the difficulty of regarding that breakdown as an accident. Historians' work will be greatly impoverished if they do not avail themselves of these keys to what was happening in the society they discuss.

When I was young we rather prided ourselves on trying to free legal history from lawyers, religious history from theologians, literary history from literary critics, the history of science from internalist scientists. Now we may perhaps add the duty of getting the

history of Parliament out of the hands of those who know nothing
but the history of Parliament. (Obviously, this does not include
Conrad Russell). Some of those whom Professor Elton might dismiss as amateur historians had perhaps a greater wisdom — Tawney,
with his expertise in religion and political theory, Louis B. Wright
and Hexter, with their feel for literature, Trevor-Roper, who recognized that Comenius, Dury and Hartlib were as important as
backwoods gentlemen, Lawrence Stone with his interest in archi-
tecture, education and marriage. We might even recall those very
great historians S. R. Gardiner and Wallace Notestein, who would
never have separated the history of Parliament from seventeenth-
century literature and the life of the common people.

NOTES

1. Underdown, *op. cit.*, pp. x, 18, 178, and *passim*.
2. *Morrill, Seventeenth-Century Britain*, p. 125.
3. Hexter, "Property, Monopoly and Shakespeare's *Richard II*", in *Culture and Politics: From Puritanism to the Enlightenment* (ed. P. Zagorin, California U.P., 1980), pp. 1-24.
4. M. Heinemann, *Puritanism and Theatre: Thomas Middleton and Opposition Drama under the Early Stuarts* (Cambridge U.P., 1980), esp. Chapters 10-12; J. Dollimore, *Radical Tragedy: Religion, Ideology and Power in the Drama of Shakespeare and his Contemporaries* (Brighton, 1984); *M. Butler, Theatre and Crisis, 1632-1642* (Cambridge U.P., 1984); D. Norbrook, *Poetry and Politics in the English Renaissance* (1984); S. Shepherd, *Amazons and Warrior Women: Varieties of Feminism in Seventeenth-century Drama* (Brighton, 1981). See also my *Writing and Revolution in 17th-century England* (Brighton, 1985), Chapter 1.

4. *Oliver Cromwell*[1]

"The historian's quarrel with the biographer ... is that he wrests a complex figure from a complex setting, seeking to epitomize history in the far too simple terms of the individual". *

I

Ever since the death of Oliver Cromwell 300 years ago his reputation has been the subject of controversy. The royalist view of him was expressed by Clarendon: "a brave bad man," an ambitious hypocrite. This interpretation was supported by many former Parliamentarians: Edmund Ludlow regarded Cromwell as the lost leader who jettisoned his early radical ideas on rising to power himself. The only aspect of Cromwell's policy that the next generation praised unreservedly was his aggressive foreign policy and support for trade. Pepys's famous phrase — "What brave things he did and made all the neighbour princes fear him" — is only one of many rueful assessments made while the last two Stuarts were squandering the heritage of the Interregnum. But after William III resumed the policy of trade wars and colonial expansion there was less reason for remembering Oliver.

When radicalism revived in the later eighteenth century, the Yorkshire Association and Major Cartwright, the Corresponding Society and Cobbett, recalled Hampden, Pym, Prynne; but Cromwell was viewed critically by radicals like Mrs Macaulay no less than by Tories like Hume. The Vicar of Wakefield looked back with admiration to the Levellers; Blake, Shelley, Byron and Wordsworth to Milton, but literary eulogies of Cromwell are far to seek. In Crabbe's *Frank Courtship* a dour and old-fashioned country trader who admired Oliver kept his portrait face to the wall, to be turned round only in the safe company of chosen friends. Crabbe may have drawn on a sub-literary tradition among the middling groups; the phrase "in Oliver's days" to describe a time of exceptional prosperity

---

* W. K. Jordan, *The Development of Religious Toleration in England*, III, p. 476.

was still in use in the West Riding in the early nineteenth century (Mrs Gaskell, *Life of Charlotte Brontë*). But men of letters were agreed, down to Sir Walter Scott in *Woodstock*, that Cromwell was both ambitious and a hypocrite.

A more balanced estimate emerged with Macaulay's Essay on Hallam's *Constitutional History*. It was clinched by Carlyle's *Letters and Speeches of Oliver Cromwell*, published in 1845. This was an epoch-making book, though today it is easier to see its defects than its virtues. By printing Cromwell's own words and relating them to his actions, Carlyle established that Cromwell was not, in the normal sense of the words, either personally ambitious or a hypocrite. What was he then? For Carlyle he was a Hero with a capital H, a God-sent leader such as, in Carlyle's view, was needed in nineteenth-century England, trembling on the brink of democracy, Chartism and other evils. But that was in 1845. In 1848 and 1867 middle-class England shot its Niagara, without needing to be saved by a military dictator; its God-sent Hero was Mr Gladstone; and it came to see Cromwell not in the light of the French Revolution or Chartism but through the spectacles of liberal nonconformity. That very great historian, Samuel Rawson Gardiner, himself a nonconformist and a descendant of Cromwell's, invented the conception of "the Puritan Revolution" to describe what Clarendon had called "the Great Rebellion". Gardiner's Cromwell was in part Puritan Hero; but he had lost the naïve simplicity of Carlyle's. Gardiner saw a man who, coming to power by military means, nevertheless wished for "bit-by-bit" reform, opposed "the exaggerations of Puritanism" and was frustrated in his attempt to found a constitutional monarchy only by the circumstances of his day. He was a liberal in advance of his time; a russet-coated Gladstone, even less successful with the Irish problem and even more apt to confuse theology with foreign policy.

This is an ungenerous caricature of Gardiner, whose work must be the starting-point for all study of the period. Like all of us, Gardiner was aware of the present whilst looking at the past, and his liberal prepossessions may well cause less distortion than the late W. C. Abbott's laboured comparisons between Cromwell and Hitler. Nevertheless, recent experience has given us new insights into Cromwell the revolutionary and dictator, whose world was so different from that of Victorian England. Moreover, research during the last fifty years has posed problems about the relation of economics to politics, and about the nature of "the Puritan Revolution", of which Gardiner was hardly aware. Professor Nef and others have shown that economic developments in the century before 1640 helped to prepare Parliament to challenge political power. Professor Tawney's *Religion and the Rise of Capitalism*, and Professor Haller's *Rise of Puritanism*, have shown the economic and political links of "Puritanism". We can no longer speak of "the Puritan Revolution" without asking further questions. Recent contributions to the *Economic History Review* from Professors Tawney and Trevor-Roper and Mr Stone agree only in assuming that the causes of the civil war are to be sought in economics rather than in religion.

Since Carlyle the English Revolution has too often been seen as Cromwell's revolution, almost as his creation. Cromwell himself needs to be placed against his background. Yet so long as no agreed interpretation has replaced Gardiner's, it is difficult to agree on the exact role of Oliver Cromwell. Mr Ashley saw him as "the conservative dictator," Professor Abbott as a proto-fascist. Professor Trevor-Roper sees him as a declining gentleman, a "country-house radical" and "natural back-bencher," who could lead a revolution of destruction but had no positive political ideals or abilities. Dr Paul sees him as the Christian trying to make God's will prevail in this world, torn between religious ideals and the necessities of political action. But the theological interpretation of Cromwell is really tautological. If we assume that God did not fact speak to him, as is perhaps safest in the present state of the evidence, we then have to consider *why* Oliver thought that God willed this, that or the other course of action. And so we are brought back again to the world in which Cromwell lived.

II

There can be such varying interpretations of Oliver's character, motives, and place in history because his character and actions bristle with paradoxes. I shall list and illustrate some of these paradoxes, and then comment on them.

(1)   First is the paradox already noted, that the revolutionary of the sixteen-forties became the conservative dictator of the fifties. At a time when Parliament claimed to be fighting *for* the King *against* his evil counsellors, Cromwell was reported as saying that "if the King were before me I would shoot him as another"; and that he hoped to live to see never a nobleman in England. In 1644 Baillie called him "that darling of the sectaries",[2] and he played a leading part in

bringing Charles I to the scaffold. Yet Cromwell was no theoretical republican. He was described as "king-ridden"; in 1652 he asked "What if a man should take upon him to be King?" (II, 589). In 1657 monarchy was virtually restored, with the Lord Protector as monarch. By that date his former radical allies had broken with him — Lilburne in 1649, Harrison in 1653, Lambert in 1657. George Fox thought Oliver deserved the ignominious treatment he received at the restoration because he failed to keep his promise to abolish tithes.

(2)   Closely allied is Cromwell's attitude to constitutional government. He organized an army to fight for Parliament against the King. It was he who in November 1641 proposed what became the Militia Ordinance of 5 March 1642 — the first direct challenge to the King's sovereignty.[3] Oliver sponsored the Self-Denying Ordinance which ordered all members of the two Houses to lay down their military commands: yet Cromwell was reappointed to his. In 1647, though he tried to mediate between Parliament and Army, in the last resort he sided with the Army in every crisis. In December 1648 he acquiesced in the Army's purge of Parliament; in 1653 he himself used the Army to dissolve Parliament. Except as Lord General he would never have become Protector. Yet from 1654 onwards he aimed, apparently genuinely, at a "settlement" by which the military basis of his rule would be ended, and a Parliamentary constitution established: and was defeated in this aim by his Army. "What's for their good, not what pleases them," had been his object in 1647 (*C.P.*I, 277). In the sixteen-fifties he could claim to be imposing liberty by the means of tyranny. Through the Major-Generals he enforced a greater degree of religious toleration than any Parliament elected on a propertied franchise could approve of. "'Tis against the will of the nation," Calamy said of the Protectorate; "there will be nine in ten against you." "But what," Oliver replied, "if I should disarm the nine, and put a sword in the tenth man's hand? Would not that do the business?"[4]

(3)   Another paradox is to be found in his attitude towards those unrepresented in Parliament. Promotion in his Army went by merit, regardless of social or political considerations. "I had rather have a plain russet-coated captain that knows what he fights for, and loves what he knows, than that which you call a gentleman and is nothing else." "It had been well that men of honour and birth had entered into these employments, but why do they not appear? ... But seeing

it was necessary the work must go on, better plain men than none."
"The state, in choosing men to serve them, takes no notice of their
opinions; if they be willing faithfully to serve them, that satisfies" (I,
256, 262, 278). Cromwell was appealing, consciously if reluctantly, to
the lower classes for the fighting support his own class had failed to
give. Yet he opposed demands for manhood suffrage. In his speeches
to his first Parliament he equated poor men with bad men, and said
that if a commonwealth must suffer, it was better that it should
suffer from the rich than from the poor (III, 435, 584). The Levellers,
with whom he worked in 1647 and in the winter of 1648-9, and whose
leaders he imprisoned and shot in the spring of 1649, had some reason
to regard Cromwell as a double-crosser.

(4)   Even in those political convictions which he most strongly
and genuinely held there are obvious contradictions. Cromwell
wrote to the General Assembly of the Kirk of Scotland: "I beseech
you in the bowels of Christ, think it possible you may be mistaken,"
and said to the Governor of Edinburgh Castle, in words that shocked
many nineteenth-century nonconformists, "Your pretended fear
lest error should step in, is like the man that would keep all the wine
out of the country lest men should be drunk" (II, 303, 339). Yet he
justified the massacre of Irish Catholics at Drogheda as "a righteous
judgment of God upon these barbarous wretches," and said: "if by
liberty of conscience you mean a liberty to exercise the mass, ...
where the Parliament of England have power, that will not be
allowed" (II, 127, 144).

(5)   Cromwell was not a hypocrite. And yet he sometimes comes
very near hypocrisy in the absoluteness of his self-deception. "He
will weep, howl and repent, even while he doth smite you under the
first rib," wrote men who had some experience of Oliver's methods.[5]
The Irish have always found it difficult to take at its face value his
declaration that "We come (by the assistance of God) to hold forth
and maintain the lustre and glory of English liberty in a nation where
we have an undoubted right to it; wherein the people of Ireland ...
may equally participate in all benefits, to use liberty and fortune
equally with Englishmen, if they keep out of arms" (II, 205).
Cromwell was never quite sure whether his main duty was to the
people of England or to the people of God. He assumed that "the
interest of Christians" was identical with "the interest of the nation"
(IV, 445), but not all the "ungodly" majority would have agreed.
Thurloe, Oliver's secretary, on one occasion differentiated sharply

between the "vile levelling party" and "the good and godly" (*C.P.* II, 245). In Cromwell's foreign policy Firth saw a mixture of commercial traveller and Puritan Don Quixote.[6] Cromwell always talked of the protestant interest; but it is difficult to think of a single instance in which he supported protestantism to the detriment of England's political and commercial interests. His famous intervention on behalf of the Vaudois seems to have done the persecuted heretics little good in the long run; but it was excellent for England's prestige, and helped to force France to conclude the treaty of October 1655. In the Baltic Oliver advocated a protestant alliance; but it was when Charles X threatened to establish Swedish power on both sides of the Sound, to the detriment of English trade, that the Protector most persistently sought to divert his energies into attacking papist Austrians and Poles. We all know of the famous scene at Whitelocke's departure for Sweden, when Oliver adjured him: "Bring us back a Protestant alliance!" But we shall search in vain in the official instructions given to Whitelocke for any such ideological purpose. It is all sordid, commercial and diplomatic.

(6)   Finally, Oliver curiously combines hesitation, waiting on the Lord, with sudden violent action. At many of the crises of the period he was either missing, or played a highly ambiguous role. In the first four months of 1647, when the quarrel between Parliament and Army was coming to a head, he took no part in the negotiations. To this day historians do not know how far, if at all, Cromwell authorized Joyce's seizure of the King at Holmby House in June 1647. We know only that after the seizure had occurred he threw in his lot with the revolutionary Army. At the time of Pride's Purge he was far away, apparently prolonging quite unnecessarily his stay at the siege of Pontefract. When he returned he said "he had not been acquainted with the design, but since it was done he was glad of it."[7] Again in the winter of 1652-3 there were long delays and hesitations, and much criticism from his fellow-officers, before Cromwell finally lost his temper and dissolved the Long Parliament. "It hath been the way God hath dealt with us all along," he commented; "to keep things from our eyes, that in what we have acted we have seen nothing before us — which is also a witness, in some measure, to our integrity" (III, 64). Cromwell's share in the dissolution of Barebone's Parliament is shrouded in mystery. He denied solemnly that he knew beforehand what was going to happen; but he accepted the *fait accompli*. Is it likely that no one ascertained his views? In 1657

there were interminable delays before the final rejection of kingship; and then in 1658 the final explosion, brushing Fleetwood's protest aside with "You are a milksop; by the living God I will dissolve the House!" (IV, 728). The conversations recorded by political opponents like George Fox, Edmund Ludlow and John Rogers make attractive reading because of Oliver's obvious sincerity; but those to whom he listened so attentively were often disappointed by his failure to adopt the point of view they had put before him. There is something mysterious about the way in which Oliver took his political decisions, about his mental processes. Did he control events, or did they control him?

Some of these contradictions can be explained by the accidents of Cromwell's personal history. He was far more tolerant than most men of his time and class. One has only to read the debates in the second Protectorate Parliament on the Nayler case to be reminded of the frightened savagery with which the average gentleman reacted to doctrines which he thought socially subversive. Only in his intolerance towards Irish papists did Cromwell fail to rise above the standards of his age. But others of the paradoxes stem from specific features of the English Revolution and from the Puritan ideas which guided its leaders. To them we now turn.

III

The Calvinist doctrine of the church contains a fundamental ambiguity. In one sense the church is all the people in a given community; in another sense it is the elect only. For the elect, Calvinism was a doctrine of spiritual equality; any good man was better than a peer or a King who was not in a state of grace. Puritan preachers sometimes presented this as though it was a doctrine of human equality: the qualifications were not always insisted on as carefully as they should have been.[8] It was easy for many laymen to proceed direct from Calvinism to Lilburnian democracy. But for the true Calvinist some men were undoubtedly more equal than others: the elect had privileges, rights and duties, because they were elect, which raised them head and shoulders above the sinful mass of mankind. In opposition the emphasis was on spiritual equality, with appropriate vagueness about the precise individuals who were equal: in power Presbyterians naturally wished to subordinate and discipline the sinful masses. Any seventeenth-century Calvinist would have agreed with the Rev. Jabez Bunting two centuries later, who opposed democracy because he opposed sin. Yet a linguistic ambiguity remained, just as it remained in the vocabulary of Locke, who talked of "the people" in a dual sense: sometimes he meant all the inhabitants, at other times he meant the propertied class, and assumed that "the people" had servants.[9] Those who loosely used Calvinist or Lockean language were liable to deceive those whose interpretation was stricter. The latter, in Wildman's expressive phrase at Putney, were "cozened, as we are like to be" (*C.P.* I, 404).

Cromwell can be identified with no sect. But he was a Calvinist, and thought democracy manifestly absurd. For those with "the root of the matter" in them, yes: for them no privileges were too great, no barriers should prevent them serving the state. But "the root of the matter," "the godly" — they are woefully imprecise phrases. In the moment of battle those who fight bravely on your side clearly have this root. But in peace visible saints are difficult to identify. It is easy to slip into interpreting "the root of the matter" to mean "agreeing with me"; then "disagreeing with me" comes to mean "ensnared by fleshly reasonings" (I, 696). Oh, Sir Harry Vane! This identification of yourself with God's cause was all the easier if, like Cromwell, you really did earnestly seek the Lord in prayer before any action; and if the Lord consistently blessed you with success, and thus gave *prima facie* proof of the rightness of your actions. So Oliver, contemptuous of the Divine Right of Kings, came close to believing in the Divine Right of Oliver. Major-General Harrison, George Fox and Lodowick Muggleton, among others, similarly identified their wishes with the will of the Almighty.

The Calvinist discipline, in France, the Netherlands, Scotland, had ensured unity during and after revolution, whilst preserving the dominance of the propertied classes through lay elders in presbyteries. But in the English Revolution the erastianism of the classes represented in Parliament made them suspicious of a full Scottish presbytery: religious toleration precluded any discipline imposed from above. So Calvinism in England disintegrated into fragments in the moment of its victory.

Puritanism in the early sixteen-forties united the opposition by concealing divergences. The doctrine of the spiritual equality of believers could sound like a doctrine of the equality of men. Add to this the comradeship in arms of a victorious Army, and we can see how those who looked to Cromwell for leadership against lordly bishops and aristocratic Presbyterians might think him more of a democrat than he was. Nay, Oliver himself, in moments of emotion, may have been deceived too: "would that we were all saints!" (I, 646). Yet after the fighting was over, after Cromwell had broken, one after another, with Lilburne, Vane, Harrison, all of whom had seemed godly at one time: where then shall we find consent? This tendency within Puritanism towards an ultimate anarchy of individual consciences seemed to Cromwell to justify military dictatorship as the only means of preserving the essential gains of the Cause. He came to see himself as the unwilling constable set not only over the people of England, but even over the good people in England.

IV

Calvinism was one formative influence. Cromwell's own political experience was another. At Huntingdon in the sixteen-thirties he opposed the transformation of the town council into a close oligarchy, and helped to protect the rights of poorer burgesses. An early letter shows him pleading with a London merchant for continuance of money to maintain a lectureship "in these times wherein we see they are suppressed with too much haste and violence by the enemies of God his truth" (I, 80). On behalf of fenmen whose common rights were endangered he opposed the drainage of the Fens by the Earl of Bedford and his associates. This was no mere philanthrophic gesture. Cromwell arranged, in a business-like manner, contributions from all the commoners affected, with which he promised to hold the drainers in suit for five years. His attitude appears to have been inherited with his estates: his uncle had also opposed fen drainage. So we have here something more than an accident of personal biography — kindness of heart, or factious opposition. Common material interests linked a section of the gentry with humbler countrymen against privileged great landlords exploiting court influence. As "Lord of the Fens" Oliver was already occupying in his county a political position similar to that which he held nationally a decade later: the country gentleman leading freeholders and people against courtiers and peers. In both cases his stand was liable to be misunderstood. Leader and led seemed to have identical aims when they only had common enemies. In the sixteen-fifties it was the Levellers who supported commoners against exploitation by fen drainage.[10] When the Lord of the Fens had become Lord General he sent troops to protect drainers against commoners; as Lord Protector he consented to an ordinance in favour of Bedford and against the fenmen.

In 1640-2 diverse groups were united against the government. Commoners, yeomen and some gentlemen opposed enclosing land-lords and court patentees. Congregations, led by their richer mem-bers, looked to London merchants to help them to get the preaching of which the hierarchy deprived them. Townsmen opposed royal attempts to remodel their government. Most men of property opposed arbitrary taxation; men and women of all classes opposed monopolies.

The House of Commons elected in the autumn of 1640 was not a revolutionary assembly. Elected on the traditional propertied fran-chise, the M.P.s were a cross-section of the ruling class. Nevertheless, they had been elected under pressure of popular opposition occa-sioned by the final fiasco of the Scottish war. The wider the franchise in a constituency, the more likely were opponents of the court to be returned. But from 1641 the atmosphere began to change. In many counties there were enclosure riots, one of which Cromwell defended in the Commons; tenants began to refuse to pay rents; in London unruly crowds got into the habit of visiting Westminster to put pressure on M.P.s. Sectarian congregations emerged from their underground existence and began openly preaching seditious doc-trines. In December 1641-January 1642, amid scenes suggestive of the French Revolution, the royalist clique of aldermen which con-trolled the City government was overthrown and replaced by radical Parliamentarians.[11] Men of property began to have second thoughts. The King took heart, withdrew from London, and started to collect an army.

Gentlemen all over England tried hard to be neutral. But neutral-ity was increasingly difficult. As the King formed his army, all but the staunchest Parliamentarians in the North and West came to heel. Nearly 100 M.P.s with estates in counties occupied by the royal forces changed to the King's side. They included a stalwart like John Dutton, M.P. for Gloucestershire, who had once endured imprison-ment for the Parliamentary cause; but now it was a matter of "the preservation of his house and estate."[12] We can imagine how men of lesser conviction behaved. Many gentlemen, especially in the North and West, abandoned Parliament when opposition was pushed to the point of rebellion. These were the "constitutional royalists," of whom Hyde made himself the spokesman. A second consequence of the social anxiety of 1641-3 was the determination of most of the solid and respectable families supporting Parliament to end the war as quickly as possible. The initiative in *fighting* the King came from socially lower groups — from the clothing districts of the West Riding, which practically forced Fairfax to lead them into battle, and from towns like Manchester; from the "Moorlanders" in Staffordshire, who banded together with little help from the gentry, and were led by "a person of low quality." [13] Within the familiar distinction between economically backward and royalist North and West, and economically advanced and Parliamentarian South and East, we must also see a division between "compromise-peace" rich and "win-the-war" plebeians. The former are those whose representatives at Westminster we call "Presbyterians".

V

Their "Presbyterianism" had two essential features: (i) It was the price of the Scottish alliance; (ii) it envisaged the preservation of a national church, subordinated to the central control of Parliament and to the local control of the men of property (elders were nominated in the acts setting up presbyteries). As against the "presbyterian" desire for a limited war, fought by county militias officered by the local gentry (or by a professional Scottish army hired for the purpose), the "Independents" were prepared for a war without limits. "It must not be soldiers nor Scots that must do this work," said Oliver Cromwell, "but it must be the godly" (I, 216). Religious toleration was the means of ensuring the widest possible unity among the Parliamentarians; for "religious" toleration in seventeenth-century terms meant freedom of assembly, discussion and organization.

So divisions at Westminster reflected divisions in the country. The counties which supported Parliament were run by committees composed of their leading gentry. As the war progressed, splits appeared in all those county committees which have so far been studied. The majority wished for a limited war, and concerned themselves mainly with safeguarding their own estates. A minority, drawn from those most active in the field, called for an all-out war. For organization and leadership they looked to London; for support they relied on lower social groups in their counties, outside the charmed circle of the ruling class. Sir William Brereton found that he had to replace the military governor of Stafford, who came from one of the best county families, by a rich Walsall merchant. Soon

Brereton was heading a party in Staffordshire, composed of religious and political radicals, which aimed at taking control of the county away from the old families. In Kent and Nottinghamshire too, county government passed into the hands of social inferiors.[14]

The Lord of the Fens had perhaps less to learn than Sir William Brereton about political alliances. Cromwell allowed his men complete freedom of political and religious discussion; appointments went by efficiency only, regardless of social rank. Contemporaries even alleged that Cromwell went out of his way to choose as officers "such as were common men, poor or of mean parentage". The logic of war brought Cromwell's principles, and Cromwell himself, to the top. What, after all, was the use of a general like Manchester, who said: "If we beat the King ninety-nine times, yet he is King still, but if the King beat us but once we shall all be hanged"? Cromwell's retort was unanswerable: "If this be so, why did we take up arms at first? This is against fighting ever hereafter" (I, 299). Since Charles had now got enough support to make him obstinate on points to which even conservative Parliamentarians attached importance, the war had to go on. It could be won only with the help of a Scottish army or by replacing the county militias with an efficient English army, nationally financed and nationally controlled. The Self-Denying Ordinance marks the triumph of Cromwell's principle of the career open to the talents: it forced the surrender of their commissions by those who owed them only to rank. In the New Model Army the vastly superior resources of the Parliamentary areas were first fully utilized. A national system of taxation — the assessment, the excise, plus the system of compounding with delinquents — allowed the Army to be paid as regularly as Cromwell's own troops had always been. Once that stage of organization was reached, the war was won. "Combination carries strength with it: it's dreadful to adversaries" (I, 128).

By the end of the war Cromwell had won a unique position. He was the idol of the Army, not only because he was a consistently successful general, but also because he had shown himself determined and courageous in sinking political differences for the sake of unity. Half of the men in the New Model were volunteers. They believed that Cromwell stood for the political principles which united them and gave them the self-imposed discipline which at Marston Moor and Naseby had proved irresistible. His resolute advocacy of toleration, his defence of Anabaptist officers against witch-hunting generals, his campaign against officers who did not really want to win the war, his readiness to serve under a general like Waller who would fight, his lead in the struggle for the Self-Denying Ordinance, even though it looked like ending his own military career — all this made Cromwell the darling not only of the sectaries but also of the Army. Outside the Army such prestige as he had was with the radicals. In Parliament he was viewed less sympathetically. Many a gentleman who in 1644-5 had supported toleration and the New Model Army as lesser evils had reason to be alarmed at the Frankenstein monster that had been created. In 1641-3 there had been agrarian disturbances and riots at Westminster; in 1647 a cross-section of the people of England, combined into the most powerful military machine in Europe, proclaimed their right to a say in settling the destinies of their country.

The royalists had been beaten: the battle now began between the old ruling families, whose representatives sat in Parliament, and the civilians in uniform living on free quarter in the Home Counties. Cromwell, unique among Englishmen, had not only a foot in both camps, but a share in the strongest feelings of both sides. With the radicals and the Army he demanded toleration; with the conservatives he wanted to preserve existing social relations. "A nobleman, a gentleman, a yeoman: that is a good interest of the nation, and a great one" (III, 435). In March 1647 Parliament took its foolish and fateful decision to disband the Army and send some of its regiments to Ireland, with their arrears unpaid. The Army revolted, and Oliver Cromwell was sent down as one of the Parliamentary Commissioners to investigate.

VI

In May 1647 Cromwell and most of the officers threw in their lot with the rank and file. The result, Cromwell explained to the House of Commons, was to bring off "the soldiers from their late ways of correspondency and actings between themselves," and reduce them "towards a right order and regard to their officers" (*C.P.* I, 98). Six months of uneasy co-operation followed. On 4 June Cornet Joyce seized the King, after the agitators had told Cromwell that "if he would not forthwith come and head them they would go their own way without him". Cromwell came, just as Fairfax had followed the West Riding clothiers when they asked him to lead them against the royalists. An Army Council, representing rank and file as well as officers, was set up, and issued its Declaration of 14 June, that this was no mere mercenary and hireling army, but a body of citizens who at the call of Parliament had rallied "to the defence of our own and the people's just rights," and so had a duty to see these rights fully established before disbanding.[15] The Army, again at the instance of the Agitators, moved on London, and the first purge of Parliament took place, the withdrawal of eleven M.P.s. named by the Army. Cromwell and Ireton then started tortuous behind-the-scenes negotiations with Charles I. Rumours of what was afoot leaked out, and the Army was in an uproar. Five cavalry regiments displaced their agitators and elected new ones; pamphlets were circulated telling the rank and file "Ye can create new officers!"[16] In debates in the Army Council at Putney which started at the end of October two conceptions of the future constitution of England confronted one another: the Heads of Proposals put forward by the Independent officers, and the Leveller Agreement of the People.

"Agreement of the People" is English for Social Contract. The Leveller theory was that in the civil war the old constitution had broken down; the Agreement was to refound the state on a new basis. Acceptance of the Agreement was to be necessary to citizenship, but all who accepted it should be free and equal citizens. The property franchise would be replaced by a much wider suffrage. The Levellers had no intention of submitting the Agreement to Parliament; for Parliament was part of the defunct constitution whose breakdown had left England in the state of nature. So radical and revolutionary a solution appalled the generals, who came from the propertied class themselves. Many of them had received substantial grants of land from Parliament. Unlike the doctrinaire Ireton, Cromwell was prepared to consider concessions to Leveller views. Some copyholders by inheritance, perhaps, might be allowed the vote; though not wage labourers or recipients of alms. But to scrap the existing constitution, he thought, would be to throw too much into the melting-pot — law, order, property, social subordination and social stability.

The profound divergences revealed at Putney explain the policy adopted by Cromwell and the Independent Grandees towards the Levellers during the next two years. In November they broke decisively with them. Aided by the timely flight of the King to Carisbrooke (so timely that unkind contemporaries suspected Cromwell of engineering it) they disbanded the Army Council, suppressed an incipient Leveller mutiny and restored traditional military discipline. Faced by a new royalist threat, soon realised in the second civil war, the Army *had* to reunite; and Cromwell's prestige was too great for it to reunite without him. When the House of Lords released Lilburne from prison in the hope that he would add to Cromwell's difficulties by attacking him, Lilburne on the contrary offered his provisional support against the common enemy.

But nothing had been solved, as was shown after the Army had won the second civil war. Levellers and "Silken Independents" again entered into conversations, since Cromwell knew that "if we cannot bring the Army to our sense, we must go to theirs, a schism being evidently destructive" (I, 569). A revised Agreement of the People was hammered out, in which the Levellers made many concessions. But when this was not forthwith submitted to the people, but only to the Rump of the Long Parliament — i.e. to one of the parties to the compromise — the Levellers not without reason felt that they had been double-crossed. They had hoped that the Rump would dissolve itself, giving way to a Parliament elected on a new franchise. A series of mutinies early in 1649 registered the protest of the rank and file. All were suppressed. In November 1648 Cromwell had told Hammond there was no need to fear the Levellers; four months later he said that unless they were broken the Levellers would break the new government. By then he probably knew that the Levellers had begun to extend propaganda activities outside London and the Army. Their programme — opposition to social and economic privileges, to enclosure, tithes, excise, conscription — might prove very attractive to the unenfranchised 80 per cent of the population if the Levellers were given a few years' freedom to propound their views. Henceforth Oliver was consistently unfair to the Levellers, deliberately using them as a bogey to scare men of property by attributing to them communist and anarchist views which most of them certainly did not hold (III, 435-8, 581-6; IV, 267-8).

VII

The break with the Levellers was a decisive moment in Oliver's career. Till then the Revolution had moved steadily to the left. Henceforth, unevenly at first, a reverse trend set in which ended only with the restoration. So it is important to realize the dilemma which Cromwell had to face in 1649. The Leveller programme seems very sensible now that it has been achieved by nineteenth-century liberal democracy. But the Levellers were democrats without an electorate. Manhood suffrage, with a largely illiterate population voting by show of hands in the presence of the parson and the squire, might well have destroyed all that had been fought for in the civil war. The Leveller attempt to circumvent this by restricting the vote to those who accepted the Agreement of the People, and by establishing certain fundamentals which were not to be changed, could have worked only if there had been a long period of dictatorship during which the Army was used, in Hugh Peter's words, "to teach peasants to understand liberty."[17] But apart from the obvious dangers of thus "forcing men to be free," the Army itself was divided. Its generals and officers did not accept the social revolution which the Agreement assumed, and were not prepared to allow the years of peaceful political education which the Levellers would have needed to achieve an electorate capable of working the new constitution.

Yet the generals had no electorate either. "A free Parliament," whether elected on the pre-1640 franchise or on any new propertied franchise that could be devised, would inevitably contain a majority of men similar in outlook to the Presbyterian majority in the Long Parliament. Yet the officers had decisively broken with the Presbyterians at Pride's Purge. So to the right there was a solid mass of opponents — Cavaliers, Presbyterians. After 1649 enemies were added on the left — Levellers, some republicans, Fifth Monarchists. After 1654 Cromwell was left sitting on a thin line of bayonets. The huge Army seemed more and more to remain in existence only to collect taxes to pay for the Army to collect taxes to pay for the Army ... After 1653 Oliver was desperately trying to arrive at a "settlement," some agreement with a Parliament by which the Army could be reduced and the burden of taxation lessened. Yet the dilemma was inescapable. Any Parliament would demand the subordination of the Army to itself. Oliver and the generals could never fully accept this, for it would jeopardize not only their lives and liberties but the whole cause for which they had fought, including toleration, to which all Parliaments were fanatically opposed. Professor Trevor-Roper's view that only a little "parliamentary management by the executive" was lacking appears to be an unwarranted over-simplification.[18]

In April 1653 Cromwell dissolved the Rump because its efforts to perpetuate itself seemed an obstacle to any settlement acceptable to those who counted in the country. Barebone's Parliament revived some of the radical policies which had been jettisoned in 1649. Its dissolution left the dictatorship of the generals naked but ashamed. The Instrument of Government spread a fig leaf over this nakedness by providing a Parliamentary constitution, which disfranchised smaller freeholders and gave votes to copyholders and leaseholders more generously than did the 1832 Reform Bill. In those days of open voting, when landlords marched "their" freeholders to the polls, such a franchise might in time have produced an independent electorate. But the first Parliament returned under the Instrument, like the first Parliaments after 1832, showed no significant change in social composition or outlook. The Instrument also endeavoured to perpetuate the veiled dictatorship of the generals by writing into the constitution, as a first charge on the revenue, an Army of 30,000 men; and by nominating to the Council the generals, their friends and relations, and making it virtually impossible to remove them. Even a purged Parliament rejected this constitution.

But the rule of the Major-Generals which followed finally demonstrated the unviability of military dictatorship without radical support. The Major-Generals were efficient. But they encountered solid opposition from precisely those groups which Parliament represented — town oligarchies, country gentry. For the Major-Generals took over command of the militia from local authorities; they purged corrupt ruling groups in corporate towns; they supervised, bullied and put pressure on J.P.s. For the last time in English history before the nineteenth century local government was run from Whitehall. It was worse than the days of Laud and Strafford, for now the representatives of the central authority were low-born intruders, with troops of horse to add persuasion to their unpopular commands. The opponents of Star Chamber had not fought a civil war to *strengthen* the power of central government. The Major-Generals ran the elections of 1656, and decided to exclude nearly 100 M.P.s, against the Protector's advice; even so they could not secure a friendly Parliament. Their rule probably did more than anything else to make the "natural rulers" of the country determined to have a constitutional monarchy — whether under Cromwell or Stuart was a secondary consideration. The long omnipotence of the J.P.s began in 1660; hatred of standing armies became a decisive political prejudice for the British ruling class — and for many radicals too.

A first attempt was made in 1657 to restore the Parliamentary constitution as it would have existed after 1642 if Charles I had been prepared honestly to accept it. The Humble Petition and Advice subordinated Council and armed forces to Parliament; taxation was to be reduced to a stated *maximum*, which precluded a large Army: "no part thereof to be raised by a land tax" (as the bulk of the revenue had hitherto been). Something as like the old House of Lords as possible was to be revived; Oliver was offered the crown. This was too much for the generals. They blackmailed Oliver by threatening military revolt if he accepted the crown. There was even talk of reviving an Army Council representing the rank and file (IV, 531). Feverish negotiations went on, in public and behind the scenes, at the end of which the constitution was accepted, without the title of King, with an enhanced revenue, with a Council subordinate to Parliament — but with the generals and their friends firmly entrenched in the second chamber, able to veto any legislation they disliked. The apparent solution had only transferred the problem to a different plane. When Parliament met, with the excluded M.P.s admitted, the Commons refused to recognize this Other House, and started a furious attack on it.

Cromwell was perhaps fortunate in the time of his death. It is difficult to see what way forward there could have been. His unique prestige with the Army made him the indispensable head of state so long as the Army was a power in the land; his genuine desire for a Parliamentary settlement continually raised hopes that he might yet square the circle. But, just because Oliver owed his position to the Army, he could never in the last resort break from it. He had created it, yet without it he was plain Mr Cromwell. For this reason no one could succeed him. Richard Cromwell had no status with the Army, and therefore no power to bargain with Parliament. None of the professional generals was acceptable to Parliament, not even the ex-royalist Monck. Oliver could ride the two horses, like a trick rider at the circus, though he could never transfer his weight from one to the other, transform military rule into Parliamentary government. But his delicate balance resulted from his unique personal position: after him — Tumbledown Dick. The Grandees were left plaintively murmuring that any constitution must include a "select senate" composed of themselves, with a right to veto legislation; until the restoration swept them away.

VIII

If we return now to the paradoxes of Oliver Cromwell, we may be able to see in them something more than the peculiarities of his personality. They were, I suggest, paradoxes of the English Revolution. All great revolutions are necessarily contradictory, ambiguous. They can begin only by a breach within the ruling class itself, a "revolt of the nobles". But in order to overthrow an old-established government and make profound changes in society, wider support is needed, especially from the unprivileged classes. To rouse them to effective political action, ideas have to be let loose which may prove inconvenient to those who later establish themselves in power. A halt at some stage has to be called: the more conservative revolutionaries break with their radical supporters, the Directory succeeds the Jacobins. The uniqueness of Cromwell is that he was Napoleon to his own Robespierre, Stalin to his own Lenin and Trotsky. Hence the accusations of self-seeking and treachery showered on him by the radicals who felt he had deceived them.

He had not deceived them. He may have deceived himself, but there was a dualism in his personality which made him the ideal leader of the revolt and the ideal leader of the Independents, those who first co-operated with the radicals and then led the move towards re-stabilization. Cromwell's passion for toleration aligned him with sectaries and Levellers against most of his own class; yet, despite his real interest in humanitarian law reform and his alleged hostility to tithes, he retained too many conservative prejudices to go far with the radicals. "We would keep up the nobility and gentry" he told Parliament in 1656 (IV, 273). He could not have law reform as well. His cousin Edmund Waller rightly saw in the Lord Protector

> One whose extraction from an ancient line
> Gives hope again that well-born men may shine.[19]

He was the ideal mediator, too, between Army and Parliament because he shared so much of the outlook of the average M.P. He always wanted "a settlement of somewhat with monarchical power in it". But he could not be "wedded and glued to forms of government" (*C.P.* I, 277), since he owed his power to the Army. God had called him there, by a series of inscrutable providences. Some of the principles which the average M.P. most deplored in Oliver, like toleration, he and his Army colleagues regarded as God's will. So considerations both of interest and of principle made it impossible for Oliver to sacrifice the Army. The most he could do was to straddle his two horses.

The paradox that Oliver's real tolerance did not extend to papists is no paradox at all if we recall that they had been "accounted, ever since I was born, Spaniolized" (IV, 264). The Armada and Gunpowder Plot were vivid memories in Oliver's youth, when the House of Habsburg seemed to be undoing the Reformation, with the connivance of the English King and bishops. In the civil war papists were preponderantly royalist. Ireland was a back door to foreign invasion; exaggerations about the "Irish massacres" of 1641 were accepted by almost all English protestants as gospel. There were sound political reasons for refusing facilities for worship and organization to men believed to be a foreign fifth column, quite apart from Oliver's genuine conviction that the mass was idolatrous and therefore forbidden by God's word. Nevertheless, the historian of toleration in England considers that the Catholics gained from Cromwell a more reasoned and consistent toleration than from the House of Stuart.[20]

Cromwell's critics lay heavy emphasis on two aspects of his Irish policy: the massacres of Drogheda and Wexford, and the "Cromwellian settlement". Cromwell is by no means free from blame for these atrocious proceedings, but there are points to be made in his defence. Of Drogheda and Wexford it can be said (i) in accordance with contemporary laws of war a garrison which had prolonged resistance unreasonably and so caused unnecessary loss of life might, after due warning, be put to the sword; (ii) civilians were not intended to be involved; (iii) the severity helped to bring to an end the ghastly Irish war, which had dragged on for eight years. Dr Paul pertinently compares the use of the atom-bomb in 1945 (although this massacred mainly non-combatants).[21] It is reasonable to condemn both Cromwell's behaviour and the use of atom-bombs; but it seems hypocritical to condemn the one whilst defending the other. The "Cromwellian Settlement" (evicting the Irish and sending them "to Hell or Connaught") was not Cromwellian at all in the sense that the West Indian campaign was. It was the putting into more drastic effect of what had been English policy since the reign of Elizabeth. The transplantation was initiated before Cromwell controlled policy; it was mitigated after he became Protector. There is no reason to suppose Oliver abhorred it, as he should have done; but only Levellers like Walwyn and Prince conceived in the seventeenth century that the common people of England and Ireland might live in peace together.[22]

Refusal of liberty of worship to "prelatists" has given rise to misunderstandings. England was not yet divided between Anglicans and nonconformists. Oliver's state church was the Church of England. The great majority of the population, ministers included, continued to accept it — as men had accepted the Church of England in its various manifestations from Henry VIII to Elizabeth. The only consistent opposition to Oliver's state church came from the Laudians, "prelatists" on principle. They formed the nucleus of the party working for the restoration of Charles II.[23] Here too there were substantial political reasons for refusing freedom of public worship and organization; though again there was much more toleration under Oliver *de facto* than *de jure*.

His foreign policy also loses some of its paradoxicality if regarded in historical perspective. The sixteen-fifties saw the beginning of that purposeful application of the resources of the state to commercial war and the struggle for colonies that characterized English foreign policy for the next 150 years. This was not Cromwell's personal policy. It goes back to Hakluyt, Ralegh, the Earl of Warwick — whose grandson married the Lord Protector's daughter in 1657 — and to the Providence Island Company which had supplied so many of the leaders of 1640. But it had never before been adopted as consistent government policy. Slingsby Bethel suggested that Oliver's alliance with France against Spain made possible the subsequent preponderance of Louis XIV.[24] But in so far as English mistakes contributed to this preponderance, it was Charles II's disbandment of Oliver's Army, neglect of his Navy, and sale of his conquest of Dunkirk that are to blame. One might argue that Cromwell's foreign policy exceeded the available resources of the country, so that a generation of consolidation and economic advance was needed before it could be resumed; or that grandiose imperial designs were not in the best interests of England. But for good or ill the sixteen-fifties mark a turning-point in English foreign policy.

The paradox underlying Oliver's attitude to foreign affairs — the protestant interest or the interest of the nation — is not peculiar to him. We find it in Gustavus Adolphus. It had existed in the minds of Englishmen ever since Hakluyt advocated colonization of America for the good of the souls of Indians and the pockets of Englishmen.

But God did seem to have put aces up the Protector's sleeve. If he had allied with Spain against France, this would have been in order to help the French Huguenots; when England in fact allied with France against Spain, it was because the Spaniard was "a natural enemy ... led on by superstition and the implicitness of his faith in submitting to the See of Rome" (IV, 261), and because France treated protestants relatively well. This may have convinced the godly; it certainly appealed to traders like Martin Noell who looked for an expansion of exports once the Spanish monopoly of American trade was broken open. If the protestant interest had been primary for Oliver he need have allied with neither France nor Spain. He could have established closer relations with the protestant Netherlands, at the price of sacrificing the Navigation Act which protected English trade and shipping. But "there were no greater considerations in England," Secretary Thurloe wrote of the Protectorate, "than how to obviate the growing greatness of the Dutch".[25] This is no place to discuss the psychological connections between Calvinism and the capitalist spirit. But the connections are deep and long-lived: they are paradoxes of the English Revolution itself.

Finally, the clue to Cromwell's delays and sudden violent actings is to be found in the famous maxim "Trust in God and keep your powder dry". Because one is fighting God's battles, one must be more, not less, careful to run no risk of failure. On the battlefield Cromwell rarely attacked until he had local military superiority. In politics, too, since the cause was the Lord's, every avenue must be explored, every contingency foreseen, before Cromwell committed himself to any course of action. In his periods of delay and hesitation Cromwell not only sought the Lord, he also consulted Ireton, Vane, Harrison, Lambert, Thurloe, Broghill — anyone whose opinion might be of significance. When he had completed his reconnaissance, and was sure of his dispositions, then he struck hard and with confidence that he was acting righteously. But to contemporaries "waiting on the Lord" might seem like waiting to see which way the cat would jump.

Again this is a paradox of Puritanism. "Trust in God and keep your powder dry" perfectly expresses that tension between pre-destination and free will which lay at the heart of Calvinism. God has his purposes for this world which are pre-ordained; but God may act through human agents. If we are privileged to be so used, we must be absolutely sure at every stage that we are genuinely striving to realise

God's will. "We are very apt, all of us," said Oliver himself, "to call that faith, that perhaps may be but carnal imagination." Just because our cause is God's we dare not fail or mistake. "The greater the trust, the greater the account", Cromwell reminded Hammond (II, 418). For Oliver's famous schoolmaster, Dr Beard, the world was "the theatre of God's judgments". God intervened directly in history. Those who acted for God would be supported by Him and tended to succeed, however weak and powerless they would otherwise have been. Their success justified them. "I can say this of Naseby," Cromwell wrote, "that when I saw the enemy draw up and march in gallant order towards us, and we a company of poor ignorant men ... I could not (riding alone about my business) but smile out to God in praises, in assurance of victory, because God would, by things that are not, bring to naught things that are. Of which I had great assurance; and God did it" (I, 365). What Marvell aptly called Oliver's "industrious valour" helped God to achieve his ends.

But "the providences of God are like a two-edged sword, which may be used both ways"[26] After 1660 Puritans had to grapple with the terrible problem posed by defeat. Had God spat in their faces, as Fleetwood thought? Or had His cause been misconceived? Perhaps His kingdom was not of this world, as Bunyan and the Quakers came to believe? At all events, in the dark hour of the crash of Puritan hopes, the ways of God needed justifying to man. It is significant that Milton started to wrestle with this cosmic problem from the mid-fifties, as he began to lose confidence in Cromwell. The restoration was for him only the outward confirmation that the cause was spiritually lost. But in the sixteen-forties not only Cromwell and Milton but thousands of lesser men had drawn tremendous moral energy from the conviction that God had chosen them to serve Him. Here again the explanation is ultimately social: problems exist, and certain men feel themselves qualified to solve them. It therefore becomes their duty to make their contribution to setting society right. A revolutionary situation breeds men with this sense of mission. Without them, revolutionary change could never take place; yet they would not act unless they were stimulated by the confidence that God, or Reason, or History, was on their side. Demanding reinforcements in 1643, Oliver wrote: "As if God should say, 'Up and be doing, and I will help you and stand by you'. There is nothing to be feared but our own sin and sloth" (I, 245). Here Oliver personifies not only the English Revolution but all great revolutions.

Perhaps the most characteristic act of his life occurred when a dispatch to the Speaker came up for signature in September 1645. Reading it through Cromwell paused at words attributing the fall of Bristol to the prayers of "the people of God with you and all England over who have waited on God for a blessing". Was that what he had dictated? It certainly was not what he meant. He took up his pen, crossed out "waited on" and substituted "wrestled with". God would help his world to be changed only by those who helped themselves (I, 377).

IX

Cromwell is the most quotable great man in English history. His sayings have a racy, earthy character. "What shall we do with this bauble? Here, take it away" (II, 643). Many of them have become proverbial. This is appropriate for the man who led a popular revolution, whom Gardiner described as "the typical Englishman of the modern world".[27] We may perhaps differentiate two types of revolutionary — the man committed to change society in accordance with preconceived ideas, like Tom Paine, Robespierre or Lenin — and the pragmatic, empirical revolutionary, like William the Silent, Cromwell or Washington. The distinction is not merely a matter of date, for Lilburne in the seventeenth century, and Calvin in the sixteenth, were clearly men with a mission. If Oliver had a political mission, it is hard to define it precisely. "I can tell you, sirs, what I would not have, though I cannot what I would";[28] "no one rises so high as he who knows not whither he is going" (I, 472). Whether Oliver used those words or not, they are certainly plausible. His theory of government always tended towards that ultimately established in 1688 by the most pragmatic and untheoretical of all revolutions.

The achievement of 1688 is summarized in two couplets:

> For forms of government let fools contest;
> Whate'er is best administer'd is best.

> There can be no pretence of government,
> Till they that have the property consent.[29]

Oliver would have accepted both. But the constitution was not his main interest. He rightly declared that religion was not the cause of the civil war, "not the thing at the first contested for, but God brought it to that issue at last" (III, 586). Religion became the great bond of union between those who opposed Charles I and Laud, and Cromwell's passionately-felt undenominational Puritanism made him the ideal leader to unite those social groups who had never hitherto been allowed to worship and discuss and organize as they pleased. If Cromwell had not been a profoundly religious man he could never have been the revolutionary leader of the sixteen-forties. If he had not accepted unquestioningly the assumptions of the propertied class he could never have co-operated as he did in the sixteen-fifties with hard-headed businessmen like Thurloe, unscrupulous politicians like Ashley-Cooper, and renegade royalists like Broghill and Monck. The very fact that he was not "wedded and glued to forms of government," that he thought them "but a moral thing," "dross and dung in comparison of Christ" (*C.P.* I, 370), made it easy for him to reflect the views of those with whom he associated — the rising revolutionary feeling of the forties and the growing conservatism of the fifties: for him political, constitutional and economic issues were secondary.

When the historian looks back at God's "working of things from one period to another" in the great turning-point of the seventeenth century, he will agree with Oliver that "such things ... have not been known in the world these thousand years" (III, 591-3). But he has to add that it was the political, constitutional and economic revolutions that succeeded: the Puritan Revolution failed. And the Protectorate, as Milton foreboded, was the period in which this outcome became inevitable. Herein lies the final paradox, the historic irony and the personal tragedy of the career of Oliver Cromwell.

NOTES

1. Originally published as a Historical Association Pamphlet in 1958. I have left it virtually unchanged: I hope readers will make allowances. I developed many points more fully later — e.g. in my *God's Englishman: Oliver Cromwell and the English Revolution* (Penguin). Quotations indicated by a volume and page number, with no further reference, are from W. C. Abbott, *The Writings and Speeches of Oliver Cromwell* (Harvard U.P., 1937-47). Quotations from *The Clarke Papers* (ed. C. H. Firth, Camden Soc., 1891-1901) are preceded by the letters C. P.

2. F. Guizot, *History of the English Revolution* (1884), p. 183; *Camden Miscellany*, VIII (1883), fifth item, p. 2; R. Baillie, *Letters and Journals* (Edinburgh, 1775), II, p. 76.

3. Ed. W. Notestein, *The Journal of Sir Simonds D'Ewes: From the first recess of the Long Parliament to the withdrawal of King Charles from London* (Yale U.P., 1943), pp. 97-8.

4. C. H. Firth, *Oliver Cromwell* (World's Classics), p. 411.

5. D. M. Wolfe, *Leveller Manifestoes* (1944), p. 370.

6. Firth, op. cit., p. 382.

7. *Ibid.*, p. 211.

8. See W. Haller, *The Rise of Puritanism* (1938), *passim*.

9. Cf. C. B. Macpherson, "The Social Bearing of Locke's Political Theory," *The Western Political Quarterly*, March 1954. See Chapter 12 below.

10. Cf. J. D. Hughes, "The Drainage disputes in the Isle of Axholme," *The Lincolnshire Historian*, Spring 1954.

11. V. L. Pearl, *London and the Outbreak of the Puritan Revolution* (Oxford U.P., 1961), Chapter 4, *passim*.

12. D. Brunton and D. H. Pennington, *Members of the Long Parliament* (1954), *passim*.

13. D. H. Pennington and I. A. Roots, *The Committee at Stafford, 1643-45* (1957), p. lxii. For the West Riding see now B. S. Manning's *The English People and the English Revolution*

14. Pennington and Roots, *op. cit.*, *passim*; A. M. Everitt, *The Community of Kent and the Great Rebellion* (1966), Chapter 5, *passim*; A. C. Wood, *Nottinghamshire in the Civil War* (Oxford U.P., 1937), Chapter 11.

15. Firth, *op. cit.*, p. 160; W. Haller and G. Davies, *The Leveller Tracts* (1944), p. 55.

16. *A Call to all the Soldiers* (1647), p. 7.

17. *Mr. Peters Last Report of the English Wars* (1646), p. 6

18. H. R. Trevor-Roper, "Oliver Cromwell and his Parliaments," in *Essays Presented to Sir Lewis Namier* (1956), p. 45.

19. Waller, "A Panegyric to my Lord Protector," in *Poems* (Muses Library), II, p. 15.

20. W. K. Jordan, *The Development of Religious Toleration in England*, IV (1940), Part iii.

21. R. S. Paul, *The Lord Protector* (1955), p. 218.

22. T. Edwards, *Gangraena* (Part II, 1646), p. 27; *Walwins Wiles* (1649), in Haller and Davies, *op. cit.*, p. 310; T. Prince, *The Silken Independents Snare Broken* (1649), pp. 6-7. See now my "Seventeenth-century English radicals and Ireland", in *Radicals, Rebels and Establishments* (ed. P. J. Corish, Belfast, 1985).

23. R. S. Bosher, *The Making of the Restoration Settlement* (1951), *passim*.

24. In *The World's Mistake in Oliver Cromwell*, *Harleian Miscellany* (1744), I, pp. 280-8.

25. S. von Bischoffshausen, *Die Politik des Protectors Oliver Cromwell* (Innsbruck, 1899), p. 221.

26. *Parliamentary Diary of Thomas Burton*, ed. J. T. Rutt (1828), I, p. xxx.

27. Gardiner, *Cromwell's Place in History* (1902), p. 113.

28. Sir Philip Warwick, *Memoirs* (1813), pp. 193-4.

29. Pope, "Essay on Man," Epistle III, in *Collected Poems* (Everyman edn.), p. 204; Defoe, *Jure Divino* (1706), Book II, p. 12.

5. *A Bourgeois Revolution?*[1]

"This kind of government [of the church] *God doth not manage according to the wisdom and thoughts, no not of his very people, but wholly according to the counsel of his own will and the thoughts of his own heart: doing things that they must not know yet, but must know afterwards; yea, such things as for the present seem absurd and absolutely destructive."* *

"Such dispensations as these cannot be looked upon by the most envious eye or profane heart as the birth and product of any fore-laid contrivances of men, biassed with corrupt and carnal interests." **

The ends of the actions are intended, but the results which actually follow from these actions are not intended ...
   The final result always arises from conflicts between many individual wills, of which each again has been made what it is by a host of particular conditions of life. Thus there are innumerable intersecting forces which give rise to one resultant – the historical event. †

The cultural consequences of the Reformation were to a great extent ... unseen and even unwished-for *results of the labours of the reformers. They were often far removed from or even in contradiction to all that they themselves thought to attain.* ††

It is impossible to discuss this subject without first clearing away some stereotypes. Many non-Marxists, even non-Marxist scholars, attribute to Marxists fixed positions of the "all Cretans are liars" type, which by definition cannot be challenged. I have learnt from long and painful experience that if I am asked the

---

* William Dell, *The Way of True Peace and Unity in the True Church of Christ* (1651), in *Several Sermons and Discourses* (1709), p. 225.

** Marchamont Nedham, *The Case of the Commonwealth of England Stated* (1650), p. 2.

† F. Engels, *Ludwig Feuerbach*, in *Karl Marx, Selected Works* (Moscow, 1935), I, p. 457; *Selected Correspondence of Marx and Engels*, (ed. Dona Torr 1934), p. 476.

†† Weber, *The Protestant Ethic and the Spirit of Capitalism* (1930), p. 90.

question "Are you a Marxist?" I must answer (however much it goes against the grain) "It all depends what you mean by Marxist." For if I answer "Yes," with however many scholarly qualifications, the next question is bound to be "What do you do when you meet a fact which does not fit in with your Marxist assumptions?" It is too late then to plead that I have no more assumptions than the next historian, or that — like him — my ideas are being modified all the time by fresh information. For my interlocutor *knows* both that Marxists have dogmatic preconceptions and that all Cretans are liars. Nothing I can say will shake him: he only becomes progressively more convinced of my dishonesty as I attempt to deny what he knows to be true.

So in discussing whether the English Revolution was a bourgeois revolution or not we must begin by defining terms. As I have argued at length elsewhere, the phrase in Marxist usage does *not* mean a revolution made by or consciously willed by the bourgeoisie.[2] Yet when I so argued, even a relatively friendly reviewer supposed that I was recognizing "a difficulty ... in the Marxist conception of a bourgeois revolution," and that I hoped "to solve it by adopting an interpretation of this term which Isaac Deutscher put forward, ...*contrary to the traditional view that the bourgeoisie ... played the leading part in it.*"[3] If this is "the traditional view" of what Marxists hold, it is held only by ill-informed non-Marxists. I quoted Deutscher as a respected and representative Marxist, not as an innovator. Lenin, who may perhaps be allowed to know something about the subject, argued at one stage in favour of bringing about a bourgeois revolution against the wishes of the Russian bourgeoisie. He mocked at those who thought that one day bourgeoisie and proletariat would line up in two opposing groups; "and this will be the revolution".[4]

The English Revolution, like all revolutions, was caused by the breakdown of the old society; it was brought about neither by the wishes of the bourgeoisie, nor by the leaders of the Long Parliament. But its *outcome* was the establishment of conditions far more favourable to the development of capitalism than those which prevailed before 1640. The hypothesis is that this outcome, and the Revolution itself, were made possible by the fact that there had already been a considerable development of capitalist relations in England, but that it was the structures, fractures, and pressures of the society, rather than the wishes of leaders, which dictated the outbreak of revolution and shaped the state which emerged from it. In our society businessmen and politicians do not will a slump, though after the event we may conclude that their attempts to avert it helped to bring it on. In the 1640s peasants revolted against enclosure, clothiers against poverty resulting from depression, the godly against Antichrist in order to bring about Christ's kingdom on earth. As a New England supporter of Parliament summed up in 1648, "Saith one, I fought and engaged for the removing evil councillors from the King; ...saith another, I engaged for the establishment of preaching; ... saith another, I fought against the King, as conceiving him rather to act than be acted of any evil councillors whatsoever; another, he fought against oppression in general." Gerrard Winstanley thought that all strove for land — gentry, clergy, commons.[5] Few indeed of the rank and file of the New Model Army fought to create a world safe for capitalist farmers and merchants to make profits in; they protested loudly when Commissary-General Ireton hinted at such a possibility. As the Revolution developed, men with ideas of what was politically desirable tried to control it, none of them very successfully. The outcome of the Revolution was something which none of the activists had willed. Once the old constraints had broken down, or been broken, the shape of the new order was determined in the long run by the needs of a society in which large numbers of unideological men minded their own business.[6]

In England by 1640 the Stuart monarchy was unable to continue governing in the traditional way. Its foreign policy was deplorably weak, partly because of lack of money; the financial measures to which it was forced to resort alienated its potential supporters no less than its enemies. To say that this situation was the ultimate consequence of stresses and strains produced by the rise of the capitalist mode of production is not to say that Charles I's government was overthrown by a gang of capitalists — it was not — nor that a more skilful policy could not have enabled it to survive longer — it could. But by 1640 the social forces let loose by or accompanying the rise of capitalism, especially in agriculture, could no longer be contained within the old political framework except by means of a violent repression of which Charles's government proved incapable. Among "the social forces accompanying the rise of capitalism" we must include not only the individualism of those who wished to make money by doing what they would with their own but also the individualism of those who wished to follow their own consciences in worshipping God, and whose consciences led them to challenge the institutions of a stratified hierarchical society. Similar stresses and strains produced analogous conflicts in other European countries,[7] and were no doubt related to the population upsurge as well as to the rise of capitalism. But the outcome in England was different from that in any other European country except the Netherlands. In Spain, France, and elsewhere the absolute monarchy survived the mid-century crisis; in England this crisis put an end to the monarchy's aspirations to build up an absolutism based on a standing army and a bureaucracy.

As Marx pointed out, one of the essential differences between the English Revolution and the French Revolution of 1789 was "the continuous alliance which [in England] united the middle class with the largest section of the great landowners"[8] — an alliance which he associated with sheep farming and dated from the sixteenth century. It is, I fear, necessary to emphasize the obvious point that in England early capitalism was strongest in the countryside, since many portentous refutations of Marxism are vitiated by confusion on this issue.[9] The rural nature of capitalism in England differentiates it from that of most continental countries, and creates difficulties for purists who regard "rural bourgeoisie" as a contradiction in terms. Linguistic arguments apart, it is hard to deny that a section of the English gentry and yeomanry, especially in the South and East, from the sixteenth century onwards took part in production for the market, notably through the woollen and extractive industries; and that this is a main difference between England and those continental countries in which absolute monarchies survived. But this will not explain individual behaviour. No Marxist to my knowledge ever suggested that the ideas of individual men and women are determined by their class origins or class position. Yet one historian thought he had shown that what happened in mid-seventeenth-century England could not have been a bourgeois revolution because some royalists were enclosing landlords and some merchants were royalists. He should have added that Karl Marx was a bourgeois intellectual, Engels a factory owner and Lenin an aristocrat, thus proving that Marxism does not exist either.[10]

The landed ruling class in sixteenth-century England was a narrow one, secure only so long as united. In the two generations before 1640 it was no longer united by fear, whether of Spain, of dynastic civil war, or of peasant revolt: it was split over economic questions, notably monopolies, and over religion. After 1618 it was divided in attitudes toward foreign policy, so closely linked with religion. The clothing depression of the 1620s and the battle for the forests alienated the common people and a section of the gentry from the crown and the great aristocrats who were enclosing forests and common lands.[11] From at least the 1620s conflicts over the Parliamentary franchise in boroughs revealed a split between the oligarchic tendencies of the crown and some of the gentry, and a willingness of gentlemen less closely associated with the court to support a wide borough franchise.[12] The gentry excluded from office, and those whose long-established control of local government was interfered with, resented the attempt to create a stronger central government and bureaucracy. Laud's policy in the church alienated middle-of-the-road traditionalists hardly less than it infuriated Puritans; it led to disaster in Scotland. Strafford's success in Ireland was as disastrous as Laud's Scottish failure, because Ireland was seen as the base for building up an army — the other component necessary to any attempt to create an absolute monarchy.

The Scottish war of 1639-40 revealed the government's inability to rule, to raise taxes or an army that would fight, and allowed plotters among the aristocracy and gentry to envisage a return to power by means of popular support. So when Parliament at last met, some of its leaders were prepared to use or accept pressure by London mobs to force concessions from the government. They were ready to connive at religious toleration as the price of popular support against bishops, to connive at enclosure riots directed especially against the crown and big landlords, to connive at riots against papists. London mobs made possible the execution of Strafford, the exclusion of bishops from Parliament and the safety of the Five Members when Charles tried to arrest them in January 1642; yeomen from many of the home counties marched up to London in a demonstration of support.[13] "The rioting soldiers of 1640", writes William Hunt, "the altar-rail burners and iconoclasts of 1641, and the plunderers of summer 1642" secured Essex for Parliament. "Potential royalists were intimidated, and would-be neutralists were coerced into active compliance, by the relatively mild reign of terror".[14] In Gloucestershire in 1642 the royalists were "crushed by the rude hand of the multitude".[15] John Rous spoke of "this insurrection" in Suffolk in 1642,[16] just as Clarendon was to speak of "these insurrections" in

London in December 1641.[17] This was the atmosphere in which Parliament proceeded to clearly revolutionary actions — first the act forbidding the King to dissolve it without its own consent — necessary if its City friends were to be persuaded to advance money — then the abolition of Star Chamber and High Commission, and finally the Militia Ordinance, which took command of the armed forces away from Charles.

Henceforth, as Mr Manning has shown, the popular party in the Commons was to some extent trapped, was no longer in control of events. The publication of the Grand Remonstrance is rightly seen as a parting of the ways between those like Hyde and Falkland whose opposition to the crown did not extend to continued reliance on popular support, and those who had no qualms about pressing on — like Oliver Cromwell, with his experience as leader of the fenmen in the sixteen-thirties, or Bulstrode Whitelocke, the popular candidate in a class-divided election in 1640. Religious toleration was a similarly polarizing question. The breakdown of ecclesiastical authority in 1640 saw the emergence from underground of lower-class heretical groups who had long been beyond the pale of respectable protestantism. Whether or not there was a continuing underground from Lollards via Anabaptists and Familists to the sectaries of the sixteen-forties,[18] the emergence of the latter did much to scare away aristocratic reformers like Sir Edward Dering. Few indeed were those who, like Milton, had a friendly word for Familists in 1642; but under pressure of military necessity and London radicalism leaders like Oliver Cromwell opted for religious liberty and promotion by merit rather than by birth (the Self-Denying Ordinance).

When civil war broke out it was not the gentry but the clothiers of the West Riding who forced the pace in Yorkshire; and Fairfax followed. In Staffordshire it was the common people who insisted on fighting, whilst the gentry havered until Brereton put himself at their head. Neutralism was popular among the gentry of very many counties. Whatever the original intentions of Parliament, other wills took over from 1642-43.[20] The waverings of the "peace party" and the "middle group" among M.Ps. were overcome by pressures from outside Parliament — first from the London populace, then from the Scottish army, then from the English army. The war was won by artillery (which money alone could buy) and by the disciplined morale of Cromwell's yeomen cavalry. The real crisis came when the fighting was over, when the Leveller democratic organization gave a dangerous political significance to what had hitherto been spontaneous activities, like those of London mobs, of anti-papist and anti-enclosure rioters, just as the more extreme sectaries made dangerous sense of radical religious ideas, some of which — like those of Ranters, Diggers, and early Quakers — had political as well as theological significance and struck conservatives as simply irreligious.[21] In the end the social anxieties to which Levellers and radical sectaries gave rise were to reunite the propertied classes. Thanks largely to the skill with which in 1649 Charles I played the only card left to him, acting out the role of royal martyr, and to the great propaganda success of *Eikon Basilike*, this reunion focused on the monarchy. But the reunion was based on strong material links between the two sections of the propertied classes as well as on the magic of monarchy.

By 1660 transformations in the English political and social scene had occurred which — whatever the intentions of those who brought them about — had the consequence of facilitating the development of capitalism. Abolition of feudal tenures and the Court of Wards (1646, 1656, confirmed 1660) "turned lordship into absolute ownership", as Professor Perkin put it. Landowners were set free from the incidence of arbitrary death duties, and their lands became a commodity which could be bought, sold, and mortgaged; thus long-term capital investment in agriculture was facilitated. This was "the decisive change in English history, which made it different from the continent". "From it every other difference in English society stemmed".[22] "A *capitalist* agricultural economy", said Emmanuel Leroy Ladurie, sprang "ready-armed from the great manorial aristocratic system", opening "a new chapter in the history of the (rural) world".[23] The abolition of feudal tenures also removed a great lever of royal control and finance, and so gravely weakened the independent position of the monarchy.

As early as 1610 the House of Commons had insisted that if and when military tenures were abolished, there should be no equivalent security of tenure for copyholders: fines, heriots, suit of court, and workdays should all remain. This point was not mentioned in the order of 1646 — not the moment for offending copyholders. But then Levellers, Diggers and others campaigned for equal treatment for copyholders; after their suppression the acts of 1656 and 1660 confirming the abolition of feudal tenures specifically excluded copyholders from securing any of the advantages which their betters were voting themselves. So far from copyholders winning security of tenure, an act of 1677 extended their insecurity to small freeholders except in the unlikely event of the latter being able to produce written title to their estates. So most obstacles to enclosure were removed. This set the stage for a rapid expansion of capitalist agriculture, employing the new techniques popularized by the agricultural reformers of the Interregnum. Food prices steadied, and there were no more famines in England, though there still were in Scotland and France. Parliament positively encouraged enclosure and cultivation of the waste, protected farmers against imports, authorized corn hoarding and established the bounty on exports. The struggle for forests, fens and commons before 1640, to which Mr Manning rightly attaches so much importance, had aimed at cultivating them more profitably. The King and the great landlords were trying to use their political power to increase their share of the surplus. Pressure to cultivate fens and wastes came from the expanding market — for food and clothing for a growing population, for cloth exports.

Experience in the Third World in the present century shows how the early processes of capitalist development lend themselves to corruption. Those with political influence batten on to schemes which may be in the national interest but can be distorted to the corrupt advantage of the privileged. In early Stuart England most monopolies could be justified on grounds of national utility but were repeatedly "smeared with the trail of finance" and corruption. In the sixteen-thirties schemes for draining the Fens were distorted to the advantage of court favourites by blatant misuse of government pressure and influence. Commoners opposed fen drainage because it brutally extinguished their way of life. But its consequence was undoubtedly to increase total food production, once the corrupt court and its instruments of government had been removed. Oliver Cromwell as Lord of the Fens had led opposition to the draining of the Great Level. He was subsequently responsible for the defeat of the Levellers which made possible the resumption of drainage under his patronage, on terms more advantageous to the drainers than to the Fenmen, but which were relatively clean from corruption.[24] By 1660 the battle for fens, forests and commons had been lost by King and commoners alike.

To quote Professor Perkin again, "the provision of land for agricultural improvement, mining, transport, factories and towns was so little of a problem in the British Industrial Revolution that it is often forgotten what an obstacle feudal, tribal or fragmented peasant land tenure can be in underdeveloped countries." This was another great difference between England and the continent.[25] After 1688 Parliament encouraged the development of mineral resources, and a series of judicial pronouncements against restraints on trade completed the pattern.

The Navigation Acts (1650, 1651, confirmed 1660, 1661), made possible the closed colonial system, which could now be enforced thanks to the vast navy inherited by the Commonwealth government and the new system of taxation evolved to pay for fighting the civil war. The Dutch War of 1652-4 was the first state-backed imperialist adventure in English history; it was followed by Cromwell's Spanish War, England's first state-backed grab for colonies in the New World. The new taxes which financed this government expenditure were doubly advantageous to businessmen, since the excise on consumption fell especially on the ostentatious expenditure of the very rich and the necessities of the poor;[26] and the land tax was based on a new assessment which hit big landowners far harder than the pre-1640 subsidy had done.

The confirmation in 1660 of legislation against monopolies and against non-parliamentary taxation, together with abolition of the prerogative courts, made any government control over economic life impossible except in agreement with Parliament. There were to be no more Cokayne Projects, no more economic interference by the Privy Council. In the late sixteenth and early seventeenth centuries, as agriculture was being commercialized, so the common law was being adapted to the needs of capitalist society and the protection of property. After 1640 arbitrary government interference with due legal process was made impossible; and due legal process now meant the law as developed by Sir Edward Coke. Parts II, III and IV of his *Institutes* could not be printed before 1640; in 1641 Parliament ordered their publication, and henceforth Coke's works, in Blackstone's delicate phrase, had "an intrinsic authority in courts of justice, and do not entirely depend on the strength of his quotations from older authorities."[27] Monopoly ended in industry though not in foreign trade, where organization and state naval backing were still required. The defeat of the Leveller-led democratic movement in the gilds, and the wartime breakdown of apprentice regulations, seriously undermined the security of small masters in industry. The period after 1660 saw both machine-breaking and the beginning of trade union organization. The liberty and mobility of the revolutionary decades also facilitated a great expansion of the class of middlemen, travelling traders, whose activities were as much encouraged by post-restoration legislation as they had been harassed by pre-1640 governments. In 1663 Pepys observed that it was cheaper for small men to buy agricultural products than to try to grow them themselves. Sixty years later Defoe said there was "hardly a parish of all the 10,000 but has some of these retailers in them, and not a few have many hundreds." We are on the way to Adam Smith's nation of shop-keepers. The revolutionary decades also saw an expansion of urban professional classes, catering in the open market for the needs of those with money, rather than relying on aristocratic patronage.[28]

After 1660, as before, the gentry dominated English society and the state. But now the social context was different. The land confiscations and sales of the Revolution, short-lived though many of them were, and the redistribution of wealth by taxation, together with the defeat of the radicals, all expedited the breakdown of traditional patriarchal relations between landlords and tenants. Royalist landlords were forced by the economic pressures of the Revolution, and by the absence of the court as a source of windfall revenue, to turn to improving their estates. These habits survived the restoration. When Sir Edward Dering lost court office in 1673, he drew up elaborate plans for reorganizing his estate management so as to increase production for the market.[29] Enclosure, which as recently as the sixteen-thirties has been officially denounced by Archbishop Laud, was defended in the pamphlet warfare of the sixteen-fifties and became a patriotic duty. General Monck, his biographer tells us,

very well knew ... how unable the nobility are to support their own esteem and order, or to assist the crown, whilst they make themselves contemptible and weak by the number and weight of their debts and the continual decay of their estates. And if the wealth of the nation come to centre most among the lower and trading part of the people, at one time or other it will certainly be in their power, and probably in their desires, to invade the government. These and the like considerations had moved the Duke of Albemarle to become as great an example to the nobility of honourable husbandry as he had been before of loyalty and allegiance.[30]

Who better?

The Royal Society, to membership of which all peers were welcome, propagandized actively on behalf of improved agricultural production. The agrarian revolution of the later seventeenth and eighteenth centuries contributed to the accumulation of capital which was to make possible the Industrial Revolution, and to a significant increase in the domestic market for its products. A smaller labour force produced enough food to maintain a landless class as superfluous labour left the land for industry.[31]

After 1660 the republican and Cromwellian foreign policy of active support for English trade and navigation was continued. Charles II may have had anti-republican interests in leading England into the second and third Dutch Wars; but for most propertied Englishmen the Dutch were the main commercial rivals. Once their competitive power had been broken, their protestantism was remembered again, and they were welcomed as allies against Louis XIV's France. The navy and the system of taxation which had made possible the Navigation Act and the first Dutch War were taken over by post-restoration governments: the second and third Dutch Wars would have been impossible without them.[32] In 1694 the Bank of England was established. A bank could not have been set up in England earlier, nor in Louis XIV's France, because "the merchants feared ... the King would get his hands on the deposits."[33]

After 1660 no doubt Charles II (from time to time) and James II (more seriously) dreamed of building up the absolute monarchy that their father had failed to achieve. But, thanks to the Revolution, there was never any chance that they could succeed. Without an army, without an independent bureaucracy, absolutism was impossible without military support from abroad.[34] The post-restoration state, and especially the post-1688 state, was strong in external relations, weak at home. The cheapest way to rule and to keep the lower orders under control was to make use of the willing but unpaid services of the natural rulers of the country, the gentry and merchant oligarchies. It had the additional advantage of maintaining habits of deference and of easing the acceptability to landowners of an expensive foreign policy.

So 1660 saw a reunion of Roundheads and Cavaliers against religious, political, and social radicalism. Although formally no legislation not accepted by Charles I was valid after 1660, enough concessions had been forced from the monarchy in 1640-1 for this not to matter. There was "a king with plenty of holy oil about him" but no risk of absolutism, bishops but no High Commission; church courts could be effective only against those thought to be socially dangerous — dissenters and the lower classes. With the abolition of the prerogative courts, the triumph of Coke's common law, and later the independence of the judiciary from the executive, institutional restrictions on the development of capitalism had been removed. Whether they wanted to or not, peers and gentry had to come to terms with it. Society could not be put back into the hierarchical strait-jacket of the sixteen-thirties. The Earl Marshal's Court, which used to fine and imprison commoners for speaking impolitely of their betters, was restored only in 1687, and then with no coercive powers.[35] Henceforth deference was paid to money, not just to land.

Peers and other great landowners still had enormous assets which could be employed in capitalist development: land, prestige, access to court office. Marx anticipated Professor Stone in stressing "the wonderful vitality of the class of great landlords" in England. "No other class piles debt upon debt as lightheartedly as it. And yet it always lands on its feet."[36] The strict settlement ensured accumulation of capital at a time when the expansion of foreign trade, navy, and bureaucracy (under Parliamentary control) offered new jobs for younger sons, when the agricultural boom was beginning to make the church once more an acceptable profession, and made available richer portions for daughters. Everything combined to reconcile the aristocracy to the victory of the new social order in which they had a secure position. By the end of the century, participating in or benefiting from England's greatest capitalist industry, its money invested in the Bank of England, the peerage was sociologically a very different class from the hangers-on of James I's court. Marx and Engels were both careful to date "the political supremacy" of the English bourgeoisie, and its acceptance by the aristocracy, from after 1688.[37] Professor Jones notes that a section of the aristocracy was more investment-minded than most of the urban middle class.[38] Edward Thompson speaks of the eighteenth-century gentry as "a superbly successful and self-confident capitalist class."[39]

Between 1660 and 1688 there was an uneasy balance. As Professor Trevor-Roper has observed, there were no problems before the civil war which could not have been solved by sensible men sitting round a table. But before the settlement was achieved, Kings and archbishops had to be taught that they had a joint in their necks, the navy and the new system of taxation had to be built up, and the country had twenty years' experience of very successful rule by Parliamentary committees. These results could not have been achieved without unleashing religious, social, and political radicalism. In the sixteen-forties, censorship and the control of church courts broke down, and a wild revolutionary ferment ensued in which every heresy under the sun was preached and printed. Mechanics and their womenfolk freely met together and publicly denied the existence of heaven and hell, of the devil, of a historical Christ, of the after life. They treated the Bible as a collection of myths, to be used for current political purposes. They rejected a state church, its clergy and its tithes. They claimed that all mankind would be saved, and that all men should have the vote. Some rejected the Ten Commandments and monogamy, others called for the abolition of landlordism and private property. Groups formed to achieve some of these ends. The deferences and decencies of all social order seemed to be crumbling.[40]

This unprecedented radicalism was slowly and painfully suppressed in the fifties, but it left a searing memory. In 1660 M.Ps. were so afraid of its revival, so anxious to disband the dangerous Army as quickly as possible, to re-establish control over lower-class sectaries, that they failed to impose precise enough terms on the monarchy. When the events of 1678-81 revived memories of the forties Charles II could get away for a short time with non-Parliamentary rule in alliance with the Tory gentry and the Church of England. He could pack corporations — the Parliamentary electorate — and James profited by this in 1685. But Charles knew the social limits within which he could safely operate. When James, after routing the Monmouthite radicals in 1685, really tried to put the clock back, and in particular when he abandoned the Tory-Anglican alliance and tried to use the social forces which the Parliamentarians had employed against his father twenty years earlier, then the ranks closed against him — and against the radicals. Even James never aspired to rule without Parliaments, as his father had done from 1629 to 1640. His unprecedented attempt to pack a Parliament in 1688 was tribute to the strength of that institution; even more so was his failure.[41] The precise terms on which the monarchy was restored had not been spelt out in 1660; that was put right in 1688-9, as in France the settlement of 1815 was corrected after 1830.

The obsessive fear of radicalism which led to the overkill of 1660 had regrettable social and political consequences. After the victory of the liberalized common law, demands for further legal reform and codification had come especially from the radicals. In the post-revolutionary panic they were jettisoned; apart from the Habeas Corpus Act of 1679, the establishment of the independence of juries from dictation by the judge, and, after 1701, of the judiciary from the executive (all of which benefited the propertied classes), legal reform, like franchise reform, was forgotten by "responsible" politicians until the nineteenth century.[42] The modest educational advances of the revolutionary decades were also abandoned. The ending of schemes for more equal educational opportunity meant that the talents of the poorer three-quarters of the population were inadequately mobilized for the Industrial Revolution which England pioneered. The exclusion of dissenters from universities as well as from political life brought about a disastrous split in the English educational system (whose consequences are still with us) between classically educated amateurs who govern, and socially inferior scientists and technologists who work.[43] Lower-class mobility was restricted by the Act of Settlement of 1662 and the poor were accepted as a permanent part of the population. The steam engine was invented but not developed. Monarchy, peerage, and the Established Church survive in England till this day.

The Marxist concept of bourgeois revolution is thus not refuted by demonstrating that the House of Commons of the Long Parliament, like its predecessors, contained a cross-section of the natural rulers of the countryside, any more than the concept of bourgeois revolution would be established if it could be shown that every M.P. was a factory owner. To say that there was a division between court and country, though true, does not get us much further than saying that the French Revolution started with a revolt of the nobility.[44] What mattered in the English Revolution was that the ruling class was deeply divided at a time when there was much combustible material among the lower classes normally excluded from politics. "The parliament men of the early 17th century were sometimes acutely aware of the political forces operating outside Westminster," Dr Hirst has demonstrated, "and on occasion attempted to present the aspirations of those forces." To win support against the court they were prepared to enlarge the electorate. But by now, as Mr Manning has pointed out, "This enlarged electorate was less easy for the gentry to control and more capable of asserting its own opinions."[45]

Though normal in composition, the Long Parliament was elected in conditions of abnormal political excitement. It is not enough to say that an M.P. was a gentleman or a lawyer. We must ask how he was elected. Some represented their counties, and others pocket boroughs; others again were returned as a result of conflict within an urban electorate, in which the successful candidate was the nominee of one particular group. For instance, at Great Marlow the richer citizens wanted the local landlord, who was also a courtier; "bargemen of the town" and "the ordinary sort of townsmen" wanted Bulstrode Whitelocke. In an atmosphere of fierce conflict Whitelocke was returned. We classify him as a gentleman and a lawyer; but his defeated opponent was also a gentleman, son-in-law of Attorney-General Bankes, and had himself been educated at the Inner Temple.[46] A sociological analysis which cannot differentiate between the two is not very helpful. When civil war was forced upon reluctant M.Ps. each individual took decisions in the light of his religious beliefs, of the location of his estates, of individual hopes, fears, ambitions, hatreds, loyalties, temperaments. Counting and classifying M.Ps. will never explain the origins of the civil war, any more than counting and classifying Fellows of the Royal Society will explain the scientific revolution, useful though each activity may be in itself.

In every county there were long-standing rivalries within the ruling gentry, which often meant that if one family chose to support Parliament, another almost automatically chose to support the King. If we restrict our gaze to a single county, this creates the impression that the civil war was either something external, forcing would-be neutralists unwillingly to choose sides, or an accidental conflict on to which local rivalries latched. But the national alignments in the civil war were the sum of alignments in individual counties: it was because the traditional structures and the traditional consensus had broken down in the localities that civil war could not be avoided.

The Long Parliament did not make the Revolution. M.Ps. coped as best they could with the breakdown of the old system of government. They had to balance the pressures of the popular forces whose hostility was directed (or came to be directed) against aristocracy, gentry, and the rich generally, against their fear of these forces. Winning the war forced actions upon the Parliamentarian leaders about which they were less than happy. If victory was to be consolidated, the Army could not be disbanded; but the Army itself became a greater liability to a stable propertied social order than even

the Stuart monarchy had been. Cromwell wrestled with these problems. In the last resort it was fear — fear of social radicalism, of
religious radicalism, of political radicalism leading to "anarchy" —
that allowed the re-emergence of the successors of the "party of
order" of the forties. They first returned to local government, and
finally brought down the government of the republic by the same
measures as had brought down Charles I's government — a tax strike
covered by an invasion from Scotland.

Nor does the Marxist concept of bourgeois revolution, as I
understand it, demand that the rulers of England in 1649 (or 1646, or
1658) should have had specific policies of "free trade," colonial
imperialism, and the like. There had been pressure for a Navigation
Act from the sixteen-twenties; the logic of the economic situation
demanded it. It became politically possible because the civil war had
forced a reconstruction of the country's tax system and the creation
of a great navy. It is no doubt true, as the Venetian Ambassador in
Madrid observed, that the rulers of republican England were more
amenable to merchant pressures than their predecessors in the
sixteen-twenties and thirties.[47] The Dutch War of 1652-4 avenged
the Amboyna massacre of 1623 to which James I had failed to react.
There is a difference between his attempts to balance between
English and Dutch merchants, both rather distasteful to him,[48] and
the truculent attitude of the Commonwealth government.

Similarly the export of the lighter New Draperies to the Mediterranean area suggested the desirability of a naval presence there. James
in 1620 sent an expedition against the Tangier pirates, but it was
ineffective; Charles I ordered English merchants to keep out of the
Mediterranean. It was not until the sixteen-fifties that Blake's fleet
ruled the Mediterranean waves. Charles I had wished to build up a
navy, but his attempt at the financial reorganization necessary to pay
for it (Ship Money) led to a civil war which was in part a revolt against
the ineffective foreign policy of a government that could not protect
merchants from pirates, even in British waters. In 1588 the Spanish
Armada had been defeated by private enterprise as much as by the
efforts of the government; by the sixteen-fifties only the state could
raise fleets adequate to the demands of English merchants. There was
continuity between the power structure and the financial structure
of England in 1649-53 and the sixteen-sixties; there was much less
continuity between pre-revolutionary and post-revolutionary England. But in the consciousness of the rulers of the Commonwealth,

dreams of a powerful protestant coalition, which the Dutch could be forced if not persuaded to join and which could then be used for an anti-Catholic crusade, may have loomed as large as merely economic considerations. Things however get very complicated when we recall that the most enthusiastic supporters both of the first Dutch War and of an international protestant crusade, the Fifth Monarchists, drew their main support from clothiers and their employees.[49]

Cromwell's conquest of Ireland took place because it was strategically and financially imperative for the young republic. But it provided state support for settlement, hitherto left, unsatisfactorily, to private enterprise, just as the colonization of North America had been left to unsupported private enterprise.[50] Behind the conquest of Ireland was the pressure of investors who had speculated in Irish land futures, and the recollections of City merchants whom Charles I's government had swindled over the Londonderry plantation. Such men no doubt appreciated the significance of the colonization of Ireland for the development of English capitalism; so did a William Petty or a Benjamin Worsley; but there is no evidence that such economic considerations played a major part in the calculations of the rulers of England in 1649. Nevertheless, in the sixteen-sixties, the Cromwellian settlement was confirmed in essentials, at the expense of the Irish and of English Cavaliers; and Ireland remained a colony to be exploited by England. Imports of sheep, cattle, butter, and cheese to England were prohibited. After the second suppression of Ireland in 1689-91 Parliament gave great weight to economic considerations in imposing restrictions on Irish trade, backed up by the penal code. The Irish clothing industry was killed.

Similar considerations applied to the war against Spain in 1655. Cromwell gave as his reasons (1) that there was a fleet in being, which it was safer and cheaper to use than to pay off; (2) that Spaniards were idolators and did not allow free trade to protestants; (3) that the Lord had brought his English people thus far in order to achieve something great "in the world as well as at home" — probably a hint at an anti-Catholic crusade.[51] I believe him. But there had been economic thinkers, from John Dee and Richard Hakluyt onward, who dreamed of a British Empire across the Atlantic which would bring economic benefits to the mother country. Sir Edwin Sandys, the Rich family, the Providence Island Company and its Treasurer John Pym, point to links between colonial interests and Parliamentary opposition. Together the pragmatists and the imperialists laid the basis for the Commercial Revolution which Professor Davis has seen as the necessary condition of England's priority in the Industrial Revolution.[52] The confirmation in 1661 of Cromwell's conquests of Jamaica and Dunkirk "had the most universal consent and approbation from the whole nation that ever any bill could be attended with." Sir Josiah Child in 1672 thought the Navigation Act had trebled "the building and employing ... of ships and seamen."[53]

Nor is the concept of bourgeois revolution, on this interpretation, refuted by the observation that rich businessmen scrambled to win privileges and monopolies under the pre-1640 régime, and that some of the richest merchants supported Charles I during the civil war. Businessmen naturally always want the greatest possible profits: such profits were best obtained in Charles I's England by establishing close links with the government in return for monopoly privileges. We have seen the same factor at work with fen drainage. Professor Ashton has described the symbiosis of crown and customs-farmers in London, which operated to the great advantage of both parties until the crash came in 1640.[54] The oligarchies of the great merchant companies were alternately "burdened and protected" by the crown, but on balance protection in their privileges against interlopers outweighed resentment of the burdens.[55] It was the price to be paid for working an unsatisfactory system. By the same token, merchants and industrialists *excluded* from monopoly privileges were always potential enemies of the crown that gave privileges to their rivals, though they might be open to offers. What was new in the early sixteen-forties was that the royal government could no longer protect the privileges of its favourites; that customs farmers and monopolists were isolated from the rest of the business community and wide open to attack from London citizens who protected the Five Members from Charles I's attempted coup. But this was in a revolutionary situation.

Similarly in local government, where oligarchies increasingly came to dominate in the decades before the Revolution. These oligarchies were ready to co-operate with the government so long as it supported their monopoly of local power and therefore of local perquisites: the crown preferred to have local government in the hands of small goups, which were easy to deal with, depended on the crown for protection, and were therefore likely to support its policies. Rank-and-file craftsmen, and merchants excluded from the oligarchy, often opposed the rulers of their town; local politics increasingly became merged with national politics because of the crown's support for oligarchy.

The House of Commons came to favour a wider electorate in most boroughs; conversely the "outs" in boroughs used elections to Parliament as part of their struggle against local rivals. So some gentlemen tended to put themselves at the head of the "outs" against the "ins" in order to get elected to Parliament.[56] The two conflicts fused, and though there were occasional exceptions, the natural result was for oligarchies to support and be supported by the crown (or, if they did not support it satisfactorily, to be purged and reconstituted by the crown), and for the middling sort of merchants and craftsmen, and craftsmen outside boroughs, to look to Parliament.[57] But we should not think of "the bourgeoisie" as a self-conscious class. Any individual merchant or industrialist was naturally prepared at any time to accept privileges for himself from the crown and to abandon support of the "outs". But in England before 1640 the numbers of those small masters and small merchants who formed the "outs" increased steadily, so that individual defections made little difference to the class alignments. They do, however, confuse those historians who suppose that a class must necessarily be conscious of itself as a class. I think of a class as defined by the objective position of its members in relation to the productive process and to other classes. Men become conscious of shared interests in the process of struggling against common enemies; but this struggle can go a long way before anything emerges which we can call "class consciousness." Otherwise the activity of Marx, Lenin, and other Marxists in trying to stimulate "class consciousness" in the proletariat becomes inexplicable.

To classify the English and French Revolutions, and the Russian Revolution of 1905, as bourgeois revolutions does not mean that they are to be forced into one mould. There are, it seems to me, interesting analogies, but the English gentry and merchants of the seventeenth century were very different from the leaders of the French *Tiers Etat*, faced by a highly privileged *noblesse* and a state machine permeated by the purchase of office; and both were very different from the timid Russian merchants and manufacturers, dependent on foreigners for ideas no less than for capital. As Marx recognized, the English gentry became a bourgeoisie of its own particular kind.[58] It continued to exploit its tenantry through manor courts, to use money as a source of political power as well as of capital. To recognize its dependence on capitalist relations of production is not to deny the specific way in which it adapted the institutions of the old society, from Parliament and common law downward, to its own needs.

Maurice Dobb long ago spelled out the reasons why in pre-1640 England many capitalists supported the old régime. He analysed the difference between the "two paths" for bourgeois revolution, the "really revolutionary way" in which radical groups representing the middling sort drive the revolution further than the moderates wish to see it go, and so clear the decks for more radical capitalist development, and on the other hand the "Prussian path," in which such popular "excesses" are avoided.[59] In its ultimate outcome the English Revolution was closer to the Prussian model than to the French, though in the sixteen-forties the radicals played a part which hints at that of the French Jacobins. The point of stabilization under the Bonapartism of Oliver Cromwell was less radical than the point of stabilization under the Bonapartism of Bonaparte.

In no capitalist state in the world today, so far as I am aware, is state power exercised directly by big businessmen. There are close links between government and business, but a Henry Ford or a J. D. Rockefeller has better things to do than attend to the details of administration. So it was in the years after 1649. Many observers noted that merchants had more political influence than previously; and that members of the government came from a slightly lower social class than their predecessors; but there was no direct takeover of power by "the bourgeoisie."

At all points, then, I wish to disclaim the imputation of conscious will, which the opponents, but not the proponents, of the idea of bourgeois revolution attribute to it. "A bourgeois revolution there may have been", wrote Dr Eccleshall, "but it was certainly not initiated by men aggressively imbued with the spirit of individualism".[60] Bourgeois revolution is not possible until capitalist relations of production have developed within a country; it comes on the agenda only when the traditional government cannot go on ruling in the old way. This inability is itself the indirect consequence of social developments, as James Harrington realised was the case for England in the sixteen-forties.

"Bourgeois revolution" is an unfortunate phrase if it suggests a revolution *willed* by the bourgeoisie, as "the Puritan Revolution" suggests a revolution made by Puritans to achieve Puritan ends.

Perhaps a better analogy is the scientific revolution, to which contributions were made by many who were most "unscientific" by the standards of the science which emerged from the revolution. Boyle and Newton took alchemy seriously, Locke and Newton were millenarians.

My emphasis has been principally on the economic transformations brought about by the Revolution, because this is a point which traditional critics of a Marxist interpretation usually stress. But a revolution embraces all aspects of social life and activity. Cromwell thought that religion was "not the thing at first contested for, but God brought it to that issue at last". Control of the church, the main opinion-forming body in the country, was as politically important as control of radio and TV today. In England, Puritanism had flourished in the economically advanced South and East, and in the industrial areas and ports of the North and West. Professor Collinson has shown that Puritan demands under Elizabeth raised social no less than religious issues. A Puritan settlement then would have meant an earlier subordination of the church to the natural rulers, whether or not contemporaries saw it in that light.[61] Professor Hunt has demonstrated the congruency of Puritan ideas with the aspirations of parish élites, though he rightly points out that the preachers' utopia was not capitalism but a society of independent producers, labouring households, with no extremes of rich and poor, the godly rich helping the deserving poor.[62]

After 1640 all institutions and ideas had been called in question, and though the episcopal church came back with the monarchy and House of Lords, and the sects ultimately decided that Christ's kingdom was not of this world, the apparent continuity is illusory. The Church of England could never again be used as a propaganda agency outside Parliamentary control. Bishops had been Charles I's most reliable instruments; it was bishops who first refused obedience to James II. Charles II's ambassador to Paris was ordered to worship from time to time at the Huguenot church at Charenton — a reversal of Laud's severance of relations.[63] Radical hostility to the English church had been motivated, among other things, by hatred of tithes, whose economic pressure notoriously bore especially on the middling and poorer sort; it was also caused by the activities of church courts against Sabbatarianism and working on saints' days, to mention only the most obvious economic connections.[64] The "Latitudinarians" carried over into the post-Restoration church Puritan attitudes toward Sabbatarianism, preaching, science, and business ethics: claims to the Divine Right of bishops or of tithes fade away after 1660. By the sixteen-eighties church courts had ceased to matter: parsons helped squires to maintain control of their villages, but dissent had established itself in the towns. What had failed was the attempt made during the revolutionary decades to modernize the church as an economic institution, to establish a living wage for every incumbent, uniting and dividing parishes for the purpose. 1660 restored pluralism together with bishops and deans and chapters. Eachard published *The Grounds and Occasions of the Contempt of the Clergy* in 1670. When reform came through Queen Anne's Bounty it was at the cost of strengthening the hold of lay patrons over the church.[65] The agricultural revolution probably helped incumbents more than Queen Anne did.

One test of a revolution is that those who live through it feel it as a unique turning point. The widespread millenarianism of the sixteen-forties and early fifties is one example of this. But detached observers like Aubrey and Hobbes, and relatively detached observers like Marvell and Harrington, no less than eager participants like Levellers, Diggers, Quakers, preachers of Fast Sermons, all believed that they were passing through an unprecedented crisis. Milton described the achievements of the English Revolution as "the most heroic and exemplary since the beginning of the world" — not excluding, apparently, the life and death of Christ.

Some will think that I overemphasize the importance of the defeated radicals at the expense of the mainstream achievements of the English Revolution. Yet without the pressure of the radicals the civil war might not have been transformed into a revolution: some compromise could have been botched up between the gentry on the two sides — a "Prussian path." Regicide and republic were no part of the intentions of the original leaders of the Long Parliament; they were forced on the men of 1649 by the logic of the revolution which they were trying to control.

The ferment of discussion which Milton had welcomed in *Areopagitica*, some of it highly sophisticated, some not, bubbled on for eight years or so before conservatives managed to get the lid back on again. The memory of it faded — more slowly and less completely perhaps than the books usually suggest. Blake remembered it, and so did Catherine Macaulay and the Wilkesites, Paine and the American rebels, Thomas Spence, William Godwin, the Corresponding

Society, and the Chartists. The young Wordsworth recalled Milton the libertarian, Shelley recalled Milton the defender of regicide. The Revolution had shown that the old order was not eternal: the possibility of estabishing God's kingdom on earth had been envisaged, especially by those normally excluded from politics. the Long Parliament itself had argued that "reason hath no precedent, for reason is the fountain of all just precedents"; Levellers, Hobbes, Locke, and many others evolved systems of rational and utilitarian politics. By 1742 David Hume could assume that no one took claims to Divine Right seriously.

It is difficult for us to appreciate how great the intellectual revolution was, to think ourselves back into a hierarchical universe dominated by precedents and authorities, where God and the devil intervened in daily life. There was, of course, no sudden break in popular acceptance of magic. Many early Fellows of the Royal Society regarded belief in witchcraft as necessary if belief in God was to survive.[66] But after 1685 no more old women were executed as witches. Aubrey among many others spotted the revolutionary decades as the period in which traditional superstitions yielded to freedom of discussion and enquiry. Parliamentary sovereignty and the rule of law made late seventeenth-century England a freer country than any in Europe, except possibly the bourgeois Netherlands. The land had "enfranchised itself from this impertinent yoke of prelaty, under whose inquisitorious and tyrannical duncery no free and splendid wit can flourish" — not as completely as Milton would have wished, but enough to allow Petty, Newton and Locke to speculate freely. From 1695 the censorship could be lifted, not in the interests of freedom of thought, but of the right to buy and sell. By now the consensus among the men of property was accepted; they could be trusted to censor themselves, and the number of those who did not conform was negligible.

In a very sophisticated article Ann Hughes recently suggested that

an examination of the nature of local-central relationships on either side suggests ... a fundamental contrast in the political processes of royalists and Parliamentarians, a contrast between an ordered, institutionalized yet flexible Parliamentarianism, and a capricious, individualized and private royalism. ... It may even be that the consolidation of a specialized public realm of politics provides the best justification for seeing the English civil war as a bourgeois revolution.[67]

Historians who have attacked the concept of bourgeois revolution would benefit by reading this elegant piece. It receives confirmation from Stephen Roberts, who shows how in Devon in the sixteen-fifties and sixties a new bureaucratic efficiency was being introduced. This "shift towards 'professionalism,' in local government" survived the restoration, which saw the emergence of 'a standing bureaucracy", with salaried officials. Similarly J.S. Morrill and J.D. Walter noted that during the Revolution "economic change undoubtedly prompted greater popular discontent but ultimately it created new structures" which made possible its containment.[68]

Nobody, then, willed the English Revolution: it happened. Adam Ferguson in 1767 quoted Oliver Cromwell's alleged remark that a man never mounts higher than when he knows not whither he is going. Ferguson added: "it may with some reason be affirmed of communities, that they admit of the greatest revolutions where no change is intended, that the most refined politicians do not always know whither they are leading the state by their projects."[69] We must look at the Revolution as a whole. Professor Pocock wisely wrote "we shall not understand the way in which the traditional constitution and the rule of the established élites were challenged and changed during the 1640s until we understand how and why they were apparently restored in 1660, and how far that restoration was apparent and how far real."[70] If we look at the outcome of the English "greatest revolution", what emerged when the idealists, the men of conscious will on either side, had been defeated, was a state in which the administrative organs that most impeded capitalist development had been abolished: Star Chamber, High Commission, Court of Wards and feudal tenures; in which the executive was subordinated to the men of property, deprived of control over the judiciary, and yet strengthened in external relations by a powerful navy and the Navigation Act; in which modern bureaucratic methods were beginning to be introduced into central and local government.

Power was now safely and cheaply in the hands of the natural rulers, and discipline was imposed on the lower orders by a church safely subordinated to Parliament. This church was as different from the church which Archbishop Laud had wished to see as the state of William III was from the state of Charles I and Strafford, as the culture of Pope, Defoe, and Hogarth was from the culture of Beaumont and Fletcher, Lancelot Andrewes, and Van Dyck. Two

ways of life had been in conflict and the outcome had transformed
life-styles and intellectual assumptions at all levels of society. With
Hume and Adam Smith we are in the modern world. Before 1640 the
English ruling class aped Spanish, French, and Italian fashions and
ideas; after 1688 Britain was to give the lead to Europe. The novel,
the bourgeois literary form *par excellence*, developed from the spiritual autobiographies of the sectaries and from Bunyan's epics of the
poor: Defoe, Richardson, and Fielding could not have written as
they did without the heritage of the seventeenth-century Revolution. They produced a new art form for the whole of Europe.

If the Revolution of 1640 was unwilled, the coup d'état of 1688-9
and the peaceful Hanoverian succession were very much willed. The
self-confident landed class had now consciously taken its destiny into
its own hands. So, as George Wither put it in 1653:

> He that would, and he that would not too,
> Shall help effect what God intends to do.
>
> Yea, they who pull down and they who do erect
> Shall in the close concur in one effect.[71]

Andrew Marvell gave this theological conclusion a Harringtonian
twist when he wrote, ironically, "Men may spare their pains when
Nature is at work, and the world will not go the faster for our
driving." The wise will "make their destiny their choice." But
destiny, the historical forces, worked through the "industrious
valour" of Oliver Cromwell and his like which had ruined the great
work of time:

> 'Tis madness to resist or blame
> The force of angry heaven's flame.[72]

The Revolution was God's work, both because it was unwilled by
men and because it was a turning-point in human history.

NOTES

1. First published in *Three British Revolutions, 1641, 1688, 1776*, ed. J.G.A. Pocock (Princeton U.P., 1980). I am deeply grateful to Eric Hobsbawm and Edward Thompson for reading a draft of this chapter and making helpful comments and criticisms. They are not responsible for what has resulted.

2. See my *Change and Continuity in 17th-Century England*, pp. 278-82.

3. Review by R.H. Nidditch in *Isis*, 68 (1977), pp. 153-4. See V.G. Kiernan, "Revolution", in *The New Cambridge Modern History*, X (Companion volume, Cambridge U.P., 1979), pp. 225-6.

4. For Lenin's views see V.I. Lenin, *Selected Works* (1934-8), I, pp. 492-3, III, pp. 134-5.

5. George Downing to John Winthrop, 8 March 1647-8, in *Collections of the Massachusetts Historical Soc.*, VI, p. 541; ed. G.H. Sabine, *The Works of Gerrard Winstanley* (Cornell U.P., 1941), pp. 373-4; cf. Rutt, *Diary of Thomas Burton*, III, pp. 145, 186-8.

6. J.H. Hexter listed some of the relevant facts in his "Storm over the Gentry"; but he failed to see where his argument was leading him (*Reappraisals in History: New Views on History and Society in Early Modern Europe*, 1979, pp. 143-8). The reader interested in what Marx and Engels actually said on these questions is referred to Marx, *Selected Works* (1935), I, pp. 210-11, 241, 456-68; II, pp. 175, 315, 344-5; Marx, *Selected Essays* (New York, 1926), pp. 69-70, 201-6; Marx-Engels, *Gesamtausgabe* (Moscow, 1927-), Abt. I, VII, p. 493; Engels, *Socialism, Utopian and Scientific* (1936), pp. xix-xxii; Engels, *Anti-Duhring* (1954), pp. 226-9; *Selected Correspondence of Marx and Engels* (ed. Dona Torr, 1934), pp. 310-11, 475-7, 517-18. What they find may surprise holders of "the traditional view".

7. R.B. Merriman, *Six Contemporaneous Revolutions* (Oxford U.P., 1938), *passim*; E.J. Hobsbawm, "The Crisis of the Seventeenth Century", *P. and P.*, 5 and 6 (1954); H.R. Trevor-Roper, "The General Crisis of the Seventeenth Century", *ibid.*, 16 (1959), and a discussion in *ibid.*, 18 (1960).

8. Marx, *Selected Essays*, pp. 204-6; *Capital*, I (ed. Dona Torr, 1946), p. 430; III (ed. Engels, Chicago, 1909), pp. 928-46.

9. See Hexter, "The Myth of the Middle-Class in Tudor England", *op. cit.*, pp. 71-116, *passim*; cf. *ibid.*, pp. 29, 140-1. It still remains to mar the otherwise excellent book by Laura Caroline Stevenson, *Praise and Paradox: Merchants and Craftsmen in Elizabethan Popular Literature* (Cambridge U.P., 1984).

10. L. Stone, "The Bourgeois Revolution of 17th-century England Revisited", *P. and P.*, 109 (1985), pp. 46-53; on the "mutual dependence" of the absolutist state and "strong peasant property" in France, see R. Brenner, "Agrarian Class Structure and Economic Development in pre-Industrial Europe", *P. and P.*, 70 (1976), pp. 68-73.

11. Brian Manning, *The English People and the English Revolution*, Chapters 1 and 7. For forests see note 24 below.

12. Derek Hirst, *The Representative of the People?*, esp. Chapters 3, 4 and 10; Ed. P. Clark and P. Slack, *English Towns in Transition* (Oxford U.P., 1976), pp. 134-40.

13. Manning, *op. cit.*, Chapters 1, 4 and p. 104.

14. W. Hunt, *The Puritan Moment*, p. 306.

15. J. Corbet, *An Historicall Relation of the Military Government of Gloucester* (1645), in *Biblioteca Gloucestrensis* (1823), I, p. 8.

16. Ed. M. A. E. Green, *Diary of John Rous* (Camden Soc., 1856), p. 122.

17. Edward Hyde, Earl of Clarendon, *History of the Rebellion and Civil Wars in England* (ed. W. D. Macray, Oxford U.P., 1888), I, p. 455.

18. See "From Lollards to Levellers" in *Religion and Politics in 17th-Century England* (1986).

19. *M.E.R.*, pp. 95-7.

20. Manning, *op. cit.*, Chapter 7. Cf. p. 52 above.

21. *Ibid.*, Chapters 9 and 10. See now Barry Reay, *The Quakers and the English Revolution* (1985), *passim*.

22. H. J. Perkin, "The Social Causes of the British Industrial Revolution", *T.R.H.S.* (1968), p. 135; cf. Daniel Defoe, *The Compleat English Gentleman* (1890), pp. 60-3. Written 1728-9.

23. E. Leroy Ladurie, "Peasants", in *New Cambridge Modern History*, XIII, pp. 133-4, 139.

24. Kennedy, "Charles I and Local Government", pp. 24-31.

25. Perkin, *op cit.*, pp. 137-8.

26. As Marx noted in 1847 (*The Poverty of Philosophy*, 1941, p. 129), Charles II received compensation for feudal tenures from the excise.

27. Quoted in *I.O.E.R.*, pp. 255-6; see also p. 227, and Chapter 5 *passim*.

28. Ed. H. T. Heath, *The Letters of Samuel Pepys and his Family Circle* (Oxford U.P., 1956), p. 3; D. Defoe. *The Complete English Tradesman* (1841), II, p. 209; cf. I, pp, 241-53 (first published 1727); A. Everitt, "Social Mobility in Early Modern England', *P. and P.*, 33 (1966); *Change in the Provinces* (Leicester U.P., 1969), pp. 43-6; D. Davis, *A History of Shopping* (1966), esp. Chapter 6, p. 181; G. W. Chalklin, *Seventeenth-Century Kent* (1975), p. 160; cf. my *Change and Continuity*, Chapter 7. See also W. N. Parker, "Industry", in *New Cambridge Modern History*, XIII, p. 71: "The difference between England and the continent lay not so much in the balance of central and local government as in who controlled that authority; ... a government of incredible strength and toughness".

29. Ed. M. F. Bond, *The Diaries and Papers of Sir Edward Dering, ... 1644 to 1684* (H.M.S.O., 1976), p. 14; cf. *A Royalist's Notebook* (ed. F. Bamford, 1936), p. 231; *The Moore Rental* (ed. T. Heywood, Chetham Soc., 1874), p. 119.

30. T. Skinner, *Life of Monck* (2nd. edn., 1724), p. 384.

31. Cf. Brenner, *op. cit.*, pp. 67-71.

32. See pp. 132, 135-9 below.

33. F. Braudel, *Civilisation matérielle et capitalisme* (Paris, 1967), I, p. 396.

34. I owe this point to an unpublished paper by Professor J. R. Jones.
35. *The Life of Edward Earl of Clarendon* (Oxford U.P., 1759), I, pp. 72-3, 76-7; G. D. Squibb, *The High Court of Chivalry* (Oxford U.P., 1959), Chapters 3, 5 and 6.
36. Marx, *Capital*, III, p. 841.
37. Marx, *Germany, Revolution and Counter-Revolution*, in *Selected Works*, II, p. 44; *Capital*, I, pp. 746-7; Engels, *Socialism, Utopian and Scientific*, pp. xxiii-iv.
38. J. R. Jones, *The Revolution of 1688 in England* (1972), p. 14.
39. E. P. Thompson, "The Peculiarities of the English", *The Socialist Register*, 2 (1965), pp. 317-18; cf. Raymond Williams, *The Country and the City* (1973) Chapters 7 and 10.
40. I have discussed these matters in *W. T. U. D.*
41. Jones, *op. cit.*, pp. 52, 128-9, and *passim*.
42. I should wish to modify this statement after reading Susan Staves's splendid *Players' Scepters: Fictions of Authority in the Restoration* (Nebraska U.P., 1979), esp. pp. 97-100, 184-9, 263, 288-92, 313. She suggests that significant changes in law were introduced piecemeal in the late seventeenth and early eighteenth century.
43. See C. Webster, "Science and the challenge to the scholastic curriculum, 1640-1660", in *The Changing Curriculum* (History of Education Soc., 1971), pp. 32-4; and *W. T. U. D.* p. 305.
44. For the conventional view see Zagorin, *The Court and the Country*. It is however interesting that the English, French and Russian Revolutions, and the Revolt of the Netherlands, all started with what may be called a "revolt of the nobles" (Kiernan, *op. cit.*, p. 227).
45. Hirst, *op. cit.*, p. 158; Manning, *op. cit.*, p. 2. In *The Debate on the English Revolution* (1977) Dr. R. C. Richardson shrewdly pointed out that, though quite fortuitously, the argument of Manning's book "followed on from where Hirst's book left off" (p. 143).
46. M. R. Frear, "The Election at Great Marlow in 1640", *Journal of Modern History*, 14 (1942), pp. 433-8; M. F. Keeler, *The Long Parliament, 1640-1641*, p. 111.
47. *Calendar of State Papers, Venetian, 1647-1652*, p. 188.
48. G. N. Clark and W. J. M. van Eysinga, *The Colonial Conferences between England and the Netherlands in 1613 and 1615* (Leiden, 1940).
49. B. S. Capp, *The Fifth Monarchy Men* (1972), pp. 82-9, 152-4.
50. Nicholas Canny, *The Elizabethan Conquest of Ireland: A Pattern Established, 1565-1576* (Hassocks, 1976), esp. Chapter 4 and pp. 158-9.
51. Ed. C. H. Firth, *The Clarke Papers*, III (Camden Soc., 1899), pp. 203-8.
52. R. Davis, *A Commercial Revolution* (Historical Association Pamphlet, 1967), *passim*.
53. C. M. Andrews, *The Colonial Period of American History* (Yale U.P., 1964), III, p. 32; R. Davis, *The Rise of the English Shipping Industry* (1962), Chapter 18; Sir Josiah Child, *New Discourses on Trade* (1751), pp. 87, xxi (first published 1672).
54. R. Ashton, *The Crown and the Money Market* (Oxford U.P., 1960), *passim*.

55. See the shrewd analysis by the Venetian Ambassador in 1622 (*Calendar of State Papers, Venetian, 1621-1623*) pp. 434-5.
56. Hirst, *op. cit.*, esp. Chapter 6; Paul Slack, "Poverty and Politics in Salisbury, 1597-1666", in *Crisis and Order in English Towns, 1500-1700* (ed. P. Clark and P. Slack, 1972).
57. Any government, including those of the Commonwealth and Protectorate, preferred oligarchies in local government because they were easier to control. The House of Commons lost its enthusiasm for wide eletorates after 1660, since popular support against the government was no longer necessary.
58. Marx, *Economic and Philosophical Manuscripts of 1844* (ed. D. Struik, 1970), pp. 100-4, 125-6, I owe this reference and some of what follows to the kindness of Edward Thompson.
59. M. H. Dobb, *Studies in the Development of Capitalism* (1946), esp. Chapter 4.
60. R. Eccleshall, *Order and Reason in Politics: Theories of Absolute and Limited Monarchy in Early Modern England* (Oxford U.P., 1978), p. 135.
61. Collinson, *The Elizabethan Puritan Movement* (1967), *passim*.
62. Hunt, *op. cit.*, pp. 138-9; cf. Wrightson and Levine, *Poverty and Piety in an English Village*, esp. Chapters 6 and 7.
63. W. L. Grant, "A Puritan at the Court of Louis XIV", *Bulletin of the Departments of History and Political and Economic Science in Queen's University, Kingston, Ontario, Canada*, 8 (1913), p. 3.
64. See my *Society and Puritanism in Pre-Revolutionary England* (Panther edn.) esp. Chapters 4 and 5.
65. See an important article by Rosemary O'Day and Ann Hughes, "Augmentation and amalgamation: was there a systematic approach to the reform of parochial finance, 1640-1660?", in *Princes and Paupers in the English Church, 1500-1800* (ed. R. O'Day and F. Heal, Leicester U.P., 1981).
66. See pp. 275-6, 284 below.
67. Ann Hughes, "The King, the Parliament and the Localities during the English Civil War", *Journal of British Studies*, 24 (1985), p. 263.
68. S. Roberts, *op. cit.* pp. 52, 127, 179; Morrill and Walter, "Order and Disorder in the English Revolution", in *Order and Disorder in early modern England* (ed. A. Fletcher and J. Stevenson, Cambridge U.P., 1985), p. 150. A valuable article in the present context.
69. Adam Ferguson, *An Essay on the History of Civil Society* (Edinburgh, 1767), p. 187.
70. J. G. A. Pocock, "Authority and Propriety: The Question of Liberal Origins", in *After the Reformation: essays in honor of J. H. Hexter* (ed. B. C. Malament, Manchester U.P., 1980), p. 332.
71. G. Wither, *The Dark Lantern* (1653), pp. 10-11, in *Miscellaneous Works* (Spenser Soc., III, 1873-4), p. 18-19.
72. A. Marvell, *The Rehearsal Transpros'd* (ed. D. I. B. Smith, Oxford U.P., 1971), p. 135; *Upon Appleton House*, line 744; cf. *On Blake's Victory over the Spaniards*, lines 141-2; *An Horation Ode*, lines 25-6, 33-4.

POSTSCRIPT

Two recent interesting books relate to matters discussed here. In *The Peculiarities of German History: Bourgeois Society and Politics in Nineteenth Century Germany*, David Blackburn and Geoff Eley argue that nineteenth-century Germany experienced a "bourgeois revolution" "from on top", since the success of capitalism in England and other west European countries convinced the German ruling class (as it did the Japanese ruling class) of the necessity and desirability of imitating England. Such a "revolution from on top" could only happen after a succession of successful revolutions from below had established the advantages of capitalism for the aristocracy as well as for business men. Blackburn and Eley stress the analogies in social position between the English aristocracy in the eighteenth century and the German aristocracy in the nineteenth century. (The concept of an "epoch of bourgeois revolutions" is elaborated by the Soviet historian M.A. Barg, in *Categories and Methods of Historical Science*, Moscow, 1984, in Russian.)[1]

In *The Great Arch: English State Formation as Cultural Revolution* (Oxford, 1985), Philip Corrigan and Derek Sayer wish to abandon the idea of a single bourgeois revolution and postulate a "complex and protracted history of state formation and transformation through which capitalist classes did come finally to achieve political dominance in England". "We are thinking of a great arch spanning centuries rather than decades", a series of " 'long waves of revolution in government' ", from the early Middle Ages to the nineteenth century.[2]

Now it may well be that my generation of historians (and myself in particular) reacted too strongly against the bland Whig assumption of "the continuity of English history", of the unbroken constitutional development of an exceptional English people, which started in the forests of primeval Germany and reached its peak in the early twentieth century. But Corrigan and Sayer not only reject "the search for an English 1789" but also say that "the revolutions that made England a nation had been (when successful) revolutions from above", and that "England was, in Trevelyan's phrase, 'hammered into a nation' *primarily* through the machinery of state".[3] For reasons given in Chapter 6 below, I am unhappy about this conception of "the state" as something continuous and undifferentiated from William the Conqueror to Queen Victoria; it is in relation to the state that I see a more decisive break in the seventeenth century than in the thirteenth century, the fifteen-thirties or the nineteenth century. The state (and the state church) of 1660 were quite different from those which existed before 1640; as was made clear finally in 1688.[4]

NOTES

1. See my review in *New Left Review*.
2. Corrigan and Sayer, *op. cit.*, pp. 11, 85, 202 and *passim*.
3. *Ibid.*, pp. 202, 192. My italics.
4. Nancy L. Matthews's important book, *William Sheppard, Cromwell's Law Reformer* (Cambridge U.P., 1986) appeared too late for me to take account of it. She argues that there was a much more serious and thought-out programme of law reform under the Protectorate than has been recognized. Fascinating thoughts about some cultural consequences of the English Revolution are raised by Michael MacDonald's trail-blazing article, "The Secularization of Suicide in England, 1660-1880", *P. and P.*, 111 (1986).

6. *Braudel and the State*[1]

"Au vrai, plus encore que des sociétés (le mot est malgré tout bien vague), c'est de socio-économies qu'il faudrait parler. C'est Marx qui a raison ... Il reste évident cependant que ces deux coordonnées, société et économie, ne suffisent pas à elles seules: l'État multiforme, cause et consequence tout à la fois, impose sa presence ..." ⃰

The Venetian Ambassador, 15 September, 1640: *"England to-day has become a nation useless to all the rest of the world, and consequently of no consideration".*†

Braudel is by common consent one of the greatest historians of our generation, and *Civilisation Matérielle, Economie et Capitalisme, XVe - XVIIIe Siècle* is his most ambitious work. The object of his three volumes is to study and classify the material bases of economic life during his chosen period, all over the world. "Men are enclosed within an economic condition, ... imprisoned within a frontier which marks the unyielding limits of the possible and the impossible" (I, p. 434). For the masses of mankind, "an omnipresent power of inertia is one of the great forces of history": in the eighteenth century 60 miles a day was still the *maximum* speed of travel, as it had been for centuries (I, pp. 325, 435). If we called on Voltaire at Ferney, we should find him to all intents and purposes our contemporary in his ideas, his intelligence, his passions; "but all the details of material existence, even the care which he took of his own person, would astonish us" (I, p. 16). For most of the world for most of these centuries climate, famine and pestilence were more important than technology. Braudel surveys the food, drink, housing, clothing, tools, transport, currency of ordinary people, drawing on a vast range of secondary authorities.

⃰ Braudel, *Civilisation Matérielle et Capitalisme (XVe - XVIIIe Siècle)* (Paris, 1967), p. 436.

† *Calendar of State Papers, Venetian, 1640-2*, pp. 27-8.

His book is the product of a lifetime's reading and research. It is as full of ideas as of facts, the former coming often from the world-view which Braudel adopts. There are two positions in the world for everyday repose, almost two biologies: the cross-legged position familiar everywhere except in Europe, and the European sitting position on chairs: the two exist side by side only in China (I, p. 219). A round (as opposed to a square) table does away with problems of precedence, but only when chairs replace benches in sufficient number, when there is no longer a single privileged "chairman" (I, p. 227). Maize, by contrast with other grains, is too easy to grow: it leaves surplus labour at the disposal of theocratic states, available for the vast building works of the Mayas and the Aztecs (I pp. 124-5). The fourteenth-century regression occurred in China no less than in Europe (I, p. 320). The water mill is owned by a feudal lord, on whom the community depends; a windmill belongs to a private individual ("on dirait, en souriant, qu'elle est 'capitaliste'" — I, p. 274). Pepper was the Worcester sauce of the sixteenth century. The new vegetables grown in Europe in the sixteenth and seventeenth centuries helped to replace spices by diversifying the flavour of meat (I, pp. 162-5). Braudel notes "a fantastic regression" in European washing habits between the fifteenth and seventeenth centuries (I, p. 247). But coaches and sedan chairs, in addition to their use as a means of transport, were also popular with the well-to-do because they guaranteed a presentable appearance after crossing the filth of a seventeenth-century city (I, p. 430). Beards go in cycles, returning to fashion after approximately a century in which clean shaving was the mode (I, p. 249). Changes of fashion in dress, however, are not to be explained solely in economic terms. "Fashion is the search for a new language for each generation" (I, p. 243) — an insight perhaps more true of the twentieth than of the sixteenth century.

Braudel is sceptical of some recent enthusiasms of historians. "They are fiscal statistics," he writes of China; "and he who says fiscal says fraudulent, or illusory, or both at once" (I, p. 23). If, as appears probable, the population explosion took place simultaneously in China and in western Europe, the Industrial Revolution cannot be held accountable for it. "We must revise many perspectives and many explanations" (I, pp. 25, 31). The author suggests that a change in climate, the ending of "the little ice age," may have been the cause for a world-wide transformation (I, p. 33). As a comment on European economic exploitation of Africa his quotation of a saying among the natives of Mozambique could hardly be improved on: if monkeys do not talk, "it is because they are afraid they would be made to work" (I, p. 76).

There is, not unnaturally, a heavy French emphasis in the evidence used: Braudel illustrates the lack of privacy in even the most luxurious seventeenth-century dwellings by the remark that Louis XIV, when he went to call on Madame de Montespan, had to pass through Mademoiselle de la Vallière's room (I, p. 229). But his breadth of view enables him to make some interesting observations about English history, even though Dekker and Pepys appear a little too frequently as sources. The English, Braudel remarks with a sniff, have always liked heavy wines. They made the reputation of malmsey, and later of port, malaga, madeira, sherry, marsala. England and the Netherlands, outside the wine-growing area, also popularized the alcoholic revolution of the seventeenth century, the mass consumption of spirits (I, pp. 174, 180, 185). Tea, chocolate, and coffee all began to be drunk in western Europe from the middle of the seventeenth century too (I, pp. 189-93): a profound change in social habits. Wolves became extinct in England many centuries earlier than on the continent, where there were no impassable water barriers (I, p. 49). Town walls soon became an unnecessary expense in England (as in Japan and the Ottoman Empire); so the expansion of London was less confined than that of other European capitals in the sixteenth and seventeenth centuries (I, p. 382). In the West generally towns, with their unparalleled freedom, were the motors of progress, without which technique would have been powerless (I, pp. 391-3). "Following the laws of a simple and compelling political arithmetic, it appears that the vaster and more centralized a state is, the greater the probable population of its capital" (I, p. 406). London remade England in its own image after the revolution of 1688 (I, p. 396) — and indeed earlier, we might think.

Braudel is a great historian in the sense in which Louis XIV is *le grand monarque*. What he does is grand in manner and style, and he has changed the map of his subject. Not everybody will agree with all of what he is trying to do, but nobody can ignore it. Much less rigorous in his economic thinking than Marx, he has something of Marx's omnivorous curiosity, and of his readiness to relate ideas fruitfully to the material life from which they spring. Nowhere is Braudel more grandly monarchical than in his attitude towards criticism. Some have complained that his broad sweeps ignore almost everything but the economic. Braudel responds obliquely:

The state is back in fashion again, even among philosophers. Any analysis which does not grant it an important place is placing itself outside a developing trend, one which has its excesses and simplifications of course, but which has at least the advantages of making some French historians think again and pay attention to something they were ready to dismiss, or at any rate neglect, in the past (III, p. 62).[2]

So he is responding not to criticism of his method but to a long-term secular trend. "We must give the state its due then: the overall economy obliges us to restore it to its very considerable place" (III, p. 314). "Us", not "me".

One of the main strengths of *La Méditerranée et le Monde Méditerranéen* was its reliance on description, its reluctance to generalize. But in these three volumes Braudel presents a thesis — cautiously — and it is a complex thesis: but a thesis none the less. Summarizing inevitably does injustice to the subtleties, but it must be attempted.

Braudel's three volumes distinguish between three levels. First is what he calls *la vie matérielle* or *la civilisation matérielle*, the self-sufficient infra-economy of pre-industrial producers. Above this is the economy of the market, "the mechanisms of production and exchange linked to rural activities, shops, workshops, exchanges, banks, fairs and town markets." It is Marx's small commodity production plus a bit more. Finally, above these two levels, there are "groups of privileged persons" who engage in activities about which most men know nothing — like controlling the exchanges to their profit.

This third level is what Fernand Braudel calls "capitalism," always most at home in the sphere of circulation. The mass of transactions about which our statistics tell us fall within "the economy of the market." But an international capitalism has existed from the great firms of the Fugger and the Welser through the seventeenth-century East India Companies to the multinationals of today — monopolistic, speculative, interested in maximum profits rather than in production or patriotism. The rules for the market of classical economics apply much more rarely in this third sphere, where power concentrates: capitalism can always control the state.

Braudel uses the example of grain. At the lowest level grain is produced for consumption; at the second level it is produced for the regular local market. The third level deals with irregular and often speculative crisis situations, where grain has to be transported from province to province or country to country. Long-distance trade is the heart of capitalism, and merchants take speculative advantage of famines and crises.

Europe, says Braudel in an agreeable phrase, invented the profession of history, and used it to its own advantage. The writing of extra-European history has hardly started, and so the superiority of Europe can be taken for granted. Braudel is convinced that a qualitative distinction between Europe and the rest of the world is a very late development — perhaps a nineteenth-century development. In studying economic history from the fifteenth to the eighteenth centuries, we must look at the world as a whole. In this period "a potential capitalism" existed in many parts of the world.

If any religion reveals a "spirit of capitalism" it is Islam, from the days of the Prophet. "The long-distance trade of the first European capitalism, starting from the Italian cities" derives "from the splendour of Islam in the 11th and 12th centuries," with its large-scale industrial production for export and long-distance trade. There was "a certain capitalism" in India under the Moghul empire. In China long-distance trade played an important role: the development of capitalism was prevented only by the power of the state.

An essential part of Braudel's thesis is that there is no necessary connection between capitalism and industrialization. Industrial capitalism is not "true" capitalism. It is only a different way of making profits. "There was no invasion by capitalism of the sectors of production until the time of the Industrial Revolution, when machinery transformed the conditions of production in such a way that industry became a sector in which profits were expanding." But even so the Industrial Revolution "was largely born on the margin of big capital, of London." It was almost a historical accident.

Braudel distinguishes a series of world economies, always with a city at the centre. Amsterdam succeeds Venice, after brief challenges from Genoa, Lisbon, Antwerp. London succeeds Amsterdam, New York succeeds London. Each world economy subdues its periphery by force — Venice and Genoa in the eastern Mediterranean, Holland in Ceylon and Indonesia, Spain in South America, England in India. An industrial base is not necessary for the centre of a world economy (III, pp. 534-5, 34).

Each city, after being the hub of world trade, then becomes the centre of world finance. Braudel sees separate "world economies", with shifting boundaries, in the Far East, the Islamic Middle East and Russia. Some of his most interesting speculations concern these economies which were left behind by Europe only in the nineteenth century. But Europe is his main theme, ending with world hegemony passing to the new world after Amsterdam and London had conquered the other world economies.

"Four successive secular cycles can be identified" in Europe, Braudel thinks. One ran from 1250 (or earlier) to 1507-10; the next from 1507-10 to 1733-43; the third from 1733-43 to 1896. In each cycle the movement is upwards until a crisis is reached (1350, 1650, 1817), after which a downward movement begins (III, p. 778). Braudel does not attempt to give causes for those precisely-dated long-term movements, which "are a rule in world history, a rule which has reached down the ages to us and will carry on operating". "Human history obeys all-commanding rhythms, which ordinary logic cannot explain." Braudel admits the possibility "that future historical studies will simply ignore the problems I am trying to formulate" (III, pp. 617-18, 85). I think he is right here; but perhaps it was useful to try out such hypotheses, if only to reject them.

Periods of exceptional social acceleration (1470-1580, 1750-1850) alternate with years in which the volume of production and the size of the population diminish (1350-1450, 1650-1750, 1850-1970). Economic upsurges are always unfortunate for the lower classes who produce the wealth for the world economy. Slavery of Indians in the mines of South America is succeeded by the import of African slaves for the plantations of the West Indies and North America. The thriving economies of Amsterdam and London are financed by exploitation of the Far East and an excise on the poorest classes at home.

In England the Industrial Revolution leads to declining standards of living, especially in the North and West which had been relatively prosperous until capitalism extended its grip there; only after 1850 did things begin to improve. On the other hand, periods in which production diminishes see an improvement in the well-being of those who survive. Braudel has no explanation for these cycles, but expects them to continue. We have just entered a new crisis period.

One conclusion that appears from Braudel's analysis is that winners always win. Once the world economy is at your disposal you can't go far wrong. The second serfdom in eastern Europe in the sixteenth century worked to the advantage of Amsterdam capitalists. England's unfavourable terms of trade with Portugal in the seventeenth century led to the subordination of the Portuguese home market and empire to England. There were plenty of parallels on the continent for the agricultural improvements which were adopted in England in the seventeenth and eighteenth centuries; but only in England was there an agricultural revolution. The backward zones of the periphery are inevitably economically dominated by the leading centres. The Industrial Revolution was a revolution of the world economy of which England happened to be the centre.

Braudel is on the side of Marx against idealist explanations of the origins of capitalism such as those to which Weber and Sombart resorted in an attempt (Braudel thinks) to escape from Marx. Braudel holds strongly that there is a two-way traffic between facts and ideas; that economics, politics, society, culture and civilisation all contribute.

All historians must select. There is therefore a subjective element in all historical writing. The greater the geographical and temporal range of the historian, the greater the selectivity. Braudel roams over the whole world for four centuries. "The important facts," he explains with agreeable common sense, "are those which have consequences." There is something appealing about Braudel's arrogance. To judge by the sources he quotes, he knows no oriental language. Yet he tells us cheerfully that all his predecessors have got oriental trade wrong, and that he has got it right. It may well be true. At least he offers exciting new hypotheses which are not based on the *assumption* of European superiority.

Braudel's strength, dare I say it, lies not in his generalizations, but in the detail with which he illustrates them, the unexpected analogies he draws. In both characteristics he rather unexpectedly recalls Arnold Toynbee. Louis XIV, his fingers deep in the dish of food, rebukes his children for their use of such new-fangled things as forks. Braudel quotes a French newspaper of the mid-eighteenth century:

The sugar from English colonies imported into London was 70 per cent dearer than the sugar of equivalent quality imported into French ports. The reason for this was the excessive price of the consumer goods which England supplied to her colonies. At that price, what can England do with her surplus sugar?

And Braudel comments: "Obviously, consume it; the home market in England was capable of it." So England got the advantage of high prices for her exports and an abundance of sugar. The sixteenth-century timber famine Braudel compares to the late twentieth-century petrol famine. The answer to the former was an extended use of coal, which in its turn led to all sorts of technological innovations.

A problem which concerns Braudel throughout his book is Why Amsterdam? Why London? Why not Paris? (III, pp. 382-4, 489). France was a bigger country, more centrally placed, with a larger and (he doesn't actually say this) a nicer and more intelligent population. Nevertheless, "the English frog managed to puff itself up to the size of the ox". Yet "France was without question the first modern nation, in political terms, to emerge in Europe". (England is presumably not part of Europe for these purposes — III, p. 315; contrast p. 293). Three-quarters of Braudel's 100 pages on "National Markets" are about France, though an interesting section on "How England became an island" between 1453 and 1558 seems also to be describing how England became a nation.

Braudel tries various explanations for France's failure. They are unsuccessful because he has not met what seems to some of his critics a major complaint — that he underestimates the role of politics in the consolidation of Amsterdam's hegemony and its replacement by London's. Similarly he recognizes that protection was essential to the rise of capitalism in nineteenth-century Germany and the USA, but not that mercantilist policies for seventeenth-century Spain and Portugal, the Netherlands and England necessitated war. Dutch world hegemony came in consequence of the sixteenth-century revolt against Spain. This revolt "ruined the aristocracy" and consolidated the power of a burgher oligarchy. It created "the real instrument of Dutch greatness" — "a fleet the equivalent of all the other European fleets put together" (III, p. 190; cf. pp. 83, 578). London succeeded after the seventeenth-century English Revolution had put power into the hands of men ready to challenge Dutch hegemony and had given them a fleet capable of beating the Dutch in three wars, and of heading off the simultaneous French challenge. Hence the Dutch and English states developed very differently from the French. An absolute monarchy with a standing army and a permanent bureaucracy may intermittently favour trade and industry for its own military purposes; but it can control them. The looser, freer Dutch and English states permitted capitalist interests to dominate permanently. In these countries there was a religious freedom unknown in France — and that, Braudel observes, is essential to any centre of a world economy, from Venice onwards (III, pp. 30-1, 115). The Netherlands and England welcomed the industrious French Huguenots whom Louis XIV drove out. The English aristocracy adapted itself to a commercial society as the French aristocracy never did.

Many things followed from these obvious facts. As Braudel notes, sale of offices in the French bureaucracy "aboutit à une féodalisation d'une partie de la bourgeoisie," their transformation into a *noblesse de la robe*, who co-operated in maintaining and advancing the power of the state on which their income and their privileges depended (II, p. 491). Savings were diverted from purchase or improvement of land into the purchase of office. (Cf. II, pp. 429-35 for the social role of the *noblesse de la robe*). In England, quite the other way, peers and gentlemen invested in trading companies. In France participation in trade led to derogation of nobility and loss of tax exemption; in England the sons of gentlemen became City apprentices, gentle families restored their fortunes by taking City wives. Hence in England (and in the Netherlands — III, p. 148) we get a full flowering of agrarian capitalism. Capitalism existed in French agriculture, but never dominated.

Braudel post-dates and underestimates the English agricultural revolution. He rightly says it was due less to technical change than to new methods of land use, and he appreciates that capitalist farming depended on large holdings and security of investment (III, pp. 559-62): but he ignores the abolition of feudal tenures in 1646 (confirmed 1656, 1660) which made these things possible. By the end of the seventeenth century England had ceased to be a corn-importing country and became an exporter of corn. The problem posed by the rapid increase in population during the century and a half before 1640 had been solved. Even when harvests were at their worst in the sixteen-nineties, there were no famines in England as there were in France (though there were famines in Scotland, a fact which facilitated the re-enactment in 1707 of the Cromwellian union of England and Scotland, as Braudel rightly says — III, pp. 317-28; cf. pp. 497-9, 508, 527). Many economic historians have thought that the English agricultural revolution of 1650-1750 laid the basis for the Industrial Revolution (II, p. 245, III, pp. 483-5).[3]

If England's economic supremacy was made possible by political revolution, it becomes pointless to enquire whether in the eighteenth century the interesting examples of advanced agriculture which Braudel cites in France could have led to France following the English agricultural model (II, pp. 245, 255-8, III, p. 330). The answer can only be "Yes, in theory; No, in practice".

It is no doubt natural for a French historian to think of the rise of capitalism in connection with the state: Sully, Colbert, eighteenth-century French statesmen generally, played a relatively positive role in the development of capitalism. But things were different in England, and I think the Netherlands. In the sixteenth century, as absolute monarchies were consolidating themselves in France and Spain, the English monarchy failed to establish a standing army: national defence was the affair of the navy, which could not be used for internal repression. Unlike the monarchies of France and Spain, the English monarchy failed to shake off the control of representative assemblies over taxation, failed to establish an independent bureaucracy to collect taxes. Taxes were voted, assessed and collected under the supervision of the "natural rulers" of the countryside, the gentry and big merchants. "The state" could function only with their co-operation: Charles I's personal government broke down in face of war, even with Scotland, when this co-operation was lacking.

Braudel has some very interesting things to say about the internal market in England. He plays down the absence of internal tolls from the end of the thirteenth century which many historians see as explaining the earlier development of the English economy than of the French (III, pp. 246-50). He stresses rather the sheer size of France, its division into regions. South-east France looked to Italy, the north-east to Flanders, the west coast to the Atlantic. And he emphasizes the rival pulls of Lyons, which should have been the economic capital, and of Paris, the political and therefore the financial capital (III, pp. 269, 275, 279, 282-3). But of course this is a question of communications too. Bordeaux had at one time better links with the Netherlands and with England than with the rest of France. Internal tolls in England may have been given up the more easily because of the ubiquity of sea transport (III, p. 275).

Braudel also perhaps underestimates the industrial as well as the agricultural contribution to the prosperity of the Netherlands. Fishing was a major Dutch industry before the English challenge in the sixteen-fifties robbed them of their monopoly (III, pp. 148, 158). So was the ship-building industry, with all its attendant crafts (III, pp. 158-60). The growing influence of French culture in the Netherlands in the second half of the seventeenth century may be symptomatic of a revival of aristocratic power (III, p. 167), just as it was the restored aristocracy in Charles II's England that looked to France. Though Braudel is right to say that England did not snatch the cultural sceptre from France in the eighteenth century (III, p. 52), he is surely remiss not to add that the English invention of the novel conquered the whole of Europe? And that the ideas of the Enlightenment were English ideas, derived from Bacon, Hobbes, Locke and Newton?

In Braudel's periodization, "une période de promotion sociale accélerée, presque, dans sa spontanéité, une poussée biologique", which started about 1470 came to an end about 1580 all over Europe *except in England and the Netherlands*. After that date,

> tout se passe en France, en Italie, en Espagne comme si, au haut de la société seigneuriale, après une période de large renouvellement de personnes en place, après une série d'annoblissements compensateurs, la porte ou l'escalier de la promotion sociale se refermait avec une certaine efficacité" (II, pp. 425-6).

In England at the same time, in the words of Professor Stone, "Charles I and his advisers also set out to enforce a social reaction to put the lid on the social mobility he found so distasteful."[4] But Charles was defeated by the English Revolution, during which the door was opened wide, never again to be effectively closed. The two societies henceforth diverged.

Braudel in fact, in my view, takes too little account of politics, and especially revolutionary politics, in the Netherlands and in England. The Dutch republic came into existence by a long struggle against Philip II; the English constitution which Braudel appears to date from 1660 was the product of the civil wars of the sixteen-forties, of regicide, of the republic. He speaks of "l'intervention décisive du Parlement dans le vote des crédits et des impôts nouveaux" as dating from 1660, which is true only in the narrowest legal sense (II, p. 469; cf. III, p. 518). This playing down of England's unique political development has the effect of exaggerating the apparent parallels between England and France. Thus Braudel says "en 1640 et encore en 1660, les finances anglaises, dans leur structure, ressemblent d'assez prèz aux finances de la France de ce temps-là". And he goes on to discuss "la réforme anglaise" which "s'est accompli avec

discrétion et de façon continue, sans toutefois que soit discernable
un fil conducteur quelconque". The "discrétion" was necessary
because these reforms were a reversion to the practices of the
revolutionary sixteen-forties and fifties (II, pp. 468-9). The excise, to
which Braudel rightly draws attention in the Netherlands and
England, was copied from the Dutch by the English Parliament in
1643; like that other drastic financial innovation of the revolution,
the land tax, the excise survived after 1660. Henceforth the poor and
the landed class were taxed more severely to pay for a commercial
foreign policy.

Braudel's discussion of English regionalism is much less interesting than what he has to say about France. He does not mention the
fundamental work of Joan Thirsk and Alan Everitt on the distinction
between champaign country and forest/pasture country. He accepts
the traditional division of England into south-east and north-west,
but does not notice its rough coincidence with the areas from which
the two sides in the civil war were drawn. Nor does he notice the
opening up of the north and west which followed in consequence of
Parliament's victory in that war (II, pp. 255-6, III, pp. 520-1).

The Netherlands shared many of England's advantages. Easily
accessible water transport facilitated the early development of a
national market there too (III, pp. 248-50). But the Netherlands
lacked the supreme advantage that Britain had in being an island.
Consequently the Netherlands could not dispense with an army,
though the navy — as for England — was far more important. The
internal conflicts between the House of Orange and the ruling
oligarchy of Amsterdam are among other things conflicts between
the military (aristocratic) and the naval interests (III, p. 163). The
crisis of 1672 showed that the Netherlands could not depend, as
England could, on the navy alone. One wonders whether the miraculous stability of sterling from 1561 to 1931 to which Braudel draws
attention and which he cannot explain may not owe something to
this insular position. The two great crises of English currency, in the
sixteen-nineties and during the Napoleonic wars, came at times when
Britain's insular position seemed least impregnable. (III, pp. 305-12).

The virtual absence of a centralized state in the Netherlands
allowed the domination of the great trading companies, which in
effect made themselves responsible for foreign policy. In England
before 1640 trading companies had to struggle against government
intervention and lack of support, but from the sixteen-fifties, and

especially after 1688, they were even freer than in the Netherlands. Braudel rightly contrasts the state of affairs in France, where the absolutist state still dominated (II, pp. 392-4, 398-9).

The role of the French monarchy in relation to its own traders changes in the seventeenth century, because — I would suggest — of the growing power first of the Netherlands, then of England. It became clear from the early seventeenth century that it was impossible to aspire to hegemony in Europe, let alone the world, without the wealth which came from trade, especially long-distance trade. Hence Colbert's policy of encouraging industry and trade under government supervision. But to ask, as Braudel does, "l'État a-t-il, ou non, promu le capitalisme? l'a-t-il poussée en avant?" (II, p. 494) seems to me meaningless unless one first distinguishes between different types of state, and takes account of the very different social structures of France on the one hand and of the Netherlands and of England (after 1640) on the other. In the two latter merchants dominate and use the state: in France the opposite is true. Braudel draws attention to the failure of the French monarchy, even in the eighteenth century, to reorganize its finances on Dutch/English lines: a revolution was necessary in France too before this could be done (II, pp. 469-79). But Braudel attributes the differences not to politics but to the position of world dominance: "seules les économies dominantes laissent circuler librement les espèces monétaires: la Hollande au XVIIe siècle, l'Angleterre au XVIIIe, les cités marchandes d'Italie des siècles plus tôt" (II, p. 487). But this economic dominance was the result of military preponderance, which had been made possible both in the Netherlands and in England by political revolution.

Holland perhaps had no need of mercantilism, "car elle a eu cette liberté d'agir que confère la puissance". Mercantilism, protectionism, is the resort of the power trying to break in — the English Navigation Act of 1651, France in the seventeenth and eighteenth centuries, Germany and the USA in the nineteenth century. But, Braudel argues, the economic liberalism of the Netherlands was an illusion: in fact its trade was monopolized by the great companies, and both the Netherlands and England fiercely maintained their colonial monopolies (established by England in 1651 — II, p. 487).

The French monarchy built up a great army, plus a paid bureaucracy which was needed to supply this army, to collect the taxes and to administer justice on behalf of the King. In England, lacking a bureaucracy, taxes were assessed and collected by the "natural rulers", the gentry and merchant oligarchies, and voted by their representatives in Parliament. The militia, the force which maintained internal order, was under the command of the same "natural rulers"; local justice was administered by unpaid J.Ps. Any attempt to maintain a standing army, whether by Charles I, Oliver Cromwell or James II — or even by William III — was hotly and successfully resisted. But after the successful revolution of the sixteen-forties, the navy never lacked for money.

By comparison with the French state apparatus, the English was exceptionally cheap. Wars were fought by the navy, and where necessary (in Europe or in India) by hiring troops of other countries to fight England's battles. Similarly, Braudel tells us, "les Provinces-Unies maintiennent la guerre hors de chez elles: sur leurs frontières, une série de fortéresses renforcent l'obstacle des multiples lignes d'eau. Des mercenaires peu nombreux, mais 'très choisis, très bien payés et bien nourris'" looked after external defence (III, p. 169). The Dutch geographical situation was less satisfactory than British insularity, but the aspirations of Dutch rulers were the same. In both countries the internal bureaucratic aspects of the state were (by French standards) miniscule; but its external power was adequate to commanding the sea routes of the world and so the trade of the world. In both countries this commercially-orientated state was a post-revolutionary creation. It was only with Blake's fleet in the Mediterranean, and with the seizure of Dunkirk in 1658, that England began effectively policing the seas on her own behalf.[5]

The interesting point to which Braudel draws attention, that in 1630 Charles I's government took over from the Genoese the transport of silver to the Spanish Netherlands, is I think evidence rather of the decline of Genoa than of an aggressive commercial policy by Charles I's government. Spain could be sure that the Dutch would not want to provoke war with England by attacking the silver fleet; they would have had no hesitation in attacking a Genoese fleet, Genoa being subordinated to Spain. The English government was anxious at all costs to avoid the hostilities with Spain which its most vociferous (and commercially-minded) subjects were demanding; and if in the process it could turn a penny or two by minting silver for the Spaniards, so much the better. As soon as the war between Spain and the Netherlands came to an end, the transport of silver was taken over by the Dutch (III, pp. 140-1, 307).

In the late seventeenth century the balance of trade between England and France appears to have favoured the latter. (But what about smuggling? — as Braudel asks — II, pp.'177-80). But neither this nor the fact that French economic growth in the eighteenth century was greater than that of England is particularly significant. The point was that the French monarchy and its attendant bureaucracy absorbed a far greater share of the gross national product than did the English (III, pp.328-30). That is why English historians so different as Charles Wilson and Eric Hobsbawm both see the Industrial Revolution as a consequence of the overthrow of the English ancien régime in the seventeenth century (III, p.508).

The Navigation Act of 1651 (re-enacted by the restored monarchy in 1660 and 1661) made possible the use of a vast new naval power for quite new imperial purposes. It led to the "Commercial Revolution", which Professor R.R. Davis has reminded us provided the necessary basis for the Industrial Revolution.

What must not be forgotten is that the policies of the great absolute monarchies facilitated the rise of the new bourgeois states, just as the rivalries of the great powers in the twentieth century helped the revolutions in Russia and China to survive. Thus Spain forwarded the prosperity of Amsterdam by destroying Antwerp's trade (III, p.177), just as France allied with England against the Netherlands in 1672-4, and with the American revolutionaries against England in the eighteenth century. The Asiento which France seized from Spain in 1701 was grabbed by Great Britain in 1713 (III, p.569).

It may also be that Braudel post-dates England's supremacy. In the three wars of 1652-74 the Dutch were at all events not the victors. They were unable to prevent England taking over the Portuguese Empire (II, pp.180-1). I find it difficult to accept so late — and rather odd — a date as 1780-5 for the establishment of British supremacy (III, p.321). Surely from the sixteen-nineties, or at latest 1713, the Netherlands had accepted a subordinate position?[6] Braudel rightly rebukes Laslett for saying that the East India Company and the Bank of England "n'ont eu avant le début du XVIIIe siècle qu'une influence infime sur l'ensemble de l'activité commerciale et industrielle de l'Angleterre" (II, p.401). And he quotes a French observer who in 1713 commented with surprise on the freedom of the economy in England from "les ordres de la Cour" (II, p.394).

Braudel argues that Holland did not take the lead in the Industrial

Revolution, among other reasons, because there was no real Dutch home market. On the eve of the Industrial Revolution the English home market was much more important than the overseas market. The beginnings of the Industrial Revolution, Braudel suggests, were of marginal interest for big capitalists in England, for London (III, pp. 253, 255, 355). Lenin was later to say that world capitalism snapped at its weakest link, Russia (and later China). An analogous explanation of the triumph of the Reformation in the North of Europe might be more satisfactory than Braudel's argument that the Reformation was victorious only outside boundaries of the former Roman Empire. For this makes it necessary for him to brush off the 500 years' occupation of Britain by the Romans as "l'épisodique présence romaine en Angleterre". But he is right, I think, to stress that the Atlantic was the scene of the real sixteenth-century fight to a finish in religion as well as in economics (II, pp. 507-8).

It is not then "the state" as such that matters. In the Netherlands and England merchants could use the state; not in France. An absolute monarchy based on a standing army and a permanent bureaucracy may intermittently favour trade and industry for its own political or military reasons, but it can control them. The looser, freer states of the Netherlands and England permitted capitalist interests to dominate permanently. Even earlier Braudel himself shows that in relation to "l'armement des bateux de course, ce qui était déjà passé dans l'Angleterre d'Elisabeth, se passe aussi vers 1730 a Saint-Malo" (II, p. 390). But the difference between the two types of state could with advantage have been used to illuminate Braudel's explanation of the rise of the Dutch and British world economies.

Again Braudel makes the point himself when contrasting the consequences of the South Sea Bubble with the Law fiasco in France. "N'est-ce pas la preuve d'une certaine maturité politico-socio-économique de l'Angleterre déjà trop engagée dans les formes modernes de la finance et du crédit pour pouvoir revenir en arrière?" (II, p. 113). Yes indeed. Braudel also rightly stresses that the centre of a world economy must enjoy religious toleration (III, pp. 20, 154, 456, 556). But religious toleration did not just happen, either in the Netherlands or in England; it was won in the course of long and bitter political struggles. There were similar struggles in France, but there the outcome was different.

Braudel's neglect of political and social change may be connected with his definition of capitalism — one of the points on which he consciously distances himself from Marx, much of whose vocabulary he has adopted. "Capitalism has been potentially visible since the dawn of history" — in first-century India, in ninth-century China, in the Mediterranean area in the eleventh–thirteenth centuries (III, p. 620). It is not a social formation which appears at specific times in history. Similarly, "imperialism and colonialism are as old as the world, and any reinforced form of domination secretes capitalism, as I have often repeated to convince the reader and to convince myself" (III, p. 285). It sounds as though he has had his doubts. He might well, since he has deprived himself of a way of escape from economic determinism.

A final point. There are a few sheer errors in Braudel's account of English institutions. "La création de l'office du Lord Treasurer en 1714" is badly astray (II, p. 469). There had been Lord Treasurers in England since the Middle Ages and throughout the seventeenth century (except during the abeyance of the monarchy). What happened after 1714 was that the office of Lord Treasurer *ceased to exist*. The Treasury was put in commission (a reversion again to interregnum practice); the commissioners were headed by the First Lord of the Treasury. I mention this with no desire to score off Braudel but merely to stress that where English history and institutions are concerned his grasp is less sure than with France. Similarly, to describe Southwark as London's "rive gauche" is agreeably true metaphorically; but it is not, I fear, "sur la rive gauche de la Tamise" geographically (III, p. 313).

NOTES

1. Compiled from reviews of various parts of Braudel's *magnum opus* in *History and Theory*, VIII (1969), *New Society*, 26 June 1980 and *New Statesman*, 20 July 1984.
2. Cf. J. H. Elliott, "Yet another Crisis?" in *The European Crisis of the 1590s* (ed. P. Clark, 1985), p. 303.
3. For the decisive significance of the abolition of feudal tenures see pp. 45-6, 102.
4. Stone, *The Causes of the English Revolution, 1529-1642* (1972), p. 125.
5. For England see pp. 102-4, 109-11.

6. Michael Duffy appears to date British naval supremacy from the sixteen-nineties ("The Foundations of British Naval Power", in *The Military Revolution and the State, 1500-1800*, ed. Duffy, Exeter Studies in History, No. 1, 1980, pp. 80-1).

III *People*

7. *The Lisle Letters* [1]

"Looked at from the worm's eye view of Lisle, the man on the spot, the Tudor Revolution in Government, allegedly engineered by Thomas Cromwell, is nothing more than a mirage. ... This was indeed centralization, but no revolution in government. ... It looks more like an Age of Plunder." *

This is I think the largest single work I have ever had to review. Epic in size and scope, tragic in the story it tells, it is also epic in its conception and execution, a remarkable triumph of persistence and determination. Miss M. St. Clare Byrne conceived the idea of editing the Lisle correspondence in 1932. Nine years later, thanks to the good offices of T. S. Eliot, she received a contract from Messrs. Faber and Faber. But the work grew and grew and grew: it seemed neverending. In 1965 Faber and Faber called in Chicago University Press to share the anticipated costs of production. But when the work was completed it had expanded to such an extent that Faber and Faber reluctantly withdrew. The Chicago University Press had to ask for subsidies to aid publication, finally receiving one from the Joseph and Helen Regenstein Foundation. Now at last this colossal work appears as an 86th birthday present for Miss Byrne. Some two thousand letters — and they are only a selection! (I. 104-7) — are embedded in the running commentary of a work totalling nearly 4000 pages.

Miss Byrne rightly claims that "the prime fact about the Lisle correspondence is its bulk". It is "a mass of unorganized material, which gives us a close-up picture both of the official dealings of the Lord Deputy of Calais with the English government in the years 1533-40, and of the private affairs of the Lisle family and its ramifications during these years (I.6, 107). Arthur Plantagenet, Lord Lisle, was an illegitimate son of Edward IV, and so Henry VIII's cousin. Miss Byrne thinks he was born about 1462, but she admits it might

*Lawrence Stone, review of *The Lisle Letters* in *The New Republic*, 3 May 1982.

have been at least as late as 1470; others say 1480. Lisle certainly does
not sound like a man in his seventies in this correspondence (I.25,
144). Miss Byrne argues that Lisle did a better job as Lord Deputy
than historians have allowed, explaining in great detail the problems
he was faced with, the contradictory instructions he received from
London, the fact that "it was important for him to be first with the
news" for Henry VIII and Cromwell (I. 331) whilst yet not bother-
ing them too often with his problems. He had the *insouciance* of the
grand seigneur, and the evidence suggests that he may possibly not
always have known everything that was going on under his nominal
command.

In 1529 Lisle married, as his second wife, Honor Basset, neé
Grenville, the daughter and widow of Devon country gentlemen (I.5,
99-100). As the world saw it, she was fortunate in marrying a
Plantagenet, even if an illegitimate one. But if Lisle married beneath
him, he married wisely. It is abundantly clear from the correspondence that Honor was twice the man her husband was. "With a few
words and a present of a penny", one of their correspondents
boasted, "he would have his lordship's good will, so that my lady was
not in the way" (V. 249; cf. 687). But she kept up appearances
splendidly. What also emerges from the correspondence, more
unexpectedly, is that she and her husband had a very deep affection
for one another and positively enjoyed being together (I. 5, 26-7, 37).
"God ... send us both shortly a merry meeting, which is the thing
that I most in the world desire", wrote Honor during one of their
rare separations (V. 316; cf. 284, 319, 652). One hopes that historians
of the relation of the sexes will note this, and also that historians of
childhood will study an "unusually detailed account of the training
and experience of the children of Lisle and his wife ... It should help
to adjust and correct the popular conception of the relationship
between parents and children" (I. 87-9). One of Honor's sons was at
Lincoln's Inn (IV.12); another went to the University of Paris at the
age of eight; two daughters were brought up in French families.

The third key figure in the correspondence is John Husee, Lisle's
agent of all work. He was totally indispensable. He looked after
every stage of his master's and mistress's land management and land
transactions. This involved lobbying Thomas Cromwell and his
henchmen, Robert Rich, Chancellor of the Court of Augmentations
where monastic lands were concerned, and the law officers of the
crown in most cases. Each transaction involved waiting on a great

man at court, often scores of times before he had time to see anyone; and then scores more times before he made up his mind. "One hour missing attendance upon my Lord Privy Seal may hinder a month's suit" (V. 97). It involved greasing every palm that might be helpful. But Husee also had the task of buying Lady Lisle's clothes, in which he showed tact and good taste, of fobbing off creditors, of collecting debts (again a matter involving many visits), looking after the interests of the Lisle and Basset children, visiting the Lisle and Basset estates, etc., etc. All this was apparently done on a stipend of £10 a year, which Husee had the greatest difficulty in getting paid, plus such occasional gratuities as his lord or lady remembered to give him. One can only suppose that, like everyone else, he lived on the tips and douceurs which the confidential agent of the Lord Deputy of Calais could expect: for there were jobs to be disposed of there.

Husee is in a way the hero of the Lisle epic. He is the liveliest of the correspondents, with many set pieces of scenes when he waited on Thomas Cromwell or Henry VIII. He spotted the up-and-coming men at court, and advised Lisle of the right moment to switch his allegiance to, for example, Henry Wriothesley, the future Earl of Southampton (cf. III. 372, 490). He watched grimly over the family's interests in their estates, warding off predators like Cromwell and the Earl of Hertford as best he could — by legal means "if the law favours us", by invoking — and paying for — court favour if it did not. In moments of crisis he turned from his easy-going, careless lord to the harder-headed and more business-like Lady Lisle. Then the two of them drafted letters for Lisle to sign, reminded him to congratulate the King on marrying Jane Seymour, coached him in the line he was to take with Cromwell, told him when it was essential for him to come over to England to discuss his financial problems personally with the King, urged him not to fail to beard Henry next time he was allowed over — of course he did fail —, not to allow Cromwell to pull the wool over his eyes again. He never acted on the good advice (I. 40, II. 256, 267, III. 396, 445, 461, 499, V. 56-7, 571, 653-8).

Husee's was a thankless task, for which he claimed to be ill-rewarded, though we may have our doubts here. Certainly he was liable to be upbraided by his master and mistress when things went wrong, usually through their fault rather than his. His expostulations make pathetic reading, but also give us insights into the nature of such a relationship. Husee appears to have devoted his whole life single-mindedly to the pursuit of the welfare of the Lisles, to have put up with abuse, insult and sheer bilking from them. Yet he was a man of stature in his own right, with whom Henry VIII would crack a joke. He was an officer of the King's retinue, holding a position in the Calais Constabulary; in 1536 he was granted the office of Scrutator or Searcher of the royal manors of Mark and Oye in the March of Calais. He died in 1548, aged 42 (I. 38, 358-60, 682, III. 385, 408).

Miss Byrne's running commentary on the letters — rather reminiscent of Thomas Carlyle on Oliver Cromwell — is endlessly informative, sometimes discursive (I. 520-8). She is always endearingly involved with her characters, and sometimes very illuminating. She even finds herself unable to dislike Thomas Cromwell (I. 434). Her unfailing gusto and infectious enjoyment carry one a long way with her, though it is difficult to share her enthusiasm all through all these volumes. Since her book has been fifty years a-writing it is inevitably repetitious and sometimes out of date. When discussing Thomas Cromwell, for instance, Miss Byrne polemicizes against H. A. L. Fisher, R. W. Merriman, W. C. Richardson (I. 421-2, 429). G. R. Elton is cited occasionally, usually with approval (but cf. V. 170, VI. 224), but one feels that his supporting evidence was added at rather a late date, and that the main lines of her argument were drawn before *The Tudor Revolution in Government* was published in 1953. "Concluding this work in 1967", the text says at one point (I. 126); what is remarkable is how her narrative manages to cohere.

Miss Byrne has amassed an incredible amount of illuminating biographical detail on every important character in her volumes — and that means almost everyone of political significance in England in the fifteen-thirties. Both Lisle and his wife receive full-scale biographies (I. 137-298, 364-5; 299-350). On a whole variety of subjects there is massive detail for those interested — family bills and accounts (I. 674-5, II. 433, IV. 457); lists of spices bought from a grocer (IV. 123), lists of Husee's expenses and complaints (II. 648, IV. 341, 459, V. 260); bills for the Basset boys' education at the Sorbonne and at Lincoln's Inn (IV. 485-7, 516-18), information about wages and prices (II, 566, 368), accounts of Mediterranean voyages (I. 294, 341, 415-20 etc.), an account for making a ship (II. 592), information about piracy and pirates (II. 76, 111, 113). There are innumerable reports on the state of affairs in Calais (I, 652-3 etc.), surveys of Calais fortifications, lists of Calais shipping (VI. 49-51),

Calais muster rolls (I. 680-8), and finally a complete inventory, occupying 40 pages, of Lisle's household goods when he was arrested in 1540 (VI. 189-210).

Light is thrown into many dark corners. The wines at Marseilles are bad; those of Valencia are too hot and have to be watered down (I. 595, V. 124-5). "Quarter shoes" — i.e. loose sandals — wear out at the rate of a pair a month (II. 434). Henry VIII refused Lisle an office in Wales "by reason it was so far from your native country [i.e. county] ... Those offices were meet for them that had land in those parts" (III. 372). Henry is terrified of the plague. Those afflicted with any "contagious or dangerous sickness" were to be "avoided" when the King thought of visiting Calais (II. 175, 179, 203).

There is evidence for mockery of the Pope and his "two wives", of priestly celibacy, of the mediation of the saints, of Purgatory and ceremonies (I. 564, 570, II. 350, 619, etc.). The prevailing cynicism is typified by Francis Hall's remark that Bishops Latimer and Shaxton were "not of the wisest sort" to resign "such promotions for keeping of opinion" (IV. 576). Even more telling perhaps is the factual description of a Good Friday dinner of fish given by the aged Bishop of Gloucester to 700 gentry and their dependants, "such ... as nor I nor none that were there ever saw, as they said, for the quantity and goodness of them" (II. 456). "Taking the world as it goeth", it was wiser for Lisle in 1536 not to include a churchman among his proxies for the House of Lords (III. 388). "As for news", the Abbot of Hyde wrote to Lisle, "we have none worth the writing, but that my Lord [Bishop] of Bangor is lately departed his transitory life and also we have need of rain" (I. 504). Landlords connive at poaching by their tenants — though on the property of another gentleman, of course (II. 443-4). An astrologer goes to prison for prophecies which were thought to be political (II. 493). Thomas Cromwell contemplates making a voyage to Calais and back for the sole purpose of purging his stomach, rather than undergo the usual medical remedy (V. 186).

Miss Byrne fights a running battle with the editors of *Letters and Papers* of the reign of Henry VIII, correcting their dating and reading of manuscripts, and their identification of individuals. No one henceforth can afford to rely on *Letters and Papers* without checking any particular document in the *Lisle Letters*. Miss Byrne very early decided to modernize the spelling and punctuation of the letters (I. 104, 107). She presents many letters in their original orthography, and their difficulty for the non-specialist reader confirms the correctness of the decision to modernize. She gives us nevertheless a great deal of information about spelling, punctuation, dialect forms, that will be of interest to specialists. She has fascinating things to say about the English language — noting the appearance of many words in the *Lisle Letters* earlier than the *Oxford English Dictionary* records them, listing proverbs familiar and unfamiliar (I. 72). She argues — very plausibly on the evidence that she gives — that English men and women could write lively, colloquial and workmanlike prose, "uncontaminated by the conscious excitement of literary experiment", long before the age of Lyly, Shakespeare and Nashe (I. 67-84, 106).

No student of sixteenth-century England can afford to ignore these volumes, which tell us so much about the culture of the times. "To what estate soever it shall please God to call [James Basset] unto", wrote John Bekynshaw sententiously, "learning shall advance him in the same estate" (IV. 482). Whether he owed it to learning, influence or money, James obtained a prebend before he was twelve years old. One hopes that any student of literacy who is tempted to argue that ability to sign one's name betokens full ability to write will carefully note the letter in which Anne Basset declares "I cannot write nothing myself but mine own name" (VI. 34). Many statistical edifices have been built on the assumption that such persons did not exist.

Most interesting however is the very full picture we gain of social relations in this transitional society, which in many respects was still feudal. Poor women tenants beg to be allowed to pay cash rather than surrender their oxen as a heriot (I. 603). Already the financial possibilities of more careful estate management were being watched and exploited (II, 160-1, III. 48). In Cornwall tin was mined (I. 624-5). Lisle owned a trading ship, though we hear more of its captain's misadventures than of profits (I. 591-2, 630. II. 72 etc.). The state is playing a bigger role: an act of Parliament ordered the pulling down of all weirs which impeded navigation or the flow of rivers, thus violating what lords regarded as their right to create fish ponds. Lady Lisle took this act very "heavily", and desperately sought ways to avoid implementing it (II. 627-45, V. 82 etc.). The "protection" which was traditionally issued to preserve a lord's servant from arrest had already become a transferable commodity which a King's trumpeter expected to get for his brother-in-law (II. 399-400).

In peasant society, when a family killed a pig, the neighbours came and gave a helping hand, receiving cuts from the carcase in return: the gift was expected to be reciprocated on a later occasion. Similarly when a gentleman went hunting he was likely to slaughter more game than his household could consume: boars' heads and sides of venison were distributed to friends and neighbours, again in the expectation of return favours. The bigger the lord, the bigger the distribution, and the greater the obligation to produce favours in return. At court the obligations tended to be one-way: gifts to the King and his ministers, in the hope of favours which might never materialize. Gift-giving at certain seasons became highly ritualized: Husee has a vignette of Henry VIII sitting in state to receive his New Year offerings, with a clerk in attendance to write them all down — the silver plate, the gold, the jewels. When Lisle's 20 sovereigns were presented (in a blue satin purse, but 6d. short, characteristically) they did not go into safe keeping with the rest: they were slapped straight into the capacious royal pocket.

The letters continually refer to gifts in kind — venison, boars' heads (I. 40-1, 297-8, IV. 379, 424), stallions, a great horse, a mule, an ox (I. 44, 390, 405-6, II. 578, V. 706), mastiffs, greyhounds, a great dog, a ship of wheat, tuns of wine and hogsheads of beer endlessly (I. 416, II. 544-5, III. 372, IV. 415, 424, 453, 460, V. 24-5, 330), rabbits, does, falcons, hawks, pheasants, partridges, capons, gulls, sprats, herrings, carp, tunny, cheeses, grapes (I. 390, 406, II, 522, 544-5, 640, 645, III. 372, IV. 130, V. 24-5, 100, 342, 476, 630). The higher the rank of the recipient, and the higher the expectations of the donor, the more exotic the gift had to be — a stallion for Wriothesley (IV. 415), horses for Thomas Cromwell and his nephew Richard ("I perceive they looketh for them", Husee said, urging speedy delivery — IV. 268, 271, V. 248). "Mr. Garter trusteth your lordship will send him a piece of wine" (IV. 374). One advantage of being at Calais was that the Lisles had access to a wider range of commodities to present. French wines for everybody, a merlin and a porpoise for Cromwell (V. 207, 519), a live seal for the Lord Admiral (which Husee had to keep at Wapping for more than five weeks, at considerable expense and inconvenience — IV. 379, 384), sprats when they were out of season in England, storks for the Prior of Christ Church (II. 578), dottrels for Henry VIII (IV. 138), barrels of sturgeon for the King, the Lord Privy Seal — and for the Lord Chief Justice of the Common Pleas at a time of legal difficulty (II. 223, 494, 500).

Lady Lisle in return was given a dozen puffins, as well as marmosets and a long-tailed monkey from Brazil offered by a French diplomat (III. 264, II. 317). Quails were given to John Basset's tutor at Lincoln's Inn until he was found to be keeping a mistress (IV. 19-20, 32, 55, 59, 153). The greatest triumph came when Henry VIII and his new Queen Jane Seymour developed a passion for the fat quails which Lisle supplied. Husee became almost delirious with excitement as he called for more and more quails, fatter and fatter quails, to meet their insatiable appetite (IV. 141-7). So successful were the quails that they provided the opportunity to get Lady Lisle's daughter introduced into the Queen's household (IV. 151). When Henry asked for more damson conserve, it was to come "as soon as may be" (V. 730).

Many gifts were not consumed by the recipient but passed on. Wine became almost a form of currency (II. 415). One recipient made it clear that he would prefer cash to the wine he was offered, and the Abbot of Westminster refused to be fobbed off with a tun of wine when he thought far more was due to him (V. 422, IV. 334, etc.). In Paris academics demanded "money beforehand" for looking after James Basset (III. 119). A tip — or at the very least a drink — was expected by the servant who delivered a gift, but was not always forthcoming (III. 29-30, 325-6, 386). Allowing someone to deliver a New Year's gift was a recognized way of ensuring that he got a gratuity of 20-40s. at someone else's expense. "5s. is but a slender reward for bringing a mule so far", Husee once commented; Cromwell gave the man who brought him two horses £3 (III. 30). "Mr. Treasurer's man paid for the charges of his piece of wine", Husee noted on another occasion, "but the others paid nothing" (III. 386; cf. V. 27 — "they may demand the charges accustomably").

At a lower social level, a nag can be swapped for damask (VI. 78). Many pathetic little tokens were presented by tenants and dependants, and greater gifts by greater people, all in the hope that the recipient would be "good lord" or "good lady" to the donor (II. 43-4, 48, 51, 69, 91-2, 161, 486-7, 513-14, III. 92, IV, 88). In some instances ready cash was offered (II. 404). Between peers it was worded more decorously: "I shall be willing and glad at your motion or request to requite [a favour being asked] accordingly" (II. 426). "With your good help the same may be brought about", wrote Lisle to Ralph Sadler, "and I assure you I will see the same recompensed unto you to the best of my power", adding casually that it was worth £40 to him (III. 528-9; cf II. 557-8).

At the stage which these letters record, the traditional system of semi-barter has been distorted in several ways. At court free (non-contractual) exchange was being transformed into a monopoly, or — from the point of view of the donor — into a lottery: returns seemed sometimes quite arbitrary. Gifts to the King were inevitably very speculative investments; yet failure to make them would put one out of the game altogether. But as government business increased, direct access to the King became more and more difficult. He had to be approached through ministers (II. 169); and they had to be gratified. Thomas Cromwell strove — successfully for a time — to ensure that no one could gain access to the King except through him. As Husee wrote to Lisle in 1535, "I perceive Mr. Secretary's mind is that your lordship should not write to any man to make mediation in your causes but only unto him" (II. 467, 275, 415, 423, 515-16). Lisle humiliatingly signed his letters to the upstart Cromwell "thus knowledging myself more bounden to you than to all men living (God and the King reserved)" (II. 505, 614-15). This meant not only that Cromwell could monopolize the King's ear, and so control policy; it also meant that he and his underlings profited exceedingly from douceurs given them in the hope of obtaining a job, a lease, a dissolved monastery, perhaps even only an interview with the King — rather than as part of a rational exchange of gifts (I. 44). The profits extended to the great man's dependants. Husee is always calculating who is the up-and-coming man in my Lord Privy Seal's entourage. It paid to allow such a man — Ralph Sadler, for instance, or William Popley — "a good fee or reward" as well as the occasional douceur — gifts which were certainly not expected to be reciprocated except in services (II. 556-7). The Lord Chancellor could demand £40 and wine (III. 591, V. 690). Fees and gratuities were necessary to ensure actual receipt of money even when it had been granted by the King (V. 424, 571).

It was important in this world of cut-throat competition to have "a privy friend" or relative acting as a spy in the household of great men, or indeed of one's potential enemies. Such a friend would supply copies of private correspondence and other vital information (IV. 45, V. 135, 187-9). William Popley and Ralph Sadler served this purpose for Lisle (or perhaps more accurately for Husee) in Thomas Cromwell's entourage: they were well worth the £10 retainer they received (II. 278, IV. 41-2, 45, 61-2, VI. 60). "There can be nothing written nor spoken against your lordship", wrote Husee gleefully in August 1537, "but it will be known, you are so friended; but this must be kept secret" (IV. 380). When Leonard Smyth, who had also been retained at £10 a year, transferred from Lisle's to Cromwell's service, the relationship of "good lordship" still remained (II. 234, 381, 438). But Lisle was no match for Cromwell at this game.

The net effect of the whole system was that aspirants to office or court favour, unless they were extremely well-connected, had to lay out a great deal of ready cash in the hope of future benefits. Money is eroding the barter economy. Lady Lisle was offered a gelding or 20 angels to be gracious lady to a suppliant (III. 598). "Tokens" such as a ring of gold worth 7 groats, or knives, for instance (I. 41, IV. 290) were a less expensive form of gift; a token was given to Lady Sussex in 1537 to take away her wrath after Anne Basset had misbehaved in her household (IV. 185).

In many cases these practices led aspirants into debt. A boar's head, a side of venison, were produced as part of a gentleman's normal mode of living; but increasingly the expectations of sitting courtiers called for cash expenditure — or an annual retaining fee, a hogshead of wine, a foreign rarity. Lord Lisle was a big but inefficient landowner, and we see him running more and more alarmingly into debt. He leaves creditors unpaid for years (V. 46). He has to make bad bargains over selling or leasing lands because he cannot wait for ready cash. Significantly, the beneficiaries of his extremity were two of the greatest courtiers — the Earl of Hertford, Queen Jane Seymour's brother, and Thomas Cromwell (III, 445). Each of them out-manoueuvred Lisle into transferring land to them, and then shamelessly failed to keep his side of the implicit bargain.

Cromwell used his knowledge of Lisle's indebtedness and his absolute dependance on a grant from the King to acquire some of Lady Lisle's lands on outrageously favourable terms (V. 227, 248, 250, 264, 268). "They pass no further than to serve their own turn", wrote Husee, using a euphemistic plural, "and care not who smart, so they may have the sweet. I doubt whether they have either conscience or soul, or believe in Heaven or Hell. God help them as they intendeth to help other!" (V. 473). Lisle was also gulled by Cromwell over grants of money from monastic lands that he thought he had obtained from Henry VIII. Lisle was often accused of being "no good husband in keeping of your house" (II 267), but he can hardly have appreciated Cromwell's poker-faced remark to Husee: "he was sorry that your lordship was no better husband" (III. 487). "Surely, my Lord," Cromwell wrote to Lisle a year later, "such a governor as you be should not ... make himself so needy that when the present thing should happen he should be forced to have more estimation of money than regard to the tale it bringeth with it" (IV. 441). Cromwell was well informed about "the tale".

Lisle's debts are a running theme throughout the correspondence. Some of them were 10, 14, 16 years old; some were still unpaid at the beginning of the seventeenth century (I. 22-3, II. 506-7, 639, III. 258, 534, IV. 123-4, V. 46, 59, 248, 340, 342-3, 486, 602, 607-8, 672, 699, VI. 16, 161-5). They included quite small sums borrowed from poor tenants and neighbours who could hardly refuse to lend yet who were left to wait years for repayment (V. 741-2). They also included large arrears of taxes (III. 220). "If extremity had been used against you", Lisle was told in 1539, "your lordship had been at outlawry seven years past and much more; but I had commandment to forbear you for a season" (V. 375). In one especially severe crisis in September 1536 Husee suggested pawning his master's plate and jewels (III, 495). Husee was often himself in danger of arrest for debts which he incurred on Lisle's behalf. When Lisle was imprisoned in 1540, the wages of his Calais household had been unpaid for over six months (VI. 151; cf. V. 645). Many of Lisle's agents went unpaid for long periods, despite their bitter complaints (II. 492, 523, 648, 652, V. 260, 610-11, 743). Faithful retainers referred their salary to the discretion of their employers: fixed contracts are not yet normal (III. 27, 102, 456, V. 272-3).

Lisle's attitude to tradesmen is revealing. He seems to have regarded them as persons who had supplied him with goods in the hope of future benefits. He was certainly not going to give them the favour of payment if that was inconvenient for him. Husee vainly reminded him, again and again, of the consequences of leaving his grocer, his draper, his apothecary unpaid for too long. "I have lost a friend of him [Blagge the grocer] forever", Husee wailed to Lady Lisle in 1539. 'I know no man in this City while I have been toward my Lord, that hath done my Lord more pleasure than he. Friends be not so soon gotten as lost" (V. 476, 486, 602). "Friendship taketh small place when money faileth"; "here is nothing but everyone for himself" (II. 463, III. 490). "Now may your ladyship see", he explained, "that ready money buyeth all things at advantage, and they that dealeth otherwise must take it at their price or go without it" (V. 59). When Lady Lisle's elder son was married in 1538, the bridal finery had to be procured on credit — thus adding to the expense, as Husee bitterly complained (IC. 75). As City men succeeded monasteries as bankers, so credit with citizens acquired a new importance. A loan of £400, even at 15 per cent, could be secured for Lisle in 1536 only if "two honest merchants ... in the City" could be persuaded to be bound for it (II. 455-6, III. 494, 499-500).

Again we can see, in this transitional world between a barter economy and a modern money economy, how important it was to grab tangible assets. "Money was never so scant since this King reigned" is the continued cry in the fifteen-thirties (III. 534). Tenants are recklessly cutting down timber on their estates for the sake of ready cash. Hence the scramble for monastic lands. "To date this was the best property investment of all time", Miss Byrne rightly observes (V. 7, cf. V. 76, 115). In 1535 Husee believed that "your lordship cannot ask of the King that thing reasonably, so it come not out of his coffers, but his Grace will grant it to you ... When the King's Highness falleth to dealing of abbeys, I doubt not but your lordship shall have one of them *in commendam*" (II. 627-8). Lisle was dealing privately with the "prior as yet" (as he described himself) of a friary in Calais which he hoped to persuade the King to grant him (V. 126, 328-9). If you delayed you would miss out. Hence too the fact that the successful monopolists of royal favour became so very rich so quickly. They were in a better position than anyone else to corner the market. Historians perhaps sometimes think too exclusively in terms of politics or religion when they discuss the faction fights of Henry VIII's reign, too little in terms of mere spoils of office. A further consequence of the dissolution of the monasteries (and of other causes) was that "masters fall very scant in our parts, and servants very plenty" (V. 15). There was accordingly a scramble for jobs at this lower level too.

Hence the even more ugly practice of begging for pickings from the property of a fallen courtier as soon as he had been *arrested*, long before he had been tried and condemned, or for an office when it was hoped that the holder was about to die. "A great horse to the value of 40 crowns of gold" or a dozen of Picardy cheeses were mentioned to Lisle by one eager applicant (III. 356-8, II. 390). An equally distasteful way of making quick money, in which Thomas Cromwell shared no less than Lisle, was by securing pardons for condemned criminals, regardless of their guilt or innocence. "If your lordship handle him well", Husee wrote to Lisle apropos a man found guilty of manslaughter, "it is not to be doubted but he will pay well for it, for the King's Highness thinketh that at least it will be worth £100 to you" (II. 627, cf. 561, 652). It was not the only occasion on which the King intervened, or was expected to intervene, to "stop the course of his common laws" when "the law of the realm" was "clearly against us" (V. 168; cf. 148, 188, 248, 304). "Without friendship" a condemned man "is like to suffer" (V. 122, 612). In 1538 a man tried to obtain his pardon by offering as a bribe a debt of £400 owing to him; but it "is worth nothing, so I have put him to execution" wrote the Lord Mayor of London (V. 202). The well-to-do could influence the course of justice by getting judges to threaten torture (I. 266-76).

Inevitably under such a system the functioning of the law is very different from what it is today. The Lisles and Husee — in this no better and no worse that their contemporaries — were willing to use influence and bribery when the law seemed to be against them (II. 91-2, 109, 214-16, 223, 648-9, III. 416, 501, V. 144). Arbitration was frequently resorted to, both as a means of avoiding legal expenses and also in the hope of influencing the arbitrators — perhaps only to gain time (II. 43-4, 48, 51, 69, 79, 91-2, 107, 109, 114, 117, 127, 191, 193-4, 212-16, 225, 275, 401, 423).

Unwillingness to pay debts reflected of course only a relative poverty. Lord and Lady Lisle were apt to snarl when the faithful Husee asked for repayment of the few pounds he had laid out in their service. But when Lady Lisle's wardrobe was confiscated in 1540, one hood and two pairs of sleeves among her clothes had 1576 pearls on them (VI. 157). Her daughter Anne, when after desperate and prolonged negotiations she was at last accepted by Queen Jane, at once informed her mother that she was expected to wear pearls. When she was given a string of six score pearls she complained that they were "too few" and "all rags" (V. 95).

Miss Byrne's story ends tragically, with Lord Lisle recalled to England, imprisoned and accused of treason in 1540. He was fortunate in being one of the very few in the reign of Henry VIII who escaped execution after such a charge. But he remained in the Tower until February or March 1542, when he was pardoned shortly before his death (VI. 180). One story attributes his death to excessive joy; but it seems more likely that he was released because he was already seriously ill. (On Miss Byrne's reckoning he was 82 years old). Honor was arrested and released at the same time as her husband. She lived on until 1566, but never remarried (VI. 188).

Miss Byrne has an intriguing and I believe novel explanation of this unexpected denouement. Up to 1540 Lisle had managed, at vast expense, to ingratiate himself with Cromwell: his position seemed secure as long as Cromwell was secure. There had always been bickering between the two men over jobs in Calais, and over religious policy. Lisle was a politique whose religious views, if he had any, were conservative (I. 433). Lady Lisle was a dangerously outspoken partisan of the old religious ways, for which she was later denounced by John Foxe (I. 31). Cromwell, Cranmer and their agents in Calais protected protestants, even against Lisle, of whose soundness in religion the Archbishop expressed doubts (II. 469). Cromwell was capable of intervening over the Lord Deputy's head to protect protestants or to promote persons unacceptable to Lisle (II. 306, 321, 556). All this was conducted in an atmosphere of growing terror with Henry himself a constant advocate of severity (VI. 73). Husee was wary of sending news to Lisle, "for if I should write it might chance that I thereby might put myself in danger of my life and also put your lordship to displeasure, for there is divers here that hath been punished for ... publishing abroad of news" (III. 551). Miss Byrne wisely draws our attention to silences in the correspondence (I. 520-1). When more eminent men did commit news to paper they asked for it to be deleted "that no man see it" (II. 79).

Husee repeatedly urged Lisle to show more favour to protestants (V. 62); support for the word of God would increase his chances of obtaining monastic lands (V. 78). He urged Honor to "conform to the world as it goeth now" (V. 9, 66). Lisle chafed under these constraints (II. 335, 339, V. 180-1, 489-90, 506). When the Act of Six Articles in 1539 showed the first signs of a decline in Cromwell's influence Lisle began to take a more independent line against heresy in Calais, on the ground that it was disrupting the unity of the garrison. In February 1540 the Duke of Norfolk, leader of the conservative faction at court, whose star was rising as Cromwell's showed signs of waning, passed through Calais on a mission as Henry VIII's special ambassador to the French court (VI. 42, 44). Miss Byrne surmises — without specific evidence, but plausibly — that Lisle used this occasion to transfer his allegiance from Cromwell to the Norfolk-Gardiner axis, on the basis of helping them with evidence from Calais that Cromwell had connived (behind the King's back) at protestant worship and agitation in the town.

It seemed a propitious moment for switching, with Cromwell already struggling to maintain his position as chief minister (V. 70, VI. 56). Precisely in the years 1539-40 Henry was hounding to death representatives of the Pole family, down to the 68-year-old Countess of Salisbury, Cardinal Pole's mother, who was executed in May 1540. Simultaneously with Lisle's switch to the Norfolk-Gardiner party, evidence came to hand of a crazy plot by a priest called Gregory Botolph to surrender Calais to the French. Botolph claimed to have visited the Pope in Rome and to have laid his plans with Cardinal Pole, the surviving male member of the House of York whom Henry VII regarded with passionate personal hatred as the one possible rival to his rule. Norfolk and Gardiner succeeded in getting a commission sent to Calais, and they were in process of collecting a lot of damning evidence against Cromwell when — according to Miss Byrne — he launched his counter-attack (V. 62, 215).

Whether Botolph had ever been to Rome or ever had seen Pole is unclear and unimportant: he said he had, and when Lisle innocently reported the affair to London Cromwell saw his chance. Botolph was Lisle's chaplain. It is virtually certain that the Lord Deputy had nothing to do with his plot (if there was one) but Lisle was a cousin and former friend of Pole (VI. 223), and it was easy for Henry in his obsessional state to believe Cromwell's suggestion that he too was involved in treason. Unfortunately Lady Lisle had been "good lady" to Botolph, and over the years Cromwell must have had reported to him many indiscreet remarks of hers in favour of the old religion. Anyway, most of the alleged conspirators were members of Lisle's household (VI. 102, 213).

It is Miss Byrne's contention that this was Cromwell's reason for engineering the recall of Lisle, his arrest and imprisonment and the seizure of his papers (VI. 215-19). After his arrest it was revealed that Lady Lisle's daughter Frances had secretly contracted marriage to a French papist. No doubt this was done in all innocence, probably through fear that her parents would oppose the match; but it was an offence to contract such a marriage without royal approval (VI. 148). It made the alignment Lisle-Pole-France just that one bit less incredible. Lisle was arrested on 19 May 1540, a month after Cromwell was made Earl of Essex and appeared to have recovered his shaken position. But on 10 June Cromwell was arrested, and by the end of July he was dead.

Miss Byrne's conjecture that Lisle was a hapless victim in the struggle between Cromwell on the one hand and Norfolk and Gardiner on the other at least merits consideration. Lisle's recall charged with treason would then be Cromwell's answer to the conservatives' attempt to attack him for conniving at protestantism in Calais. What still remains mysterious is how Norfolk and Gardiner gained the upper hand. Evidence was produced by the Calais commission that Cromwell had continued to support protestants in Calais after Henry's wishes to the contrary had been given statutory form in 1539; and this may have outraged the King. Perhaps Lisle's papers so conspicuously failed to implicate the Lord Deputy in Botolph's conspiracy that the charge rebounded against Cromwell. It could be made to look like a smoke-screen raised to cover his own misbehaviour — as indeed on Miss Byrne's account it was. Anyway, Lisle was almost the only personage related to the royal family who survived arrest on a treason charge. Miss Byrne surmises that once the accusations against him were abandoned he was forgotten and remained in the Tower for two years because no one dared to mention to Henry VIII the name of a man who had once been charged with adherence to Reginald Pole.

Lisle was neither a nice man, nor a very effective politician. Apart from the fact that George Monck, the hero of the restoration of Charles II in 1660, was descended from him (VI. 260), Lisle's most lasting memorial is this vast correspondence, seized in order to be of use to Cromwell in his power struggle, and fortuitously preserved when that failed. In Miss Byrne it has found the ideal editor. It will be her memorial too.

NOTE

1. Ed. Muriel St. Clare Byrne, Chicago U.P., 6 vols., 1980. This chapter is a review published in the *New York Review of Books*, 11 June 1981. I have restored some phrases which were cut editorially. Figures in brackets refer to volume and page numbers.

8. Radical Pirates?

"And then they minded to get a ship or two more, and good fellows to the number of two or three hundred tall men, and then they would keep the seas in two parties, . . . to obtain many great booties: . . . and so to go to a certain island, whose name he remembreth not, where they should have a groat or 8d. a day a man, saying that within few days there shall no clean man be able to live within the realm of England but that he shall be sought out and hanged up, till there shall be an insurrection within the realm." *

I

For the purposes of this paper, which deals with the period after 1640, "radical" refers to those who rejected a state church, supported full religious toleration, and often carried this over to advocacy of democratic, communist or antinomian ideas — beyond the pale of respectable Puritanism.

I start from the problem of what happened to radicals and their ideas after 1660, after defeat. What became of all the fine ideals and idealists who impress us so much in the sixteen-forties and sixteen-fifties? Did it all run away into the sand? Even so, how? Did the nonconformist sects lead men off to abandon heaven in this world in return for pie in the sky? Did economic expansion absorb the energies of all those New Model Army soldiers who returned to their vocations in 1660? Or was it emigration? Was the off-white terror of the restoration period more successful than such persecutions usually are?

For some of my historical colleagues this is a non-problem. They assume that the extreme radicals in the sixteen-forties and sixteen-fifties were just a loud-mouthed minority whose apparent influence was due to a succession of historical accidents; so their disappearance when "normality" was restored in 1660 calls for no explanation. I don't believe this myself, but no doubt many of the radical spokes-

*Michael James of Hampton, pirate, 1534, in *The Lisle Letters*, II, p. 113.

161

men of those years did run far ahead even of those who thought they agreed with their ideas.

The disappearance of radical ideas after 1660 may be an optical illusion caused by the restoration of a more severe and all-inclusive censorship. We can find some such ideas in the last four decades of the century if we look for them. In *The World Turned Upside Down* I indicated a few. After 1688 there are more. The end of the Licensing Act in 1695 set the press nominally free, but by then an upper-class consensus had re-established itself sufficiently for censorship to be unnecessary. Toland reprinted Milton, Ludlow, Harrington, Sidney, not Levellers, Diggers, Ranters. In 1708 the Leveller William Rumbold's epigram was cited: "No man was born with a saddle and bridle on his back, nor any booted and spurred to ride him".[2] It must have been in common currency, for three years earlier Defoe had paraphrased it in relation to kings and subjects.[3] There was a Calves Head Club in London in the sixteen-nineties, of which predictably Milton's nephews, Edward and John Phillips, were members.[4] In the sixteen-nineties there were men called Ranters in Scotland, and in Long Island, America, who proclaimed recognizably Ranter doctrines, singing and dancing at their meetings. Similar figures are found later in Nottingham and Cumberland. They believed that God was in them, so that "for man to judge is vain, since those actions he may censure may be done in the motion of the holy seed and spirit of Christ: under which pretence", our reporter adds, "they cover many lewd and vile practices".[5]

The nearest I have come to finding an *organization* which continued to debate the issues of seventeenth-century radicalism in the eighteenth century is the Robin Hood Society, composed of London artisans, which used to meet weekly in 1756. They were said to ridicule religion, morality and the clergy, and to air their doubts about the Trinity, the authenticity of the Scriptures and of the gospel miracles.[6] In the seventeen-eighties Ranter doctrines were still being preached in London: there is no God but man, the preacher himself was God.[7] These stray facts suggest that more might be unearthed with a little effort. What about radical influences in America? What was the effect on the European Enlightenment of English radicals who emigrated to the continent after 1660? So far as I know, only Margaret and James Jacob are beginning to follow these trails.[8]

II

I want to use some hints from Defoe's *History of the Pyrates*, published in 1724, to draw attention to another area in which research might reveal more survivals of utopian and radical ideas. Many of Defoe's pirates are bloodthirsty thugs, whose careers contain little of intellectual interest. But among them is Captain Misson, who, like many real-life buccaneers, was French. As with Luther, Misson's faith was shaken on a visit to Rome: unlike Luther, he decided that all religion was "no more than a curb upon the minds of the weaker, which the wiser sort yielded to in appearance only".⁹ A "lewd priest", Caraccioli, utilized this promising start to make "a perfect deist" of Misson; he came to believe that all religion was no other than human policy, that the Bible was self-contradictory, the miracles described in the New Testament inconsistent with reason. God gave us reason, he concluded in Miltonic vein, "to make use of for our present and future happiness, and whatever was contrary to it ... must be false". Like Milton too his favourite targets were "avarice and ambition". "Every man was born free", Misson continued, "and had as much right to what would support him as to the air he respired." Monarchy existed to defend inequality. Governors were legitimate only when they allowed no excesses of wealth or poverty, and prevented the rich and powerful from oppressing the weaker. The slave trade "could never be agreeable to the eyes of divine justice". Christians who "sold men like beasts ... prove that their religion was no more than grimace".¹⁰

Caraccioli told Misson's crew that they were no pirates, "but men who were resolved to assert that liberty which God and Nature gave them and own no subjections to any, farther than was for the common good of all". Misson "might lawfully make war on all the world, since it would deprive him of that liberty to which he had a right by the laws of nature". Mison's crew "the more readily embraced" these views since a great number of them were "Rochellers", later joined by thirty Englishmen. Among these "new-fangled pirates ... regularity, tranquillity and humanity" prevailed. Officers were elected, captured slaves were liberated and encouraged to join the crew, on equal terms.¹¹ Swearing was strictly prohibited — not quite so surprisingly, in view of the Calvinist background of the crew; when a buccaneering crew mutinied in 1681 their new captain saw to it that the Sabbath was observed as a holy day.¹² A temporary settlement on Providence Island in 1687 had an elected governor, "an Independent" who "usually preached to the inhabitants every First Day of the week".[13]

Misson's crew finally founded a settlement, which they called Libertalia, on Madagascar. The booty and cattle were divided equally among them all. It was not, however, a communist society, as some critics have assumed from the fact that all money was held in a common treasury, "money being of no use where everything was in common, and no hedge bounded any particular man's property". In fact Defoe clearly tells us that "such lands as any particular man would enclose should for the future be deemed his property, which no other should have any claim to if not alienated by a sale". The government of Libertalia took "a democratical form where the people were themselves the makers and judges of their own laws". Every ten men elected a representative to a constituent assembly which drafted "wholesome laws for the good of the whole". Government was in the hands of a single individual (the Conservator), but he was to be elected every three years. A representative assembly was to meet at least once a year, oftener if the Conservator and his Council thought it necessary. Nothing of moment should be undertaken without its approval. The laws were printed and dispersed among the people ("for they had some printers and letterfounders among them")[14]

This interesting experiment did not last long. The natives, in an unprovoked attack, destroyed Libertalia before its theories could be tested in practice. What are we to make of Defoe's fascinating, full and specific account, in the middle of a history of fierce and unideological pirates? He is sometimes portrayed as an ideologist of early capitalist individualism. If he were simply that, he could have made Libertalia collapse because its institutions were contrary to Calvinist or bourgeois ideas of human nature; some commentators have incorrectly alleged that he did this.[15]

Libertalia has been described as the realisation of a Lockean ideal. It seems to me also to echo Levellers, Winstanley and Milton. Did Defoe invent it? It is not the only odd thing in the *History of the Pyrates*. Another pirate community, also on Madagascar, elected by lot a man to be governor for three months, after which he was ineligible to be chosen again until every man had had his turn.[16] The articles of another pirate, Captain Roberts — elected by his men — provided for the sharing of prizes among the crew; one pirate had one

vote in all "affairs of moment". Discipline was maintained by an
elected Quarter-Master, who shared out the booty.[17] Another crew
voted its captain out of office for cowardice.[18] We meet in the
History class-conscious characters like the lady pirate Mary Read,
who found her shipmates morally preferable to "those who are now
cheating widows and orphans and oppressing their poor neighbours
who had no money to obtain justice",[19] and Captain Bellamy, who
refused to "submit to be governed by laws which rich men have made
for their own security ... They rob the poor under cover of law
forsooth, and we plunder the rich under the protection of our own
courage." Captain Bellamy had no use for "snivelling puppies who
allow superiors to kick them about deck at pleasure; and pin their
faith upon a pimp of a parson — who neither practises nor believes
what he puts upon the chuckle-headed fools he preaches to". His
crew rather surprisingly occupied their leisure by writing and
performing plays in rhymed couplets. One of them, a Yorkshireman,
had been transported to Jamaica for "borrowing" (his word) an
excellent gelding. There he promptly joined "these marine heroes,
the scourge of tyrants and avarice and the true assertors of liberty".
Captain White told his men it was cruel to rob innocent children,
whereupon by unanimous consent 500 dollars and some silver
objects were returned to two young captives.[20]

Such are not perhaps the views usually held of early eighteenth-
century pirates. We need not believe all Defoe's stories, but we know
that most of his pirates did exist in real life, and we know that in the
course of his professional activities for *Applebee's Journal* in the early
seventeen-twenties Defoe had many conversations with former
pirates.[21] Given his Shakespearean capacity for entering into and
enjoying the most diverse personalities — Robinson Crusoe and
Moll Flanders as well as Mary Read and Captain Misson — I think we
may conclude that he was reproducing the substance of what he had
been told. Some pirates must have seen themselves as egalitarian
avengers. How are we to explain the radical element in these pirate
yarns or fantasies?

III

Who says pirates says West Indies. There is a long history of interest
in American colonization by anti-Spanish protestants in England.
The elder Hakluyt thought that "a place of safety might there be
found, if change of religion or civil wars should happen in this

realm". The idea was often repeated.[22] Sir Walter Ralegh became a popular hero after his execution in 1618 at the behest of Spain in consequence of his attempt to open up Guiana. Prince Henry was alleged to have wished to carry out Ralegh's western design. No less than four *Ralegh's Ghosts* were written between 1620 and 1631, either published abroad or circulating in manuscript. One was by Thomas Scott, the popular radical pamphleteer, who combined a call for conquest of the West Indies with denunciations of pro-Spanish courtiers and great landowners who rigged Parliamentary elections. Not unnaturally he was "generally approved of ... by the meaner sort".[23] Another *Raleigh's Ghost,* which a Secretary of State thought "as seditious a book as the other [i.e. Scott's], if not much worse", was by Captain Thomas Gainsford, later editor of newsbooks.[24]

In the sixteen-thirties the Providence Island Company seized an island off the Spanish Main as a refuge for religious malcontents and a base from which to prise open the Spanish monopoly of central and southern America. This company, of which John Pym was treasurer, acted as focus for opposition to Charles I in the sixteen-thirties: it organized Hampden's defence in the Ship Money case. But on Providence Island itself the settlers were "by the hard and undue dealings of such as then swayed the affairs of this realm" — that is, Charles I's government — "exposed to the rapine of the public enemy, Spain".[25] First they took to selling slaves to other settlements: in 1638 Providence Island experienced a slave revolt.[26] Ultimately they took to piracy — anti-Spanish piracy. In 1642 a follow-up voyage to Providence Island by Captain William Jackson was financed by Maurice Thompson. Thompson was a link figure who had been a contractor for the original Providence Island colonists and was to be first the architect of the Navigation Act of 1651, and then the right-hand man of Cromwell's Western Design which conquered Jamaica in 1655.[27] In 1649 Thompson supported an interlopers' scheme for colonizing Assada, an island off Madagascar.[28]

These are not radicals on my definition. But in 1645 Hugh Peter, back from New England, urged the conquest of the West Indies, in a sermon preached to the Lord Mayor and aldermen of London, both Houses of Parliament, and the divines of the Westminster Assembly. Thomas Edwards saw this proposal as part of a radical plot.[29] In October 1649, the year of Leveller defeat, John Lilburne offered to lead his adherents to the West Indies, if the government would finance them.[30]

A surprising number of English radicals emigrated to the West Indies either just before or just after 1660. Joseph Salmon the Ranter went to Barbados. In the sixteen-eighties a Joseph Salmon, shoemaker, was in trouble for trying to organize an Anabaptist congregation there.[31] Another émigré was Robert Rich, a wealthy merchant whom orthodox Quakers denounced as a Ranter. He supported a succession of Quaker heretics — James Nayler, Perrot, and the Story-Wilkinson separation — strong in Barbados in the late sixteen-seventies.[32] John Perrot, who joined Rich in Barbados in 1662, had also been attacked by Fox as a Ranter, and was a former associate of Nayler. In Barbados he wore a sword and was called "Captain".[33]

In the early sixteen-forties there had been "divers sects of Familists", some of "mean quality", in Barbados.[34] Their practices were "turbulent"; their influence may help to explain the prevalence of extreme radical and non-pacifist views among the "several hundred" Quakers on the island from 1655 onwards.[35] The Governor of Barbados in the early sixteen-forties begged for "some godly ministers and other good people" to be sent from Massachusetts to remedy the "distracted condition" of his island.[36] George and Richard Leader, merchants of Barbados, were Muggletonians. There were also Muggletonians in Antigua and in Guatemala.[37] Jews built a synagogue in Barbados in the early sixteen-forties; in the next decades there were Jews in Jamaica.[38] There were Quakers in Jamaica, in the Leeward Islands and on Nevis.[39] In 1656 Samuel Highland advised Parliament not to sentence James Nayler to transportation lest he infect other settlers.[40] Greene the feltmaker took refuge in Trinidad from 1644 to 1646 before returning to preach in an alley of Coleman Street, where Thomas Edwards did not fail to locate him.[41] In Jamaica there was the Fifth Monarchist Captain William Rightson, an amateur lawyer and smuggler.[42]

George, brother of the republican, M.P. Henry Marten, went to Barbados about 1647, and was later in Surinam. Aphra Behn celebrated him in *Oroonoko* as one of the few humane white colonists. Mrs Behn also met William Scott, son of the regicide, among other political refugees in Surinam. There were many Quakers.[43] Richard Norwood took refuge from Archbishop Laud in Bermuda.[44] John Oxenbridge, expelled from Magdalen Hall in 1634 for encouraging student unrest, was a minister in Bermuda until in 1641 he returned to England. In 1660 he fled again, initially to Surinam, before settling in New England.[45] Charles Hotham, an early admirer of Milton's prose style, went to Bermuda after ejection from his fellowship at Peterhouse in 1662. Both Norwood and Hotham corresponded with the Royal Society.[46]

Fulke Greville wrote a sonnet moralizing the dangers of Bermuda's coast,[47] but the island's paradisaical beauty was celebrated (at second hand) by both Waller and Marvell, the latter adding "and cast, of which we rather boast,/ The gospel's pearl upon our coast". Indeed, Bermuda's most outstanding minister, Lewis Hughes, was accused in the sixteen-twenties of "railing upon bishops" and describing the prayer book as an "old wife's tale".[48] In 1633 the Puritan Governor of the island invited the greatest of the Puritan émigrés, William Ames, to move there from the Netherlands,[49] and in the following year a letter from Bermuda said "we are ... far more secure from the hierarchical jurisdiction than New England". In 1639 Laud was informed about opposition to "the government and discipline of the Church of England" in Bermuda and tried — too late — to take remedial action.[50] It would have been appropriate if George Wither had accepted the Governorship of Bermuda which he believed he had been offered in the mid-forties; only the arrears of army pay and losses in the civil war for which he had received no compensation prevented him accepting.[51] There were many Quakers on Bermuda: from 1661 they enjoyed liberty of worship.[52]

Just off Bermuda was the significantly-named island of Eleutheria, to which undesirables and rebellious slaves were banished. An unusually complete religious toleration prevailed there.[53] In 1647 a broadside published in London on behalf of a "Company of Eleutherian Adventurers" advocated a near-republican constitution for the island, a single legislature, and continuation of religious toleration, though property and social privilege were to be preserved.[54] In 1660 Samuel Hartlib's associates saw Bermuda as an ideal site for his utopian community, Antilia or Macaria.[55] So already the West Indies gave rise to utopian ideas as well as offering a refuge for persecuted radicals.

After 1660 the West Indies received much more tolerant treatment, as a matter of deliberate government policy, than did England. The Governor-in-Chief of the Leeward Islands was specially instructed in 1670 to dispense with the oaths of allegiance and supremacy.[56]

Apart from the desirability of attracting immigrants, the nature of those already in the Caribbean area enforced toleration. The inhabitants of the islands were a hodge-podge of pauper immigrants (Barbados was described in 1627 as a "city of refuge for poor impoverished persons", in 1655 as "a dunghill whereon England doth cast forth its rubbish".)[57] There were many deportees, especially Irish. Nevis was first settled with Irish colonists, Montserrat was virtually an Irish island: survivors from Drogheda were shipped to Barbados. By 1669 it was estimated that there were 12,000 Irish in the West Indies.[58] Among others were beggars from Liverpool[59] royalist prisoners from Scotland,[60] and from England after Penruddock's plot in 1655,[61] highwaymen taken on the Scottish border,[62] pirates caught on the English high seas,[63] a royalist agent arrested in 1659,[64] dissenters under the Clarendon Code,[65] Monmouthites after 1685.[66] On St Christopher there were Huguenots and other Frenchmen.[67]

Some of these were men of high principle, who had emigrated or been transported for conscience' sake; others were described in 1665 as 'convict gaol birds or riotous persons, rotten before they are sent forth, and at best idle and only fit for the mines". "They be all a company of sodomists", a lady said of Antigua's colonists in the same year.[68] Both types were there, making a curious mixture.

From the earliest days Barbados was an unruly island. John Winthrop's son Henry went to the bad there in the late sixteen-twenties.[69] In 1629 "disloyal servants" deserted to Spanish ships invading the island. Sixty years later their successors were prepared to betray it to the French. In 1634 white servants revolted. With the expansion of sugar planting in the sixteen fifties, a greater threat came from the rapidly expanding slave population, estimated at less than 6000 in 1645 and at over 80,000 in 1667.[70] Some think 50,000 a more plausible figure; even so, there had been at least an eightfold increase in twenty years.[71] The first serious slave revolt occurred in 1649.[72] In the same year white servants organised a rebellion in which, it was said, they would have massacred all masters. It was severely repressed, eighteen leaders being executed.[73] It was ominous when in 1655 Irish servants joined black slaves in rebellion.[74] In Bermuda, slave revolts were forestalled in 1656 and 1661, but here, too, the Irish were liable to join rebel blacks. The Irish on St Christopher and Montserrat revolted in 1666.[75] Monmouthite rebels transported to Jamaica after 1685 allied with "maroon" Indians in creating disturbances.[76]

Sugar-planting transformed the social structure of Barbados, squeezing out the "yeomen". By 1647 no more land was available for indentured servants who had completed their time; they had to go to the Leeward Islands. Shortage of land and heavy taxation caused massive emigration, especially to Jamaica after its conquest in 1655. By 1667, 12,000 were said to have emigrated to other islands since 1643, when the white population of Barbados reached its peak. "Disaffection will continue," Governor Willoughby told Charles II, "unless some way be found to give a comfortable livelihood to the meaner sort." There was similar emigration from St Christopher and Nevis.[77]

Between 1641 and 1650 Barbados was virtually an independent state.[77] Its politics, Dr Puckrein tells us, are to be interpreted in the light of the tensions I follow him in describing. Quarrels on the island culminated in 1650-2 in a civil war, normally described in terms of royalists versus Parliamentarians, but which Dr Puckrein thinks was between a traditional élite (royalist) and an upstart group of too successful planters which the old guard was trying to get rid of. The upstarts — like the English Parliamentarian leaders in the sixteen-forties — were prepared to use radical sectarian support.[79] When the "royalists" won control their governor rejected in a single sentence "the toleration of independency or admitting of free trade".[80] They sequestrated their rivals' plantations and imposed heavy financial penalties on conventiclers. When their opponents came to power all coercive ecclesiastical legislation was repealed.[81]

The need to maintain white solidarity against the slave population forced toleration on the turbulent and disparate inhabitants. By 1655 "that liberty of conscience which we so long have in England fought for" had been established in Barbados.[82] One clergyman held a living in the Church of England for twenty-four years before 1681 without Anglican ordination. Many schoolmasters were Quakers and Anabaptists. After a brief interlude under the Stuart reaction religious toleration was restored in 1689.[83] An eighteenth-century attempt to establish a church court in Barbados failed.[84]

Not tolerated was any attempt to convert or educate black slaves.[85] In Bermuda the Reverend Samson Bond tried to liberate Christian slaves and educate black children. He was twice dismissed from the ministry. It is not surprising to learn that he was a preacher of the Everlasting Gospel — a fairly certain sign of radicalism.[86] In 1670 a Quaker was in trouble for converting slaves in Barbados.[87] Seven years later a former captain who had allowed slaves to attend a Quaker meeting, and who refused to contribute to payments for the parish minister or for the militia, was banished.[88] However, many Quakers themselves owned slaves, so this was not yet an issue for the Society as a whole.[89] In Jamaica, too, slaves were not allowed to obtain their freedom by becoming Christians.[90]

In the early days slave organisation was impeded by the fact that the Africans came from different tribes and could not communicate with one another sufficiently to conspire.[91] As English became a common language, the danger increased. The dramatic decline of the yeoman population, the endemic state of war in the West Indies, and the reluctance of the planter oligarchy to arm their servants, still less their slaves, meant that the ruling group in Barbados, as on other slave islands, became absolutely dependent on British military and naval support.[92]

By 1666, Barbados was said to be seventeen times as rich as before sugar-planting began. The take-off period was the decade of virtual independence, the sixteen forties, and it was made possible by liberal injections of Dutch capital and credit. In 1650, Amsterdam was the "metropolis of the Caribbean". The island might well have become a Dutch dependency but for the Navigation Act of 1651. For a time the Barbadians tried to ignore the act: they "doted on the Dutch commerce", observed Edward Winslow in 1655.[93] But after the British conquest of Jamaica, Barbados — a regular port of call for naval vessels *en route* to the larger island — had to accept the Navigation Act, though with many complaints.[94] England's victory in the First Dutch War was thus the necessary preliminary to the Western Design and the enforcement of the Navigation Act on the West Indies.

This prompts complicated thoughts about the relationship of free trade and liberty of conscience, so confidently asserted by the Governor of Barbados in 1647 (page 170 above). Free trade meant free access to the West Indies for the Dutch. Parliament's Navigation Act in theory shut them out, and after the conquest of Jamaica theory began to become practice. It was no doubt the smaller men who favoured free trade — those who had difficulty in holding on to their land. The bigger planters accepted the government of the Commonwealth when its policy was backed by a powerful navy, and when the English market began to recover. They could equally well shift their allegiance to the restored monarchy when that monarchy accepted the Navigation Act and maintained a strong navy.

Liberty of conscience survived, despite unsuccessful attempts to abolish it in 1681-9; but the smaller planters were being driven from their land, because they could not keep up with the big producers in competition for the English market. For some of them piracy was the only alternative occupation.[95] Piracy could be suppressed only when the domination of the big planters, and of the English navy, was finally established.

Barbados, then, the first rich West Indian colony, had to establish religious toleration because the planters needed the loyalty of all the heterogeneous white population.[96] Religious radicals were attracted by this congenial atmosphere. But then the cancerous growth of slave plantations ate up the island and forced all but the rich and the lucky into further emigration. Most of them went to Jamaica, conquered in 1655.

Jamaica was similarly heterogeneous in its immigrant population — Irishmen in large numbers, old Cromwellian troops from Venables's expeditionary force,[97] whose members were, in Gardiner's measured words, "for the most part those of whom their colonels were most anxious to be rid, and ... the riff-raff of the London streets". They had been recruited from "the men most abject in all companies, and raw fellows", said Venables himself.[98] "Loose wenches" were sent from London in 1656.[99] They found in Jamaica a "floating population" of time-served bond-servants and victims of heavy taxation from Barbados.[100] After 1660 they were joined, voluntarily or through transportation, by Quakers,[101] and by followers of Monmouth after 1685.[102] Henry Newcome's ne'er-do-well son was sent to Jamaica in 1670.[103] As in Barbados, heterogeneity made religious toleration essential, even of Quakers. No oaths of allegiance or supremacy were imposed.[104] Jews were permitted to build synagogues in the sixteen-eighties. There was more liberty, a minister claimed in 1687, than in most protestant countries.[105] In 1718 it was agreed that in Jamaica there was no ecclesiastical law or jurisdiction to impose fines or punishments.[106]

Jamaica's politics were also influenced by surviving settlers from the Cromwellian army. In 1660 there was a mutiny, led by an ex-Cromwellian officer, with the support of some of his troops.[107] Jamaica was always a poor second to Barbados as a sugar island; from the earliest days its wealth came from privateering, which "old standers and officers of Cromwell's army" continued to favour.[108] "Young and lusty men" were out privateering, we hear in 1669. Colonel Thomas Modyford, an ex-royalist cousin of General Monck, who had led the pro-Commonwealth faction in Barbados in 1651-2, urged a revival of Ralegh's scheme for conquering Guiana, and greatly influenced Cromwell's Western Design.[109] After becoming vastly rich as a Barbados planter, he moved to Jamaica, where as Governor in 1660 he earned his pardon and a baronetcy by proclaiming Charles II. From 1664 to 1670 he was Governor again, and deliberately promoted privateering.[110] After peace was signed with Spain in 1670 a brief attempt was made to end Jamaica's role as "a Christian Algiers" (Charles II's phrase). Ex-privateers took up a clandestine trade to the Spanish colonies. Long-cutting at Campeachy swiftly turned into full-time buccaneering, initially directed only against Spain.[111] Ships often sailed with a French commission but English crews. (We recall Defoe's Captain Misson). In the sixteen-thirties Providence Island, initially established as a Puritan colony of refuge, had degenerated into a buccaneering centre.[112] Something similar happened in the sixteen-seventies to Jamaica's privateers, who may originally have been motivated by ideological hostility to Spain.

The buccaneer's chief was Henry Morgan, another old Cromwellian officer knighted by Charles II. Morgan was said to have been an indentured servant on Barbados. He joined Venables in 1655 and settled in Jamaica.[113] He and Modyford dominated the island's politics until the sixteen-eighties, apart from the interlude of 1670-4. Morgan gave Modyford, Governor again from 1674, 10 per cent of his booty. The old Cromwellian buccaneering interest proved stronger than that of the planters.[114]

To summarize: many radicals sought refuge in the West Indies, especially in Barbados; squeezed off that island, some — like Morgan — went to Jamaica, where they were a source of recruits for the privateers and buccaneers patronized by that island's former Cromwellian rulers.[115] Some no doubt carried with them ideas which had originated in revolutionary England. But the dependence of the West Indian economy on slaves and subjected Indians must have made these ideas hard to sustain, especially when piracy seemed to offer the only means of livelihood. Morgan's brutal raid on Panama in 1671 was made, a historian tells us, by "troops in the faded red coats of the New Model Army".[116] Bermuda's surplus population similarly overflowed into the Bahamas, another privateering centre, whose inhabitants lived "a lewd licentious sort of life". In 1681 they shipped their Governor off to Jamaica.[117] He was succeeded by Robert Lilburne, whose surname is interesting in this context. He commissioned privateers from 1682 onwards.[118]

In the short run buccaneering may have been a convenient investment for big planters.[119] But in the long run the buccaneers were a nuisance, expendable once the Caribbean was policed. So long as there was no regular and perpetual revenue either from England or from the West Indies themselves for the maintenance of naval and military stations, the Caribbean remained a prey to smugglers and pirates. There could be no such revenue, no such military and naval power in the West Indies, until the fear of military absolutism in England had been removed by the removal of the Stuarts. Meanwhile, in time of war or emergency, governors in the West Indies needed the buccaneers. Only after 1688 did it begin to be possible to dispense with them; repudiation of the buccaneering interest in Barbados coincided with a victory for big sugar-planters over small farmers. But not until 1718 was the ex-privateer Woodes Rogers made Governor of the Bahamas with instructions to suppress piracy in the West Indies.[120] In the next few years the long war of attrition against smugglers and pirates was finally won, and the seas were left free for English merchants to make profits in.[121]

We may conclude that the survival of some radical ideas among the pirates whom Defoe describes is not impossible: it is, indeed, likely. We find, for instance, expressions of sympathy for Monmouth's rebellion made by West Indian pirates and privateers.[122] But in real life the ideas of Morgan's men can hardly have been those of the Putney Debates. Given the choice, many ex-radicals may have thought privateering a more honourable occupation than cultivating sugar plantations with slaves under the lash. Others may have felt that if they restricted themselves to preying upon Spaniards (or Papists generally) they were continuing the war against Antichrist which had been lost in England.[123] But most men had no choice. At the end of their indentured servitude they were turned loose with no capital and no opportunities. "Being ... naked and destitute of all human necessities, not knowing how to get my living", a Dutch ex-servant turned pirate. His early companions, he tells us, were "very faithful among themselves", dividing booty equally and releasing prisoners.[124] As in England after 1660, former radicals had to adapt to a world in which their cause had been defeated, their ranks hopelessly thinned. The rough equality of pirate life may have been psychologically more congenial than the tensions and economic hazards of a slave-owning society, or the harsh discipline of a merchant vessel. The original buccaneers of the sixteen thirties had no chiefs among them, and no priests.[125] Morgan was first elected captain by a buccaneering crew and then admiral-in-chief of their confederacy: his royal commission merely confirmed his status.[126] Some of the old ideals may have survived to the second or third generation, among them utopian dreams of establishing a free and egalitarian community — say in Madagascar — which would offer escape from the pressures of the real world.

IV

This brings us back to Defoe. We must remember his radical past. Intended as a nonconformist minister, he took part in Monmouth's rising in 1685, and was lucky to escape a traitor's death. In William III's reign he frequently discussed public affairs with the old Leveller plotter, John Wildman.[127] Defoe's *True-Born Englishman* is a magnificently class-conscious attack on the aristocracy: *Legion's Memorial* calls Parliament to account in the name of the people; *The Shortest Way With the Dissenters* is a dramatically effective plea for religious toleration. All these were published in 1701-2. In 1706 he wrote an introduction to a new edition of the nonconformist martyr, Thomas Delamaine's, *Narrative* of his sufferings (first published 1684). But radicalism was on the way out in England too. Bankrupted once, pilloried once, Defoe gradually came to terms with his world and sold his pen to Robert Harley. By the seventeen-twenties he was denouncing the wickedness of servants. Nevertheless, something remained: it is very hard to be sure exactly where Defoe stands in his later years.

His interest in piracy seems to date from the seventeen-twenties, when it was being suppressed. The pirates to whom he talked were presumably those who had retired at about this time. In *A History of the Pyrates* Defoe stresses the reluctance of English juries to return verdicts of guilty in trials of pirates.[128] We recall the folk songs which attest to the popularity of pirates, as of highwaymen, as earlier of Robin Hood, no doubt for similar reasons.[129] Defoe frequently tells us of men who describe themselves as "a kind of pirates, known and declared enemies to the Spaniards; yet it was to these only and to no other" — not the French or the Dutch, still less the English.[130]

Secondly, Defoe continually plays with the ambivalent attitude of Quakers, members of the most radical religious sect, towards piracy. In *Captain Singleton* the Quaker William insists on accompanying a pirate voyage, but also insists that it is made clear he acted under compulsion. On many occasions he masterminds the pirates' activities. It is he who proposes settling in Madagascar. William is against slavery, but helps the pirates to sell their slaves.[131] In *The King of Pirates* a Quaker who commands a trading vessel is prepared to defend it when attacked.[132] This may well reflect the nature of early "Quakerism" in the West Indies. Many had emigrated before 1661, when Fox first imposed the peace principle on the Society. The word "Quaker" in any case was a loosely used term of abuse, often covering those whom after 1661 the Society would have repudiated: Ranters, men like Perrot with his sword, Rich with his support for the Story-Wilkinson separation (see p. 167 above). They may supply the background for Defoe's fighting or ambiguous Quakers. Even the Muggletonians, pacifists long before the Quakers were, obtained special permission from the prophet to use arms in defence of Antigua in 1679.[133]

V

Finally, Madagascar. As a calling station on the route to India, Madagascar had attracted would-be interlopers on the East India trade since at least the sixteen-thirties, when Sir William Courteen seems to have enticed Prince Rupert and the Earl of Arundel to give their blessing to schemes for colonization. "Absurd", "a desperate and fruitless action", Sir Thomas Roe described Rupert's scheme of 1637: the Prince's mother was equally sceptical. Arundel is said to have planned to go to Madagascar himself: he had his portrait painted by Van Dyck beside a globe on which his finger points to the island. Sir William Davenant's *Madagascar* (1638) relates to this project. Davenant prudently avoided saying anything about the island: for most of his poem it was simply a source to be plundered, despite the alleged innocence of the inhabitants.[134] Suckling mocked Davenant's armchair colonizing exploits: "Davenant's come/ From Madagascar, fraught with laurel home", but without anything more useful.[135]

Charles I, always prepared to make money by selling licences to breach monopolies he had already sold to others, authorized another project in 1639.[136] But in April 1640, anxious to appease the East India Company on the eve of the Short Parliament, he withdrew his permission for this project, as well as disavowing Courteen.[137] The captain involved in the 1639 plan managed three years later to obtain authorization from the House of Commons to sail with 250 men and 40 women "to erect a new commonwealth in Madagascar". 140 men, women and children actually sailed, under a different captain, but the colony was a failure and was abandoned in May 1646.[138]

A piece of promotional literature by Walter Hamond, ship's surgeon, was published in 1640 as *A Paradox Proving That the Inhabitants of the Island, called Madagascar ... (in Temporal Things) are the happiest People in the World.* In this early example of the literature of the noble savage Hamond followed Davenant in praising the naked simplicity of the "affable, courteous and just" inhabitants, their wholesome and simple diet, and their lack of ocean-going vessels or gunpowder: "barbarism civilized".[139] A second pamphlet by Hamond, *Madagascar, the Richest and Most Fruitfull Island in the World* (1643, reprinted 1649) was followed by the attempted settlement in 1645-6 which failed dismally, leaving eighty dead.

At least three other pamphlets appeared before 1650, one by Robert Boothby attributing to Bishop Morton an undertaking that, if bishops should "continue in disrespect" with King and Parliament, they (or the majority of them) would settle in Madagascar in order to convert the natives. Fortunately the latter were already hostile to images. Boothby suggested that the inhabitants would welcome English settlers to set against the cruel Portuguese. Madagascar would also be a refuge for truly religious protestants if it should please God to punish the nation for its crying sins by the prevalence of malignants and tyrannous papists.[140] Another pamphlet was by Robert Hunt, former Governor of Providence Island, who in 1650 became Governor of a settlement on Assada, an island off Madagascar. Hunt more than once compared Assada to Barbados. Hunt died and the colony was abandoned in the year his pamphlet was published.[141] The Harringtonian Henry Neville's polygamous utopian novel, *The Isle of Pines* (1668), was set on an island just off Madagascar.

Later in the century utopian legends about settlements on Madagascar got transferred to pirates. Defoe's *Review* gave considerable space to Captain John Avery, one of many pirates who settled

on the island in the sixteen-nineties.[142] Pamphlets of 1709 describe
how Avery's crew made "an exact dividend ... according to the law
of pirates". "This republic of pirates" attracted other pirates to
settle there too.[143] Defoe, it might seem, was obsessed with Madagascar. In *The King of Pirates* (1720), "an Account of the famous
Enterprises of Captain Avery, the mock-king of Madagascar", Defoe
stressed the libertarian aspects of Avery's settlement. "In a free state,
as we were, everybody was free to go wherever they would".[144] In *A
History of the Pyrates* we are told that Captain North's crew settled
for some years on Madagascar, where they were "strictly just both
among themselves and in composing differences of the neighbouring
natives". All quarrels were tried by the Captain, assisted by judges
chosen by lot. They "grew continent and sober. . . .It's true they were
all polygamists". Captain Thomas Tew, an ally of Misson's, thought
no place so fit to receive him as Madagascar. His crew, and some of
Misson's, also practised polygamy with native women.[145] We are told
that Edward Condent's crew broke up after "getting their fortunes",
and many of them settled in Madagascar some time around 1720.
One of them, James Plantin, lived at a place to which he had "given
the name of Ranter Bay". A pirate of Captain Davis's crew was
strongly anti-papist because his father had been a sufferer in Monmouth's rebellion — as Defoe nearly had been.[146] Madagascar recurs
in *Robinson Crusoe, Captain Singleton* and *A New Voyage Round the
World.*[147]

Defoe's use of Madagascar as a vehicle for social criticism makes it
seem likely that — as is often suggested — he had a hand in *The
Pleasant and Surprizing Adventures of Mr. Robert Drury during his
15 Years Captivity on the Island of Madagascar* (1729). The title, with
its echoes of *Robinson Crusoe,* is that of the second edition (1743).
The first was entitled *Madagascar, or Journal during Fifteen Years'
Captivity on the Island.* Drury certainy existed, but it is more
probable that his fifteen years (ending in 1717) were spent in piracy
than in captivity.[148] Defoe may have edited the story — contributing
for instance Drury's amusingly naïve inability to answer the theological queries of the natives, which recalls Crusoe's conversations with
Friday and the failure of the narrator of *Oroonoko* to convince its
hero of "our notions of the Trinity". Drury's editor rejected in
advance any suspicion that his "account of the religion of the
natives" was "a mere fiction", intended to "advance some Latitudinarian principles".[149] Drury's historical reflections also suggest Defoe.

He compares the inhabitants of Madagascar with the early inhabitants of Britain in order to establish the origins of government in popular consent. Drury married two women of Madagascar, in each case insisting that a mutual declaration of love and loyalty was the essential basis of matrimony, as Milton did in *Paradise Lost*. Drury however did not divorce his first wife; he left her — reluctantly — in an attempt to escape from the island. Drury expresses a familiar Miltonic sentiment: "every man here, the poor man as well as the rich lord, is a priest for himself and his family".[150]

VI

Defoe himself can hardly have regarded Libertalia as an ideal community. Ambivalent though he was in his attitude towards capitalist society, he respected individualism and the bourgeois virtues, and did not believe in an artificial equality of property. That is what makes the fairness of his description of Libertalia so remarkable. This would be surprising if he had invented the whole thing, less so if he had been listening to old sailors' tales and saw the possibility of using Libertalia to criticise aspects of capitalist society which offended him. He made similar use of the French thief Cartouche, frustrated in his attempt "to have made his retreat from the world, as other merchants do".[151] It is never easy to be sure exactly what Defoe is up to. The tolerance professed by some pirates may have appealed to him; he always emphasized the economic advantages of toleration. Amicable relations between protestants and Catholics in the New World were necessary if trade was to be most profitably pursued.

I did not re-read Eric Hobsbawm's *Primitive Rebels* and *Bandits* until I had finished writing this piece. There are no pirates in *Primitive Rebels*, and only occasional mention of them in *Bandits*, but they fit pretty well into his picture. Hobsbawm defines social bandits as "peasant outlaws", though "in Asian deltas and archipelagoes there was no clear distinction between bandits and pirates".[152] "Banditry tended to become epidemic in times of pauperisation and economic crisis", especially in "those forms of rural economy ... which have relatively small labour demands". (In the West Indies in the late seventeenth century demand for free labour was shrinking, in sharp contrast to the mainland colonies.) Banditry was "a form of self-help" for "the rural surplus population" who "*must* look for other sources of income". But the West Indies lacked the cohesiveness of a traditional peasant society. Some servants came from Ireland or the Scottish Highlands, others from English towns. Eric Hobsbawm contrasts with peasant bandits, orthodox in religion, the urban or vagrant underworld which "provided a refuge for libertinist or antinomian sectaries such as survivors of central-German Anabaptism", but he accepts that the distinction is not absolute.[153] The ideas of Misson and others I have quoted have more in common with Hobsbawm's urban underworld than with trad-itional peasant bandits who "remain within peasant society and are considered by the people as heroes" and avengers, as some pirates saw themselves.[154]

So I suggest, first, that it might be worth investigating more carefully the West Indies as a refuge for political radicals after the defeat of the Revolution. A Jamaican historian recently remarked that "it would be a most curious work to trace the Levellers and Diggers among the earliest settlers".[155] Secondly, we might look more seriously at the social basis of West Indian piracy. And, finally, we might scrutinise the utopian literature associated with pirates and islands — "a certain island whose name he remembreth not" as the epigraph to this chapter has it, and later more specifically with the West Indies and Madagascar. We may not learn very much; we might however be helped to understand how those on the margins of society adapted themselves to a world which seemed increasingly hostile. "Piracy ... is freedom for hill peoples", Gwyn Williams said.[156]

I referred earlier to the Robin Hood Society of 1756 as a repository of seventeenth-century radical traditions among London craftsmen. But I failed to mention one member whose significance may now be clearer: an old man from the West Indies.[157] He would have to be very old to remember the seventeenth century himself, but perhaps, like Defoe, he had talked to superannuated pirates in the seventeen-twenties.[158]

NOTES

1. A paper delivered at a conference on The Origins of Anglo-American Radicalism held in New York in November 1980; printed in a volume with that title, edited by Margaret Jacob and James Jacob, 1984.
2. *W.T.U.D..*, Chapter 17; B. S. Capp, *Astrology and the Popular Press: English Almanacs, 1500-1800* (1979), p. 249.

3. Daniel Defoe, *The Consolidator* (1705), in *Novels and Miscellaneous Works* (1840), Vol. IX, p. 216.
4. Edmund Ludlow, *A Voyce from the Watch Tower* (ed. A.B. Worden, Camden fourth series, 21, 1978), p. 19.
5. *A Journal of the Life of Thomas Story* (Newcastle upon Tyne, 1747), pp. 70-2, 192, 290, 676-7. For further examples see my *Religion and Politics in 17th-century England*, Chapters 7 and 11.
6. Richard Lewis, *The Robin Hood Society: A Satire by Peter Pounce* (1756), pp. v-vi, 19, 79. I owe this reference to Dr. Vincent Caretta. I have benefited by discussing this society with Arthur Clegg.
7. J.F.C. Harrison, *The Second Coming: Popular Millenarianism, 1780-1850* (1979), p. 14.
8. See especially M.C. Jacob, *The Radical Enlightenment: Pantheists, Free Masons and Republicans* (1981); J.R. Jacob, *Henry Stubbe, radical Protestantism and the early Enlightenment* (Cambridge U.P., 1983).
9. Defoe, *A General History ... of the Pyrates* (ed. M. Schonhorn, South Carolina U.P., 1972), pp. 283-4. The book was published as by Captain Charles Johnson. I assume Defoe's authorship: see Schonhorn, Introduction. There were Huguenot Missons who were well-known in England from the sixteen-nineties (Hillel Schwarz, *The French Prophets: the History of a Millenarian Group in 18th-century England*, California U.P., 1980, pp. 48-9, 258, and Index, *passim*).
10. *History of the Pyrates*, pp. 384, 388-92, 403-4. For Milton see *M.E.R.*, Chapter 19 and pp. 185-97.
11. *History of the Pyrates*, pp. 389, 391-2, 400, 406-7, 426-7.
12. P.K. Kemp and C. Lloyd, *The Brethren of the Coast* (1960), p. 48; cf. H.N. Brailsford, *The Levellers and the English Revolution* (1961), pp. 688-9: Sabbatarianism was included in a *Manifesto* accompanying a French translation of the Leveller *Agreement of the People* made in Bordeaux in the early sixteen-fifties.
13. *A Relation of the Great Sufferings and Strange Adventures of Henry Pitman, Chirurgeon to the Late Duke of Monmouth* (1689), in *An English Garner* (ed. E. Arber, 1895-7), VII, p. 366.
14. *History of the Pyrates*, pp. 417, 427, 432-4.
15. For example, M.E. Novak, *Economics and the Fiction of Daniel Defoe* (California U.P., 1962), p. 109.
16. *History of the Pyrates*, pp. 434-5.
17. *Ibid.*, pp. 211-13.
18. *Ibid.*, p. 139; Kemp and Lloyd, *Brethren of the Coast*, pp. 4-5.
19. *History of the Pyrates*, pp. 153-9. Anne Bonny, another lady pirate, changed husbands by means of a properly written and witnessed document (*ibid.*, p. 625). Divorce by mutual consent seems to have been recognized, at least in Bermuda (J.H. Lefroy, *Memorials of the Discovery and Early Settlement of the Bermudas or Somers Islands, 1515-1685*, 1877, II, pp. 46, 100, 197-8, 224-5). Cf. p. 216 below.
20. *History of the Pyrates*, pp. 585-8, 485.
21. *Ibid.*, pp. xxx-xxxi.
22. "Notes on Colonization, by Richard Hakluyt, Lawyer" (1578), in *The*

Original Writings and Correspondence of the two Richard Hakluyts (ed. E. G. R. Taylor, Hakluyt Soc., 1935), I, pp. 119-20. The point was made more tactfully by the younger Hakluyt in *A Discourse of Western Planting* (1584), *ibid.*, II, p. 318. For later examples, see my *Religion and Politics in 17th-century England*, pp. 86, 278-80, 324, 328.

23. *I.O.E.R.*, pp. 206-7, 218.
24. S. L. Adams, "Captain Thomas Gainsford, the 'Vox Spiritus' and the *Vox Populi*", in *Bulletin of the Institute of Historical Research*, XLIX (1976), pp. 141-4. I have benefited from reading an unpublished paper on Gainsford by Pete Steffens, cited on p. 61 note 132 above.
25. See my *God's Englishman* pp. 32, 153.
26. A. P. Newton, *Colonizing Activities of the English Puritans* (Yale U.P., 1914), pp. 149, 258-61.
27. Ed. V. T. Harlow, "The Voyages of Captain William Jackson (1642-1645)", *Camden Miscellany*, XIII (1924).
28. Ed. E. B. Sainsbury, *Calendar of the Court Minutes of the East India Company, 1644-1649* (Oxford U.P., 1913), pp. xxi-xxv, 358-84; II, *1650-1654*, pp. ix-x. See p. 177 above.
29. H. Peter, *Gods Doings and Mans Duty* (1646), p. 30; T. Edwards, *Gangraena* (1646), III, p. 133.
30. J. Lilburne, *The Innocent Mans Second Proffer* (1649).
31. R. S. Dunn, *Sugar and Slaves: The Rise of the Planter Class in the English West Indies (1624-1713)* (1973), p. 103; J. F. McGregor, "Ranterism and the development of early Quakerism", *Journal of Religious History*, 9 (1977), p. 356.
32. *W.T.U.D.*, pp. 219, 254-5; W. C. Braithwaite, *The Second Period of Quakerism* (1919), pp. 348-9.
33. *Ibid.*, pp. 235-40; McGregor, "Ranterism", p. 362; K. L. Carroll, *John Perrot, Early Quaker Schismatic* (Friends' Historical Soc., 1971), *passim*.
34. *Winthrop's Journal, 1630-49* (ed. J. K. Hosmer, New York, 1908), II, pp. 142-3.
35. Braithwaite, *The Beginnings of Quakerism* (1912), pp. 224, 337-8, 401-4; Braithwaite, *Second Period*, pp. 43-6, 216-17, 603, 618-21; G. Fox, *The Short Journal and Itinerary Journals* (ed. N. Penney, Cambridge U.P., 1925), pp. 298, 324, 332, 335; Dunn, *op. cit.*, pp. 104-5, 183-4. For an early call to Barbados, see *Early Quaker Writings, 1650-1700* (ed. H. Barbour and E. Roberts, Grand Rapids, Michigan, 1973), pp. 123-4; cf. E. Burrough, *The Memorable Works of a Son of Thunder and Consolation* (1672), pp. 544-50.
36. William Hubbard, *A General History of New England* (Boston, 1848), p. 346. Written around the sixteen-eighties.
37. B. Reay, in *The World of the Muggletonians* (ed. C. Hill, B. Reay and W. Lamont, 1983), Chapter 3.
38. C. and R. Bridenbaugh, *No Peace beyond the Line: The English in the Caribbean, 1624-1690* (New York, 1972), pp. 147, 326-7.
39. Fox, *Short Journal*, p. 298; Braithwaite, *Second Period*, pp. 46, 620.
40. *Diary of Thomas Burton*, I, p. 40.

41. Edwards, *Gangraena*, III, p. 248.
42. Capp, *Astrology*, pp. 223, 260.
43. *Oroonoko* was published in 1688 but probably written twenty years earlier. I am grateful to Professor C. M. Williams for help with Marten. He tells me that there are some letters from George in Barbados to Henry Marten, 1652-7, in the Marten-Loder collection of papers in the Brotherton Library, Leeds.
44. *The Journal of Richard Norwood* (ed. W. F. Craven and W. B. Hayward, New York, 1945), *passim*.
45. Lefroy, *op. cit.*, I, pp. 571-98; *Calamy Revised* (ed. A. G. Matthew, Oxford U.P., 1934), pp. 377-8.
46. *The Correspondence of Henry Oldenburg* (ed. A. R. and M. B. Hall, Wisconsin U.P., 1965 -), III, pp. 276, 442-4; IV, pp. 547-52, V, pp. 172-3, VI, pp. 535-6.
47. Ed. G. Bullough, *Poems and Dramas of Fulke Greville* (Edinburgh, n.d., ? 1939), I, p. 109.
48. W. F. Craven, "Introduction to the history of Bermuda", *William and Mary Quarterly*, second series, 17 (1938), pp. 50-1.
49. K. L. Sprunger, *The Learned Doctor William Ames* (Illinois U.P., 1972), p. 251.
50. Lefroy, *op. cit.*, I, pp. 535-6, 560.
51. G. Wither, *Justifarius Justificatus* (1646), p. 13, in *Miscellaneous Works*, Third Collection (Spenser Soc., 1874); A. Pritchard, "George Wither and the Somers Islands", *Notes and Queries*, new series, VIII, pp. 428-30.
52. Lefroy, *op. cit.*, II, pp. 132-3, 161, 215, 249-50, and *passim*.
53. *Ibid.*, II, pp. 94-6, 111-12.
54. [Anon.], *A Broadside Adventuring Eleutheria and the Bahamas Islands*, quoted in M. Craton, *A History of the Bahamas* (1962), pp. 57-62. The Adventurers seem never to have succeeded in getting a charter.
55. C. Webster, *The Great Instauration: Science, Medicine and Reform* (1975), pp. 87, 368.
56. C. S. S. Higham, *The Development of the Leeward Islands under the Restoration, 1660-1688* (Cambridge U.P., 1921), p. 78.
57. *Acts of the Privy Council, Colonial Series*, I, p. 403; cf. pp. 426-7; Henry Whistler's Journal, quoted in *The Narrative of General Venables* (ed. C. H. Firth, Camden Soc., 1900), p. 146.
58. Ed. T. W. Moody, F. X. Martin and F. J. Byrne, *A New History of Ireland* (Oxford U.P., 1976), III, pp. 363-4, 601-3.
59. Ed. G. Chandler, *Liverpool under Charles I* (Liverpool, 1965), pp. 411-12.
60. M. Ashley, *General Monck* (1977), pp. 138-9.
61. P. G. Rogers, *The Fifth Monarchy Men* (Oxford U.P., 1966), p. 62.
62. Ed. C. H. Firth and R. S. Rait, *Acts and Ordinances of the Interregnum* (H.M.S.O., 1911), II, p. 1264 (26 June 1657).
63. V. T. Harlow, *A History of Bermuda, 1625-1685* (Oxford U.P., 1926), p. 297.
64. Ed. H. M. Margoliouth, *Poems and Letters of Andrew Marvell* (Oxford

U.P., 1926), II, p. 295: Marvell to Downing, March 1659.

65. Harlow, *History of Barbados*, p. 297.
66. Higham, *Leeward Islands*, p. 176. This came after St Christopher's hope of a large number of deportees following the Rye House Plot had been dashed (*ibid.*, p. 172).
67. *Ibid.*, pp. 108, 145, 148.
68. *Calendar of State Papers, Colonial, America and the West Indies, 1661-1665* (1860), 5 August 1665; and Bridenbaugh, *No Peace*, p. 394.
69. E. S. Morgan, *The Puritan Dilemma: the Story of John Winthrop* (Boston, 1958), pp. 35-7.
70. Dunn, *op. cit.*, pp. 120, 258.
71. Harlow, *History of Barbados*, pp. 43, 309-10.
72. J. H. Parry, *The Age of Reconnaissance, 1450-1650* (1963), p. 278.
73. R. Ligon, *A True and Exact History of the Island of Barbados* (1657), pp. 45-6.
74. G. A. Puckrein, *The Acquisitive Impulse: plantation society, factions and the origins of the Barbadian Civil War (1627-52)*, D. Phil. Thesis, Brown University, 1978, p. 74. I am very grateful to Dr Puckrein for allowing me to read and quote from this thesis.
75. Lefroy, *op. cit.*, I, pp. vii, 94-5, 159; Bridenbaugh, *No Peace*, pp. 174, 214-15.
76. Kemp and Lloyd, *op. cit.*, pp. 62-3.
77. Harlow, *History of Barbados*, pp. 43, 307, 339; Bridenbaugh, *No Peace*, pp. 171, 175, 179, 214-15, 222; Richard B. Sheridan, "The Plantation Revolution and the Industrial Revolution, 1625-1775," *Caribbean Studies*, 9 (1969), p. 12.
78. Harlow, *History of Barbados*, p. 25.
79. Puckrein, *op. cit.*, pp. 219, 224; Harlow, *History of Barbados*, pp. 26-7, 31; Lefroy, *op. cit.*, *passim*.
80. Lefroy, *op. cit.*, I, pp. 630-1, 642, 650-4.
81. Harlow, *History of Barbados*, pp. 50, 58-9.
82. Dunn, *op. cit.*, p. 77.
83. Harlow, *History of Barbados*, pp. 127, 249-51.
84. Puckrein, *op. cit.*, p. 17.
85. Ligon, *op. cit.*, pp. 50, 82.
86. A. Day Bradley, "Friends in Bermuda in the 17th century", *Journal of the Friends' Historical Soc.*, 54 (1976), pp. 9-10; Jean Kennedy, *Isle of Devils: Bermuda, 1609-1685* (1971), p. 230.
87. Dunn, *op. cit.*, p. 104. Fox was in favour of educating blacks with a view to their conversion to Christianity, but they must be discouraged from rebellion (*Journal*, 1902, II, pp. 149, 157-8).
88. Fox, *Short Journal*, pp. 346-7.
89. Dunn, *op. cit.*, p. 105; Braithwaite, *First Period*, p. 495.
90. [Anon.], *A New History of Jamaica* (1740), p. 218.
91. Ligon, *op. cit.*, p. 46.
92. Puckrein, *op. cit.*, pp. 60-1, 78.
93. Harlow, *History of Barbados*, pp. 41-2; Bridenbaugh, *No Peace*, pp. 67.
94. Harlow, *History of Barbados*, pp. 86, 93-4.

95. Bridenbaugh, *No Peace*, p.176; Sheridan, *op. cit.*, p.12.
96. Puckrein, *op. cit.*, pp.60-1, 78.
97. *A New History of Ireland*, II, p.603. Some 2000 indentured servants are said to have been liberated in Barbados to take part in the Jamaica campaign (*Memoirs of Edmund Ludlow* ed. C.H. Firth, Oxford U.P., 1894, I, p.384).
98. S.R. Gardiner, *History of the Commonwealth and Protectorate* (1903), IV, p.128; C.H. Firth and G. Davies, *The Regimental History of Cromwell's Army* (Oxford U.P., 1940), II, p.700.
99. Ed. A. Macfarlane, *The Diary of Ralph Josselin* (Oxford U.P., 1976), p.163.
100. Harlow, *History of Barbados*, pp.117, 152, 175, 207.
101. Braithwaite, *Second Period*, p.45; Fox, *Short Journal*, p.324. The Rev. Henry Vaughan, "a worthy man", was so discouraged that after five years' conflict with sectaries he returned to England in 1669 (R. Baxter, quoted in *Calamy Revised*, p.501).
102. Higham, *Leeward Islands*, p.174.
103. Newcome, *Autobiography* (ed. R.Parkinson, Chetham Soc., XXVII, 1852), pp.184, 192-3.
104. Harvey L. Dacosta, "The first constitutional struggles",*Jamaica Historical Review*, 3 (1957), p.19.
105. *A New History of Jamaica*, p.248; H.J. Cadbury, "Conditions in Jamaica in 1687", *Jamaica Historical Review*, 3 (1959), p.53-5, 57.
106. *A New History of Jamaica*, p.191.
107. E[dmund] H[ickeringill], *Jamaica Viewed* (2nd. edn., 1661), pp.77-9; [Anon.], *The Present State of Jamaica* (1683), p.38.
108. *A New History of Jamaica*, pp.92-3; A.P. Thornton, *West-India Policy under the Restoration* (Oxford U.P., 1956), p.222 and *passim*.
109 .*Calendar of State Papers, Colonial, 1574-1660*, pp.373-4.
110. Ligon, *op. cit.*, p.96; Thornton, *op. cit.*, pp.149, 250.
111. G.L. Beer, *The Old Colonial System, 1660-1754* (New York, 1912), I, p.121; II, pp.70, 73, 89; Thornton, *op. cit.*, pp.227, 232.
112. A.P. Newton, *European Nations in the West Indies* (1933), pp.173-4.
113. J. Esquemeling, *The History of the Bucaniers of America* (1699), p.79; Thornton, *op. cit.*, pp.219, 255.
114. H.R. Allen, *Buccaneer: Admiral Sir Henry Morgan* (1976), pp.2, 18-20, 27, 36, 70, 140 and *passim*; Thornton, *op. cit.*, p.222; cf. *A New History of Jamaica*, pp.92-3.
115. Esquemeling, *op. cit.*, pp.80, 123.
116. Kemp and Lloyd, *op. cit.*, p.17.
117. Craton, *op. cit.*, pp.64-5.
118. Beer, *op. cit.*, II, p.89.
119. J.A. Williamson, *A Short History of British Expansion* (2nd. edn., 1941), I, p.290.
120. *History of the Pyrates*, p.xvi. Defoe may have known Rogers.
121. Thornton, *op. cit.*, pp.237, 257.
122. *A Relation of ... Henry Pitman*, pp.355, 364. See now Robin Clifton, *The Last Popular Rebellion: the Western Rising of 1685* (1984), p.129.

123. Cf. Captain Bartholomew Sharp, who "robbed all nations but especially the King of Spain" (Kemp and Lloyd, *op. cit.*, p.18).

124. Esquemeling, *op. cit.*, pp.11-12, 40, 61.

125. Newton, *European Nations*, p.170.

126. Allen, *op. cit.*, pp.10, 18, 27.

127. F. Bastian, *Defoe's Early Life* (1981), p.159.

128. *History of the Pyrates*, pp.xix, 285. There was a long tradition of such lenience by juries: see Evelyn Berckman, *Victims of Piracy: The Admiralty Court, 1575-1678* (1979), Chapter 6.

129. A.L. Lloyd, *Folk Song in England* (1975), pp.259-60.

130. Defoe, *The King of Pirates* (1895), p.11. First published 1720.

131. Defoe, *The Life ... of Captain Singleton* (1840), pp.177, 194, 204-5. First published 1720.

132. *The King of Pirates*, p.14.

133. Ed. A. Delamain and T. Terry, *A Volume of Spiritual Epistles ... by John Reeve and Lodowicke Muggleton* (1820), pp.468-70. First published 1755.

134. Davenant, *Shorter Poems and Songs from Plays* (ed. A.M. Gibbs, Oxford U.P., 1972), pp.10-21, 343-4; cf. E. Warburton, *Memoirs of Prince Rupert and the Cavaliers* (1849), I, pp.59-61.

135. Sir J. Suckling, *Poems, Plays and other Remains* (ed. W.C. Hazlitt, 1892), I, p.21. See L.B. Wright, "The Noble Savage of Madagascar in 1640", *Journal of the History of Ideas*, IV (1943) — an instance of Wright's flair for spotting the significant subject.

136. Sainsbury, *Calendar of the Court Minutes of the East India Company, 1635-1639*, pp.245, 304.

137. *Ibid.*, *1640-1643*, pp.25, 296. There were French plans to colonize Madagascar at this time (*ibid.*, p.56).

138. *Ibid.*, *1640-1643*, p.xxviii; *1644-1649*, pp.vi, 25, 195.

139. In *Harleian Miscellany* (1744-6), I, pp.256-62. This tract was reprinted in 1643.

140. Richard Boothby, *A Briefe Discovery or Description of Madagascar* (1646), pp.8, 18. Boothby's pamphlet was tactfully dedicated to the King and both Houses of Parliament. He argued that Madagascar was the key to ruling all India.

141. R. Hunt, *The Island of Assada* (1650); Sainsbury, *op. cit.*, *1650-1654*, pp.ix-x. The other pamphlet was Powle Waldegrave's *Answer to Mr. Boothbies Book of the Description of Madagascar* (1649). Waldegrave had been a member of the ill-fated colony of 1645-6, and was justifiably indignant with promotional material written from a safe distance. Waldegrave was paid £5 for his *Answer* by the East India Company, which regarded Madagascar as coming within its monopoly area (Sainsbury, *op. cit.*, *1644-1649*, p.327). For Assada see p.166 above.

142. Defoe, *Review*, IV, pp.425-8; cf. *Captain Singleton*, pp.225-6; *History of the Pyrates*, pp.52-4.

143. Van Brook, *The Life and Adventures of Captain John Avery* (1709), pp.39, 43, 46; *History of the Pyrates*, p.683. A play entitled *The Successful Pirate*, by Charles Johnson, was published in 1713. It is set

in Madagascar; Arverargus, King of the island, is said to be based on Avery. But it is an unserious play, about court intrigue and mob violence, and makes no attempt at local colour. Its main interest for us is the fact that "Captain Charles Johnson's" name is on the title-page of Defoe's *History of the Pyrates*. I am deeply grateful to Martine Brant for drawing my attention to this play.

144. *The King of Pirates*, p. 81; cf. p. 32 for the advantages of Madagascar as a place to settle.

145. *History of the Pyrates*, pp. 58-61, 133, 421-39, 498-9, 526-8. For radical advocacy of polygamy, see *M.E.R.*, esp. pp. 136-9.

146. *History of the Pyrates*, p. 93; information of Clement Downing, 1724, High Court of Admiralty, January 1655, f. 79. There is another reference to Ranter Bay, *ibid.*, f. 77. I am indebted for both these references to the kindness of Marcus Rediker. Recollection of the Ranters seventy years after their suppression is remarkable.

147. *Robinson Crusoe*, Part 2, Chapter 9; *Captain Singleton*, pp. 55, 225-6; *A New Voyage Round the World* (1840 edn.), pp. 28, 57. First published 1725.

148. Cf. P. Oliver's Introduction to the 1890 edition of Drury's work.

149. *Pleasant and Surprizing Adventures* (1743 edn.), pp. v, 181, 187-8; Aphra Behn, *Oroonoko, or, The Royal Slave. A True History*, in *Shorter Novels, Jacobean and Restoration* (Everyman), p. 192.

150. *Pleasant and Surprizing Adventures*, pp. 148-9, 231, 233, 413; *Paradise Lost*, Book VI. See p. 218 below.

151. Defoe, "A Narrative of the proceedings in France" (1724), in *The King of Pirates*, p. 110.

152. E. J. Hobsbawm, *Bandits* (Penguin edn., 1969), pp. 13, 26.

153. *Ibid.*, pp. 17, 20, 25, 31.

154. *Ibid.*, p. 13.

155. D. J. Buisseret, "Subjects and sources in the history of seventeenth-century Jamaica", *Jamaica Historical Review*, 10 (1973), p. 20.

156. Gwyn Williams, *When Was Wales? A History of the Welsh* (1985), p. 4.

157. Lewis, *Robin Hood Society*, p. 80.

158. Since I wrote this paper there have appeared *Misson and Libertatia* [*sic*], retold by Larry Law (1980), and Marcus Rediker, " 'Under the banner of King Death': the social world of Anglo-American pirates, 1716 to 1726", *William and Mary Quarterly*, third series, 38 (1981), pp. 203-27. The latter in particular meets my second suggestion, at least for the last period of piracy. Professor Rediker emphasizes the pirates' demo-cratic procedures, and their lack of any sense of deference such as some historians think ought to have come naturally to them. See also J. S. Bromley, "Outlaws at Sea, 1660-1720: Liberty, Equality and Fraternity among the Caribbean Freebooters", in *History from Below: Studies in Popular Protest and Popular Ideology in Honour of George Rude* (ed. F. Krantz, Concordia University, Montreal, 1985), esp. pp. 306-10, 314-15, 317.

9. *Sex, Marriage and Parish Registers* [1]

"A noble family's stud books and pedigrees were maintained with a precision which ... probably exceeded that bestowed on many parish registers." *

"When historians use so-called 'literary sources' there is every prospect that these will be re-read and re-evaluated by other scholars: it is far less likely that figures will be re-calculated." † [2]

I

Thirty-five years ago John Buckatzsch opened up a new approach to history by using parish registers for demographic purposes. [3] Demography has boomed in England since then. Mr Peter Laslett produced a rather unfortunately premature book, *The World We Have Lost*, in 1965, but a great deal of serious work has been done by the Cambridge Group for the History of Population and Social Structure, which in time should lead to solid conclusions. Two journals, *Population Studies* and *Local Population Studies*, testify to the vigour of the new discipline. Meanwhile the family as an institution rather suddenly became fashionable, perhaps as a by-product of the women's liberation movement. Dr Joan Thirsk's article on "The Family" in *Past and Present*, 27 (1964), was the harbinger of a great deal of writing — good, bad, and indifferent. This has come mainly from the United States where there is a *Journal of Marriage and the Family*. Interest in childhood was stimulated by Philippe Ariès's book translated as *Centuries of Childhood* (1962), and there is now a *History of Childhood Quarterly*, some of the writers in which seem to think that attitudes towards children in present-day America put all previous civilizations to shame. If this is so, it is an example of the phenomenon, not unknown to economists, that the most sophisti-

---

*K.V. Thomas, *Man and the Natural World: Changing Attitudes in England, 1500-1800* (1983), p. 59.

†K.H.D. Haley, review in *English Historical Review*, 359 (1976), p. 390.

cated methods of production do not necessarily always yield the most pleasing article.

The sixteenth, seventeenth, and eighteenth centuries seem by general consent to be a period in which interesting things were happening to the family in western Europe, though there is perhaps less agreement on what those things were. For England, Professor Lawrence Stone's *Crisis of the Aristocracy, 1558-1641* (Oxford U.P., 1965) had nearly 100 fascinating pages on marriage and the family. So both the very different books under review are by old hands, and their subjects overlap. Mr Laslett's is a collection of articles and papers, some of which have been in print for a long time. It is a great improvement on *The World We Have Lost.* The insecure, boastful tone is less in evidence, though he still insists that he has invented something called historical sociology, which he thinks is different from and better than anybody else's sociology (pp. 113, 174). But there are interesting things in the book. It was well worth stressing that children in present-day English society are less, not more, likely to be deprived of their natural parents than in seventeenth-century England. Professor Stone takes the point over, and as usual expresses it more trenchantly. The family was "statistically speaking, a transient and temporary association, both of husband and wife and of parents and children. . . . It looks very much as if modern divorce is little more than a functional substitute for death" (pp. 55-6). "We are hardly justified", Mr Laslett continues, "in historical terms, in sympathizing with ourselves for the prevalence of broken marriages in our time and its deplorable effect on our children" (p. 170). But it may matter more in our society, where families are more isolated from each other and from any community.

On the other hand, the problem of the elderly in modern society is new, because more people live longer (pp. 180-1). When death terminated marriages earlier, more single parents lived with their children, unless the children were rich enough to pay for them to live elsewhere (chapter 5). Professor Stone argues that "most widows in peasant families lived in the same house with one of their children" (pp. 24-5; cf. p. 28). Mr Laslett pushes further back in time "the origins of the interrelated characteristics of the Western family. As of [*sic*] the present state of our knowledge we cannot say when 'the West' diverged from the other parts of Europe" (p. 48). Why indeed should one assume divergence from a common pattern? Are there not perhaps other phenomena which demographers have too easily assumed must date from the sixteenth century, simply because there begins to be more evidence then — the mobility of the English population for instance?

Mr Laslett sensibly observes that it would be unwise to deduce from literary evidence "what the whole content of the attitude to children was amongst the élite minority, still more so to make a reliable decision on how far this attitude represented what all, or nearly all, persons experienced as children or acted upon as parents" (p. 19). Professor Stone would never have written so clumsily; but they are words whose content he might have taken to heart.

Mr Laslett's point that "only the United Provinces are so far known to have had as many — perhaps even more — craftsmen in the rural villages" in the seventeenth century as England, is a good one (p. 64). He appreciates that pre-nuptial pregnancy may have nothing to do with "illicit love", but may rather reflect the survival of earlier marriage customs (p. 104). But he appears to forget this when he comes to discuss what he calls "the perduring sub-society of the illegitimacy-prone" (pp. 3-4). Again, the phenomenon may be one of class differentials in marriage customs (pp. 149-51) — a point to which I shall return.

But some idiosyncracies remain. It is odd to speak of "the Western family pattern" and "Westernness" when the family pattern in question seems limited to northern France, the Netherlands, England and a few parts of Germany (pp. 14, 16, 24, 29, 31). Southern France, the Baltic countries, Hungary, Italy, Serbia, and Russia are excluded (pp. 12-16, 24, 29, 35). It is odd to speak of French as "the alien language which they used — or so it must appear to the English reader" when speaking of its use by French curés (p. 76).

The main doubt, however, about Mr Laslett's work remains his uncritical attitude towards his principal source, parish registers. This is the more remarkable since many historians and even demographers have warned against their inherent weakness. The pioneering article of John Buckatzsch recognized and clearly stated the difficulties as long ago as 1949.[4] Professor Flinn doubted "whether it will ever be possible to derive conclusions of any real value from parish registers". The warning was repeated by Professors Chambers and many others.[5] It is not only that parsons and parish clerks might be lazy or incompetent or corrupt, important though these considerations are. Many nonconformists disapproved on principle of baptism, marriage or burial in the parish church. Professors Collinson and Everitt, Drs

Richardson, Spufford and Clark, give many examples of ministers coming from outside a parish to baptize children, who presumably would not be registered, of families moving out of their own parish for the birth, which therefore would be registered in another parish. Until 1590 Bedlam churchyard was used for burials by people "out of sundry places of the City of London".[6] It was, said Mrs Chidley in 1641, "the cheapest place that I know".[7] Quakers rejected church baptism altogether, and though they sometimes conformed to marriage in church, they avoided it whenever possible. In the decade 1691-1700 unregistered Quaker baptisms in the parish of Weston, Lancashire, amounted to 16 per cent of the total for the parish; unregistered burials were 8 per cent, unregistered marriages 20 per cent.[8] But it is rare to have this sort of knowledge. Wherever parish records can be checked against other sources, they turn out to be hopelessly inaccurate.[9] The modern editor of Josselin's *Diary* points out that Josselin "refers to a considerable number of burials, marriages and baptisms which . . . do not appear in the parish register . . . His *Diary* provides a warning concerning the inadequacy of local records." Of 21 sample cases of infanticide in early seventeenth-century Essex, none was registered as born or baptized; only two as buried.[10]

Some parishes refused to baptize the children of paupers.[11] The high mobility of the sixteenth and seventeenth centuries makes labourers especially difficult to trace: many of them remained for only a short time in a parish. How many vagrants got into parish registers? Such considerations led Drs Hirst and O'Day to searching criticisms of family reconstitution.[12] In towns the hazards were greater. We have no idea how many residents even attended church regularly: in many London parishes only a small proportion of them could have got into the church at one time. Mr K. V. Thomas quotes a writer of 1759 on the "perhaps not inconsiderable number among the lowest class of the people who never are brought to be baptized at all".[13] Social mobility must have affected the age-structure of different parishes and different families in different ways: this also increases the problems of family reconstitution. Some villages had access to a main road or a navigable river; others had not. Many children put to wet-nurses around big towns must have died in a parish different from that in which they were born. The tendency of demographic interpretations is to assume continuity: they are conservative. Historical interpretations stress mobility, change.[14]

In addition to the conscientious scruples of nonconformists there must always have been a desire to avoid paying fees. Even in the nineteenth century many deaths escaped registration altogether. In the eighteen-thirties and forties the *majority* of those buried in non-Anglican churchyards were technically Anglicans: burial in their parish church would have cost three times as much. There is no reason to suppose that this was a new development; seventeenth- and eighteenth-century conformists disliked paying fees too. On the other hand, dissenters who had never received Anglican baptism might be buried in Anglican churchyards. Parish registers varied enormously in their recording of unbaptized children, still births and abortions, and in the interval between birth and baptism.[15] Many conformists were unwilling to pay the fee for baptism.[16] Dr Razzell has suggested that in the eighteenth and early nineteenth centuries up to one-third of all births were never recorded in rural parish registers.[17] There were great variations from place to place; and there would be variations over time as dissent became legally established and church courts lost their punitive powers. As early as 1671 an M.P. was urging the prohibition of nonconformist celebration of baptisms, marriages and funerals.[18] For twentieth-century statisticians it is a pity this proposal was rejected.

The point to stress is that we do not know whether a parish register is reliable or not, unless it can be checked from some other source.[19] We certainly cannot assume, as Mr Laslett does, that irregularities will cancel out. A moment's reflection will show the absurdity of supposing that conscientious objectors who sought baptism outside their own parish would be "counterbalanced by exactly similar persons coming in to the village" (Laslett, pp. 55-6). For the objectors leave one parish because they object to the ceremonies used there, and go to another in which the services are "lower". But the "high-church" parishioner is much more likely to believe in the desirability of baptizing (or burying) his children in his own parish. There are many examples of men trying to evade ceremonies by going to another parish: very few of men coming into a parish in order to enjoy ceremonies.[20] There can be no compensation for the distortion: at all events we must not assume that there is.

Mr Laslett believes that the number of bastards in England suddenly and significantly decreased in the sixteen-forties and sixteen-fifties. What he has found, however, is almost certainly not a reduction in illegitimate births but a reduction in *registered* illegitimate births. Mr Laslett himself tells us that there are "evident signs of a sudden collapse in registration after 1643, which may not have been put right until after 1662" (p. 125).[21] He speaks of "the disconcerting irregularity of the registrations" (p. 144; cf. pp. 108-11, 132). He is cautious in drawing conclusions, believing only that his statistics represent "with rough and ready accuracy the objective story of bastardy levels in England" (p. 115). But he does say that "it might in fact have been true that Puritans did succeed in reducing the amount of irregular intercourse in England during the sixteen-fifties, and enforcing an unwonted chastity" (p. 110; cf. p. 120). Unfortunately, what Mr Pennington called "the spurious authority of a column of figures" tends to prevail over the warnings of those who compile the figures.[22] Professor Stone reproduces Mr Laslett's graph of illegitimacy, attributing the startling dip between 1640 and 1660 to "Puritan control" (Stone, p. 613). He assumes that "Puritans were likely to be more strict in registering bastards than conventional Anglicans" (pp. 144-6). His reference to "the great Puritan experiment at moral regeneration from 1640 to 1660" (p. 262) contradicts Mr Veall, the latest and best historian of the subject. After a careful survey of the evidence, Mr Veall describes as "quite erroneous" the view that "the victory of Parliament over the King ...introduced a period in which offences against sexual morality were heavily punished." How indeed is "Puritan control" supposed to have worked? Even the most ruthlessly efficient of modern repressive governments have been unable to check copulation. Church courts were abolished in 1646, and no Presbyterian disciplinary system took their place. Such harrying of unmarried mothers as occurred was done by J.P.s for traditional financial reasons, not by Puritan parsons for theological reasons. In the absence of church courts, the means of enforcing laws against fornication were inadequate, Mr Veall tells us; the panic law of 1650 against adultery was never effective. From 1650 to 1657 non-attendance at one's parish church ceased to be a legal offence; from 1653 to 1657 marriage was a civil ceremony. The sex lives of lower-class Englishmen and women were freer between 1641 and 1660 than they had been for centuries.[23]

It is therefore probable that before 1640 and after 1660 many more convinced Puritans than Mr Laslett has recognized managed to avoid marrying or baptizing their children or burying their dead in the parish church. Professor Stone himself admits the possibility that "most illegitimate children were either not registered at all or were

registered as legitimate" (p. 144). It seems to me certain that this
tendency was accentuated in the forties and fifties. So we need not
suppose that the thunders of Puritan preachers produced "an unwonted chastity". Mr Laslett's graph depicts the failure of parochial
authorities to *register* bastards. When Professor Stone says that "the
family life of the poor was more heavily regulated by public pressures
between 1580 and 1660 than at any time before or since" (p. 146), he
may be right about the decades between 1580 and 1640. But it seems
likely that anxiety about the cost of maintaining bastards, rather
than Puritanism, led to the tightening up of controls in these years,
especially after the slump of the sixteen-twenties.[24] And the break
came in the sixteen-forties, not in 1660.

II

But apart from being misled by Mr Laslett on this matter, there are
many excellent things in Professor Stone's book. He recognizes the
force of the point recently made by Professor Finley, that "all the
possible statistics about age of marriage, size of family, rate of
illegitimacy, will not add up to a history of the family."[25] Professor
Stone is not afraid to use "literary sources", and does so with
learning and wide-ranging sympathy. He has a short way with "a
sociological theory based on an overarching concept of moderniz-
ation marching relentlessly through the centuries" (p. 660), and with
the "sheer historical fantasy" that "adolescence only became a social
problem in the nineteenth century" (p. 512; cf. pp. 35, 107-8, 139,
245, 376-7). He has not much use for the eternal categories of Freud.
"Nothing could be more false than that the sexual experiences and
responses of middle-class Europeans in the late nineteenth century
were typical of those of all mankind in the past, or even of Europeans
in the previous three centuries, or even of all classes in late Victorian
society" (p. 16; cf. pp. 161, 484, 681). "The sexual drive is itself not
uniform, but is heavily dependent on an adequate protein diet and
the amount of physical exhaustion and psychic stress." It is possible
to overemphasize the significance of swaddling, weaning, and toilet-
training (p. 15).

But if Professor Stone is sceptical of some conventionally received
orthodoxies, he has a historian's awareness of the difficulties in
recreating the thoughts and emotions of men and women in the past.

"The nature of the surviving evidence inexorably biases the book towards a
study of a small minority group, namely the literate and articulate classes,

and has relatively little to say about the great majority of Englishmen ...
Much correspondence of an explicit sexual or embarrassingly intimate
character has undoubtedly been destroyed ... What appears to be a growth
of affect [by which Prof. Stone appears to mean love] may in fact be no more
than a growth in the capacity to express emotions on paper ... Any
behavioural model of change over time imposes an artificial schematization
on a chaotic and ambiguous reality" (pp. 11-14).

Literary evidence can be deceptive: the wide acceptance of Locke's
theories may have been less the consequence of his writings than of
"a deep-seated change in the response of the readers, which...made
them more receptive to the advice" (p. 20).

This is a promisingly sceptical start, and gives us confidence in
many of Professor Stone's conclusions. About half the population
was under the age of 20, despite the death of a very large number of
infants; only a handful lived till over 60. Marriage was delayed longer
than in any other known society. "The delayed marriage system
makes good economic sense", since it was necessary to set up an
independent household to join in production (pp. 51-2). All these
points derive from Mr Laslett. What perhaps is novel is the audacity
with which Professor Stone draws conclusions affecting delicate
areas of human sensibility. The short duration of marriage "funda-
mentally affected all human relationships". Infants "could only be
regarded as expendable" (p. 81; cf. p. 32). These bold conclusions do
not necessarily follow from the demographic data.

With equal confidence Professor Stone periodizes the evolution of
the family in England. First there was "the Open Lineage Family,
1450-1630", with arranged marriage, subordination of women, neglect and fostering out of children, harsh parental discipline, little
affection, no sense of domestic privacy. This was modified into "the
Restricted Patriarchal Nuclear Family, 1550-1700". The consolidation of the national state led to a decline of the ties of kin and
clientage, and this was "a major cause of the rise of the nuclear
family". The Tudor monarchy deliberately fostered "the power of
the husband and father within the conjugal unit" (pp. 134-5). The
Reformation, by destroying traditional rituals, simultaneously
strengthened the power of the state and of the head of the household
who in so many respects replaced the priest (pp. 140, 152). These
changes were accompanied by an "almost hysterical demand for
order at all costs". Men were "a prey to acute insecurity and anxiety.
The material world was more threatening and unpredictable than it

had ever been ... Salvation was thought to lie in the ruthless persecution of dissidents." In the lower-middling and labouring classes "economic co-operation in the running of the family business dictated a certain measure of sharing of responsibility," and greater freedom of choice in marriage for children. But children were "probably subjected to physical and moral coercion from an early age in order to maximize their productivity before they left home".

"The Closed Domesticated Nuclear Family, 1620-1800" reversed the trend towards domestic patriarchy, at the same time as absolute monarchy was overthrown. The influence of kin and neighbourhood declined. Choice in marriage was freer, and was now based "as much on expectations of lasting mutual affection" as on economic considerations. The authority of husbands over wives and of parents over children declined. "Professional, upper-bourgeois and gentry families became much more child-oriented, and some adopted remarkably permissive attitudes to child-rearing." The upper-class family carried "a much greater load of emotional and social commitment ... Among the higher aristocracy adultery by both sexes again became extremely common"; prostitution increased. More and more middle-class wives were withdrawing from economic production, aping the life-style of their social betters. Among the propertyless poor illegitimacy greatly increased (pp. 652-8).

One can admire the sweep and courage of Professor Stone's scheme, even as crudely summarized here. He is careful to say that he is dealing with "trends and not absolutes", and that there are wide variations over time and between social classes. In many ways this periodization makes sense, and it leads to some fascinating *aperçus* by the way. The artificial revival of the cult of chivalry and heraldry was an attempt "to relight the dying embers of lineage loyalty" (p. 30). The triumph of newer marriage styles led to

a major reorientation of consumption patterns, caused by the growth of a more inward-looking, more private and more urbanized life-style for the aristocratic family. It was characterized by the withdrawal of the family from the great hall to the private dining-room and by the increasing habit of residing for long periods in London to enjoy the 'season'" (p. 125).

"To the extent that saleable offices increased in the seventeenth century, as they did, this undermined the importance of kinship" (p. 128). The household "helped to keep in check potentially the most unruly element in any society, the floating mass of young unmarried males" (p. 27). A prentice sub-culture was a constant threat to public order in London, especially in the sixteen-forties when traditional controls had broken down (p. 376). The subjection of women to husbands and fathers was so axiomatic that even the Levellers never raised the question of votes for women (p. 195; cf. p. 240). The national marriage market of the eighteenth century helped to reconcile the aristocracy to greater freedom of matrimonial choice for their children (p. 317).

There are interesting if inconclusive discussions of birth control, whether deliberately by *coitus interruptus* or abortion (pp. 63, 66, 398, 417, 432, 480, 651), or accidentally by the breast-feeding so strongly urged by Puritan preachers. Ladies who farmed their children out to wet-nurses had more children than the poor — though malnutrition among the latter may also have played a part. Professor Stone has a chapter entitled "Plebeian Sexual Behaviour", but he assumes without argument that "the two lead sectors in society . . ., the upper bourgeoisie of the towns and the squirearchy of the country, . . . provided a pattern which was followed, at varying intervals of time, by the propertied lower middle class and by the highest levels of the court aristocracy" (p. 652). "The literate and articulate classes" were "the pacemakers of cultural change", and there was "stratified diffusion downward" (pp. 10, 12, 222, 274, 340, 362-3). "It is fairly clear", Professor Stone admits, "that neither kinship nor clientage had played anything like the same role among peasants, artisans and poor as they did among their betters" (p. 142). So "the Open Lineage Family" presumably did not exist among the bottom 80 per cent of the population. Many features of the new family type "never penetrated the poor at all until the nineteenth or even the early twentieth centuries" (pp. 657-8). If that is so, is it really helpful to try to trace trends or developments in "the family"?

Much of what Professor Stone has to say about the upper 10 per cent of the population is fascinating and convincing because based on solid knowledge. For classes below that level it is difficult indeed to find evidence. But it would be no less plausible to assume, as a starting hypothesis, that for long before 1500 there had been a class differential relating to marriage. The upper landed class necessarily regarded marriage as a property transaction, with which love had little to do. But why should this attitude have been "diffused downward" among the unpropertied? It is at least possible that, as

Keith Thomas long ago suggested, permanent monogamy had never been the rule among the lowest classes.[26] Professor Stone refers from time to time to "surviving folk customs" which indicate this. "Bundling" may have been one of them (pp. 605-7, 637-8). He recognizes the existence of different lower-class conventions, including "handfast marriages" in the North. But he seems to forget this later. He stresses that the propertyless poor were "fairly free to choose a spouse for themselves" (pp. 30-2, 91, 191-2). Professor Stone gives evidence for the ease with which a poor man could desert his wife, disappear, and remarry elsewhere — *de facto* divorce, however much the church officially prohibited it *de jure*.[27] The "unofficial folk-custom" of wife-sale among the lower clases, for which much eighteenth-century evidence exists, is surely at least as likely to be a survival as a novelty? (pp. 38, 40-1). In Mary's reign, for instance, a priest "sold his wife to a butcher", since the return of Catholicism had made her inconvenient.[28] Robert Greene refers to wife-sale in 1592.[29] Professor Stone notes that "the changes in child-rearing", to which he attaches much importance, affected primarily the upper classes (p. 449). He even hints that the ale-house may be a centre of lower-class culture rivalling the church (p. 140). But he never subjects lower-class conventions to the same sort of analysis as he does those of the aristocracy and gentry.

He postulates "a sharp rise in pre-marital intercourse" after about 1700. "Among the propertyless poor ... sexual relations before marriage *became* normal from the late seventeenth century" (p. 657 — my italics). Professor Stone attributes this (among other things) to "the rise of a landless labourer class, which placed less value on virginity than on fertility", and perhaps "a revival of the recognized mediaeval custom" of sexual intercourse after public betrothal but before the church wedding. Laslett gives evidence for the practice in Leicestershire in the sixteenth century: why should we suppose that it "spread" to other areas? One wonders indeed how new all this was; or for that matter "the rise of bundling", "the emergence of a hereditary bastardy-prone subculture among the poor",[30] and a "growing army of abandoned and murdered infants" (Stone, pp. 615, 628-31, 645-8).[31] Mr Thomas suggested that "what indignant observers ...mistook for the effects of the Industrial Revolution upon the morality of the cotton mills represented merely the standards which the labouring classes had always known, ... the tradition of promiscuity."[32] Mr Laslett's "perduring sub-society of the illegitimacy-prone" is a non-historian's way of describing the same phenomenon. It is surely possible that we are dealing not with "rises", "revivals", or "emergences" but with a change in social attitudes. As the standard of living of the middle classes improved, long-established lower-class habits would seem less acceptable; and urbanization forced lower-class sexual conventions upon the attention of their social betters.[33]

I do not think that Professor Stone has established that "the culture of sexual promiscuity in the large submerged class of the very poor" was growing during the Industrial Revolution (p. 617). It may have been its greater visibility that caused Evangelicals to work hard "to suppress the deplorable folk-customs of the poor". The "hedonistic popular culture of the rural poor" which had "to be made to conform to urban middle-class morality" did not originate in the eighteenth century (p. 667, cf. pp. 616-17). When some households began producing for the market on a significant scale, they would naturally differentiate themselves from the mass of the lower classes by a new stress on monogamous marriage, the wife acquiring a certain status as junior partner in the family firm. (Beavers, I am told, are the only monogamous rodents, because the nature of the tasks they undertake makes it advantageous to work in couples). The household ideology came to be expressed in England by protestantism, as Professor Stone rightly argues. But the new marriage ethic antedates the Reformation: it is not unknown in Roman Catholic countries. I think Mrs Davies is far more right when she argues that the Puritan preachers "were not advocating new ideals for marriage but were describing the best form of bourgeois marriage as they knew it. They were describing behaviour by husbands and wives which had in fact changed very little, in spite of considerable changes in theological views about the status of marriage itself."[34] I am not myself convinced that literacy and printing "*created* great divergences between high and low cultures" (Stone, p. 21 — my italics), though no doubt they accentuated them. What was new in the seventeenth century was that "the thrifty and prudent habits" of the household culture "appealed to some of their social superiors".[35]

Professor Stone traces the economic roots of the monogamous ideology to the household economy (pp. 258-62, 637-41), and makes the point that "there had been bourgeois cultures before and elsewhere, but nowhere else had they spread their values through the landed élite as well" (p. 261). (This was hardly a diffusion downwards from the "lead sectors"). Professor Stone fails to emphasize that in England as nowhere else the gentry were participating in production for the market through sheep farming and the clothing and extractive industries. The ultimate victory of "bourgeois" ideas among the squirearchy owes more, it seems to me, to their involvement in an increasingly capitalist way of life than to the theologians or to "a series of changes in child rearing, which created among adults a sense of trust instead of one of distrust" (pp. 261, 268). Professor Stone is at pains to argue that the "great secular change in sexual attitudes and sexual behaviour" which occurred in the late seventeenth and eighteenth centuries had nothing to do with "the rise of capitalism"; but he can do so only by equating capitalism with industrialization in a way that I for one would not accept (pp. 646-8, 661-5).[36]

Professor Stone himself produces evidence that it was not "among the landed, professional and upper bourgeois classes" that the "individualistic ideology" emerged which "changed the character of internal and external family relationships", any more than it was (we may agree) "among the propertyless industrial poor". It was among small householders that capitalist relations and "the new family type" emerged, in England and in New England (pp. 361-2, 637-41, 653-4, 661-6). The upper bourgeoisie and squirearchy were not the pace-makers.

Such a chronology would perhaps help to explain England's priority over France in adoption of breast-feeding by the upper classes (pp. 432, 479), and in abandoning swaddling of infants (pp. 424-6), both by something like the century which separates the English from the French Revolution (cf. p. 636). It would not explain why England lagged behind France in the use of contraception by the lower classes, and in abandoning beating in schools (p. 480).

Before the middle of the seventeenth century, though the new marriage ethic could be used in criticism of the landed ruling class, its main thrust was directed against the traditional unconcern with marriage of the mass of the population — rogues and vagabonds, and the inhabitants of the outlying areas least influenced by the London market. In Lancashire as in Ireland in the sixteenth century "adultery, fornication and bawdry" were much in evidence, and illegitimacy carried no social stigma.[37] The immorality of the Welsh was attributed to the intoxicating mountain air, but it seems more likely that this, like the "multiplication without marriage" of the Gubbings in Devon, was a description of older marriage conventions by modern protestants. The percentage of Elizabethan brides pregnant on marriage was two and half times higher in Devon than in the city of York. Of vagabonds a pamphlet of 1567 complained "not one among them are married". How few beggars, asked John Donne, "were ever within church, ... christened or ... married?" Pamphlets of 1631 and 1654 agreed.[38] But Simon Forman at the end of the sixteenth century shows a "high level of casual fornication and adultery" in London's "lower-middle-class, middle-class and even upper-class circles" (Stone, p. 550). Common-law courts, which controlled property, recognized only church marriage; church courts, which had to deal with the unpropertied masses, recognized a contract without a wedding (p. 32). What the respectable called polygamy was alleged to be widespread in the mid-eighteenth century (p. 36). It had attracted many radical thinkers from the Anabaptists through Milton to Samuel Richardson, not to mention James Boswell (pp. 574, 586).

Only if we have some such understanding of the deeply rooted older sexual habits of the poor can we understand the marriage practices of the radical sects. A royal proclamation of 1548 denounced seditious preachers who advocated polygamy, or divorce on the initiative of either sex, allegedly arguing that immutable monogamy was enjoined "not by God's law but by the Bishop of Rome's law".[39] In the early seventeenth century divorce was much easier among the emigré churches in the Netherlands than in England. There was a long history behind the outburst of antinomian "immorality" in the sixteen forties and sixteen fifties, which Professor Stone mentions but does not explain. Antinomian opinions, he asserts, were "more shocking than attractive to the great majority of their contemporaries" (p. 627) This would be a very difficult statistic to establish. Such opinions proved attractive to the Ranters against whom governments legislated in the sixteen-fifties, and to the young John Bunyan.[40] Contemporaries who drew analogies between the sexual ethics of the Ranters and of vagabonds may have had a point: for the first time older sexual habits were able to express themselves in ideological form. After 1660 the expression was suppressed again, but the habits seem to have remained unchanged.

Professor Stone actually says that "England in 1650 was probably less secular than it ever had been" (p. 659),[41] and argues that the "frank and hedonistic eroticism" of Aphra Behn and Bernard de

Mandeville was "unthinkable" in England at an earlier date (pp. 528, 530, 538, 543, 675-9). It was however very thinkable in the sixteen-fifties: Milton's nephews were among those who enjoyed it. Printed English pornography dates from 1650.[42] Awareness of this fact and recollection that civil marriage had existed from 1653 to 1660 would have saved Professor Stone from having to postulate that "the custom of marriage in church partly broke down after the Restoration," and that there was a "very striking increase" in pre-marital sexual activity (pp. 603, 616-48). Libertinism of the Ranter type caused alarm again when the Industrial Revolution brought large numbers to live in cities, free from the constraints of J.Ps. and parsons in the countryside (pp. 611, 750). I see not two tidal waves of moral regeneration and repression, one in the sixteenth and early seventeenth centuries, the other in the nineteenth century (p. 9), but rather a continuing struggle to impose the new ethic. The decline in infant mortality is as likely to have economic and medical causes as to be due to "a rise of maternal affection and consequent child care" (pp. 677-9). Continuity of lower-class attitudes towards the relation of the sexes, whose evolution is quite distinct from that of their betters, seems to be a more plausible explanation of the course of events than Professor Stone's "long-term see-saw oscillations" (p. 545), or his theory that only in the eighteenth century was "the libido ... released from its long period of religious containment" (p. 657).

Professor Stone's assumptions about the harshness of Puritanism (and its effectiveness), and his failure to allow for the complexities of the interaction between middle-class Puritanism and the heresies of the lower classes, repeatedly lead him astray. The vigour and repetitiveness of the preachers' propaganda on behalf of patriarchal authority over wives and children, and of breaking children's wills, suggests that such attitudes were by no means so universally accepted as they would have wished (Stone, pp. 151, 158-9, 168-9, 193-5, 198-200).

Rejection of the Calvinist doctrine of original sin in the later seventeenth century may have contributed to kindlier attitudes towards children, if such were indeed developing. But "the root cause" is more likely to have been a general modification in attitudes towards inflicting pain; use of torture was declining at the same time, and Calvinists had not invented torture. Mrs. Aphra Behn's *Oroonoko* may be "early evidence" of the view that children are born good but corrupted by society (p. 406);[43] but this had been argued forty years earlier by Gerrard Winstanley, not to mention Thomas Traherne. There are similar post-datings at pages 275 (Mary Astell), 326 (Defoe), and 363 (Place). That Puritan favourite, the great educational liberator, Comenius, should surely not figure only as one who threatened children with divine vengeance for sin (p. 410)? I cannot regard it as proven that "a majority [in the sixteenth and early seventeenth centuries] ... found it very difficult to establish close emotional ties to any other person" (p. 99), or that "love before marriage, however rare it may have been in the sixteenth century, may have been on the increase in the early seventeenth century and after." I do not know how one would prove that statement, even for the upper classes; but it is surely going beyond the evidence to assert that "romantic and sexual love ... played little or no part in the daily lives of men and women of the late seventeenth and early eighteenth centuries." Is there any reason to suppose that contemporaries were right to suggest that "the growth of marriage for love in the eighteenth century was caused by the growing consumption of novels"? (pp. 249, 272, 283; cf. pp. 387, 465, 685). All the historian is entitled to say, surely, is that *talk about* marriage for love increased.

Professor Stone recognizes that he disagrees with other scholars on this point (p. 700), and he has to admit the existence of Shakespeare (pp. 102-3, 700). He might also have thought of Chaucer, or for that matter of the love poets of the ancient world. Chimpanzees establish continuing sexual preferences, which might or might not be called love.[44] If Arthur Young was prostrate when his beloved daughter died, so were Nehemiah Wallington and Oliver Cromwell nearly a century and a half earlier (p. 248). Is it necessarily true that the abandonment of children in time of famine, or the use of child labour to augment family income, are evidence of lack of affection? (p. 114). The latest born might have to die so that the others could survive. Not many of us have had to make this choice, but it must have faced many people in the fifteen-nineties and sixteen-twenties.[45] Professor Stone uses evidence from the law courts to establish "the lack of warmth and tolerance in interpersonal relations", and improvidence, neglect, and brutal treatment of children (pp. 98-9, 392-4. 451, 470, 476, 519, 655, 663, 683-7). But similar sources would provide similar evidence for our own society, which Professor Stone believes to be so different in these matters.

The assumption throughout that values percolate downwards

from the upper to the lower classes seems to me dubious. How can
we know that "for those without property, affective and companion-
ate marital relations did not develop before the nineteenth century"
(p. 389)? There may not be much evidence the other way, but
Elizabethan ballads, Winstanley and Harrington would suggest that
Professor Stone's flat generalization is wrong.[46] He considers that
for the lower middle-class "patriarchal authority seems to have been
in full decay by the late seventeenth century, if not earlier" (my
italics). But has its previous existence been demonstrated? "*As early
as* [my italics] the middle of the seventeenth century", Ralph Josselin
was "struggling vainly to control the marriage of his children"
(pp. 292-3). Professor Stone's obsession with 1660 rather than 1640
as a turning-point leads him to make misleading statements. The
Court of Wards was not abolished at the restoration (p. 242); it was
abolished in 1646, and this abolition was confirmed in 1656 and again
at the restoration. The "strict settlement", which Stone thinks
undermined patriarchal authority, had developed well before 1660,
from which he dates it (p. 89): it seems to have arisen as a reaction to
the abolition of wardship and feudal tenures.[47]

Professor Stone's argument, then, gives plenty of room for disagreement and controversy. He could not have written a book of this
sweep if he had not intended to provoke. His subject is much more
important than any likely to be tackled by most of those who will
snipe at him from the academic undergrowth. Quantification can be
a useful servant if the historian satisfies himself exactly what has been
counted: it is a dangerous master if the historical background has not
been fully taken into account in assessing the accuracy of population
figures. For this reason historical demography is far too serious a
subject to be left to the demographers. Professor Stone has begun
the task of assimilating and interpreting their statistics in the light of
what historians know about seventeenth-century society. A lot more
work and discussion will be needed before agreement is reached, and
I for one could have wished he had been more critical of the
demographic raw material at certain points. But we must be grateful
to him for starting the process off with such panache. Though I have
dwelt on some of my disagreements with some of Professor Stone's
interpretations, it is the positive side of his achievement that we
should end by stressing. His work on the aristocracy and gentry is
likely to prove pretty definitive, and he has shown the areas in which
more research and analysis are needed before we can make statements

about the sexual and family relations of the rest of the population with equal confidence. Few living historians would have had the courage to try to bring order into such a large and amorphous subject; none could have written 800 pages on it with such sustained gusto and power and readability.

NOTES

1. A review of Lawrence Stone, *The Family, Sex and Marriage in England, 1500-1800* (1977) and Peter Laslett, *Family Life and Illicit Love in Earlier Generations*, (1977), originally printed in *Ec. H.R.*, second series, 31 (1978).
2. Professor Haley's words might be applied to much work based on archive sources, as well as to figures.
3. E. J. Buckatzsch, "Occupations in the Parish Registers of Sheffield, 1655-1714", *Ec.H.R.*, second series, 1 (1949) pp. 148-9.
4. Buckatzsch, *loc. cit.* pp. 148-9; cf. J. T. Krause, "Changes in English Fertility and Mortality, 1781-1850", *Ec.H.R.*, second series, II (1958), pp. 52-70.
5. M. W. Flinn, "Population in History", *Ec. H.R.*, 20 (1967), pp. 141-3, criticising Mr Laslett specifically; cf. now his "The Population History of England, 1541-1871", *ibid.*, 35 (1982), p. 449, reviewing Wrigley and Schofield; J. D. Chambers, *Population, Economy and Society in Pre-Industrial England* (Oxford U.P., 1972), pp. 59-64, 105-14; my *Change and Continuity in 17th-Century England*, pp. 209-16.
6. Collinson, *The Elizabethan Puritan Movement*, pp. 143, 373-4, 390-1; A. Everitt, *The Community of Kent and the Great Rebellion* (Leicester U.P., 1966), p. 215; R. C. Richardson, *Puritanism in North-West England: A Regional Survey of the Diocese of Chester to 1642* (Manchester U.P., 1972), pp. 27, 79, 114, 165; M. Spufford, *Contrasting Communities: English Villagers in the Sixteenth and Seventeenth Centuries* (Cambridge U.P., 1974), pp. 20, 27, 236, 296, 301; P. Clark, "Review of Periodical Literature, 1973: 1500-1700", *Ec. H.R.* 28 (1975), p. 141. See pp. 211-14 below.
7. Katherine Chidley, *The Justification of the Independent Churches of Christ* (1641), p. 58.
8. H. Barbour, *The Quakers in Puritan England* (Yale U.P., 1964), pp. 176-7; R. Speake, "Under-Registration in the Weston (Lancashire) Registers", *Local Population Studies*, 15 (1975), p. 45.
9. Cf. D. V. Glass, "London Inhabitants Within Walls, 1695", *London Record Soc. Publications*, 2 (1966), xxxv-vii; *idem*, "Two Papers on Gregory King", in D. V. Glass and D. E. C. Eversley, eds. *Population in History* (1965), pp. 170-2; J. T. Krause, "The Changing Adequacy of English Registration, 1690-1837", *ibid.*, pp. 381-3, 391; D. E. C. Eversley,

"A Survey of Population in an Area of Worcestershire from 1660 to 1850"; *ibid.*, pp. 396-7; E. A. Wrigley, "A Simple Model of London's Importance", *P. and P.*, 37 (1967), p. 46.

10. *The Diary of Ralph Josselin*, p. xxii; K. Wrightson, "Infanticide in Earlier Seventeenth-Century England", *Local Population Studies*, 15 (1975), p. 18.

11. Clark, *op. cit.*, p. 141.

12. Review by R. O'Day in *Ec. H. R.* second series, 28 (1975), p. 322; review by Derek Hirst in *Social History*, 3 (1976), p. 382.

13. *A Collection of the Yearly Bills of Mortality from 1657 to 1758* (1759), p. 4, quoted by K. V. Thomas, *Religion and the Decline of Magic* (1971), p. 166.

14. S. B. Baxter, "The Later Stuarts, 1660-1714", in *Recent Views on British History: Essays on Historical Writing since 1966* (ed. R. B. Schlatter, Rutgers U.P., 1984), p. 161; cf. P. J. Greven, *Four Generations: Population, Land and Family in Colonial Andover, Massachusetts* (Cornell U.P., 1970), p. 267; B. Coward, *The Stuart Age: A History of England, 1603-1714* (1980), p. 36. See now Angus McLaren, *Reproductive Rituals: The Perception of Fertility in England from the 16th to the 19th century* (1984), and Dorothy McLaren, "Marital fertility and lactation, 1570-1729", in *Women in English Society, 1500-1800* (Ed. Mary Prior, 1985). G. R. Quaife, *Wanton Wenches and Wayward Wives: Peasants and Illicit Sex in Early Seventeenth Century England* (1979), p. 251. On mobility, cf. M. J. Ingram, *Ecclesiastical Justice in Wiltshire, 1600-1640, with Special Reference to Causes Concerning Sex and Marriage* (unpublished Oxford University D. Phil. Thesis, 1976), pp. 348-55. P. J. Greven, "Historical Demography and Colonial America", *William and Mary Quarterly*, 24, 1967, pp. 451-3, notes Laslett's self-contradictions on this point.

15. B. M. Berry and R. S. Schofield, "Age at Baptism in Pre-Industrial England", *Population Studies*, 25 (1971), pp. 453-63; E. A. Wrigley, "Births and Baptisms: The Use of Anglican Baptism Registers as Sources", *ibid.*, 31 (1977), pp. 281-312. Mr Wrigley recognizes this as a weakness in parish registers as sources. He mentions, without attempting to evaluate, other inadequacies, which seem to me even more serious (p. 281). Cf. his "Clandestine Marriages in the Late Seventeenth Century", *Local Population Studies*, 10 (1973), pp. 15-21.

16. Krause, "Changes in English Fertility and Mortality", p. 55; cf. D. Levine, "The Reliability of Parochial Registration and the Representativeness of Family Reconstitution", *Population Studies*, 30 (1975).

17. P. E. Razzell, "The Evaluation of Baptism as a Form of Birth Registration", *ibid.*, 26 (1972), p. 131.

18. D. T. Witcombe, *Charles II and the Cavalier House of Commons* (Manchester U.P., 1971), p. 121.

19. Spufford, *op. cit.*, p. 167.

20. For one example, see Richardson, *op. cit.*, p. 79.

21. This point is confirmed, at least for the period before 1653, by Dorothy McLaren, "The Marriage Act of 1653: Its Influence on the Parish

Registers", *Population Studies*, 28 (1974), pp. 319-27. I have rewritten this passage, since Mr Laslett claims that I misrepresented him ("Introduction" to *Bastardy and its Comparative History*, ed. P. Laslett, K. Oosterveen and R. M. Smith, 1980, p. 51).

22. D. H. Pennington, *Seventeenth-Century Europe* (1970), pp. 17-18.
23. D. Veall, *The Popular Movement for Law Reform, 1640-60* (Oxford, 1970), pp. 139-41.
24. I owe this point to M. J. Ingram's Thesis, pp. 370-81. That there was no illegitimacy bulge in the sixteen-fifties has now been satisfactorily established by Wrightson and Levine ("The social context of illegitimacy in early modern England", in *Bastardy and its Comparative History*, pp. 158-75). As Alan Macfarlane put it, "the bulge in bastardy of the Jacobean period faded away before the Puritans came formally to power" ("Illegitimacy and illegitimates in English history", *ibid.*, p. 81). The point is delicately made by the title of Wrightson's "The nadir of English illegitimacy in the 17th century" in the same volume, pp. 176-91. Mr Laslett seems to accept defeat on this point ("Introduction", *ibid.*, pp. 25, 51).
25. M. I. Finley, "'Progress' in Historiography", *Daedalus*, 106 (Summer 1977), p. 139.
26. K. V. Thomas, "The Double Standard", *Journal of the History of Ideas*, 20 (1959), p. 206; cf. J. Thirsk, *op. cit.*, pp. 120-1: "It is almost certainly true that the history of the rich family was not also that of the poor." Mr P. Clark suggests that "the growth of poverty and subsistence migration in the sixteenth century undermined the institution [of of marriage] even further." — *English Provincial Society from the Reformation to the Revolution: Religion, Politics and Society in Kent, 1500-1640*, p. 156. The weakness of Stone's theory is confirmed by P. Slack, *Poverty in Early Stuart Salisbury* (Wiltshire Record Soc. 31, 1975), *passim*; cf. Clark and Slack, eds., *Crisis and Order in English Towns, 1500-1700*, pp. 135, 159-60, 167, and P. Clark, "The Ecclesiastical Commission at Canterbury, 1572-1603", *Archaeologia Cantiana*, 89 (1974), p. 195.
27. J. A. Sharpe, "Crime and Delinquency in an Essex Parish, 1600-40", in *Crime in England, 1550-1800* (ed. J. S. Cockburn, 1977), pp. 99-100, confirms the point.
28. Ed. J. Nichols, *The Diary of Henry Machyn* (Camden Soc., 42, 1848), p. 48.
29. R. Greene, *The Blacke Bookes Messenger*, in *Coney-Catching and Bawdy-Baskets* (ed. G. Salgado, 1972), p. 325; cf. Thomas, "the Double Standard", p. 213. See now S. P. Menefee, *Wives for Sale: An Ethnographic Study of British Popular Divorce* (Oxford, 1981), *passim*, and Capp, *Astrology and the Popular Press*, p. 125.
30. This is a concept which Professor Stone has taken over, perhaps unwisely, from Mr Laslett (*The World We Have Lost*, pp. 141-2).
31. Cf. Professor Stone's more plausible reference to the "long history of fairly generalized infanticide in Western Europe" (pp. 473-4, 476; cf. pp. 340, 375).

32. Thomas, "The Double Standard," 206.

33. Cf. Professor Stone's assumption that May Day frolics came under criticism only in the eighteenth century (p. 640).

34. Kathleen M. Davies, "The Sacred Condition of Equality — How Original were Puritan Doctrines of Marriage?", *Social History*, 5 (1977), p. 577; cf. Stone, pp. 180-1.

35. Davies, *op. cit.*, p. 578; cf. Stone, pp. 261-2, 321.

36. For a much more convincing economic analysis, see H. Medick, "The Proto-Industrial Family Economy", *Social History*, 3 (1976), esp. pp. 297, 305-6, 313-15.

37. N. P. Canny, "The Ideology of English Colonization: From Ireland to America", *William and Mary Quarterly*, third series, 30 (1973), pp. 584-5; T. W. Moody, F. S. Martin, and F. J. Byrne, eds., *A New History of Ireland*, III (Oxford, 1976), p. 1; C. Haigh, *Reformation and Resistance in Tudor Lancashire* (Cambridge U.P., 1975), pp. 374-81.

38. *W.T.U.D.* p. 320; A. L. Rowse, *The Elizabethan Renaissance: The Life of the Society* (1971), p. 158; Thomas Harman, *A Caveat or Warening for Commen Cursetors* (1566), in Salgado, ed. *op. cit.*, pp. 101-2, 121; C. Ricks, ed., *Sphere History of Literature in the English Language*, II, (1971), p. 401; Wye Saltonstall, *Picturae Loquentes* (1631), Luttrell Soc. Reprints, No. 1 (Oxford, 1946), p. 39.

39. D. M. Loades, *The Oxford Martyrs* (1970), p. 95.

40. Bunyan, *Grace Abounding to the Chief of Sinners* (1666), in *Works* (ed. G. Offor, 1860), I, pp. 11, 17-20, 49-50.

41. Contrast the very well-informed Professor Olivier Lutaud: "Never has the tendency towards secularization been so clear as in the years 1649-52" — *Winstanley: Socialisme et Christianisme* (Paris, 1976), p. 426.

42. Martine Brant, *The Literature of the London Underworld. 1660-1720* (Newcastle Polytechnic M. Phil., 1982), pp. 373-4. I am grateful to Ms Brant for permission to read and quote from this thesis.

43. *Oroonoko* was probably written twenty years or so before it was published in 1688 (contrast Stone, p. 231).

44. I owe this information to the kindness of Prof. P. A. Jewell. It is based on observations made at Jane Goodall's study site in Tanzania. I am also indebted to Prof. Jewell for beavers, p. 199 above.

45. Mr Hair suggests that an apparent increase in infanticide in Elizabethan England merely means that more notice was taken of it. — P. E. H. Hair, "Homicide, Infanticide and Child Assault in Late Tudor Middlesex", *Local Population Studies*, 9 (1972), pp. 45, 48; cf. F. G. Emmison, *Elizabethan Life: Disorder* (Chelmsford, 1970), pp. 156-7; Wrightson, *op. cit.*, pp. 10-19; J. S. Cockburn, ed., *Western Circuit Assizes Orders, 1629-48*, Camden fourth series, 17 (1976), pp. 144-5; R. W. Malcolm "Infanticide in the Eighteenth Century", in *Crime in England, 1550-1800*, esp. pp. 189-90. For Wallington see P. S. Seaver, *Wallington's World: A Puritan Artisan in Seventeenth-Century London* (1985), p. 87.

46. A. Clark, ed., *The Shirburn Ballads, 1585-1616* (Oxford U.P., 1907), pp. 109-11, referring to 1701; Sabine, *Works of Winstanley*, p. 599;

Harrington, *Works* (1737), pp.109-10. See now M.Spufford, *Small Books and Pleasant Histories: Popular Fiction and its Readership in seventeenth-century England* (1981), pp.157-8, 181.

47. The idea that the strict settlement "undermined patriarchy" has been challenged by Eileen Spring: "The Family, Strict Settlement and Historians", in *Law, Economy and Society: Essays in the History of English Law* (ed. G.R.Rubin and D.Sugerman, Abingdon, 1984), pp.168-91, and in "Law and the Theory of the Affective Family", in *Albion*, 16 (1984), pp.1-20. Professor Spring is one of the many who think Stone wrong about love.

People

POSTSCRIPT

D.M. Palliser recently accused me of "statistical Luddism" in *Economic History Review*.[1] Since the publication of Edward Thompson's *The Making of the Working Class* I thought that "Luddism" had lost some of its derogatory flavour. Not all Luddites wanted to smash all machines; they discriminated, and had wider objectives in mind. As the reader will have noticed, in the above pages I was not attacking the demographic machine, but suggesting that it might be made more effective. I have not attempted to rewrite this piece. But I should like to clarify the nature of my concern. I am not alone in my doubts about parish registers.[2] J.D. Chambers spoke of demographers "making bricks without straw"; D.C. Moore asserted that no really confident statements about birth and death rates can be made before 1838, when the first accurate survey of the population was made.[3]

It is not demography that is at fault but the over-enthusiasm of some demographers, and their apparent ignorance of or unconcern about the circumstances in which parish registers were compiled. Thus Dr Schofield after admitting that there are suspicions about the adequacy of parish registers, nevertheless concludes blithely that "to reject a system of registration on these grounds is as much an act of faith as accepting it at its face value".[4] I am against any acts of faith in the search for historical truth; but the onus of proof is surely on those who believe, not on the sceptics. The demographer who has taken most pains to refine his statistical techniques to correct under-registration resulting from delays in baptizing and delays due to inefficiency says insouciantly "the extent of under-registration due to the spread of nonconformity is a separate subject".[5] It is surely a most important source of under-registration? Wrigley and Schofield in their monumental *Population History of England* assume that "before the late 18th century the problem of residual escape from ecclesiastical registration becomes progressively less serious, until in Tudor and Stuart times it was probably too slight to be a source of serious concern".[6] I suspect that this assumption may be quite wrong; it is certainly unproven; it is not accepted by many historians of the period. The fact that we know more about the defects of later registration does not prove that they did not exist earlier: it may prove the opposite. Assumptions about universal acceptance of the Tudor and early Stuart church are analogous to Mr Laslett's assumptions about universal acceptance of monogamy: both derive from very out-of-date history.[7]

I do not myself think it likely that parish registers can ever be made a wholly reliable source of statistics; but a great deal more sophistication is needed before they become even a usable blunt instrument. T.H. Hollingsworth made the obvious point that methods of correcting statistics of infant mortality which work for modern periods may not work for the seventeenth century.[8] Parish registers at best recorded baptisms, not births; burials, not deaths; marriages performed in the parish church, not elsewhere.

Margaret Spufford suspected "considerable under-registration" in Cambridgeshire nonconformist parishes, citing the Willingham register in 1697: "Note that some dissenters fanatically inclined are not taken notice of here". Perhaps nearly three-quarters of the population of this parish were "inclined towards Congregationalism". In Orwell, another dissenting parish, marriages "certainly went unregistered"; so did burials. The register refers to "some . . . who say they are married, by lawless ministers at lawless churches, as they call them".[9] Parish registers contain data which do not harmonize with other evidence. "All the work done on obtaining an apparently 'complete' analysis from more adequate documents begins to seem merely a painful exercise in futility".[10]

When Mr Earle, searching for Monmouthite rebels, checked the parish registers of Taunton, Lyme Regis and Colyton against other records, he found that marriages were very seriously under-registered — as is not surprising in that nonconformist area.[11] The Wimbledon registers were kept meticulously from 1598 to 1606, when they almost came to a full stop with the arrival of a new parson. Only two marriages were recorded between 1607 and 1617, no burials between 1607 and 1615. Matters improved after he left. But between 1637 and 1640 "there was no infants registered". No marriages were recorded between 1645 and 1660, no funerals 1653-60. Some baptisms for the late sixteen-fifties were added after the restoration, not always in the right place.[12] In Tetbury, Gloucestershire, in the late seventeenth century, Dr Wrigley found that nearly half the parents of children whose baptism was recorded were — so far as the parish register goes — unmarried.[13] Similar under-registration of marriage was noted in Eyam, Derbyshire, for the sixteen-forties and fifties.[14] Victor Skipp made allowances of between 5 and 12½ per cent for recusancy and defective registration in his Warwickshire parishes.[15] Wrightson and Levine speak of "a shortfall in marriage registration" between 1660 and 1680 in Terling and many other English parishes.[16] "Even with an apparently reliable set" of parish registers like those of Salisbury, Dr Slack recognized "the probability of some under-registration".[17] Maureen Duffy found at Thaxted, Essex, that the number of recorded marriages dropped from an average of 15 a year before 1642 to 4 in 1644, and only one each in 1646 and 1650. In 1655 there were 25. Nor was this an exceptional lapse due to civil war: there was another bad patch after 1786.[18]

Parish registers might be at the mercy of lazy or incompetent incumbents and clerks. "The arrival or departure of an especially scrupulous clerk", says Dr Hunt, "is apt to produce a mirage, vivid but insubstantial, of astounding demographic change".[19] Parish registers might circulate around the parish; entries might be forged.[20] Even regularly maintained registers, Dr Flynn argued, under-registered.[21] Pepys tells us how in the exceptional circum-stances of 1665 plague deaths in London were under-estimated — he thought by at least 25 per cent — "partly from the poor that cannot be taken notice of, through the greatness of the number, and partly from the Quakers and others that will not have any bell ring for them". There was much deliberate concealment. The parish clerk of St Olave's said "there died 9 this week though I have returned but 6".[22] In time of plague, men and women did not always die (and so were not buried) in their own parish.[23]

Pepys's mention of "the poor that cannot be taken notice of" no doubt refers specifically to plague conditions; but it reminds us of the possibility that a significant proportion of the population may have eluded parish registers altogether. Many children of vagrants were never baptized, and their parents no doubt were often unmarried. Clark estimates that in late sixteenth-century Kent probably one-third of the population never went to church.[24] What happened to them? The responsibility of the incumbent, D. V. Glass reminds us, was to record the baptisms, burials and marriages of members of his congregation; not those which occurred in his district.[25] It is impossible even to guess the numbers of vagabonds, or of men and women living in moorland, forest and fen parishes, who slipped through the net altogether; *a priori* one would expect it to be much greater in the sixteenth and seventeenth centuries than later. Dr Jones notes that in north Shropshire the many children who died before being baptized never got into the parish register; he reckons their number at some one-third before 1700, almost half in the eighteenth century. This raises, as he mildly observes, serious questions about the viability of family reconstitution.[26] Refusal of baptism to pauper children in some parishes was no doubt in order to avoid giving them a settlement.[27] Some clergymen would not baptize bastards: others made no distinction between legitimate and illegitimate offspring.[28] What about infanticide? Of twenty-one cases in Essex which Dr Wrightson examined, none were registered as born or baptized; only two as buried — these in parishes with exceptionally well-kept registers. Wrightson thinks — and he is surely right — that infanticide may have been common in weakly-controlled areas of the North and West.[29] But — even more statistically disturbing — it must also have varied over time and place, rising in starvation years. In the bad year 1624 an act of Parliament put the onus of proof that a child had not been murdered on the mother. In 1655 the Lord Mayor of London ordered a precept to be read against the murder of bastard children by their mothers — so frequent was the practice thought to have become.[30]

The evidence for nonconformists either taking their children out of the parish to be baptized, or importing a suitable minister to perform the ceremony, is overwhelming.[31] Sometimes women, or whole families, moved out of an uncongenial parish for the birth; "and my child kept secret", said Thomas Shepard proudly.[32] Or they made private arrangements for lying in so as to avoid the ceremony of churching.[33] In Elizabeth's reign Sir Henry Sidney and others had their children baptized in the French strangers' church.[34] In Glossop, Derbyshire, of 169 births recorded in the parish register between 1653 and 1659, apparently only 45 were baptized.[35] In Cranbrook, Kent, there were 500 unbaptized persons in 1663.[36] Were children not baptized in church always registered? In Thaxted, Essex, the burial is recorded of children who had never been baptized. There are examples of baptism of adults, one "upwards of 70".[37] Defoe's baptism was not registered — either because he was not baptized or because he was baptized in a nonconformist meeting house.[38] Couples also went out of their own parish to be married.

Town registers, Peter Clark tells us, were especially likely to under-record. In the earlier period towns were flooded by poor immigrants, outside the pale of the parish; later, dissenters were heavily concentrated in towns.[39] In London and other cities, eighteenth-century burials were taking place outside the central parishes, while baptisms were still recorded there. In Newcastle nonconformists buried their own dead and refused to pay fees; they were estimated at one-third of the population.[40] Catholics in Lancashire and Cheshire buried their dead secretly and at night.[41] On the other hand, in some Cambridgeshire villages in the later seventeenth century nonconformist deaths were occasionally recorded in the parish register though they were not buried in the churchyard.[42]

Nor was nonconformity the only reason for leaving a parish. On the evidence of Myddle, it appears that newly-married couples frequently went to live in another parish until they inherited the family property.[43] At Earls Colne only twelve per cent of men and twenty-four per cent of women were born and married in the same parish. But some women returned to the parish of their birth to have children. Children often went out to service in another parish.[44]

By all accounts registration in the sixteen-forties and fifties was at its most chancy. In Wiltshire the social status of parish officers appears to have declined during these decades;[45] there was far less supervision. Between 1650 and 1657, when church attendance ceased to be compulsory, the parochial system must have come near to breaking down.[46] Mr Milward noted that there was in Wimbledon a steady increase in the number of recorded baptisms from 1620 to 1700 — except in the sixteen-fifties.[47] Dr Quaife found Wiltshire registers so faulty for most parishes in the sixteen-fifties that he had to ignore them for statistical purposes.[48] Dr Wrightson reported general under-registration in seventeenth-century Lancashire.[49] The parish registers of Myddle recorded only one per cent of all baptisms in the sixteenth and seventeenth centuries as those of illegitimate children; "but this figure is very unreliable when set against Gough's evidence" for the late seventeenth century. "Probably many illegitimate children were never baptized", says Dr Razzell; "this should make one wary of using these statistics [from parish registers] uncritically".[50]

One conclusion on which many scholars agree is that family reconstitution on the French model is much more difficult in seventeenth-century England, where parish registers are less reliable than in France. The very idea of reconstituting families assumes a society "nearly always socially quiescent", as Laslett put it, a population which stays put in its villages.[51] No one these days would describe seventeenth-century England in such terms. There an immobile village is an untypical village. "Fully reconstituted families" concludes Peter Clark, "are likely to be the least mobile; ... the reconstruction of mobile families can only be partial because of the inconstant quality of parish records overall".[52] How can you with confidence reconstitute a family in which children are baptized whose parents' marriage is unrecorded in the parish register? D. G. Hey, Keith Wrightson and David Levine, among others, have argued that no amount of statistical sophistication can help here, if it is divorced from the social history of the community.[53] Miranda Chaytor has indeed called in question many of the assumptions about the prevalence of the nuclear family, and with them, "the usefulness of the concept and the appropriateness of the terminology".[54]

Magnificent work is however being done by demographic historians who are aware of the pitfalls and realise that population changes are not a *deus ex machina* explaining social shifts but are themselves the product of social reactions and social controls. Wrightson and Levine reject Laslett's idea of a "bastardy-prone culture", for instance. It is a survival of an independent popular culture. The rise in bastardy figures between 1591 and 1610 is related "to a point of crisis in a growing disequilibrium between customary attitudes, expectations and sexual behaviour and deteriorating social and economic circumstances".[55] "Formal regulation of sexual behaviour was dependent on local support for its efficacy".[56] Margaret Spufford, D. G. Hey and Miranda Chaytor also recognize that the religious life and the social and kinship relationships of a community must be taken into account before demographic analysis can become meaningful.[57] Such an approach offers hope that demography can become really useful to historians.

What was the object of parish registers? Clearly not to provide statistical evidence for historians. They were introduced in 1538, just after the incorporation of Wales into England and the setting up of the Councils in the North and in Wales.[58] No doubt the main object of parish registers was fiscal; and later in the sixteenth century, as poverty increased, registration became important to the finances of local communities when questions of settlement were at issue. But the fifteen-thirties were the decade of the Reformation, and one object of parish registers was to impose monogamous marriage as against traditional marriage patterns, which in Wales and the North and West of England were very different from those approved by the Church of England and beginning to be accepted in the South and East.[59] English Lollards, and some of the sects of the radical Reformation, also had their own views about marriage. Official registration of baptism was introduced at Zurich in the fifteen-twenties specifically against Anabaptists.[60] In England, where the mediaeval church had been satisfied to leave matrimonial problems to private litigation between the parties except in cases of open notoriety in the parishes, the Elizabethan church attempted to see that no improper marriages took place, chivvying the local authorities for this purpose.[61]

But what was improper? There was great confusion in sixteenth- and seventeenth-century England as to what was a lawful marriage. The classic authority, Henry Swinburne, recognized that marriage (and therefore the legitimacy of children) was to a significant degree still determined by local customs which varied from region to region. His object (and that of the church courts) in accepting that local custom might authorize the legitimacy of customary marriages seems to have been to insist on the indissolubility of such marriages: it is all part of the same campaign. But was marriage contracted before witnesses without church ceremony recorded in parish registers?[62] Ivy Pinchbeck in two neglected articles stressed the different marriage customs of the lower classes and the lack of social stigma on bastardy.[63] Mr Laslett regarded this as "a dubious supposition", apparently because "we can be confident that officials, secular and official, disapproved of bastardy".[64] We can be equally confident that the police today disapprove of theft. It was because there were different marriage customs that sixteenth-century officials were so anxious to impose the approved rules. Evidence like that of P. E. M. Hair on bridal pregnancy shows how far church marriage was from being accepted as the essential preliminary.[65] So does the ease with which it was abandoned by settlers in the West Indies.[66] Hollingsworth calculated that 70% of the marriages at Colyton between 1674 and 1694 were clandestine, though the figure fell to 50% in the next 20-year period.[67] In Tetbury in the sixteen-nineties approximately half the marriages took place outside the parish church.[68] Stone recently recognized that "large numbers ... were living in casual concubinage", but he still confined this to "the urban proletariat" and to the nineteenth century.[69]

An interesting article by Martin Ingram argues that by the late sixteenth century the church's "centuries-long campaign to secure popular recognition of the need for solemnization [in church] seemed all but won". "Around 1640 . . . the wedding service of the Church of England had been absorbed as part of popular culture". This ignores the evidence for resistance to church marriage, especially in the fifteen-nineties.[70] And it ignores contemporary agitation about the "immorality" of the lower classes in the North and West, and of vagrants. Even Mr Laslett recognized that the West and North-West were the most "bastardy-prone" regions of England.[71] Ingram mentions the possibility that church marriage may not have been accepted by "the vagrant poor", but does not explore the implications of this admission.[72] How many "vagrant poor" were there? Where did they come from? From the reign of Elizabeth, he admits, "there was probably also concern about the marriages of very poor people", because these were likely to prove expensive for the parish.[73] Ingram's approach is more sophisticated than Laslett's, but he still seems to me too bland in his belief that church marriage was somehow "normal". He ignores the possibility of intellectual dissent from it, and he is too sceptical about the existence of distinct lower-class marriage customs before the seventeenth century.[74] Susan Amussen, on the basis of much wider research, stresses the contrasting attitudes towards church marriage of ecclesiastics and villagers, and the acceptance by the latter of informal divorce as well as of informal marriage.[75] The "concern" about marriages of the very poor could extend to refusal of church marriage by the parish. What were they to do?[76]

Apart from such external constraints, there were many quite distinct reasons why men and women might wish to avoid the church ceremony. The dissolute, the careless, the footloose and the very poor either were outside the pale of parish government or could not afford to pay its fees. Nonconformists, increasingly organized after 1660, disapproved on principle of having set forms imposed on them whether for baptism, burial or marriage. But others might share these objections on general libertarian as distinct from libertine grounds. Such people no doubt supported Barebone's Parliament's act for civil marriage, which seems to have been widely observed. The number and frequency of marriages increased between 1653 and 1660 in the only area so far investigated, which may suggest that some types whose marriages would previously have been "clandestine" had no objection to being married by a J.P. Those who

welcomed civil marriage may have included some Ranters; but also
Milton.

In Book IV of *Paradise Lost* Milton went out of his way to stress
the informal nature of the marriage of Adam and Eve.

> Other rites
> Observing none, but adoration pure,
> Which God likes best, into their inmost bower
> Handed they went ....
> Whatever hypocrites austerely talk
> Of purity and place and innocence,
> Defaming as impure what God declares
> Pure, and commands to some, leaves free to all.

Church marriage ("place") is totally superfluous. Adam and Eve had
fulfilled the necessary conditions for a valid informal marriage.
"Heavenly choirs" of angels were witnesses. This defence of informal marriage (sharply distinguished from "casual fruition") had
to be made covertly to get past the censor. As with his inclusion of
polygamy in his hymn to wedded love, Milton went to such devious
lengths because he attached importance to the permissibility of non-
church marriage and of polygamy.[77] The evidence suggests he was
not unique in either case.

Parish registers for demographers are rather like the words on the
page for literary critics. Both — let us start by insisting — are the
essential starting point. But some literary critics have managed to
carry on as though there was nothing but the words on the page.
They analyse them, interpret them, argue about them, generalize
from them, as though they had not come into existence in a real
world: without asking how and why these particular words and no
others got on to the printed page, why some words could never get
into print at all. Under censorship, what gets printed is the orthodox,
the accepted, what the society's ideologists want to think actually
happens or is believed. Similarly some demographers compile large
statistics on the assumption that parish registers tell us the whole
truth about the community whose officers produce them. With a
myopia very like that of words-on-the-page critics, they do not press
hard enough in their search for social misfits and "deviants" (loaded
word), for infanticide and concealed illegitimate children, for irregular marriages, by sale or exchange or by declaration before the
congregation, for the nonconformists who would avoid registration
if they possibly could and would go to another parish to avoid one

they had particular reason to dislike, for the complex facts of migration in a highly mobile society, and for the dislike of paying fees that was not peculiar to seventeenth-century England. Parish registers tell us what orthodoxy thought (or hoped) was the case about baptisms, marriages and burials. Whenever historians have tried to get beyond the written page of parish registers, they have found that they are far from accurate. Like the printed page, they are the end-product of countless social pressures, censorships, evasions, compromises, cowardices, fears of penalties for "deviancy".

One of the highest standards of accuracy so far discovered in seventeenth-century parish registers comes from six selected London parishes.[78] But by 1740 informal Fleet marriages in London very nearly equalled the total number of marriages which demographers would expect from their estimate of London's population. No doubt many Fleet customers came to London specially for the purpose, but even so there seems to be something to explain here. Those marrying in the Fleet came mainly from the artisan sector of society.[79]

In the "dark corners" of England informal marriage gave concern all through the 17th century. In Scotland until the 19th century the law still accepted the old tradition that consent made a marriage; couples could be accepted as married "by habit and repute" — i.e. the law recognized non-church marriages accepted by neighbours and friends.[80]

The object of the censorship in sixteenth- and seventeenth-century England was to present the appearance of a one-minded community, to prevent the expression of unorthodox ideas.[81] Hence general agreement on such matters as the great chain of being, social hierarchy, degree, the wickedness of popery and Anabaptism, etc., etc. If all had been one-minded, of course, censorship would have been unnecessary. But there were ways round — illegal printing presses in England, books smuggled in from the Netherlands, use of Aesopian language, etc.

What was the object of parish registers? If we assume that it was, at least in part, to impose the monogamous family on a population many of whom had different marriage customs, then we should hardly be surprised if sixteenth- and seventeenth-century parish registers show the monogamous nuclear family to have been overwhelmingly the rule, anything else a rare exception.[82] This may of course have been the case, just as it may be true that all Englishmen and women thought the same orthodox thoughts. But — *a priori* grounds apart — there is evidence in each case to suggest that the apparent consensus orthodoxy may have been more apparent than real. The problem is to evaluate that evidence. It will seem, in each case, to be evidence about exceptional persons, "deviants," abnormal survivals. But if the object of censorship, and of registration of baptisms, marriages and burials is precisely to turn those who do not fit the officially approved modes into "deviants", we have to probe very carefully. On the one hand there may be more "deviants" than are allowed to meet the eye. On the other hand, we must not let such an assumption affect our handling of the available evidence. The important thing is to be open to the possibilities, not to assume one-mindedness because that appears on the surface, nor to assume pluralism because of the occasional glimpses which we catch. Above all, not taking for granted either that censorship is natural and proper, that nobody struggles against it, or that parish registers serve no social purposes and are subject to no social influences. Neither censorship nor compulsory registration are value-free.

I add nothing to what I have said about Professor Stone's view that married love, and the love of parents for their children, were invented in the eighteenth century. There is much to be said; but Stone's critics have been almost unanimous in rejecting this idea of his, and have drawn on a powerful body of seventeenth-century (and earlier) evidence to the contrary. I am sure Bernard Capp is nearer the mark when he says "the literature suggests very strongly that young people [of the lower classes] regarded love as the chief consideration in marriage".[83]

NOTES

1. Palliser, "Tawney's century: Brave New World or Malthusian Trap?" *Ec.H.R.*, 35 (1982), p. 341.
2. See M. Drake, "An Elementary Exercise in Parish Register Demography", *Ec.H.R.* 14 (1962); D. V. Glass, J. T. Krause and D. E. C. Eversley in *Population History: Essays in Historical Demography* (ed. Glass and Eversley, 1965), esp. pp. 170-2, 380-93, 394-8; J. H. Hollingsworth, *Historical Demography* (1969), esp. pp. 166, 184-96; D. Levine, "The Reliability of Parochial Registration and the Representativeness

of Family Reconstruction", *Population Studies*, 30 (1976), pp. 107-22; R. E. Jones, "Infant Mortality in Rural North Shropshire, 1561-1810", *ibid.*, pp. 305-17; E. A. Wrigley, "Births and Deaths: The Use of Anglican Baptism Registers as a Source of Information about the Numbers of Births in England before the Beginning of Civil Registration", *ibid*, 31 (1977), *passim*, Wrigley and R. S. Schofield, *The Population History of England*, 54-1871 (1981), esp. pp. 1-5, 15-16, 19-32, 166-73, 454-7, 705-7; Paul Slack, *The Impact of Plague in Tudor and Stuart England* (1985), pp. 55, 83, 106, 149; J. Gillis, *For Better, for Worse: British Marriages, 1600 to the Present* (Oxford U.P., 1985), esp. pp. 6, 16, 186, 219; P. S. Seaver, *Wallington's World*, pp. 227-8.

3. Chambers, *op. cit.*, p. 107; D. C. Moore, "In Search of a New Past, 1820-1870", in Schlatter, *Recent Views on British History: Essays on Historical Writing since 1966*, pp. 257-8.

4. R. S. Schofield, "The Representativeness of Family Reconstitution", *Local Population Studies*, 8 (1972), pp. 15-16.

5. Wrigley, "Births and Baptisms", p. 310.

6. *Op. cit.*, p. 103. Cf. M. W. Flinn's review of this book in *Ec. H. R.*, 35 (1982), pp. 443-57.

7. Glass, *Numbering the People: the 18th-century Population Controversy and the Development of census and vital statistics in Britain* (1978), Chapter 4.

8. Hollingsworth, review in *Ec. H. R.*, 35 (1982), p. 306; cf. his *Historical Demography*, esp. Chapter 5.

9. Spufford, *Contrasting Communities*, pp. 20, 27.

10. *Ibid.*, pp. 166-7. Deaths of dissenters were sometimes recorded even though they were not buried in the churchyard (*ibid.*, p. 301).

11. P. Earle, *Monmouth's Rebels* (1977), pp. 209, 225.

12. R. J. Milward, *Wimbledon in the Time of the Civil War* (Epsom, Surrey, 1976), pp. 41-3, 106, 124.

13. Wrigley, "Clandestine Marriage in Tetbury in the late 17th century", *Local Population Studies*, 10 (1973), pp. 15-16; cf. "Births and Baptisms", p. 281.

14. L. Bradley, "Common-law Marriage: a possible cause of under-registration", *Local Population Studies*, 11 (1973), p. 43.

15. V. Skipp, *Crisis and Development: An Ecological Study of the Forest of Arden, 1570-1674*, p. 121.

16. Wrightson and Levine, *op. cit.*, p. 47; cf. p. 168n, and Wrightson, "The Nadir of English Illegitimacy in the 17th century", in *Bastardy and its Comparative History*, pp. 184-91.

17. P. Slack, "Poverty and Politics in Salisbury, 1597-1666", in *Crisis and Order in English Towns*, p. 316.

18. Maureen Duffy, *Inherit the Earth: A Social History* (1980), pp. 47, 135; cf. P. J. Corfield, *The Impact of English Towns, 1700-1800* (Oxford U.P., 1982), p. 118: growing deficiency of registration in eighteenth-century London, Leeds, Nottingham and Exeter.

19. Hunt, *The Puritan Moment*, pp. 77-8. He gives examples.

20. I owe this point to Dr. John Gillis.

21. Reviewing Wrigley and Schofield's *The Population History of England*, in *Ec.H.R.*, 35 (1982), p. 449.

22. Pepys, *Diary*, 30 and 31 August 1665; cf. *Diary* (ed. R. Latham and W. Matthews, X (companion vol., 1983), p. 33.

23. A review by T. H. Hollingsworth, quoting Dekker, in *Ec.H.R.*, 35 (1982), p. 301.

24. P. Clark, *English Provincial Society from the Reformation to the Revolution*, pp. 156, 437; Quaife, *Wanton Wenches and Wayward Wives* pp. 56-7; P. A. Slack, "Vagrants and Vagrancy in England, 1598-1664", *Ec. H.R.*, 27 (1974), p. 360. Cf. p. 19 above.

25. Glass, *Numbering the People*, p. 15. Except, he adds meticulously, between 1653 and 1660 and 1694 and 1704.

26. Jones, *op. cit.*, pp. 305-17.

27. Cf. Milward, *op. cit.*, p. 121. See review by Peter Clark in *Ec.H.R.*, 28 (1975), p. 141.

28. Quaife, *op. cit.*, p. 57; cf. A. Macfarlane, "Illegitimacy and Illegitimates in English History", pp. 78-80.

29. Wrightson, "Infanticide in earlier 17th-century England", *Local Population Studies*, 15 (1975), pp. 17-19.

30. Quoted by H. J. C. Grierson, *Cross-Currents in English Literature of the 17th Century* (1948), p. 295. Dr Macfarlane quotes a Colchester man in 1638: "Tush, it was not the first she had made away" (*op. cit.*, p. 77).

31. Collinson, *Godly People: Essays on English Protestantism and Puritanism* (1983), pp. 9-10, 13; Duffy, *op. cit.*, p. 123; Spufford, *op. cit.*, pp. 27, 236, 258, 296; E. J. I. Allen, *The State of the Church in the Diocese of Peterborough, 1601-1642* (unpublished Oxford B. Litt. Thesis, 1972), pp. 99-100, 114-15, 123.

32. Ed. M. McGiffert, *God's Plot: The Paradoxes of Puritan Piety, Being the Autobiography and Journal of Thomas Shepard* (Massachusetts U.P., 1972), p. 34; Avihu Zakai, *Exile and Kingdom: Reformation, Separation and Millennial Quest in the Formation of Massachusetts and its Relationship with England* (Microfilm, Ann Arbor, 1982), p. 49.

33. P. M. Higgins, *Women in the English Civil War* (unpublished Manchester University M.A. Thesis, 1965), quoted by A. Fraser, *The Weaker Vessel: Woman's Lot in seventeenth-century England* (1984), p. 72.

34. Collinson, *op. cit.*, pp. 262-8.

35. J. M. Brentnall, *William Bagshawe: The Apostle of the Peak* (1970), p. 32.

36. Reay, "Popular Religion", in Reay, *op. cit.*, p. 96; R. S. Paul, *The Assembly of the Lord*, pp. 373-4.

37. Duffy, *op. cit.*, pp. 76-85, 92-8, 108, 123; cf. Macfarlane, *op. cit.*, p. 81.

38. R. Weimann, *Daniel Defoe: Eine Einführung in das Romanwerk* (Halle, 1962), p. 9.

39. P. Clark, "Introduction", *The Transformation of English Provincial Towns* (ed. Clark, 1984), p. 15; Corfield, *op. cit.*, pp. 118, 192.

40. Joyce Ellis, "A dynamic society: social relations in Newcastle-upon-Tyne, 1660-1760", in Clark, *The Transformation of English*

Provincial Towns, p. 209.

41. Reay, *op. cit.*, p. 109.
42. Spufford, *op. cit.*, p. 301.
43. R. O'Day, *Economy and Community* (1975), p. 25.
44. A. Macfarlane, *The Family Life of Ralph Josselin* (Cambridge U.P., 1970), pp. 114, 205-6. As Dr Macfarlane notes, all these practices increase the hazards of family reconstitution. I have benefited from hearing a paper by Dr Macfarlane on "Studying 17th-century village life".
45. Quaife, *op. cit.*, p. 21.
46. Cf. Milward, *op. cit.*, p. 106; Duffy, *op. cit.*, p. 74.
47. Milward, *op. cit.*, pp. 106, 113.
48. Quaife, *op. cit.*, pp. 21, 56-7; cf. pp. 190-1 above.
49. Wrightson, "The nadir of English illegitimacy", pp. 184-5.
50. Richard Gough, *The History of Myddle* (ed. P. Razzell, 1979), p. xxvii. Dr. Razzell refers specifically to Laslett's unwariness. Laslett himself admits "there was persistent, perhaps reasonably consistent, under-representation", but seems to regard this as unimportant (Laslett, "Introduction" to *Bastardy and its Comparative History* pp. 50-1). "Reasonably consistent" can only be a guess, if not wishful thinking. Cf. Professor Haley, cited as epigraph to Chapter 9.
51. Laslett, *The World We Have Lost*, p. 175.
52. P. Clark, "The Migrant in Kentish Towns, 1580-1640", in *Crisis and Order in English Towns, 1500-1700*, p. 154; cf. R. E. Jones, *op. cit.*, p. 316; O'Day, *Economy and Community*, p. 25; Macfarlane, *The Family Life of Ralph Josselin*, pp. 89, 114, 205-6. Cf. D. Woodward, "The Impact of the Commonwealth Act on Yorkshire Parish Registers", *Local Population Studies*, 14 (1975).
53. D. G. Hey, *An English Rural Community: Myddle under the Tudors and Stuarts* (Leicester U.P., 1974), p. 208; Wrightson and Levine, "The Social Control of Illegitimacy", pp. 174-6, 188-91.
54. M. Chaytor, "Household and Kinship: Ryton in the late 16th and Early 17th Centuries", *History Workshop Journal*, 10 (1980), pp. 25-60.
55. Wrightson and Levine, "The social context of illegitimacy", pp. 169-75. It is to Mr. Laslett's credit that he now recognizes that his premature hypothesis of a "bastardy-prone culture" has been effectively called in question (Laslett, "The bastardy-prone sub-culture", in *Bastardy and its Comparative History*, pp. 229, 238-40).
56. Wrightson, "The nadir of English illegitimacy in the 17th century", p. 176.
57. See also a sympathetic comment on Miranda Chaytor by Wrightson, *History Workshop Journal*, 12 (1981), pp. 151-8.
58. G. E. Howard, *A History of Matrimonial Institutions* (Chicago U.P., 1904), p. 363.
59. Laslett obscures this point by referring to the Western and North-western regions as "the most bastardy-prone" (*Family Life and Illicit Love*, p. 136). Those adhering to older marriage conventions by no means regarded their love as "illicit".

60. Ed. J. Hillerbrand, *The Reformation in its own words* (1964), p. 233; cf. p. 201 above for mid-sixteenth-century sects in England. For the official assumption that fifteenth-century Lollards would oppose church marriage, see *Heresy Trials in the Diocese of Norwich, 1428-31* (ed. N. P. Tanner, Camden fourth series, 20, 1977), *passim*.

61. R. E. Rodes, *Lay Authority and Reformation in the English Church: Edward I to the Civil War* (Notre Dame U.P., 1982), pp. 137-40, 178.

62. Wrightson, "The nadir of English Illegitimacy", p. 178; cf. Laslett, "Introduction", pp. 10-11. Swinburne's *A Treatise of Spousals or Matrimonial Contracts* was not published until 1686, though he died in 1623.

63. Ivy Pinchbeck, "Social Attitudes to the Problem of Illegitimacy", *British Journal of Sociology*, 5 (1954), p. 315; "The State and the Child in 16th-century England", *ibid.*, 7 (1956), p. 283.

64. Laslett, "Introduction", p. 49.

65. P. E. H. Hair, "Bridal Pregnancy in Rural England in Earlier Centuries", *Population Studies*, 20 (1966-7), pp. 235-40.

66. See note 19 to Chapter 8 above.

67. Hollingsworth, *Historical Demography*, p. 190. For informal marriage and divorce see now Gillis, *op. cit.*, pp. 17-20, 38, 44-65, 50-2, 78-9, 84, 88-102, 110, 209-11; S. Amussen, "Gender, Family and the Social Order, 1560-1724", in Fletcher and Stevenson, *op. cit.*, p. 209.

68. E. A. Wrigley, "Clandestine Marriage in Tetbury in the late 17th Century".

69. Stone, "Sex in the West", *The New Republic*, July 1985, p. 35.

70. Gillis, *op. cit.*, p. 46.

71. Laslett, *Family Life and Illicit Love, p. 136.*

72. M. Ingram "The Reform of Popular Culture? Sex and Marriage in early modern England", in Reay, *Popular Culture in 17th-century England*, p. 143. Cf. M. Spufford on the irrelevance of marriage for those too poor to have dowries ("Puritanism and Social Control?", in Fletcher and Stevenson, *op. cit.*, pp. 48-56).

73. *Ibid.*, pp. 144-6.

74. Cf. pp. 197-9 above. Ingram is contradicted in the same volume by Capp, "Popular Literature", Reay, *op. cit.*, p. 213.

75. Susan Dwyer Amussen, "Feminin/Masculin: Le Genre dans l'Angleterre de l'Epoque moderne", *Annales*, March-April 1985, pp. 274, 284-5, 290.

76. W. Hunt *The Puritan Moment*, pp. 74-6.

77. *Paradise Lost*, IV lines 689-775; cf. A. Rudrum, "Polygamy in *Paradise Lost*" *Essays in Criticism* (1970): *M.E.R.*, pp. 136-9.

78. R. A. P. Finlay, "The accuracy of the London Parish Registers, 1580-1653", *Population Studies*, XXXII, 1978, pp. 95-112.

79. R. L. Brown, "The Rise and Fall of the Fleet Marriages", in *Marriage and Society: Studies in the Social History of Marriage* (ed. R. B. Outhwaite, 1981), Chapter VI, *passim*; cf. Outhwaite's "Introduction", p. 13. By the beginning of the 19th century Rickman estimated that one-third of London deaths escaped registration (Chambers, *op. cit.*, p. 78).

80. T.C. Smout, "Scottish Marriages, Regular and Irregular", in Outh-
    waite, *op. cit.*, pp. 206-7 and *passim*.
81. Kathleen Davies suggests that the censorship may have prevented open
    approval of divorce before 1640 ("Continuity and Change in Literary
    Advice on Marriage", *ibid.*, p. 74).
82. See Laslett, *The World We Have Lost*, pp. 71-3, 130, for particularly
    naïve acceptance of appearance for reality in such matters.
83. Capp, "Popular Literature", pp. 212-13.

10. *Male Homosexuality in 17th-century England*[1]

"I think there is no crime in making what use I please of my own body".[*]

Alan Bray's short book opens up quite a new subject in English social history, in a way that is at once meticulously scholarly but human and democratic. Such passing references as historians have made to homosexuality in seventeenth-century England have been limited to gossip about James I and the Duke of Buckingham (and other handsome young men), or to Charles II's courtiers, including the second Duke of Buckingham. This was the coterie from which the scandalous play *Sodom, or the Quintessence of Debauchery* emerged, in which King Bolloxinion established buggery by law.[2] There has to my knowledge been no serious attempt to study homosexuality among ordinary English people in the seventeenth century.[3]

Alan Bray starts with a chapter "Word and Symbol" in which he tries to find out what contemporaries thought about male homosexuality. This is less straightforward than one might suppose. The words "sodomy" and "buggery" were used, and the practices so described were violently denounced; but the exact meaning of the words, Alan Bray convincingly shows, is unclear. "Sodomy" covered sexual licence of any kind, hetero- as well as homo-; "buggery" could include bestiality, intercourse with animals. The educated would know what homosexuality was; in his younger days the future James I described it as one of the few "horrible crimes" that a King was "bound in conscience never to forgive" (p. 62). But the ritual denunciations of what Sir Edward Coke called the "detestable and abominable sin, amongst Christians not to be named" (p. 61) may have conveyed nothing precise to simpler members of parish congregations listening to sermons against sin.

*Unknown young man, 1726: see p. 233 below.

Sodomy was associated with luxury, with sexual licence, with conspicuous self-indulgence. It was a sin of the rich, not of ordinary Englishmen: more likely to flourish in courts than in cottages. It was also a sin of the clergy, especially of celibate popish priests, monks and friars. In a play of 1538 by the protestant reformer John Bale, the character "Sodomy" was "decked ... like a monk of all sects".[4] In John White's *The First Century of Scandalous Malignant Priests* of 1643 more than one parson was charged with homosexual practices. Under the sixteenth-century statutes which made buggery a felony, those found guilty could not plead benefit of clergy.[5]

The Earl of Castlehaven fitted into this picture. He had homosexual relations with his servants, it is true; but he also encouraged one of them to rape his wife. And he was a papist. So it was easy to accept the strong language of the attorney-general at his trial: his crimes were "of that pestiferous and pestilential nature that if they go not punished will draw from heaven heavy judgments upon this kingdom .... That God may remove and take away from us all his plagues, let this wicked man be taken away from amongst us." He was duly executed in 1631 (pp. 29-31).

There was then a generalized denunciation of the sins of Sodom and Gomorrah, which God had punished by raining down fire and brimstone. But those who approvingly read the pamphlets about the Castlehaven trial would fit him into a picture of luxurious popish upper-class vice; it was remote from the friendly practices which went on among consenting males in the English countryside. Those who heard similar denunciations of Christopher Marlowe would note that the poet was notorious as an "atheist" and "blasphemer" (pp. 63-4). When the Bishop of Waterford and Lismore was executed for buggery in 1640 the crime here too had dreadful associations — adultery, incest and rape; nor was 1640 a year in which there was much sympathy to spare for Laudian bishops (pp. 14, 18). He too was the subject of a popular pamphlet.

Alan Bray's case is perhaps strengthened by linguistic usage. "Fuck" covered hetero- and homosexual intercourse, as in Rochester's line "Whether the boy fucked you or I the boy" (*The Disabled Debauchee*); and buggery was applied to bestiality even more regularly than to homosexuality, as in popular ballads about the Quaker and his mare.

Having cleared the ground in this way, Alan Bray turns to less exalted people. He points out that such persons married very late —

in the late 20s or early 30s for men — because of the difficulty of saving enough money to set up a separate household (pp. 78-9). That left a very long period between puberty and marriage, even if puberty came later in the seventeenth century than today, and for the poor was further delayed by undernourishment. What did men and women do in the years between puberty and marriage? There must have been a great deal of pre-marital heterosexual intercourse. A large number of brides were pregnant when they got married. But the illegitimacy rate was not high by comparison with late eighteenth-century England, when the age of marriage had fallen markedly; yet we have no satisfactory evidence for widespread knowledge of contraceptive practices, nor of infanticide on a significant scale.[6] A seventeenth-century clergyman accused of eighteen instances of buggery claimed that he was practising a form of birth control: he had a horror of fathering bastard children.[7] Was he alone?

Alan Bray also points out that large numbers of male servants and apprentices lived in very close proximity in their employers' small houses and cottages; bed-sharing was the rule rather than the exception. Although homosexuality was punishable by death, so far as the legal records tell us it was rarely punished at all unless other aggravating circumstances accompanied it[8] (as they did the Castle-haven case). "Homosexuality", Alan Bray tells us, "was effectively tolerated in the educational system". The headmaster of Eton, Nicholas Udall, was involved in 1541 in a homosexual relationship with a former pupil; but he was arrested only when the boy was found to have stolen school silver. The schoolmaster of Great Tey in Essex was charged in 1594 with being "a man of beastly behaviour among his scholars", teaching them "all manner of bawdry". But nothing seems to have happened to him. Udall was sacked from Eton, but his reputation and his career in the church, and his favour at court, do not seem to have been affected (pp. 52-3). Samuel Butler was perhaps conveying a point when he wrote, with an execrable pun, "as cautiously as paedants bugger".

In other cases which came before the courts, there were almost always aggravating circumstances — a violent sexual assault, or the seduction of the son of an influential neighbour (pp. 73-4).

In each of these instances what was at issue was primarily the maintenance of the social order, in particular the maintenance of parental rights, and only secondarily the enforcement of the legislation against homosexuality. So long as homosexuality was expressed through established social institutions, in normal times the courts were not concerned with it; and generally this meant patriarchal institutions — the household, the educational system, homosexual prostitution and the like .... Noticeably absent are prosecutions for homosexuality between masters and servants unless undue violence was involved or for offences involving homosexual prostitution, although the literary evidence shows how common homosexual prostitution was (p. 74.)

In this respect England may have differed from continental Europe. "This was not tolerance", Alan Bray insists. We should accept at face value "the expressions of fear and loathing which are to be found so readily in the literature of the time". English travellers wrote detailed and horrified accounts of homosexuality among relatively more tolerant societies — associating it with popery whenever possible. Sir Edward Coke remarked that "bugeria is an Italian word". Sir Thomas Browne thought "le bougre Italien" fairly represented the Italian national character (p. 75). John Garfield's *The Wandering Whore* (1660) derived from Pietro Aretino's dialogues; its main character, Julietta, "an exquisite whore" is Venetian. It refers to "effeminate men, ... whose vicious actions are only to be whispered amongst us".[9] Ten years earlier John Bulmer had associated sodomy with Turks.[10]

It was not tolerance; it was rather a reluctance to recognize homosexual behaviour, a sluggishness in accepting that what was being seen was indeed the fearful sin of sodomy. It was this that made it possible for the individual to avoid the psychological problems of a homosexual relationship or a homosexual encounter, by keeping the experience merely casual and undefined: readily expressed and widely shared though the prevalent attitude to homosexuality was, it was kept at a distance from the great bulk of homosexual behaviour by an unwillingness to link the two. Inevitably the evidence for a mechanism of this kind, although in this case very strong, is largely indirect.

He skilfully uses evidence from a number of legal cases to show that male homosexual practice was not in fact regarded too seriously. In one particularly well-documented case a labourer who was up before the justices for sexually abusing an apprentice with whom he shared a bed was not punished and was not even removed from the boy's bed (pp. 76-7). Interesting confirmation of Bray's thesis comes from two cases before the Admiralty Court. In 1608 an accusation which had been proved by two witnesses and the confession of the accused was dismissed by the jury: "We do not know". Twenty-eight years later Robert Hewitt was accused of "that crime detestable and abominable of sodomy, in English of buggery" with three separate individuals on a single voyage. But the jury found him not guilty.[11] It may have been different when in the Hampshire assizes of 1647 a negro was accused of buggering a white boy. But we do not know the outcome.[12]

Alan Bray's argument is then that despite the death penalty and pulpit rhetoric, there was widespread practice of male homosexuality in sixteenth- and seventeenth-century England, and that it was connived at so long as it did not upset the social order. There was no homosexual sub-culture. The only man who is known to have definitely asserted his homosexuality is Marlowe, an intellectual sceptic who enjoyed shocking, as when he suggested that Christ had a homosexual relationship with St John (pp. 63-4). And Marlowe came to an edifyingly bad end. Even on the restoration stage it was Nero in Lee's play of that name who gloried in his homosexuality.[13]

By the late seventeenth century all this has changed. There were now in London a series of "molly houses", open meeting places for homosexuals either in private houses or taverns. Here there was drinking and dancing, and the possibility of sexual intercourse. The molly houses, Alan Bray insists, were by no means the gentlemen's clubs described by Lawrence Stone. "They cut across social classes with a bias rather towards the lower and lower-middle classes; the aristocracy were almost entirely absent." (p. 138). Clients of the molly houses were united by "ways of dressing, of talking, distinctive gestures and distinctive acts with an understood meaning." They had their own private language. What most scandalized "contemporary journalists writing about the molly houses was the extravagant effeminacy and transvestism they could involve; and this was at the root of the way they worked" (p. 86.) This was for the first time a self-conscious male homosexual sub-culture, whose warmth and friendliness Alan Bray describes movingly (Chapter 4).

We should not suppose that "the more socially diffuse homosexuality of the earlier period ceased to exist, especially in rural areas; it is scarcely possible for example to imagine a network of molly houses existing outside a large city." (p. 88.) But what now appeared in the capital was something new.

Up to the closing years of the 17th century prosecutions for buggery were nearly always of isolated individuals and never of groups of people, and when they do occur they appear in a limited number of identifiable circumstances. Something fundamental has changed ... There was now a continuing culture ... and an extension of the area in which homosexuality could be expressed and therefore recognized: clothes, gestures, language, particular buildings and particular public places (p. 92.)

We may speculate about the reasons. The breakdown of traditional norms of behaviour and expectation during the Revolution of the sixteen-forties and the congregation of an unusually large number of males together in London, the Army and navy may have contributed. So, almost certainly, did the vast increase in long-distance commercial sea-voyages. By 1755 Samuel Johnson could define bugger as "a term of endearment among sailors". After 1688 there was a further weakening of ecclesiastical discipline. Above all the ideas of the 'forties and 'fifties, proclaiming many of Marlowe's positions, and the propaganda and practice of the Ranters, must have opened new doors. Sin, Lawrence Clarkson said in the 'forties, "hath its conception only in the imagination .... If that within thee do not condemn thee, thou shalt not be condemned." Clarkson was a heterosexual, but his loudly proclaimed principles could have wide application. The 1650 Blasphemy Act, with Ranters in mind, had condemned those who should claim divine inspiration to justify sodomy.[14] Later in the century men did not fail to notice that John Hoyle, "atheist, sodomite professed", "always loved the Rump".[15]

Alan Bray dates the public appearance of the male homosexual sub-culture back to at least the sixteen-nineties, possibly earlier. In 1669 the madame of a seamen's brothel in London, Damaris Page, also supplied sailors for gentlemen — and no doubt others. In 1726 there was what is described as a homosexual brothel in London.[16] The existence of molly houses was seen as a provocation by the forces of law, order and godliness, and they were periodically raided. These raids seem to have been instigated by the Societies for the Reformation of Manners which took upon themselves, with fresh vigour, many of the tasks formerly carried out (or not carried out) by the church courts. After 1688 the godly were freer to undertake this kind of activity: this may explain why the homosexual culture was exposed then. (It is also further evidence against Stone's idea that the molly houses were gentlemen's clubs. The Societies for the Reformation of Manners specialized in suppressing the pleasures of the poor: they did not risk tackling their betters.) In raids of 1699, 1707 and 1726 there were many arrests, followed by several executions, suicides and deaths in prison from disease.

Persecution of this "continuing culture" must have increased the consciousness of identity among male homosexuals, just as religious persecution had earlier consolidated the sectarian congregations (p. 93). There was now "little room for the quiet social and nominal adjustments of Elizabethan and Jacobean society: there was a sharp and painful choice to be made. It could still of course be avoided altogether, but now only at the price of a continuing confusion of identity, which increased in importance as the individual succeeded in making homosexual contacts, inevitably in exposed and dangerous circumstances." (p. 93).

The molly houses and the homosexual sub-culture survived:

Effectively they were tolerated, although in a tense and hostile atmosphere; and that accords ill with the violence and downright savagery of the periodic pogroms. For all the protestations to the contrary, one cannot avoid the conclusion that they served a function wider than the needs of those who took refuge in them: that society, however ambivalent its attitudes, had an interest in them. The alternative identity and society they were taken up with had an ambiguous result, and here the explanation lies: they served, in effect, a dual purpose, for they must have restricted the spread of homosexuality at the same time as they secured its presence .... For the same reason that for some the molly houses provided a solution and a means of escape, for others they effectively closed the door: too much was involved. They thus served the needs of persecutor and persecuted alike (p. 102).

Again the analogy of the nonconformist congregations in the years of persecution after 1660 is valid.

Alan Bray sees the word "molly", replacing "sodomite" or "bugger", as symbolic of this change. "Molly" encapsulates "behaviour that was not intrinsically sexual at all" but implied "a particular social identity" — "a sub-culture, a miniature society within a society, in its own right ... What had once been thought of as a potential in all sinful human nature had become the particular vice of a certain kind of people, with their own distinctive way of life. The change is revolutionary" (pp. 103-4).

Why? Here Alan Bray is at his best. "There is no linear history of homosexuality to be written at all, any more than there is of 'the family' or indeed of sexuality itself. These things take their meaning from the varying societies which gave them form; if they change, it is because these societies have changed." (p. 104). His argument is too subtle to be fairly summarized: it runs rapidly through the "crisis of a culture" in this period. The statutes of 1533 and 1563 had been directed against homosexual acts, not persons.[17] "The new ideas of homosexuality that appeared in England towards the end of the seventeenth century are not isolated phenomena: they are part of the emergence of that concern with the individual and the particular which is peculiarly modern" (p. 109). Mr Bray clinches his point by quoting a young man who was trapped by an agent provocateur in Moorfields in 1726, and arrested for alleged homosexuality:

"I did it because I thought I knew him", he replied, "and I think there is no crime in making what use I please of my own body". To have made such a claim in Jacobean England would have meant shaking off the accepted conventions and beliefs of society to a far greater extent than it required a century later (p. 114).

One might add that in between had come the Leveller Richard Overton's argument for democracy on the grounds that "every one as he is himself, so he hath a self-property, else could he not be himself."[18]

The appearance in England [Alan Bray concludes] of a separate homosexual culture and a distinctive homosexual identity were part of that far-reaching transformation which English society underwent in the course of the 17th century, a transformation which played its part in making the world in which we now live. The figure of the homosexual, either as we see it there in its first and early form among the molly houses or as it is now after more than two centuries of change, has never been a welcome part of the society, the atomized pluralistic society, which gave rise to it. But it is its reflection (p. 114).

In so far as the male homosexual sub-culture is a part of the culture of the English people we should welcome with enthusiasm the great understanding of its evolution which Alan Bray gives us. "This book should be judged", he wrote in his introduction, "firstly by its capacity to explain the many fragments from the past bearing on homosexuality which are now coming to light, and secondly by its ability to illuminate the world around us as history has given us it and — this above all else — to play a part in changing it" (p. 11). His will not be the last word, as he recognizes: but it is a splendid beginning.

NOTES

1. Review of Alan Bray, *Homosexuality in Renaissance England* (Gay Men's Press, 1982); first printed in *History Workshop Journal*, 18 (1984). Page references in brackets are to Alan Bray's book.
2. *Sodom* is sometimes, but wrongly, attributed to Rochester.
3. R.R. Burg's *Sodomy and the Perception of Evil: English Sea Rovers in the Seventeenth-Century* (New York, 1983) contains some interesting guesswork, but it relies on behavioural theory and twentiety-century analogies more than on serious historical research. R. Trumbach, "London's Sodomites" (*Journal of Social History*, 11, 1977) deals mainly with the eighteenth century. R.F. Oaks, "Things Fearful to Name: Sodomy and Buggery in Seventeenth Century New England", *ibid.*, 12 (1978), is useful on America. Cf. David Rollinson "Property, Ideology and Popular Culture in a Gloucestershire Village", *P. and P.*, 93 (1981).
4. G. Wickham, *Early English Stages, 1300 to 1660*, II, Part 1, *1576-1660* (1963), p.17.
5. J.A. Sharpe, *Crime in seventeenth-century England: A county study* (Cambridge U.P., 1963), p. 24.
6. All these remarks assume that the facts in parish registers, as interpreted by demographers, bear a reasonably close approximation to reality — perhaps a higly dubious assumption; but we have nothing else. See Chapter 9 above.
7. Burg, *op. cit.*, p.11.
8. In the eighteenth century, if not earlier, this appears to have been true of other crimes punishable by death (Douglas Hay, "Property, Authority and the Criminal Law", in *Albion's Fatal Tree: Crime and Society in Eighteenth Century England*, ed. Hay *et. al.*, 1975).
9. *Op. cit.*, Part 4, p.5. Reprinted by The Rota, Exeter U.P., 1977.
10. Bulwer, *Anthropometamorphosis* (1650), quoted by John Wilders in his edition of Samuel Butler's *Hudibras* (Oxford U.P., 1967), p.408.
11. Evelyn Berckman, *Victims of Piracy: The Admiralty Court, 1575-1678* (1979), pp. 51-2. There seems to have been a similar reluctance to enforce the death sentence in New England (Oaks, *op. cit.*, pp. 269-73).
12. Cockburn, *Western Circuit Assize Orders, 1629-1648*, p. 247.
13. Staves, *Players' Scepters*, p. 248.
14. J.F. McGregor, "Seekers and Ranters", in *Radical Religion in the English Revolution* (ed. McGregor and B. Reay, Oxford U.P., 1984), p. 132.
15. Cf. Maureen Duffy, *The Passionate Shepherdess: Aphra Behn, 1640-1689* (1977), p. 131; *Poems on Affairs of State* (ed. G.F. Lord, Yale U.P., 1963-76), IV, p. 213. When Hoyle was accused of buggering a poulterer in 1687 the grand jury's verdict was "Ignoramus" (Duffy, *op. cit.*, p. 255).
16. Ed. R. Latham and W. Matthew, *The Diary of Samuel Pepys*, X (1983), p. 307; P. Clark, *The English Alehouse: A Social History, 1200-1830* (1983), p. 236. I am grateful to Peter Clark for confirming the date of the

brothel. Trumbach rejects the idea that a homosexual sub-culture emerged at this time (*op. cit.*, p. 11).

17. Jeffrey Weeks, *Coming Out: Homosexual Politics in Britain from the Nineteenth Century to the Present* (1977), p. 12.
18. Richard Overton, *An Arrow against all Tyrants* (1646), quoted with useful comments by C. B. Macpherson, *The Political Theory of Possessive Individualism* (Oxford U.P., 1962), pp. 137-9.

11. *Karl Marx and Britain* [1]

"Can one be more clueless than in England, for example, where cluelessness has been made into a system?" *

Marx lived most of his life in England after coming here in 1849 at the age of 31. He never became anglicized in the way that Friedrich Engels did, the fox-hunting Manchester businessman who was his lifelong fellow-worker.

At first Marx lived the life of a poverty-stricken exile in Dean Street, Soho, and for many years he had to maintain himself by hack journalism. But as Engels's factory prospered he was able to subsidize Marx more generously.

Marx regarded himself as "a citizen of the world," but one suspects that he remained a German in accent and habits. Wilhelm Liebknecht tells a story of Marx in 1850 leaping from a London bus to go to the rescue of a woman shrieking "murder, murder!" She and the husband with whom she was having a drunken quarrel at once turned on the "damned foreigners," and Marx and Liebknecht had to be rescued by the police.

But Marx adapted himself to some English customs. He started calling Engels "Fred." Most weekdays he worked in the British Museum or wrote at home, but he accepted the English Sunday as a day of rest. After a long lie-in, there were family walks on Hampstead Heath gathering wild forget-me-nots and hyacinths, lunch at a pub, donkey rides and fairy stories for the children. By 1855 Marx was defending England against the criticisms of later refugees. "No language," he claimed, "is as rich as English" for jeering and abuse.

In 1855 Marx wrote for a German newspaper a hilarious description of a demonstration in Hyde Park against a bill prohibiting shops from opening on Sundays (yes, 1855!). To Marx's delight the

* Karl Marx, "Critical Remarks on the Article, 'The King of Prussia and Social Reform'" (1844), in *Karl Marx: Early Texts* (ed. D. McLellan, Oxford, 1971), p. 215.

demonstration encountered "English high society", parading in the Park "in their high coaches-and-four, with liveried lackeys in front and behind", and "a few mounted venerables slightly under the weather from the effects of wine". They were greeted with "a cacophony of grunting, hissing, whistling, squeaking, snarling, growling, croaking, shrieking, groaning, rattling, howling, gnashing sounds", together with "outbursts of genuine old-fashioned English humour peculiarly mixed with long-continued seething wrath. 'Go to church' were the only articulate sounds that could be distinguished". But when "one lady soothingly offered her prayer-book in orthodox binding .... 'Give it to your horse to read!' came the thundering reply". "Noble lords and ladies ... were forced to alight and use their own legs". When the police came they were "received with the popular ditty

"Where are the geese?
Ask the police".

This was a hint at a notorious theft of geese recently committed by a constable in Clerkenwell. Alas, even in the solidly virtuous Victorian days the police were not spotless.

"Marx could only become what he has become in England", Liebknecht wrote. Germany was too underdeveloped economically and politically: only in England could he arrive at his analysis of capitalist production and his critique of political economy. English technology indeed fascinated Marx as some are fascinated by American technology today. The sight of a model electric train filled him with "fire and enthusiasm". "Now the problem has been solved", he declared, "the consequences are unpredictable. The economic revolution must be followed by a political one, for the latter is only the application of the former." His attitude towards British Rail would not have been that of the present government.

Marx's academic training had been that of a philosopher. In England he made himself an economist, whose contribution has lasted better than that of any of his contemporaries. As early as 1850 he was giving a course of lectures on economics in London, which suggests that his English was already adequate. In the British Museum Marx found a wealth of unused material on the British economy, in government blue books which he was the first to exploit fully. He also bought his own copies from a waste-paper dealer in Long Acre.

In the Preface to *Capital* (1867) he paid handsome tribute to the authors of these reports, doubting whether it would be possible to find in any other country "men as competent, as unbiased and as free from respect of persons" as English factory inspectors and commissioners of inquiry into working conditions, health, housing and food.

Marx called England "the demiurge of the bourgeois cosmos," "the despot of the world market." World economic crises originate in England, he observed, as now in the U.S.A. Marx had come to England after experiencing the revolutions of 1848 in France and Germany, whose defeat he attributed in part to English diplomacy — another role which the U.S.A. has inherited.

Marx was impressed and astonished by the stolidity of the English social system, whose greatest crises in "the year of revolutions" had been large demonstrations on Kennington Common. When he asked Englishmen about the possibility of a revolution in their country, they all thought it out of the question. He observed with sardonic pleasure that English economic experts were congratulating themselves on "the prosperity and soundness of business just a month before the eruption of the crisis of August, 1857." But his own expectations of revolution in England were equally faulty, as he came to recognize.

Marx made contact with the Chartists on his arrival in England. In 1855-6 he was writing articles for Ernest Jones's Chartist *People's Paper*. In 1856 he made a speech in English at an anniversary meeting of this paper. English working men, he said, were "the first-born sons of modern industry," and he expressed his confidence that they would "not be the last to aid the social revolution produced by that industry — a revolution which means the emancipation of their class all over the world."

But in the difficult circumstances of the third quarter of the nineteenth century Marx soon came to realise that revolution was not on the cards in England. Emigration to newly-discovered goldfields, he said in 1864, "led to an immense exodus, leaving an irreparable void in the ranks of the British proletariat"; relative economic prosperity killed off the Chartist movement and its press. In the eighteen seventies Marx envisaged the possibility of a peaceful revolution by Parliamentary means in England, Holland and America.

It was Engels who remarked that "this most bourgeois of all nations is apparently aiming ultimately at having a bourgeois aristocracy and a bourgeois proletariat as well as a bourgeoisie", adding "for a nation which exploits the whole world this is of course to a certain extent justifiable".

Marx himself wrote in 1863 of the "apparent bourgeois infection" of the English workers. "The English working class", he wrote in 1878, "had been gradually more and more deeply demoralised by the period of corruption since 1848 and had at last got to the point where they were nothing more than the tail of the great Liberal Party — i.e. henchmen of the capitalists". They were led by "corrupt trade union leaders and professional agitators".

In 1868 Marx praised American trade unionists for treating working women with complete equality, unlike "the English, and still more the gallant French. ... Anybody who knows anything of history knows that great social changes are impossible without the feminine ferment. Social progress can be measured exactly by the social position of women". But the American proletariat was perhaps even less class-consciously militant than the English.

Marx's appreciation of the difficulties of the English working-class movement did not prevent him often losing his temper with individual Chartists and trade unionists. Normally he blew off steam in private correspondence with Engels, as when he spoke of "these thick-headed John Bulls whose brainpans seem to have been specially manufactured for constables' bludgeons." But in his published writings Marx reserved his eloquence and wit for those whom he regarded as class enemies.

Tories, he wrote as early as 1852, are distinguished from Whigs "in the same way as the rent of land is distinguished from commercial and industrial profit. Rent of land is conservative, profit is a dissenter by birth." The Church of England "will more readily pardon an attack on 38 of its 39 Articles than on 1/39 of its income." Whigs were "Grand Masters of corruption, hypocrites in religion, Tartuffes of politics." Fortunately, "the mass of the English people have a sound aesthetical common sense" which makes them despise both parties.

Whatever reservations or impatience Marx felt privately, he seems to have got on well with English trade union leaders. This was shown when the International Working Men's Association was founded in 1864. For years Marx had been concentrating all his energies on research for *Capital*, and was politically isolated. He knew little about the trade union personalities who invited him, at the last moment, to attend the foundation meeting of the International. Yet

within a matter of weeks, by sheer power of intellect and personality,
he became its spokesman.

He proved unexpectedly skilled at finding compromise formulae
to preserve unity and agreement among the heterogeneous body
during the next eight years. He drafted nearly all the statements
issued in the name of its General Council. After the publication in
1871 of Marx's *The Civil War in France*, glorifying the Commune of
Paris in the name of the International, two members of the Council
resigned.

"This is the only instance,' Chimen Abramsky tells us, "when
members disassociated themselves from a statement of the General
Council after it was published."[2] This was the more remarkable in
that *The Civil War in France* caused an uproar. The French and
Spanish governments called for suppression of the International, a
demand which Gladstone, then Prime Minister, rejected. In consequence Marx, hitherto an obscure and isolated figure notwithstanding the publication of *Capital*, became world famous or
notorious.

One of Marx's favourite ironical techniques in his writing was to
quote political enemies to make points for him. In Volume III of
Capital (not published in his lifetime) he cited a speech by the radical
John Bright in 1865: "Can we not say truly that the mass of the
nation, excluded from the suffrage, toils and toils again and knows
almost no rest? Compare them with the ruling class — but if I do that
I shall be accused of communism. . . ." Marx took especial pleasure in
quoting on his side that "systematic falsifier of history," Lord
Macaulay, and the Tory Sir F.M. Eden — whom Marx treated with
respect as a scholar in spite of his "crafty special pleading."

Marx showed his knowledge of the British intellectual scene by
those whom he cited in *Capital* — Babbage, Darwin's "epoch-
making work," which Marx had been praising in private for years;
Thorold Rogers's "patient and diligent labour," notwithstanding
the fact that he had been "Professor of Political Economy in the
University of Oxford, the hotbed of Protestant orthodoxy," was
quoted on "the pauperisation of the mass of the people by the
Reformation."

Marx enjoyed stressing the anti-clericalism of Sir William Petty
and Adam Smith. He always referred to Adam Smith and Ricardo
with great respect, but he missed no opportunity to be rude to
Bentham ("a genius in the way of bourgeois stupidity"), Parson

Malthus ("that master in plagiarism"), J. S. Mill (though "it would be wrong" to class him "with the herd of vulgar economic apologists") and Carlyle (of whom Engels once thought rather well).

When Marx was asked who were his favourite poets, he named Shakespeare, Aeschylus and Goethe, in that order. His daughters had so much Shakespeare read to them that they knew whole scenes by heart. Marx used Shakespeare's writings to make economic or political points. In *Capital* he quotes *Henry IV* (Mistress Quickly) to illustrate the nature of commodities, *The Merchant of Venice* to show the insecure position of the labourer ("You take my life/When you do take the means whereby I live") and elsewhere to illustrate the ruthlessness of capitalism.

Marx's citation of *Timon of Athens* on the power of gold has often been imitated: it derives from a fuller discussion in a then unpublished manuscript. One wonders how many of the audience at Marx's speech for *The People's Paper* in 1856 recognized the allusion to *Hamlet* in his toast to "the old mole that can work in the earth so fast, that worthy pioneer — the revolution!" There was a similar allusion in *The Eighteenth Brumaire of Louis Bonaparte*, published in German in 1852. This work also refers to *Henry VI*, and to Bottom in *A Midsummer Night's Dream*. Marx's *Address to the General Council of the International* in 1865 cites Menenius Agrippa from *Coriolanus*. In an unpublished manuscript Marx referred to the problem raised for him by the fact that "certain periods of the highest development of art stand in no direct connection with the general development of society. ... Witness ... Shakespeare".

On page 3 of *Capital* Marx quotes Samuel Butler's *Hudibras* to make a point about exchange value. In a famous passage he discusses Robinson Crusoe as an example of "economic man". He cites Hobbes on labour power, Bishop Berkeley on division of labour, Burke to illustrate "surplus labour", De Quincey on female labour. Others quoted include More's *Utopia*, Francis Bacon, Bernard de Mandeville's *Fable of the Bees*, William Harrison, John Strype, Adam Ferguson, and a host of others. All are used appropriately: none are dragged in.

We must add exhaustive references to early British economists — Edward Misselden, Thomas Mun, William Petty, Dudley North, John Bellers, Arthur Young. In footnotes Marx rebuked Adam Smith for cribbing from Mandeville, and gave unacknowledged sources for one of David Hume's *Essays*. Predictably, Marx cited Swift on Ireland.

Among his favourite poets were Burns and Shelley, whom he preferred to Byron. Marx thought the latter might have gone politically to the bad if he had lived longer: Shelley he believed would always have belonged to socialism's avant garde. Just to show that his literary judgments were not determined by political considerations, Scott was one of his favourite novelists; he particularly admired Fielding. Others were Dickens, Thackeray, Miss Brontë (Charlotte?), Mrs Gaskell, Charles Lever, Captain Marryat and Fenimore Cooper.

Marx was a great historian as well as a great economist. But — unlike Engels — he wrote no formal historical work; his writings are full of insights, tucked away in unexpected places, mostly unpublished in his lifetime. But they add up to a coherent view of English history.

Much of Marx's work focused on elucidating what the French historian Guizot called "the English Revolution." Marx was more inclined to compare the English and French Revolutions than — with Guizot — to contrast English moderation with French violence. "The revolutions of 1648 and 1789 were not English and French Revolutions," Marx wrote, "they were revolutions of European significance."

"At the outset," Marx reminded Guizot, "the French Revolution was just as conservative as the English, if not more so." "The free thought of the French Revolution which makes [Guizot] shudder so convulsively, was imported into France from no other country than England." Similarly, "socialism and communism did not originate in Germany, but in England, France and North America."

Marx spotted the existence of several contemporaneous revolutions all over Europe in the middle of the seventeenth century, a subject which has attracted the attention of historians recently. He anticipated Lawrence Stone's work on "the decline of the aristocracy." He spoke of

the wonderful vitality of the class of great landlords. No social class lives so sumptuously, no other claims like it a right to traditional luxury in keeping with its "estate," regardless of where the money for that purpose may come from, no other class piles debt upon debt as lightheartedly as it. And yet it always lands on its feet — thanks to the capital invested by other people in the soil, whereby the landlord collects a rent which stands in no proportion to the profits to be drawn out of the soil by the capitalist.

Historians might with advantage pay more attention to Marx's insistence on the capitalist nature of agricultural production in England from the sixteenth century onwards. He had grasped the crucial importance for subsequent English history of the abolition of feudal tenures during the Revolution. He noted that "in an age and in a country where royal power, aristocracy and bourgeoisie are contending for mastery, ... the doctrine of the separation of powers ... is expressed as an 'eternal law'". It is thanks to Marx and Engels that one of the few points on which the U.S.S.R. and China agree today is that modern history begins in 1640, with the English Revolution.

In 1844 Marx mocked those who looked for "the history of freedom ... in the Teutonic primeval woods, ... the freedom history of the boar". This hoary Whig theory has recently been revived as the last word of modern historical wisdom. Marx also devoted much attention to the history of India, and of Anglo-Indian relations. ("Whatever may have been the crime of England, she was the unconscious tool of history" in bringing about a fundamental revolution in the social condition of Asia). He discussed with Engels at great length the history of Ireland, "England's first colony," on which Engels was gathering materials for a large historical work.

The American Historical Association recently passed a resolution calling for a nuclear freeze. Drawing on its specialized historical knowledge, it asserted its duty to warn that a continuing arms race will almost certainly lead to world war. Some eyebrows were raised at this claim that historians have a right and a duty to warn, but Marx would have agreed.

He noted that in the seventeenth century "the English reaction in England had its roots ... in the subjugation of Ireland": many of the revolutionaries allowed their energies to be diverted to the conquest of Ireland in the name of anti-Catholicism. "The English working class," he wrote, "can never do anything decisive here in England until it ... makes common cause with the Irish."

Since the creation of the Irish republic and partition, Anglo-Irish relations have become more complicated; but Marx's sense of urgency is still relevant. "The English republic under Cromwell met shipwreck in Ireland," he said in 1869; "Non bis in idem" — don't make the same mistake again. Alas: not again, but again and again and again.

So Marx came to know England better than any other country, its economics, its politics, its history, its literature. It was from England that he influenced the German Social Democratic Party and the international socialist movement. Yet by and large the English did not reciprocate. After the Chartists, H.M. Hyndman was one not very satisfactory disciple. The greatest nineteenth-century English Marxist, William Morris, found Marxism only after Marx's death.

The British Labour Party is virtually the only working-class party which is not Marxist even in name. There have been splinter groups in plenty, but no Marxist mass movement. This calls for a fuller Marxist analysis than it has yet received.

NOTE

1. Published in *The Guardian*, 12 February 1983. I have restored one passage by Marx which was cut editorially.
2. Chimen Abramsky, "Marx and the General Council of the International Workingmen's Association", in *La Première Internationale: L'Institution, L'Implantation, Le Rayonnement* (Colloques Internationaux du Centre National de la Recherche Scientifique, Paris, 1968), pp. 78-82.

IV Ideas

12. *The Poor and the People*[1]

"The poorest man ought to have a voice [in Parliamentary elections];... *it was the birthright of the subjects of England".**

"England is a prison ... and poor men are the prisoners".†

I

One obvious point to start with. The word "people" is often abused today, as when politicians say "the people want this", or "the people won't stand for that", when they haven't a clue statistically about what the people want. But the fact that we can see that they are abusing the word shows that there is an agreed meaning. "The people of England" means the inhabitants of England, all of them, male and female, rich and poor. As we shall see, things were not quite so simple in the seventeenth century. Very few indeed used what Patrick Collinson called "that deceptive expression, the people" to include all inhabitants.[2]

Linguistic usage related to political practice. Only in the present century have all adults been regarded as people in the sense of having a vote for Parliament. Nineteenth-century historians took quite seriously seventeenth-century claims that the House of Commons represented the people of England, because it seemed to them that the Commons in their day represented the people, even though only a minority of the population had the vote. As so often, history has to be rewritten not because new evidence has been discovered but because of changes in the society in which the historians live. Introduction of universal suffrage has made historians aware of its absence in the seventeenth century.

When civil war broke out between King and Parliament in 1642, Parliament had to find arguments to justify its stand against the

* Sir Simonds D'Ewes, *Journal* (ed. W. Notestein), p. 43: 19 November 1640.

† Gerrard Winstanley, *A New-years Gift for the Parliament and Army* (1650), in *The Law of Freedom and other Writings*, p. 170.

King. He was accepted as the Lord's Anointed, ruling by Divine Right, and also by tradition, by historical and legal right. What moral claim had Parliament to oppose him? The answer found was that Parliament represented the people of England, and that the whole people was superior even to the King. Some even claimed, to the horror of conservatives, that the Biblical text "Touch not mine anointed" "refers to inferior subjects. ... This dangerous tenet", wrote a pamphleteer as early as 1642, "hath been buzzed into the ears of the people, as if they only were anointed, none but they".[3] But even if the people were superior to the King, awkward questions were raised in the free discussion of the sixteen-forties about the extent to which Parliament was really representative. The royalist Sir Robert Filmer had great fun pointing out that, so far from representing the people of England, the Parliamentary electorate in fact included perhaps one out of every ten Englishmen — the upper ten. Levellers made the same point from the other side; but they — unlike Filmer — thought that the franchise should be widely extended so as to make Parliament more representative.

Parliamentarian political thinkers got themselves into deep waters here. The rhetoric of the prosecution at Charles I's trial, when he was condemned to death as a traitor to the people of England, made great play with the superiority of "the people" to the King; so did the legislation abolishing monarchy in 1649. But even if the Long Parliament did represent the people, it was notorious that before the King could be brought to trial a majority of M.Ps. had to be purged by Colonel Pride. The Rump that was left of the Parliament, sitting on the bayonets of the New Model Army, hardly looked like the people of England — less so even than the Army itself, many contemporaries thought.

But then who were the people? The question remained. It had been asked a century earlier. When one of Henry VIII's propagandists, William Marshall, translated Marsiglio of Padua's *Defensor Pacis* in 1535, he had to interrupt irritably from time to time with marginal notes explaining to his readers that, despite appearances, when Marsiglio spoke of the people he did not mean the whole people. "In all this long tale he speaketh not of the rascal multitude but of the Parliament"; "wheresoever he speaketh of such multitude he meaneth when it is assembled in the Parliament". Machiavelli similarly distinguished between "i grandi" and "i popoli", those who own property and those who own none.[4] In Elizabeth's reign Sir

Thomas Smith declared that the "commonwealth consisteth only of freemen". "Day labourers, poor husbandmen" and others who have no free land "have no voice nor authority in our commonwealth, and no account is made of them but only to be ruled".[5] The point was insisted on by a frightened baronet in 1641: "the *primates*, the *nobiles*, with the *minores nobiles*, the gentry, consult and dispose the rules of government; the plebeians submit to and obey them". By 1641 the plebeians were not submitting and obeying quite as was expected of them. But after 1660 George Monck, now Duke of Albemarle, was able with more confidence to reassert that "the poorer and meaner people have no interest in the commonwealth but the use of breath".[6] Men of property in the seventeenth century inherited a horror of the Many-Headed Monster, an ignorant, irrational populace.[7]

So upper-class writers tended to exclude the poor from "the free people", though in no very precise or self-conscious way. They just did not think of the lowest classes (any more than they thought of women) when speaking of "the people" whom Parliament represented. The poor were non-persons. They did not serve in the militia, the army of property, but they could be conscripted into army or navy for service overseas. They could be compelled to work. They did not act as jurors or local government officers; they were not worth fining for non-attendance at church. They made no wills, left no inventories. Their daughters had no dowries. The anonymous *The Laws of England*, probably written by a Puritan in the sixteen-twenties or thirties, gave as one of the rights of "the people" — "those *jura familiae*, consisting in wives, children, servants, goods and lands", over which all fathers of families are "lords and kings in their own houses".[8] The best-known distinction between the poor and the people was drawn by Captain Adam Baynes, Yorkshire M.P., speaking in the Parliament of 1659. Discussing the causes of the civil war, he said "the people were too hard for the King in property, and then in arms too hard for him. . . . Property generally is now with the people. . . . All government is built upon property, else the poor must rule it". The poor appear not to be people, because they have no property.[9]

The question had come up earlier, in October-November 1647, in the General Council of the Army, meeting at Putney. The Army had just won the war against the King, and this General Council, consisting of the generals, some officers, elected representatives of the rank and file, with some London Levellers, was discussing what should be the future constitution of England — a unique occasion. Colonel Rainborough and some Levellers called — or appeared to call — for manhood suffrage, on the ground that every man had a natural right to the vote. The Levellers and their supporters at Putney were very confused when Commisary-General Ireton suggested that the same arguments could be used to defend a natural right of all men to property — i.e. to justify communism. Most of the Levellers were in favour of private property, and perhaps had not fully thought out the implications of resonant phrases like Lilburne's "the poorest that lives hath as true a right to give a vote ... as the richest and greatest".[10]

Rainborough uttered the famous words: "the poorest he that is in England hath a life to live as the greatest he; and therefore ... I do think that the poorest man in England" ("every man born in England") "is not at all bound in a strict sense to that government that he hath not had a voice to put himself under". Wildman repeated that "all government is in the free consent of the people"; therefore each person must "by his own free consent be put under that government". Ireton, echoing Sir Thomas Smith, retorted that "a man's being born here" gives him no right to a vote: the franchise is attached to property. By the people, Ireton maintained, is meant those that are possessed of "a permanent fixed interest in this Kingdom" — i.e. landed property. Colonel Rich added that if master and servant should be equal electors, then "the majority may by a law ... destroy property". If any property qualification at all was retained, he said, five-sixths of the people would be excluded from the franchise. What guarantee have you, Rich and Ireton asked, that if you give the vote to the poor they will not vote for communism and share out the property of the rich?[11]

The Levellers had no thought-out answer. They were probably divided among themselves. One of them distinguished between the free people and the poor. "All inhabitants that have not lost their birthright", said Maximilian Petty, "should have an equal voice in elections". He suggested that the poor had lost their birthright freedom by becoming — at least temporarily — dependent on others. This also applied to apprentices and living-in servants. A few days later the General Council of the Army voted to extend the franchise to all except servants and beggars.[12]

But Petty's was rather a sophisticated distinction. Most Parliamentarian spokesmen continued to talk of "the people", making it clear only when pressed that they did not include the poor. Thus Serjeant Thorpe, in his charge to the York Grand Jury on 20 March 1649 was reported to have qualified his assertion that kings were accountable to the people by adding "I do not mean the diffused humours and fancies of particular men in their single and natural capacities: but to the people in their politic constitution, lawfully assembled by their representative".[13] Similarly Marchamont Nedham, propagandist for the republican government in the fifties, declared "when we mention people we do not mean the confused promiscuous body of the people"; "by the people we mean such as shall be duly chosen to represent the people successively in their supreme assemblies".[14] Both might have been reading Marshall's marginal notes to his translation of Marsiglio; it is the nearest Nedham ever gets to a definition. Robert Norwood in 1653 asserted that Parliaments are "the people meeting together", who "choose from all parts of the land men from amongst themselves". Answering the question, who are to judge the justice of Parliament's laws, he replied "Why all Englishmen, the whole people of England, in and by their several courts and officers . . ., hundred courts, county courts, courts of inquest, sheriffs, juries and the like".[15] Here "the whole people" means at most all householders.

Thomas Hobbes came near to a break through when he argued that the state was founded on the consent of the people, and that all men were in this respect equal. But Hobbes had included competitive individualism within his basic psychology of man, and the object of his analysis was far from being the establishment of a democracy. Rather he argued that the form of government is irrelevant so long as subjects are protected from the anarchy to which their inherent competitiveness would otherwise inevitably lead. So the effect was to defend the *status quo* — any old *status quo* — against change of any sort: though once change had taken place it must be accepted. In his *De Cive* Hobbes had argued that the people must be distinguished from the multitude: "the people rules in all governments ... In a democracy and aristocracy, the citizens are the multitude, but the court is the people. And in a monarchy, the subjects are the multitude and the King is the people". Sir William Davenant in 1651 saw "the gentry" on the defensive against "the people".[16]

James Harrington (Baynes was a Harringtonian) elaborated a

republican political theory in which he always speaks of government as based on the people, but in his ideal commonwealth servants were not citizens. The distinction between freemen and servants seemed to him "as it were natural", not deriving from the constitution but existing before the state was set up.[17] Servants neither had the vote nor were allowed to bear arms. In England, he argued, economic power in the century before 1640 had passed to "the people" who had upset the traditional balance by purchasing land from crown, church and aristocracy. The revolution of the sixteen-forties had simply been a matter of adjusting the political superstructure so as to restore the balance. By people Harrington clearly meant men of some property. "The peasantry, partaking not of the balance, can (in relation to government) be of no account", and therefore "is not called the commons but only the third estate; whereas the yeomanry in England" are the commons, the true people.[18] So there are distinctions to be drawn between people and people. In one of Harrington's dialogues Publicola asks: "The Parliament declares all power to be in the people; is that in the better sort only?" Valerius (who appears to represent Harrington) replies: "The Parliament consisted wholly of the better sort.... It was, you will say, no democracy .... Yet this derived from the free election of the people". Publicola was still dissatisfied. "How free? Seeing the people then under lords dared not to elect otherwise than as pleased those lords". "Something of that is true", Valerius admitted; "but I am persuaded that the people, not under lords, will yet be most addicted to the better sort". "That is certain", Publicola agreed.[19]

In October 1659 Henry Stubbe, who had read his Harrington, distinguished between on the one hand "the nation" (all men except servants) who ideally should have the right to vote in a free commonwealth, and on the other "the people". Stubbe recognized that this was not the usual use of "people", asserting that "to be a part of the people, it is not necessary that one actually have land in such and such a country". Yet "to become a part of the people it is not sufficient that I do live in this or that country". "They only are the people who upon the erection of a government have empowered the legislators to act, being avowedly ready to stand by and uphold them in their actings". The people were in effect those who had actively declared for Parliament at the time of Booth's rising in August 1659. "Neuters ...are not considered as the people". On this showing Presbyterians were not people: all sectaries and many landless soldiers were. Only "the people" are entitled to bear arms. They would elect the Senate; Parliament would be "chosen by the whole nation, not the people only".[20]

For Algernon Sidney too (later the hero of the Whigs) not all the people were full citizens. "No man whilst he is a servant can be a member of a commonwealth, for he that is not in his own power cannot have a part in the government of others".[21] Locke echoed Harrington. "The people" whose social contract founded Locke's state had servants in the state of nature before the state existed: "the turfs my servant has cut" belong to me. The Earl of Shaftesbury, in about 1680, declared that "every paterfamilias ... has ... the votes of all his family, man, woman and child, included in his". Locke took it for granted that the poor, servants and women were all disfranchised.[22] For similar reasons "the meaner sort of people and servants" were normally excluded from service in the militia. "Rogues, vagabonds and other evil, dissolute and masterless persons" were however the main source of conscripts for military service overseas.[23]

James Tyrell, friend and follower of Locke, thought that "fathers of families, or freemen at their own dispose, were really and indeed all the people that needed to have votes." Servants without property in goods or land had no more reason than women or children to have a say in the institution of government.[24] (This attitude helps to explain why even the Levellers never advocated votes for women. The famous seventeenth-century phrases which proclaim the rights of man — "every he", "the poorest man" — all explicitly exclude women from sharing these rights).

Freeholders are the proper owners of the country, thought Defoe in 1702.[25] "When we talk of the people with regard to elections", said Henry Fox, father of Charles James, "we ought to think only of those of the better sort, without comprehending the mob or mere dregs of the people".[26] In early nineteenth-century America artisan republicans still differentiated between the people and the poor.[27]

The liberties of Englishmen had been fought for in the first half of the seventeenth century by the educated, politically-conscious sector of the people; they therefore believed that the fruits of victory should accrue to them. Voltaire made the point in 1734: "the people, the most numerous, the most virtuous, and so the most respectable part of mankind, composed of those who studied law, the sciences, of merchants, of artisans, ... the people were regarded by [the lords and bishops] as animals below the condition of men".[28]

Seventeenth-century practice was clearer than seventeenth-century theory, but equally unfavourable to the poor. In 1640 it was "the sense of the House" (of Commons) that "no beggar or man that received relief or is not subject to scot and lot is capable of giving his voice in election of burgesses". This was normal practice in elections in Parliamentary boroughs.[29] Similarly in parish elections those who did not pay poor and church rates had no vote.[30] This seemed to seventeenth-century men of property only just: those who were elected spent the money of tax- and rate-payers; therefore they should be elected by and responsible to them. In the countryside, moreover, Richard Baxter pointed out, "in most parishes the major vote of the vulgar ...is ruled by money and therefore by their landlords". Those whose poverty is "so great as to make them servants of others and deprive them of ingenious freedom" should lose their right to vote.[31] In the heady days of November 1640 Sir Simonds D'Ewes won some support in the Commons for his view that the poor ought to have the vote. But he qualified this a year later so as to exclude vagrants. Even so he was more liberal than most of his contemporaries.[32] The Presbyterian minister Thomas Edwards for instance regarded it as a *reductio ad absurdum* of any idea of universal suffrage that it would give the vote to paupers and women.[33] "Had women and children and servants and madmen and fools", asked Archbishop Ussher, "freedom of suffrage as well as men of age and fortune and understanding?"[34]

II

There is a theological background to such attitudes. In the reign of Elizabeth, Presbyterian Puritans had argued that laymen should share with the minister in administering the discipline of the state church, and therefore that lay elders should be elected by parish congregations. There were loud outcries that this would mean "the dregs of the people" selecting those who would supervise the moral behaviour of their social betters. Archbishop Parker deplored any system which allowed "the people to be orderers of things".[35] Defenders of Presbyterianism were at great pains to explain that they did not intend that sort of democracy. Only heads of households would be involved, said Thomas Cartwright.[36] Matthew Sutcliffe took him up on this in 1592, pointing out that on Cartwright's logic not only householders "but women and servants and young men, and all that are the people of God, should have a voice in the election, for all these have like interest in their pastor with householders". So "clowns and men of occupation should determine matters of religion".[37] William Stoughton in 1604 spoke of the "birthright" of the people whilst specifically excluding "the multitude" from the right to elect elders. "The multitude" were the poor as distinct from "the people". "Men of occupations", Stoughton insisted, would be elected elders. There should be no fear of the word democracy, provided the thing which the word represented was not dangerous.[38] Only Anabaptists advocated equality of servants and masters, William Gouge asserted.[39] "The Anabaptists are men that will not be shuffled out of the birthright of the freeborn people of England", one of them later claimed.[40]

Richard Hooker in 1593 drew attention to the ambiguity in Presbyterian arguments:

When they hold that ministers should be made with the consent of many, they understand by *many* the multitude or common people; but in requiring that many should evermore join with the bishop in the administration of church censures, they mean by *many* a few lay elders, chosen out of the rest of the people to that purpose.

Half a century later the Levellers were equally "going round in a circle by failing to define what they meant by 'the people'".[41]

Later Puritans were more cautious than Stoughton. When the Pilgrim Fathers sailed to America, "some of the strangers amongst them" let fall "discontented and mutinous speeches" suggesting that "none had power to command them", and that "when they came ashore, they would use their own liberty". "The people therefore", as Thomas Prince put it a century later, "before they landed, wisely formed themselves into a body politic ... by solemn contract" — which effectively excluded servants as well as "strangers".[42] In New England exclusion from church membership meant exclusion from the franchise. This made explicit what was implicit in England, where the parish had become a political as well as an ecclesiastical unit. The same persons had the vote in each. "Rogues, beggars, vagabonds", William Perkins and other Puritans argued, "commonly are of no civil society or corporation"; "they join not themselves to any settled congregation for the obtaining of God's kingdom". They were outside church and commonwealth unless and until they could be restored by labour discipline and hard work.[43]

There is a curious analogy between the idea that some of the people are full citizens whilst servants and the poor are not, and the dual meaning which Calvinists gave to the word church. It is the whole community; but it is also the godly within that community. In an ideal world both church and state would be run by the godly minority. This was rarely achieved in practice. It was difficult to identify the elect on earth: there were backsliders and hypocrites. But the theoretical distinction remained clear. It derived from theology. The elect were predestined to salvation from all eternity. Therefore in one sense Christ died for all men, in another he died for the elect only. Persons brought up in this theological tradition, who thought of the church as both the whole community and the elect minority within that community, easily slid from thinking of the people as all inhabitants to "the people" as the respectable minority. Dutch rebels at the end of the sixteenth century argued that their States-General not only represented but was selected ("made") by the people. But excluded from the people were "what we call the rabble ... as against the good, the decent citizens".[44]

The two concepts were linked in Stoughton's assumption that elected elders would be "men of occupations", respectable citizens. In the Parliamentary ordinance of 1646 which set up a Presbyterian state church in England, elders were to be elected by members of congregations who were not "servants that have no families".[45] Nor indeed was the slide from people to elect peculiar to Presbyterians. Bishop Lancelot Andrewes likewise had distinguished between "the common sort" and "true Christians".[46]

III

Religious thinking thus contributed by analogy to explain why men forgot "the poor" when speaking about "the people". But social developments helped. In the first place we must recall the patriarchal nature of seventeenth-century society. A very large part of the population — probably the majority — lived in households which were units of production, whether industrial workshops or family farms. The head of the household was manager of the firm, supervising not only his wife and children but also his apprentices and living-in servants. He was held responsible for their moral and religious welfare, and for their education and vocational training, no less than for that of his own children. The exclusion of women, children, servants and prentices from the vote was justified on the assumption that they were "virtually represented" by the head of their household.[47] When an apprentice or living-in servant married and set up his own household, then he too became "free" and possibly eligible for the vote. In 1647 it was arnged that "very many in the Army" were "servants and prentices not yet free", and so by definition were *incapable* of representing anybody.[48] Paupers and vagrants did not count at all.

Secondly of course, all political ideas were formulated by intellectuals, by men of some education. This was true even of interregnum radicals like Levellers, Diggers and Ranters. Of the three leading Levellers, Richard Overton had had a university education, William Walwyn — grandson of a bishop — was a very sophisticated reader of Montaigne; Lilburne — a gentleman's son — had had some legal training. Winstanley the Digger was educated at a grammar school and quoted Latin. The century before 1640 is the century of what Professor Stone has called the "educational revolution". There are far more schools in England, thanks largely to generous endowments by merchants and gentlemen. As English society was increasingly commercialized, far more people were needed who could read, write and keep accounts.

But the century of the educational revolution was also the century of the great economic divide. Those who prospered were a minority; but they were an up-and-coming self-confident minority, from whom much of the support for the radical revolutionaries was soon to be drawn. The mass of the population had to face an inflation in which the price of food rose faster than that of other commodities, and the price of the food of the poor rose more sharply than that of the food of the rich. One consequence was that landlords were encouraged to meet rising prices by racking rents, enclosing and over-stocking commons, and by a myriad other devices which saved them at the expense of the poor. Enclosure by agreement between the richer occupants of a village fortified their power over the community.

The net result was that a class of permanent poor established itself, at a time when economic opportunities were opening up for the fortunate few. Mass poverty was of course nothing new: what was new was the possibility that some members of social groups below the gentry might break through the barrier between indigence and prosperity. Education was vital to crossing this barrier. The poor could not spare the labour of their children, could not afford to maintain them at school once they had reached the age at which they were able to contribute to the income of the household — 7 or 8 years.[49] Only a tiny minority of the children of the poor were lucky enough to find a patron who would pay for them to receive a grammar school education, still fewer went on to a university. The universally observed phenomenon, that children of the gentry were usurping free places in schools that were originally designed for poor children, is not so much evidence of the greed and self-interest of the gentry as of the economic helplessness of the poor. So the lines of social division hardened; the vast mass of the children of the poor were excluded from access to the educational ladder up which some of the children of their more fortunate betters were climbing rapidly. It was almost impossible for a pauper to escape from the inheritance to which he was born. The consequence was stated brutally by the advocate of women's education, Bathsua Makin, in 1673. "Women are of two sorts: the rich, of good natural parts; the poor, of low parts". The former are educable, the latter not.[50]

The Elizabethan poor law had been codified after the famine years of the fifteen-nineties. Accepting the existence of a permanent class of paupers, it recognized and legitimized payment of relief to the deserving poor, as distinct from idlers, rogues and vagabonds; and it put the administration of the poor law, under J.Ps., into the hands of village constables and churchwardens. These were normally drawn from the middling sort, below the gentry, from the upper 10 per cent of the villagers who were relatively prosperous. As a class of permanent poor differentiated itself from these parish élites in the desperately hard days of the fifteen-nineties, sixteen-twenties and sixteen-forties — economic crisis and wartime taxation — so the problem of maintaining law and order became one which increasingly preoccupied parish élites as well as the gentry.[51] The poor were rightless, helpless, illiterate: their only resource in near starvation was riot. Not only did they exist only to be ruled: maintaining them in subjection and making them work was a major object of government and the possessing classes, joined now by the middling sort.

An act of 1610 declared that any able-bodied man or woman who should *threaten* to run away from his or her parish was liable to be sent to the house of correction and treated as a vagabond. The poor could be conscripted to labour as they were conscripted into the armed forces when necessary; but "the meaner sort of people and servants" were normally excluded from the militia, the army of property, because "the government feared to arm and train the lower orders".[52] This increasingly sharp division between "the poor" and the rest of the population may help to account for the trend in English Puritanism, from William Perkins in the fifteen-nineties onwards, which stressed the wickedness, the apparently irredeemable wickedness, of many of the poor. Calvinist doctrines of the predestination of the majority of mankind to eternal damnation reflected the social realities of English life in the early and mid-seventeenth century. Oliver Cromwell in a speech to his Parliament of 1654 said that Levellers wanted to reduce "all to an equality", an aim he thought likely to appeal to "all poor men and... all bad men". Harrington similarly spoke of "robbers or Levellers".[53] (Most of the Leveller leaders in fact were defenders of private property. Cromwell and Harrington were probably thinking of Winstanley and the True Levellers, whom I shall be discussing shortly).

The supposed wickedness of the poor also helps to explain Puritan and Parliamentarian emphasis on labour discipline, on the sinfulness of idleness. The "debauched" and "profane" lower classes notoriously preferred idleness to work, observed every saint's day as a holiday in a regrettably papist way: the poor law distinguished sharply between the deserving poor and idle rogues. Men assumed that the poor would work only to avoid starvation. A statute of 1550 had protected small cottagers building on wastes and commons. They formed a convenient pool of the cheapest labour for new rural industries. Commons and wastes gave them something to live on when there was no employment. "There are fewest poor where there are fewest commons", observed Samuel Hartlib. But improvement of England's agricultural production, and the profits of farmers, depended on bringing waste land under cultivation. The well-to-do came to dislike these "housed beggars", as Bacon called cottagers.[54] Enclosure, said Adam Moore in 1653, "will give the poor an interest in toiling whom terror never yet could inure to travail". Workhouses were deliberately made unpleasant in order to discourage applicants for relief.[55]

The ability to squat on uncultivated land was the last refuge of the vagrant poor. In the course of the seventeenth-century forests were brought under cultivation, some fens were drained, and other steps were taken to curb lower-class mobility. The 1662 Act of Settlement was accompanied by a drive against cottages. This was possible because the population explosion had ended: indeed, soon it was necessary to allow limited mobility for economic reasons.[56] At the beginning of the century, fear of over-population; at the end, fear of shortage of hands: from import to export of corn. Dalby Thomas expressed the new view when he said in 1690 that people are the wealth of the nation. But he hastened to add that by "people" he meant the laborious and industrious people, not the unemployed such as serving-men and beggars — and, he naughtily added, "gentry, clergy, lawyers".[57] Swift similarly distinguished between poor artisans, meaner tradesmen and labouring men on the one hand, and the idle rabble on the other.[58]

Richard Sibbes had spoken of "a company of men that have the image of God upon them [though he could not call them "Christian souls"], men that live miserable poor,... without laws, without church, without commonwealth, irregular persons that have no order taken for them".[59] Forty years later Sir William Petty described the poor as "the vile and brutal part of mankind".[60] "The stereotypes of the poor expressed so often in England during the late seventeenth and eighteenth centuries", Edward Morgan observed "were often identical with the descriptions of blacks in colonies dependent on slave labour, even to the extent of intimating the sub-humanity of both".[61]

Looked at from the other side, we must recall the hatred which many of the poor felt for a life of wage-labour as unfreedom. Permanent wage-labour and the poor law arose together.[62] Bernard Mandeville in the early eighteenth-century expressed the distinction between the poor and the rest of society by saying "we have hardly poor enough to do what is necessary to make us subsist" (Note the distinction between "them", the poor, and "us", for whom they work). "Men who are to remain and end their days in a laborious, tiresome and painful station of life, the sooner they are put upon it at first, the more patiently they'll submit to it *for ever after*" (my italics).[63]

If we look at seventeenth-century developments in this perspective several points relevant to our theme emerge. John Morrill recently argued persuasively that the seventeenth century had no word to cover those yeomen, artisans and merchants who were prospering at the time of the great economic divide; and he argued, less convincingly, that therefore historians should not try to distinguish them as a special social group linked by their economic position.[64] But I think we can see by now that the seventeenth century did have a word for them, though the usage of the word is so different from our own that we have failed to notice it. The word is "people" — those between the gentry above them and the permanent poor below them from whom they are in process of distinguishing themselves.

Secondly, the work of Derek Hirst on Parliamentary elections has shown how in the early seventeenth century the electorate — the middling and lower sort above the very poor in the towns, yeomen and freeholders in the counties — was taking a quite novel and increasingly active interest in national politics.[65] In the severe economic depression of the twenty years before 1640 — which Professor Bowden sees as perhaps the worst in all English history for the poor[66] — there was continuing fear of popular revolt. In the early sixteen-forties leaders of the Long Parliament used appeals to the people and the threat of mob violence to pressurize the King, though ultimately they got more than they bargained for.

Thirdly, the most radical Parliamentarian revolutionaries were drawn mainly from the middling sort in town and country, from those self-confident prospering men who were excluded from social and political privileges but who were distinguished by education and knowledge of affairs from the permanent poor. Such men were prepared to break with tradition and convention. There were many of them in the New Model Army: Oliver Cromwell deliberately recruited his Ironsides from "freeholders and freeholders' sons", "plain russet-coated captains". Such men from the middling sort were ready to emphasize the rights of the people as against the privileges of peers, gentry and big merchants: they wanted the franchise to be extended to them, and had no inhibitions about using lower-class support. But — except in moments of emotion — they did not really want the poor to be enfranchised. The well-to-do in urban and rural parishes wanted their growing say in affairs to be officially confirmed; but in the last resort such men of small property had more in common with the gentry than with the unpropertied. That is why the Levellers collapsed once they had failed to capture the Army. 150 years later middle-class French revolutionaries proclaimed the Rights of Man, and seem to have been genuinely taken aback when the Fourth Estate claimed that they too were human.

Fourthly, the role of Archbishop Laud and his followers perhaps looks rather different in this perspective. Laud was criticized by Puritans because his theological and ceremonial innovations were thought to be leading England back to popery. But the Laudians were objected to on social no less than on theological grounds. The Book of Sports issued in 1633 encouraged men and women to engage in traditional village pastimes on Sundays. Puritans thought they ought to have been improving their minds, or at least resting after their six-days' labour; parish élites agreed with Puritans that the pagan fertility rites which underlay the traditional sports were disruptive of the labour discipline they were struggling to impose. Laud opposed enclosure, because eviction from smallholdings meant loss of tax-payers, of trained men for the militia and of tithe-payers for the church, as well as creating the danger of riots and unrest. In the sixteen-thirties the Privy Council interfered with local control of poor relief and of wage regulation. The Laudians were not so much *for* the poor as *against* parish élites, against the growing control of local affairs by the middling sort in alliance with town oligarchies and the gentry.[67]

IV

All this may perhaps help us to understand the restoration of monarchy in 1660. After the civil war things looked like getting out of hand — Agitators in the Army were demanding manhood suffrage, mechanic preachers were collecting congregations and preaching sedition with no control at all. Regicide and the abolition of the House of Lords seemed to call all social subordination in question. Levellers, Diggers, Ranters, early Quakers were organizing the middling and lower classes. The more moderate revolutionaries felt genuine outrage and fear. They had been let down by those whom they had liberated. An Independent in 1650 said that the rule of the Great Turk would be better than that of the rabble rout.[68] Such social anxieties were to lead the men of property to restore Charles II — not quite the Great Turk, but certainly better than the rabble rout.

For a time in 1647-9 it had been claimed that the New Model Army *was* the people and indeed it was arguably a fairer cross-section than the electorate, since it included conscripts from the poor. "The people in gross", declared William Sedgwick in 1649, are "but a monster, a rude unwieldy bulk of no use; but here they are gathered together into one excellent life.... For an army has in it all government and parts of government, order, justice, &c, in highest virtue". So in the Army the defects of the poor, their ignorance and helplessness, were overcome; "they are truly the people, not in a gross heap, or a dull, heavy body, but in a selected, choice way".[69] The Army was controlled by "the people".

That may have been plausible in 1647-9, when the New Model Army, claiming to be "no mere mercenary army", took over power. But in the fifties the Army was repeatedly purged of radicals, was professionalized and used increasingly to repress the people it claimed to represent. So though a pamphleteer of 1653 still argued that the Army was "the people's power, chosen by the people, entrusted with people's welfare and defence", he had to admit that "by people is meant the sound, well-affected part, the rest are the conquered or subdued part, who can challenge no right in that free election which is the fruit of conquest".[70] The Army became increasingly unpopular as the fifties wore on, and left a lasting heritage of dislike for standing armies, which was shared by radicals no less than conservatives. It was merely pathetic when in 1659 a pamphleteer claimed that: "The Army is the principal body of the people", representing "the ordinary and common bulk of the people" better than Parliament. Power should rest with "the good people embodied in an army together with those that adhered to them". We may compare Christopher Feake, also in 1659: "the people (I mean the faithful among them)."[71]

I am suggesting that the distinction between "the poor" and "the people" was deeply embedded in the social reality of seventeenth-century England. The dilemma of the radicals in the English Revolution — and the dilemma reappeared in later revolutions — was that the poor had for centuries been kept away from politics and education. In 1642 Milton denounced the bishops who first "with a most inhuman cruelty ... put out the people's eyes" and then "reproach them of their blindness". Milton was happy with the way in which "that iron flail, the people" rather roughly overthrew the bishops' government in 1640-1. But Milton rapidly lost confidence in the people when he had seen more of them in action. ("Licence they mean when they cry liberty".) In the sixteen-fifties he among others realised that the likely consequence of introducing the wide franchise the Levellers advocated would not be a democratic republic but a return of the royalists to power: he contrasted "the people" with "the mob". The governors of the commonwealth "are themselves the people".[72] "Everywhere the greater party are for the King", wrote an Independent in October 1648. "If the common voice of the giddy multitude rule, ... how quickly would their own interest, peace and safety be dashed and broken?"[73] In the sixteen-forties Richard Overton had listed "Rude Multitude" among the supporters of Mr. Persecution.[74] The Presbyterians had shown that they could use City "mobs" for conservative purposes, no less than did the Independents for their purposes. In the revolution of 1688 Roger Morrice ominously noted that "there was another power (though it was unwarrantable) that the *mobile* had" beside that of the "natural rulers" of the country.[75] But by the end of the century "the mob" was notoriously fickle: Tories could stir up church and king mobs to rabble dissenters.

So what could the answer have been? Cromwell advocated "what's for their good, not what pleases them". The republican Thomas Scot spoke of "our new people, scarce yet proseletized". "We ... would have enfranchised the people", declared the regicide John Cook, "if the nation had not been more delighted in servitude". Hugh Peter spoke of using the Army to teach peasants to understand liberty.[76] It is Rousseau's paradox of forcing men to be free, the dilemma which the Soviet Communist Party tried to resolve by the dictatorship of the proletariat. But the C.P. became divorced from the people just as Cromwell's army did: what Trotsky called "substitutism", the rule of a minority in the name of a people whom in theory they represent, inevitably degenerates into something less admirable. The problem did not cease with the seventeeth century's failure to solve it: Shelley in 1817 admitted that "the consequences of the immediate extension of the elective franchise to every male adult would be to place power in the hands of men who have been rendered brutal and torpid and ferocious by ages of slavery".[77]

Laurence Clarkson, later a Ranter, in October 1647 was one of the very few who tried to stir up the poor to act upon a class analysis of politics. It is, he declared, "naturally inbred in the major part of the nobility and gentry to oppress the persons of such that are not as rich and honourable as themselves". They

judge the poor but fools and themselves wise, and therefore when you the commonalty calleth a Parliament they are confident such must be chosen that are the noblest and richest ... Your slavery is their liberty, your poverty is their prosperity ... Who are the oppressors but the nobility and gentry? And who are the oppressed, is it not the yeoman, the farmer, the tradesman and the labourer? ... Have you not chosen oppressors to redeem you from oppression?'[78]

Starting from similar assumptions to those of Harrington (see pp. 251-2 above), Clarkson advocated startlingly different conclusions.

Many reformers spoke with alarm, especially in the starvation years 1648-9, of the dangerous consequences that might result if something was not done to relieve the lot of the poor, hard hit by bad harvests on top of heavy wartime taxation, free quarter and plunder. In January 1648, "the poor" were seizing corn going to market and dividing it "among themselves, before the owners' faces, telling them they could not starve".[79] On 3 April 1649, Peter Chamberlen declared his fear lest the many who were starving for want of bread would proceed to direct action unless something was done for them. He advocated the nationalization of lands confiscated from church, crown and royalists for the poor to cultivate, together with commons and fens.[80] But only one thinker, I believe, followed Clarkson in looking at the problem from the point of view of the poor, and advanced beyond him in proposing specific, thought-out measures which would not have been merely palliatives but which aimed at the total abolition of poverty — a possibility which Bacon had conceived, but which no one had done anything to realise. This was Gerrard Winstanley, spokesman for the True Levellers or Diggers.

V

The Diggers started digging up the common land near Cobham, Surrey, in April 1649. In defending their action, Winstanley quite deliberately spoke on behalf of "all the poor oppressed people of England" and indeed of "the whole world". "All laws", he declared in 1652, after the supression of the colony, "were made in the days of the kings to ease the rich landlord ... The poor labourers were left under bondage still". These laws enslaving the poor to the rich were backed up by the clergy, who promised the poor recompense in heaven, in the afterlife. Winstanley and the Diggers wanted a more tangible heaven, on earth, now. Victory over the King in the civil war had been won by the people, including the poor, who indeed had done most of the fighting as well as bearing the heaviest burden of taxation and free quarter: it was only right that they should now benefit by victory over kingly power.[81]

Winstanley believed that "that Scripture which saith, the poor shall inherit the earth" was "really and materially to be fulfilled"; the reluctance of the gentry to share the fruits of victory with the common people, "the gentry's hardness of heart against the poor", might lead to disaster in case of foreign invasion. For "the poor see, if they fight and should conquer the enemy, yet . . . they . . . are like to be slaves still". They say "We can as well live under a foreign enemy working for day wages as under our own brethren". It was therefore on all grounds essential to recognize that "the common people" (among whom Winstanley specifically included "poor labourers") are "part of the nation".[82] It was a direct challenge to traditionalists who held that the poor "existed only to be ruled".

"This is the bondage the poor complain of, that they are kept poor by their brethren in a land where there is so much plenty for everyone". A rational economic organization, based on collective ownership, would end the oppression and exploitation of the poor; this was the only way in which real equality could be established. Winstanley's solution was similar to Chamberlen's, but instead of urging the rich to make charitable concessions he called on the poor themselves to occupy and cultivate waste and common lands, which by right belonged to them and were withheld only by "murdering governing laws". For "the poorest man hath as true a title and just right to the land as the richest man". So he extended Leveller "natural rights" arguments from the franchise to property, just as Ireton had predicted in the Putney Debates. The Diggers thought it their duty to demonstrate that "everyone" should as his just inheritance "have the benefit and freedom of their creation, without respect of persons". "Will you be slaves and beggars still when you may be freemen?" they asked.[83]

"The declaration of righteous law shall spring up from the poor", Winstanley believed. "Magistracy signifies the greatest bond . . . that ties people together in love"; it should preserve all and despise none. And he asked: "Is the magistracy of the nations like this?" The answer could only be No: it favours the rich, despises and slights the poor. "In many parishes", Winstanley noted, "two or three of the great ones bears all the sway in making assessments, over-awing constables and other officers" — the parish élites to whom we have referred. Yet true magistracy is to be sought "among the poor despised ones of the earth, for there Christ dwells". Winstanley hoped that the Revolution in England would mark the beginning of a better state of affairs, in which true freedom would be made possible by the abolition of private property and wage labour and the establishment of an egalitarian communist society.[84] In the ideal commonwealth which he sketched in outline, manhood suffrage would be established, though supporters of Charles I during the war and speculators in confiscated lands would be disfranchised. Apprentices were also disfranchised during their prenticeship (for the traditional reasons), as were those who should be deprived of their "freedom in the commonwealth" for particularly heinous offences such as buying and selling or preaching for money. All magistrates were to be elected annually (including judges, peace-makers and ministers) by "the whole body of the parish"; they and M.Ps. were to be responsible to "their masters, the people who chose them". The sanction which Winstanley invoked was the might of the whole armed people, who would defend the liberty of the commonwealth against a foreign enemy, against "degenerated officers" or against any others who "through treachery do endeavour to destroy the laws of common freedom". There was to be no standing army.[85]

Winstanley, then, took seriously the equality of servants and masters proclaimed earlier by Anabaptists (p. 255 above). He envisaged a reorganization of society which would enable the poor to assert themselves as part of the nation. He was the only man, to my knowledge, who really tried to grapple with the problem of fitting the whole people to run a democracy. He came to recognize that this would call for a long period of education and political re-education to liberate people from dependence on the gentry and clergy from whom they had always taken their political ideas. In *The Law of Freedom* he proposed laws and institutions which would incorporate what he regarded as the true interests of the people, but the people itself would always retain control over the representative government which administered the laws, backed by the ultimate authority of the armed people. And by people Winstanley really did mean all the people. We may think his proposals inadequate (though they are worked out in far more detail than I have been able to indicate). He himself finally despaired of their being accepted. But at least they try to face some of the problems in setting up a communist society —in this he was well ahead of his time.

As the failure of Levellers and Diggers demonstrates, the poor in the seventeenth century were not only ill-educated but also divided by their economic situation. The Levellers appealed to men of small property, and Lilburne attacked the Diggers' communist experiment, though some of his followers were more sympathetic. The Levellers drew their initial support mainly from London and the Army. In 1649 they initiated a propaganda campaign in towns outside London, and began to turn to the countryside, laying a new stress on opposition to enclosure and defence of the property rights of small occupiers. They were immediately suppressed. The Diggers came at the socially dangerous point where rural and urban poor joined hands. They too were suppressed, perhaps coincidentally, after they had sent emissaries from Surrey to ten or more groups of sympathizers scattered through the Midlands. What later alarmed the respectable classes most about the very unrespectable and un-pacifist early Quakers was that they repeated many Leveller and Digger ideas and that they had a national organization. Such anxieties played a big part in creating the social panic which led to the restoration of Charles II.[86]

VI

We started then with a problem in political theory: how was it that serious thinkers in seventeenth-century England could not see that the poor were people? I suggested a possible analogy in Puritan theology: Christ died for all men, but especially for the elect. But we have been led ultimately into social history: differentiation between people and poor can be understood (which does not mean justified) only if we grasp something of the depressed and ignorant state of the poor in seventeenth-century English society, just as we can only understand the similar blind spot in relation to women if we recognize how totally patriarchal that society was.

I want to end by stressing not the inability of the men of the seventeenth century to include the poor within the people: that might lead us to conclude smugly that we are cleverer and nicer than they were. I want to emphasize that the thinking of some of them got far enough for the question of whether the poor were people to arise at all. It was raised nowhere else in Europe in the seventeenth century, so far as I know, and not again in England till the nineteenth century, after the Industrial Revolution had transformed "the poor" into the working class. It was not solved in practice, formally at least, until the present century. Seventeenth-century radicals made a fantastic intellectual leap in the revolutionary forties, culminating in Winstanley's proposals for an egalitarian reorganization of society which would enable the poor to assert themselves as "part of the nation". The intellectual leap, I suggest, was made possible by the rapid evolution of the household economy as capitalism developed in agriculture and industry. The unique preponderance of the household in the English economy, and of householders among supporters of Parliament, made the conception of the sovereignty of the people theoretically possible; but stratification among householders still prevented the poor being accepted as people.

NOTES

1. Delivered as a William F. Church Memorial Lecture at Brown University, 1981. Originally written for a Festschrift for George Rude, ultimately published in 1985 as *History from Below: Studies in Popular Protest and Popular Ideology* (ed. F. Krantz, Concordia University, Montreal).
2. P. Collinson, *The Puritan Movement*, p. 94.
3. [Anon.] *The Soveraignty of Kings: Or An Absolute Answer and Confutation* (of schismatics) (1642), Sig. A lv.
4. G. R. Elton, "The Political Creed of Thomas Cromwell", *T.R.H.S.*, (1956), p. 86. In *The Tudor Constitution* (Cambridge U.P., 1960), Elton appears to share this assumption that Tudor Parliaments represented the people, "everyone" (pp. 230, 300, 303). Cf. Bob Hodges, "Marlowe, Marx and Machiavelli", in *Literature, Language and Society in England, 1580-1680* (ed. D. Aers and others, Dublin, 1981), p. 10.
5. Ed. L. Alston, *De Republica Anglorum, A Discourse of the Commonwealth of England* (Cambridge U.P., 1960), pp. 20-2. Cf. Sir Walter Ralegh, *Works* (1751), I, p. 9.
6. Sir T. Aston, *A Remonstrance against Presbytery* (1641), Sig. I 4v; G. Monck, Duke of Albemarle, *Observations Upon Military and Political Affairs* (1671), p. 146.
7. I have discussed this at greater length in *Change and Continuity in 17th-Century England*, Chapter 8.
8. Quoted by M. A. Judson, *The Crisis of the Constitution* (Rutgers U.P., 1949), p. 337.
9. Rutt, *Diary of Thomas Burton*, III, pp. 147-8.
10. J. Lilburne, *The Charters of London* (1646), p. 4.
11. Ed. A. S. P. Woodhouse, *Puritanism and Liberty* (1938), pp. 53-6, 63, 66.
12. *Ibid.*, p. 53; D. E. Underdown, "The Parliamentary Diary of John Boys, 1647-8", *Bulletin of the Institute of Historical Research*, XXXIX (1966), pp. 152-3.
13. As reported by Roger L'Estrange, *Considerations and Proposals In Order to the Regulation of the Press* (1663), p. 20.
14. *Mercurius Politicus*, No. 78, 27 November — 4th December, 1651, p. 1237; cf. No. 77, p. 1222, and Marchamont Nedham, *The Excellencie of a Free State* (1656), p. 244.
15. Robert Norwood, *An Additional Discourse* (1653), pp. 44-8.

16. Hobbes, *De Cive* (ed. S.P. Lamprecht, New York, 1949), p.135; ed. D.F.Gladish, *Sir William Davenant's Gondibert* (Oxford U.P., 1971), pp.29-30.
17. Pocock, *The Political Works of James Harrington*, pp.786-8.
18. *Ibid.*, pp.436-7.
19. *Ibid.*, pp.786-8; cf. p.764.
20. H.Stubbe, *A Letter to an Officer in the Army* (1659), pp.52-4, 59-62.
21. A.Sidney, *Discourses Concerning Government* (1698), p.79.
22. Shaftesbury, "Some Observations", in *Somers Tracts* (1809-15), VIII, pp.400-1; J. Dunn, *The Political Thought of John Locke* (Cambridge U.P., 1969), pp.122-3, 131. Cf. H.R.Fox Bourne, *Life of John Locke* (1876), II, pp.377-91; Locke, *Works* (1823), V, p.71.
23. See pp.257-9 above. Cf. *Sir Henry Whithed's Letter Book*, I, *1601-1614* (Hampshire County Council, 1976), pp.11, 13 (1602): J.S. Cockburn, *A History of English Assizes, 1558-1714* (Cambridge U.P., 1972), p.129.
24. James Tyrell, *Patriarcha non Monarcha* (1681), pp.83-4; cf. pp.73-4, 118.
25. Defoe, *The Original Power of the Collective Body of the People* (1702), p.10.
26. H.T.Dickinson, *Liberty and Property* (1977), pp.78, 128, quoted in *1642: Literature and Power in the Seventeenth Century* (ed. P.Barker and others, University of Essex, 1981), p.230; cf. C.Robbins, *The Eighteenth-Century Commonwealthman* (Harvard U.P., 1959), p. 16; G. Rude, *Paris and London in the 18th century* (1969), p.293.
27. S. Wilentz, *Chants Democratic: New York City and the Rise of the American Working Class, 1788-1850* (New York, 1984), pp.93-5.
28. Voltaire, *Lettres Philosophiques* (1734) (ed. G. Lanson, Paris, 1909), I, p.103.
29. M.R.Frear, "The Election at Great Marlow", *Journal of Modern History*, XIV (1942), p.435; M.F. Keeler, *The Long Parliament, 1640-1641*, pp.33, 35; Derek Hirst, *The Representative of the People?*, Chapter 5.
30. H.Prideaux, *Directions to Churchwardens* (Norwich, 1701), p.51.
31. R.Baxter, *The Holy Commonwealth* (1659), pp.243, 218-19.
32. See epigraph to this chapter; cf. G.P.Gooch, *The History of English Democratic Ideas in the Seventeenth Century* (Cambridge U.P., 1898), p.154.
33. Edwards, *Gangraena*, II, p.16c.
34. J.Ussher, *The Power communicated by God to the Prince* (3rd. edn., 1710), Sig. D 6v-7. First published 1661. Ussher died in 1656.
35. Quoted by P.Collinson, *Archbishop Grindal: The Struggle for a Reformed Church* (1979), p.289; cf. pp.205, 247-8.
36. A.F.Scott Pearson, *Church and State: Political Aspects of Sixteenth-Century Puritanism* (Cambridge U.P., 1928), p.48.
37. Matthew Sutcliffe, *An Answer to a Certain Libel* (1592), p.188.
38. W.Stoughton, *An Assertion for true and Christian Church-Policie* (1604), pp.193-5, 362-72.
39. W.Gouge, *Of Domesticall Duties* (1626), pp.331-2.
40. [J.Sturgion], *Queries for His Highness to Answer* (1655), quoted by

D. B. Heriot, "Anabaptism in England during the 17th century", *Transactions of the Congregational History Soc.*, XIII (1937-9), p. 29.

41. R. Hooker, *Works* (Oxford U.P., 1890), II, p. 405; J. Frank, *The Beginnings of the English Newspaper, 1620-1688* (Harvard U.P., 1961), pp. 190-1, 343, referring to *A Modest Narrative of Intelligence*, No. 7, 12-19 May 1649.

42. W. Bradford, *History of Plymouth Plantation* (Massachusetts History Soc. Collections, III, 1856), pp. 89-90; T. Prince, *A Chronological History of New England*, Part 2, Section 1 (1736), in *An English Garner* (ed. E. Arber, 1895-7), II, pp. 410-11.

43. See my *Puritanism and Revolution*, pp. 225-7; *Society and Puritanism in pre-Revolutionary England*, pp. 274-5.

44. P. Geyl, "The Interpretation of Vrancken's *Deductio* of 1587 on the Nature of the Power of the State of Holland", in *From Renaissance to the Counter-Reformation: Essays in Honor of Garrett Mattingly* (ed. C. H. Carter, New York, 1965), p. 239.

45. Firth and Rait, *Acts and Ordinances of the Interregnum*, I, p. 749.

46. L. Andrewes, *XVI Sermons* (2nd. edn., 1631), p. 459.

47. See for instance John Eliot, *The Christian Commonwealth* (1659), pp. 5-6.

48. [Anon.], *The Case of the Army Soberly Discussed* (1647), p. 6.

49. Joan Simon, *Education and Society in Tudor England* (Cambridge U.P., 1966), pp. 195, 217, 370; D. Cressy, *Literacy and the Social Order: Reading and Writing in Tudor and Stuart England* (Cambridge U.P., 1980), *passim*; K. Wrightson, *English Society, 1580-1680, passim.*

50. Bathsua Makin, *An Essay To Revive the Ancient Education of Gentlewomen* (1673), p. 22.

51. R. H. Tawney, "The Assessment of Wages in England by the Justices of the Peace", in *The American Labour Movement and Other Essays* (ed. J. M. Winter, Brighton, 1979), pp. 179-80; Wrightson and Levine, *op. cit., passim;* W. Hunt, *The Puritan Moment, passim*; cf. my *Puritanism and Revolution*, p. 233; *Change and Continuity*, p. 202.

52. L. Boynton, *The Elizabethan Militia, 1558-1638* (1967), pp. 62, 108-11, 220-1.

53. Harrington, *Works*, p. 292; cf. pp. 429-30, 657-60, 840.

54. See my *The Century of Revolution* (revised edn., 1980), pp. 18-21, 131, 177-8; *Reformation to Industrial Revolution* (Penguin edn., 1969), pp. 56, pp. 56, 98-9.

55. Adam Moore, *Bread for the Poore* (1653), p. 39.

56. P. Styles, *Studies in Seventeenth-Century West Midlands History* (Kineton, 1978), pp. 186-93.

57. Dalby Thomas, "An Historical Account of the Rise and Growth of the West India Colonies" (1690), in *Harleian Miscellany* (1744-56), II, p. 343.

58. J. Swift, *Works* (1814), VIII, pp. 111-12.

59. R. Sibbes, *Works* (Edinburgh, 1862-4), III, pp. 40-1. Note that order is taken *for* them.

60. Petty, *Economic Writings* (ed. C. H. Hull, Cambridge U.P., 1899), I, p. 275.
61. E. S. Morgan, *American Slavery, American Freedom* (New York, 1975), p. 325.
62. I argued this in "Pottage for Freeborn Englishmen: Attitudes to Wage-Labour", *Change and Continuity*, Chapter 10.
63. [Bernard de Mandeville], *The Fable of the Bees* (3rd edn., 1724), I, pp. 328-30; cf. pp. 210-13.
64. J. S. Morrill, *Seventeenth-Century Britain*, pp. 108-9. Cf. pp. 46-7 above.
65. D. Hirst, *op. cit.*, *passim*.
66. P. J. Bowden, "Agricultural Prices, Farm Profits, and Rents", in *The Agrarian History of England and Wales*, IV, *1500-1640*, p. 621.
67. See pp. 50-1 above.
68. John Price, *The Cloudie Clergy* (1650), p. 14.
69. William Sedgwick, *A Second View of the Army Remonstrance* (1649), p. 13; cf. M. Kishlansky, *The Rise of the New Model Army* (Cambridge U.P., 1979), p. 251.
70. T. Lock, *The Extent of the Sword* (1653-4), p. 2.
71. [Anon.], *The Armies Vindication of This Last Change* (1659), pp. 3-6, quoted by Austin Woolrych, Introduction to Vol. VII of *M.C.P.W.*, pp. 124-5; Feake, *A Beam of Light Shining In the midst of much Darkness and Confusion* (1659), p. 51. I have discussed the further complications caused by distinctions between "the good people", "the saints" and the people generally in *The Experience of Defeat: Milton and Some Contemporaries* (1984), esp. pp. 288-90.
72. *M.C.P.W.* I, pp. 932-3, IV, p. 635.
73. [Anon.], *Salus Populi Solus Rex* (1648), quoted by H. N. Brailsford, *The Levellers and the English Revolution* (1961), pp. 345-6.
74. R. Overton, *The Araignement of Mr. Persecution*, in *Tracts on Liberty in the Puritan Revolution* (ed. W. Haller, Columbia U.P., 1933), III, p. 213.
75. Quoted by Howard Nenner, "Constitutional Uncertainty and the Declaration of Rights", in *After the Reformation: Essays in Honor of J. H. Hexter* (ed. Barbara C. Malament, Manchester U.P., 1980), p. 294.
76. J. Nickolls, *Original Letters and Papers of State* (1743), p. 28; [Anon], *A Complete Collection of the Lives and Speeches of those persons lately executed* (1660), p. 49; *Mr. Peters Last Report of the English Warres* (1646), p. 6.
77. P. B. Shelley, *A Proposal for Putting Reform to the Vote* (1817), in *Prose Works* (1912), I, p. 365.
78. L. Clarkson, *A Generall Charge or Impeachment of High Treason in the name of Justice Equity, against the Communality of England* (1647), pp. 10-18. "The commonalty," of course, did not "call a Parliament."
79. J. Wildman, *Truths Triumph* (1648), p. 4.
80. P. Chamberlen, *The Poore Mans Advocate* (1649), *passim*.
81. Gerrard Winstanley, *The Law of Freedom and Other Writings*, pp. 97, 108-9, 136, 170, 201-2, 373-4.
82. *Ibid.*, pp. 182, 372-4. Cf. epigraph to this chapter.
83. *Ibid.*, pp. 49, 104-6, 340; Sabine, *Works of Gerrard Winstanley*, p. 408.

84. *The Law of Freedom and Other Writings*, pp. 244-5, 281; Sabine, *op. cit.*, p. 205; "The Religion of Gerrard Winstanley", in my *Religion and Politics in 17th-century England*.

85. *The Law of Freedom and Other Writings*, pp. 314-21, 324, 345, 356-7, 361-2, 383-9.

86. See now Barry Reay, *The Quakers and the English Revolution* (1985), esp. Chapter 5.

13. *Science and Magic*[1]

Lady Loadstone: *You must give losers*
*Their leave to speak, good doctor.**

There are few subjects on which the attitudes of historians have changed more in the last few decades than the origins of modern science in the seventeenth century. We used to think of a conflict between religion and science in that century as in the nineteenth. We then argued about whether protestanism or Catholicism was the more stimulative/permissive to science. The assumption in most of these discussions was that science and religion were polar opposites; magic hardly came into the picture at all. But recently historians, especially those influenced by anthropological studies, have become increasingly aware how entangled with magic science still was in the seventeenth century. I am thinking especially of the work of K. V. Thomas, Frances Yates, Charles Webster. In trying to deal with my subject I shall draw very largely on their writings, though confining myself mainly to England.

Part of the problem is to define our terms. There is a great deal of superstition in our society today, as witness the astrological columns in popular newspapers. We say "touch wood", no longer thinking of the holy cross; we think Friday and thirteen at table unlucky, no longer thinking of the crucifixion on Good Friday or Judas as the thirteenth at the Last Supper; we avoid walking under ladders, though not because of Tyburn. But all these are vestigial: the fact that we speak of them as "superstitions" shows that we know they won't do really. We may not know much about science ourselves, but we accept as authoritative the superficially implausible view that the earth goes round the sun; we accept that the planets don't influence our personalities, that diseases are caused by germs, not by witches. Magic today is something that happens in pantomimes; or it is

---

*Ben Jonson, *The Magnetic Lady* (1632), Act V, scene v.

something that people pretending to be witches play about with. It is by definition irrational, anti-scientific, often consciously so. But magic did not seem either irrational or anti-scientific in the seventeenth century. If we start from J. D. Bernal's dictum, "magic was evolved to fill in the gaps left by the limitations of technique",[2] then we can see magic in more anthropological terms, as an attempt to control the outer world by methods which seem irrational in the light of modern science and technology, methods which assume the existence of entities and forces in the universe which are neither material nor susceptible of what we would regard as scientific analysis. In this sense there was a great deal of magic about in the seventeenth century, some of it intellectually respectable. Sorcery and witchcraft probably meant as much as Christianity in the lives of most Englishmen. Mr Laslett's notorious statement, "all our [seventeenth-century] ancestors were literal Christian believers, all of the time",[3] is true only if we give a very unfamiliar meaning to the word "Christian". Almost every English village had its "cunning man", its white witch, who told those who had been robbed how to recover their property, advised on propitious times for journeys, and foretold the future. Nor were such beliefs limited to ignorant villagers.

The best and most authoritative opinions favoured magic, in the sense in which I have defined it. In Roman Catholic countries bread and wine were miraculously turned into body and blood; holy water, crossing oneself, exorcism, wonder-working images, were all met with every day. In theory these had been abolished in England in the sixteenth-century Reformation, but it is likely that they still had a strong hold over ordinary people. The Laudians tried to revive many "magical" religious ceremonies in the sixteen-thirties. Belief in the existence of witches was still widespread. It was coming under criticism, and by the eighteenth-century prosecutions for witchcraft had virtually ceased in the English-speaking world. But in the early seventeenth century witches were still executed; defenders of their existence included not merely an amateur theologian like James I but many eminent scientists. The second wife of Oliver Cromwell's grandfather was believed to have been killed by a witch, who was hanged for it in 1593. Oliver's grandfather endowed a sermon against witchcraft, to be preached annually at Huntingdon for all time. Oliver must have heard many. In 1646 a witch was executed at Huntingdon. Yet times were changing. Cromwell's army in Scotland in the sixteen-fifties enforced a virtual cessation of witch persecution there. On the other side, Sir Thomas Browne and the Rev. Joseph Glanvill, F.R.S., still argued that those who denied the existence of witches denied the existence of spirits, and so ultimately of God. They had a point, as I shall suggest later.

Consider too what are now regarded as the pseudo-sciences of astrology and alchemy. Most astronomers took astrology seriously — the science which studied the influence of the stars upon events on earth, the belief that the conjunctions of planets under which a man was born would affect his whole future life and personality, and that at certain times and seasons the heavens were propitious for certain types of action. Words like "saturnine", "jovial", "martial", meaning born under Saturn, Jupiter or Mars, remind us of those beliefs. Most royal persons had their court astrologers: the great astronomers Tycho Brahe and Johann Kepler were so employed at the court of the Holy Roman Emperor Rudolf. It was primarily for astrological purposes that Tycho Brahe made the vast collection of observations which enabled him to redraw the map of the night sky. Isaac Newton first took up the study of mathematics because of his interest in astrology. John Locke and Robert Boyle used astrological reckonings to find a time favourable for planting peonies.[4]

Conversely, professional astrologers were well-versed in up-to-date scientific methods. Simon Forman's astrological studies stimulated a "constant and conscientious striving after accuracy". In the sixteen-fifties the astrologer Nicholas Culpeper was making use of the recent invention of logarithms to aid his astrological calculations.[5] Come to that, the man who invented logarithms sixty years earlier, John Napier, was said to value them most because they speeded up his calculation of the mystic figure 666, the number of the Beast in *Revelation*. Interpretation of the Biblical prophecies was the job of mathematicians, from Napier to Isaac Newton. There was an astrological millenarianism which agreed with the scholarly consensus among protestant theologians in thinking the end of the world was likely to come in the sixteen-fifties or perhaps 1666.[6] Fifth Monarchists like John Spittlehouse and Peter Chamberlen accepted astrology.[7] The fiercest opponents of astrology were orthodox theologians, whether Popes or Calvinists. Pope Sixtus V condemned astrology and magic in 1586; Urban VIII condemned both astrology and Galileo — though he practised astrology himself.[8]

To the defence of astrology came — the scientists: John Dee,

Tycho Brahe, Kepler. There was a very respectable academic Society of Astrologers in London a dozen years before there was a Royal Society. Serious rational characters like Jean Bodin in France, in England John Selden, Bulstrode Whitelocke, John Lambert, William Rainborough, Mrs. John Lilburne, consulted astrologers; important politicians like Elizabeth's Earl of Leicester, the first Duke of Buckingham, and Wallenstein, as well as monarchs, kept their own astrologers. The Earl of Clarendon in a speech to Parliament in September 1660 quoted astrologers who prophesied good things for the reign of Charles II.[9] Keith Thomas has suggested that astrology represents an attempt to explain social and human behaviour in scientific terms, in terms of law as against apparent arbitrariness; in some respects it anticipated sociology, he thinks. There was as yet no recognition that heredity or environment influenced human behaviour: astrology was a serious attempt at scientific explanation — and so ultimately at control. That is why many orthodox theologians opposed it — as a rival system of explanation of events otherwise inexplicable, and a rival system of control.[10] Although the idea of planets influencing human behaviour now seems absurd, it did not in the seventeenth century. And indeed, what was the supreme scientific achievement of that century, Newton's theory of gravitation, but an explanation in terms of a single heavenly force working across vast spaces — in ways that Newton himself had difficulty in explaining?

Similarly with alchemy — serious alchemy, not the mere hunt for quick means of converting base metals into gold satirized by Ben Jonson and many others. Bacon and Boyle thought it a worthwhile subject. Newton was fascinated by it all his life, and left hundreds of pages of unpublished manuscripts on alchemy. Sir Richard Steele believed in it.[11] Chemistry, from Paracelsus in the early sixteenth-century to Van Helmont in the mid-seventeenth century, was responsible for many of the main advances in medicine. Paracelsus and the alchemists strongly emphasized the need for experiment, for working in laboratories with one's own hands, trying out new chemical combinations. This led to real discoveries in medicine and distillation.

In addition to astrology and alchemy, there was in the sixteenth and seventeenth centuries a revival — or intensification — of interest in natural magic; and it is here that our definition of terms becomes crucial. Those serious scholars who worked in this tradition did not regard themselves as conjurors who produced rabbits out of hats or made brazen heads speak (though some of them might enjoy skilful mechanical tricks like the latter). Natural magic was defined as "the wisdom of nature" by Sir Walter Ralegh, "that which bringeth to light the inmost virtues and draweth them out of nature's bosom to human use", for "the help and comfort of mankind".[12] *Magi* who worked in this tradition — Robert Fludd, for instance [13] — believed that the wisdom which gives control over nature had been known to the ancients — especially to Milton's "thrice-great Hermes" — Hermes Trismegistus — whose writings were believed to have been composed in Egypt at the time of Moses. Much of this occult wisdom, it was thought, had been lost, much had been corrupted. The ancient philosophers — Moses in the early books of the Bible, as well as Hermes Trismegistus — expressed themselves in parables, wrapping up truth in mystery for later generations to unravel. But because Hermeticists believed in ancient knowledge which had been lost, they worked for its recovery by the direct study of nature, by experiment, rather than by the study of books. Francis Bacon's *Wisdom of the Ancients* was in this tradition, an attempt to elucidate the scientific wisdom concealed in classical myths; and Isaac Newton was convinced that he had merely rediscovered the law of gravity, which he believed was hinted at in many ancient texts.

There was then a continuing magical tradition of some intellectual respectability, which flourished down at least to the end of the seventeenth century, though by then it was growing a little shame-faced. Now magic of course is as old as human history, as men have attempted by various devices to control the forces of nature. What is new in the fifteenth–sixteenth centuries — or what seems to be new — is the renaissance of a serious intellectual magic, the Hermetic renaissance. I use the word renaissance advisedly. "The Hermetic texts", writes Dr French, "encouraged a basic psychological change that released the human spirit and thus prompted *magi* like Dee to experiment with the powers of the universe".[14] Dee was the greatest sixteenth-century English mathematician, who tried to establish contact with spirits and may well have been the model for Marlowe's Dr Faustus — possibly even for the friendlier portrait of Prospero in *The Tempest*, whose relationship with Ariel was not unlike that to which Dee aspired. Such men hoped to acquire new powers for the domination of nature.

The magical revival was based on rediscovery in the fifteenth

century of the texts attributed to Hermes Trismegistus. The spread
of these texts and commentaries on them was made possible by the
invention of printing. The scholarly Hermetic tradition bears the
same sort of relation to popular magical beliefs as protestant theology bears to traditional popular heresy. The secret wisdom of the
ancients had had a long life before the invention of printing: manuscripts *necessarily* circulated privately, reading was a skilled art. But
printing, combined with a new emphasis on literacy in protestant
countries so as to be able to read the Bible, made possible a wider
popularization of Hermeticism.

The salient features of the Hermetic tradition are the assumption
that the world is a living soul, not a dead machine; that no part of the
world is devoid of consciousness. Also assumed is the analogy
between the microcosm and the macrocosm, that there are resem-
blances and parallels between what modern science would regard as
different levels of organization of matter. Robert Fludd gave a
chemical description of the circulation of the blood which parallels
the circular motion of the sun.[15] Such assumptions draw on age-old
popular beliefs, which died hard even among the scientists. Certain
herbs — like the mandrake root — cure certain illnesses because they
look like the relevant parts of the body. Certain colours repel or
attract the influences of particular planets. Just as the seed is buried
in the earth, dies and is resurrected as grain: so metals can be
transmuted by fire and resurrected in a nobler form. Christianized
alchemy is thus an outward symbol of internal regeneration. Pursuing another analogy, heat in chemical experiments is seen as
parallel to the action of digestion in the human body. Chemical
processes can also be regarded as analogies of sexual intercourse, with
a new procreation as the outcome.[16]

The concept of analogy is the basis for belief for sympathetic
magic; the idea that an application of medicine to the *weapon* which
caused a wound can cure the patient. This belief was held by Francis
Bacon, Sir Kenelm Digby and other Fellows of the Royal Society.
Digby's importance in the history of biology is rated high by modern
scholars; it may be that his sympathetic powder did in fact achieve
cures because whilst the powder was applied to the weapon, the
wound itself was left clean and without the noxious ointments
seventeenth-century doctors favoured. Anyway the poet Thomas
Flatman, later Fellow of the Royal Society, was cured of a wound by a
plaster applied to the offending knife; the powder of sympathy was

administered to the rationalist Earl of Shaftesbury by the rationalist Dr John Locke[17]. Here is a prescription for relieving "violent nephritical pains" (pains of the kidneys): "take three stone quart jugs — fill them with the urine of the patient, stop them close, bury them a yard underground and lay a tile over them that the earth fall not close upon them". The date is 1681: the doctor is John Locke.[18]

This all derives from a traditional animism which also died hard. Giordano Bruno and Campanella believed that the earth and other planets were alive. Kepler said "once I firmly believed that the motive force of a planet was a soul" and he continued to assume that planets had an inner motive force. The universe above the moon was thought to be composed of a matter different from and superior to that of the sublunary sphere: it was a great shock when Galileo's telescope revealed that the moon was not a perfect sphere, that there were spots on the sun. Kepler believed that the universe was constructed around geometrical forms and musical harmonies.[19] There was a similar belief that minerals grow in the earth, and that every now and then a mine should be left alone to give it time to replenish; or that, as Bacon and others held, worms and other small insects are spontaneously generated in mud and slime — as well they might seem to be before the invention of the microscope. All these beliefs were still perfectly respectable in the early seventeenth century, and indeed reasonable in the then state of technical knowledge: spontaneous generation was first clearly challenged by Harvey in 1651. In such a world there was nothing outrageous about alchemy, astrology, witchcraft or magic: they all fitted well into universally held assumptions.

Giordano Bruno in the late sixteenth century fused Copernicus's heliocentric doctrine with the Hermetic tradition. As late as the seventies and eighties of the seventeenth century the Secretary of the Royal Society, Henry Oldenburg, and John Flamsteed, Astronomer Royal, both regarded the Copernican hypothesis as not yet scientifically established.[20] Recent students of Francis Bacon, the ideological founder of modern science, have stressed Hermetic and millenarian elements in his thought. Exponents of the Paracelsan and Hermetic traditions in the seventeenth century were no less critical of the established scholastic Aristotelianism of the universities than were experimental mechanical philosophers. In 1654 John Webster, just as much as his opponents Wilkins and Ward, looked back to Bacon.[21] Indeed, *serious* study of the folk magic practised by

cunning men is strictly analogous to the Baconian insistence on
scientists learning from the rule-of-thumb techniques practised time
out of mind by industrial craftsmen — iron-workers, bakers, brewers.
(Cf. popular medicine in China today). As Dr French put it: "only by
viewing applied science as 'real artificial magic' can the Renaissance
relationship between *magic* and science be fully understood ...
Practical science can be seen to have developed, at least in part, out of
the renewed interest in magic" — and he quotes Dee as the man who
most of all bridged this apparent gap, or combined these two roles.[22]

The magical desire for power [Mr Thomas sums up] had created an
intellectual environment favourable to experiment and induction; it marked
a break with the characteristic mediaeval attitude of contemplative resignation. Neoplatonic and Hermetic ways of thinking had stimulated such
crucial discoveries in the history of science as heliocentrism, the infinity of
worlds and the circulation of the blood. The mystical conviction that
number contained the key to all mysteries had fostered the revival of
mathematics. Astrological enquiries had brought new precision to the
observation of the heavenly bodies, the calculation of their movements and
the measurement of time.[23]

This illustrates Bernal's important point that "the discovery of
problems ... is more important than the discovery of solutions ...
The greatest effort is required not so much in discovering new things
as in breaking obsolete ideology sanctified by custom or religion".[24]
The bold speculations of Renaissance magicians, alchemists and
astrologers helped to pose new problems, and to thrust aside obstacles set by conventional ways of thinking.

One of the remarkable features of England in the three generations
before the civil war is the number and high quality of popular scientific books published in the vernacular, and the opportunities for
education in mathematics and science which existed in London.
These scientific books are inextricably entangled with alchemy, astrology and magic, as the names of their leading authors indicate — John
Dee, Thomas Digges, William Gilbert. The early acceptance of the
Copernican system in England owed much to astrologers and to
writers of popular almanacs preoccupied with astrology as well as
astronomy. By 1650 the English had the reputation of being "great
astrologers".[25] If you asked me — or anyone else — to name the most
rational and forward-looking of the Leveller intellectuals, we should
think of Richard Overton and John Wildman. Yet the former
consulted astrologers for advice on political action in 1648 (of all

crucial years); Wildman in the sixteen-eighties invoked the aid of devils, spirits and fairies in a search for hidden treasure. John Dryden made an astrological prognosis of one of his son's illnesses. Robert Hooke, reporting on the weather for 19 November 1672, added the words "conjunction of Saturn and Mars. Fatal day" on which John Wilkins died [26]. Not only Sir Thomas Browne but also John Milton still believed in the existence of guardian angels "appointed to preside over nations".

The most interesting problem in my view is to account for the change by which, by the end of the seventeenth century, the mechanical philosophy had replaced animism; and the magical/alchemical movement, which in the early years of the century had seemed at least as well-established and influential as the Baconian movement, lost its intellectual appeal. No doubt the ultimate reasons for this are economic and social; the mechanization of the world picture could only happen in a society in which machines of some complexity, and the principles of mechanical causation, were already familiar. But both Hermeticism and the mechanical philosophy are ideologies, the affair of intellectuals: a change in the "world picture" is a change in ideas, through which economic changes are mediated.

I see a complex of interlocking and sometimes contradictory causes at work in the century or so which preceded the triumph of the mechanical philosophy. First, there is the point I have already made: the fiercest early opponents of magic were not scientists but theologians, and among theologians especially protestant theologians, among protestant especially Calvinist theologians, starting with John Calvin. The Laudians in England, including the Archbishop himself, were much more interested in astrology. There are perhaps analogies between the Roman Catholic emphasis on unwritten tradition and the Hermetic doctrine of a secret law handed down by the *magi*. What is politely called neo-Platonism was strongest in Roman Catholic countries, notably Italy and Germany — Ficino, Pico della Mirandola, Cornelius Agrippa, Bruno, Campanella, for England's lone John Dee — and Dee went to Prague for his most active magical period: in England his house was wrecked in a popular demonstration against him as a magician. [27] Syncretism, the ability to absorb into the popular faith elements from pagan and other non-Christian sources, had always been a feature of Roman Catholic thought. Puritan protestantism, with its stark emphasis on the Bible and its monotheism, was less all-embracing.

Protestantism, and especially Calvinism, protested precisely against the magical elements in mediaeval Catholicism, from the sale of indulgences to buy souls out of Purgatory onwards. Thousands of protestant preachers in thousands of pulpits denounced the miracle of the mass in terms which were often crudely rationalistic and materialistic. Catholic wonder-working images were exposed to rational criticism, and so were Catholic practices like use of holy water, crossing, exorcism, etc. Saints and the Virgin lost their power to intervene in events on earth. The abolition of Purgatory made belief in ghosts less easy.[28] Protestants tended to push all miracles into the distant past, to the age of Christ and the Apostles; and to assume that events which apparently transcended the normal laws of cause and effect were *either* improperly understood *or* the result of the intervention of the devil and his agents. Mr K. V. Thomas has acutely pointed out that the abolition of mediating saints and of magical practices generally appeared to *enhance* the power of the devil, to leave men and women more naked and exposed to his assaults. "The Reformation, ... by taking away the protective ritual of Catholicism, made witchcraft appear a serious danger to ordinary people."[29] Holy water, relics, incantations, crucifixes, exorcisms, no longer protected men as they had done. Yet this did not immediately lead to an internalization of the struggle against the forces of evil. It led rather to a growth in the importance of the cunning man, the lay magician, who filled the place vacated by the priest.

Many things happened in the world of sixteenth-century men and women for which there appeared to be no rational explanation. I quote from an account of Henry Hudson's voyage to find the North-East passage in 1608:

On the morning of 15th June, in latitude 75 on a clear day, two of the company (their names Thomas Hills and Robert Rayner) saw a mermaid. She came close to the ship's side, looking earnestly on the men. A little after a sea came and overturned her. From the navel upwards her back and breasts were like a woman's; her body as big as ours; her skin very white; and long hair hanging down behind, of colour black. In her going down they saw her tail, which was like the tail of a porpoise and speckled like a mackerel.[30]

Since we often (rightly) emphasize that the cold matter-of-fact reporting of observations made on voyages led men to be sceptical of some old-wives' tales, it is worth remembering that they might also create new ones.

Reverting to belief in the devil, Mr Thomas suggests that a sense of the power and menace of witchcraft *increased* in Britain in the century after the Reformation, not because there were in fact more witches, but because men had lost the traditional magical remedies against the devil and his agents (and also because social tensions were increasing). We can see in some of the investigations of Calvinist divines — e.g. Perkins, and Increase Mather in New England — a combination of scientific scepticism with a firm belief in the ultimate power of the Evil One. In case after case certain phenomena are dismissed as the result of fraud, hysterical deception, malice; until in the end some facts are left for which there appears to be no rational explanation: and these are attributed to machinations of the devil and to witches who have sold themselves to the devil.[31] Mr Pennington has pointed out that there is better historical evidence for the existence of the devil in the seventeenth century than for many facts which we should today regard as established.[32] The Bible asserts the existence of witches and the duty of punishing them. So we get a curious combination of scepticism about magic leading to increased persecution of unpopular old women; and scientific techniques of investigation being used to convict them — though it remains true that witch persecution ended first in protestant countries, starting with the Netherlands.

It was then only a short move forward for the philosopher, in Hobbes's *Dialogue . . . of the Common Laws of England*, to say that he could not "conceive how the devil hath power to do many things which witches have been accused of", though divines still continued to say "Deny spirits and you are an atheist". Sir Thomas Browne thought scepticism about witchcraft was propagated by the devil himself. Commentators like John Aubrey, again and again, and Sir William Temple, testify that belief in witches, fairies and magic generally took a downward turn with the free discussion and enlightenment of the civil war decades.[33] "The searching into natural knowledge began but since or about the death of King Charles I", wrote Aubrey with some precision. "Till about the year 1649 'twas held a strange presumption for a man to attempt an innovation in learning". But "civil wars . . . extinguish . . . superstition".[34] The doctrine that the soul dies with the body, taught by many radical sectaries during the revolutionary decades and accepted by Milton and Hobbes, made belief in spirits difficult.

There were other factors. By and large protestantism and especially Calvinism appealed to the urban middle and lower-middle classes: citizens of Geneva, Amsterdam, La Rochelle and London; by and large witch beliefs were strongest in the countryside. The Puritan attack on witches is part of an attempt to impose new *mores*, new standards, on the traditional paganism of the countryside, just as the Puritan (and Shakespearean) ethic of marriage is an attempt to impose new social patterns on the easier-going sexual habits of traditional society.

But for these very social reasons, the sects which protestantism so rapidly spawned, and which flourished most among the middling and lower classes of society, were closer to popular beliefs, including belief in magic, than urban Calvinism. And so, as Mr Thomas has abundantly shown, although "the Reformation took a good deal of the magic out of religion, leaving the astrologers and cunning men to fill much of the vacuum, ... the sectaries brought back much of the magic which their early Tudor predecessors had so energetically cast out". Radical sects in England and New England retained more magical beliefs and practices than the high Calvinism of the *haute bourgeoisie* and of the universities: a Familist midwife was asccused of being a witch in Massachusetts in the sixteen-forties:[35] the accusation was frequently directed against midwives, and later against Quakers.

Calvinist theologians' opposition to magical techniques tended to make them suspicious of certain types of experiment: the sects with their very strong emphasis on personal experience as the sole test of the validity of religious truth were far more receptive to the experimental approach. The sects were strongest among craftsmen, many of whose technical processes were drawn upon by early experimental scientists. However we explain it, there seems to be a clear connection between alchemical beliefs, especially chemical medicine, and religious and political radicalism — from Paracelsus in the early sixteenth century. In Germany, Dr Yates has argued, alchemical Rosicrucians in the second decade of the seventeenth century were associated with a political radical movement looking to the Elector Palatine, which established links between England, Bohemia and Germany. In France in the sixteen-twenties there was a witch-hunt against Rosicrucians, who were alleged to be socially dangerous: this was the intellectual background from which Cartesianism emerged, in which Mersenne attacked the mystical tradition and built up the mechanical philosophy in opposition to it.[36]

In England too there were close links between the Hermetic

tradition and politico-religious radicalism. In the revolutionary decades hitherto unpublishable works on astrology and alchemy were printed in profusion: Mr Thomas speaks of an "unprecedented vogue" for astrology. More Paracelsan and mystical chemical books were published in English translation in the sixteen-fifties than during the whole preceding century. In 1646, we are told, "the Familists are very confident that by knowledge of astrology and the strength of reason they shall be able to conquer the whole world".[37] The Comenian group around Samuel Hartlib combined plans for social, economic and educational reform with an interest in chemistry. The group included men like William Petty, Gabriel Plattes, John Hall and Robert Boyle. Nicholas Culpeper, republican and sectary, who was wounded fighting for Parliament at Newbury, was the leading alchemical reformer, the chief enemy of the monopoly of the College of Physicians. He published astrological almanacs and, like William Lilly, used them to make anti-monarchical and anti-clerical propaganda.[38] John Webster, chaplain and surgeon in the parliamentary army, was associated with the religious radical William Erbery, accused of being a Seeker if not a Ranter. Webster published an attack on Oxford and Cambridge which combined a rational critique of traditional scholasticism and a demand for Baconian reforms with a simultaneous insistence that chemistry, astrology, Hermeticism and natural magic should be taught in the universities. He was denounced as an exemplar of the "Familistical-Levelling-Magical temper". When the Ranter Lawrence Clarkson took up physic in the sixteen-forties, its natural accompaniment was astrology, and it led him to aspire to the art of magic.[39] Gerard Winstanley, the Digger, most consistent radical of all, wanted astrology to be taught in his ideal commonwealth. He carried the Hermeticist idea that God equals reason so far as virtually to deny the existence of any personal God above the skies.

There is thus a sharp contrast between anti-magical high Calvinism, on the one hand, and the leanings towards astrology, alchemy and magic of many of the political and religious radicals, though both were opposed to the Aristotelean scholasticism of the universities. Calvinism, with its emphasis on the overwhelming power of God, and on predestination (like Augustinian Jansenism in France) prepared for the reception of the mechanical philosophy. The radicals were closer than the Calvinists to the ideas of ordinary people, among whom magical assumptions were still commonplace. For this very reason their ideas contained — or were thought to contain — a political threat to the men of property in the revolutionary decades. Respectable opinion in the late sixteen-fifties and the restoration era in England opposed "fanaticism", "enthusiasm", whether in religion or in politics, in science or in medicine.[40] The long-term effect of the mechanical philosophy was to reject magic: it was a secularized Calvinism.

The Royal Society, and especially Thomas Sprat in his propagandist *History*, trumpeted their rejection of any belief in portents, prodigies, prophecies — though Sprat in 1659 had not been above citing the "wonders" and "miracles" which accompanied Oliver Cromwell all his life. The Society wanted science henceforth to be apolitical — which then as now meant conservative. Some astrologers and alchemists were Fellows of the Royal Society, but they abandoned the democratic associations of their bodies of ideas. With the restoration of the Church of England, many leading scientists became bishops; Charles II, wisely, became patron of the Royal Society as well as head of the church. Thomas Hobbes, who had the reputation of being an atheist, was excluded from the Society; so was the radical Samuel Hartlib. Sprat played down the role of Hartlib's colleague, Theodore Haak, in its pre-history, and historians have perhaps mistakenly followed him. In 1664 Joseph Glanvill was anxious to differentiate the mechanical philosophy of the Royal Society from the mechanic atheism of the radicals. "The mechanical philosophy yields no security to irreligion", he proclaimed.[41] Despite the efforts of the Society of Chemical Physicians, alchemy, astrology and magic sank into the intellectual underworld of cranks and charlatans; their rejection was thus self-validating. The Royal Society and the College of Physicians eclectically accepted some of the practical achievements of Paracelsan and Helmontian chemistry: the cosmic speculations and the social-reforming applications of alchemy and natural magic were abandoned. Newton never published his voluminous alchemical writings. Charles II took an alleged astrologer to Newmarket and told him to spot winners.[42] By the end of the century the Archbishop of Canterbury was a Copernican. "Latitudinarian" is the word used after the restoration to describe conformist Puritans like Wilkins.

It is important to realize in human terms what the triumph of the mechanical philosophy meant. I have known and quoted for more than forty years Pascal's famous remark, "the eternal silence of those infinite spaces terrifies me" but I think only when I came to prepare this lecture did I feel on my pulses what Pascal meant. We have got used to boundless space; but it is very new in human history. "The infinite is unthinkable", Kepler said when he heard what had been revealed by Galileo's telescope; yet he and Pascal and all men had to learn to live with the unthinkable. The idea of an infinite universe was not unknown to the learned before Copernicus and Galileo; but now it was slowly coming to be accepted by at least the literate part of the population. Galileo's discoveries seemed perhaps less startling in England, where Thomas Digges's *Parfit Description of the Celestial Orbes* had gone through at least seven editions — in the vernacular — between its first publication in 1576 and Galileo's observations.[43] The science fiction of John Wilkins and many others helped. C. S. Lewis called Milton "our first poet of space": Satan's journey through space from hell to earth seems to have been Milton's invention.

Pascal's terror came from the transformation of the universe from something relatively cosy, bounded and understood, to a vast blank nothingness. The music of the spheres was silenced; the heavens were no longer populated by hundreds of thousands of spirits, pushing the spheres around, going on divine errands, bearing influences. The universe had become *void*. Moreover, it had suddenly enormously increased in size. Cosmic equality under the sun, whether the units were planets, atoms or (for the Levellers and Hobbes) men, took the place of hierarchy, of the great chain of being. The universe, hitherto a series of concentric spheres each neatly enclosing its own bustle of spirits, was now infinite in extent as well as empty. The full significance of the changes in outlook which the new astronomy demanded took time to penetrate the general consciousness; but the beginnings date from the mid-seventeenth century.

The Christian pattern of fall and redemption had already been shaken by exploration of America, Africa and Asia, which revealed that millions of men and women had no means of knowing the truths of the gospel, traditionally held to be necessary for salvation. But now even vaster perspectives opened up, of other worlds, possibly inhabited; how could they be fitted into the traditional Christian pattern? This earth was no longer the centre of the universe, the object of God's particular attention: it was difficult to go on thinking of it as created solely for man. Then why did it exist at all, and what was man's place in it? — located by some accident in a corner of an infinite and unfriendly universe — why here rather than elsewhere? — and with eternity stretching out into the past and future as space stretched out until it was lost in infinity.

> And yonder all before us lie
> Deserts of vast eternity.[44]

The political crises of the mid-seventeenth century rendered God's purposes suddenly far less clear than they used to be — or at least man's knowledge of these purposes. The new cosmology accentuated the withdrawal of God from the affairs of mankind, in which he used to intervene so regularly. Copernicus thought of heliocentrism as a mathematical formula, and could live with it on those terms. Galileo glimpsed something of its physical reality; a profoundly religious mathematician like Pascal was struck by the full horror of the empty universe. No wonder he could not swallow, as well, the impersonal God of Cartesianism. For Pascal knew that, in addition to the vacancies of infinite space, on earth truth on one side of the Pyrenees might be a lie on the other; truth was relative, the human mind fallible. Geometry had stripped the universe of all human qualities, depersonalized it. Pascal flung himself on to the bosom of a personal God, the God of Abraham, of Isaac and of Jacob, not of philosophers.[45]

All depends on the telescope now, Henry Oldenburg (future secretary of the Royal Society) wrote in 1659, "the vulgar opinion of the unity of the world being now exploded, and that doctrine thought absurd which teacheth the sun and the heavenly host, which are so many times bigger than our earth, to be made only to enlighten and quicken us".[46] The sun and the heavenly host — a phrase now used purely as a metaphor — no longer exist for man's sake and for no other purpose. The discovery of the microscope also stretched the human imagination, to comprehend the infinitely small as well as the infinitely large. By revealing things invisible to the naked eye, the microscope helped to call in question commonsense reliance on the human senses, and to show that forms of life existed with which it was not easy for men and women to feel affinity. A similar isolation of humanity resulted from the discrediting of alchemical metaphors. "When metals no longer 'marry', 'copulate', 'die' and are 'resurrected', they appear alien to us. Although we can manipulate them, they remain stubbornly *other*. We dominate them, but we are separated from them by a gulf; they do not share our consciousness or our purposes."[47]

"The mechanization of the world picture" occurred as men became more accustomed to living in a world of machines, a world which was beginning to appear rational and predictable, less at the mercy of forces outside human control, — even before the upsurge of technology which we call the Industrial Revolution. "The decline of magic", says Mr Thomas, "coincided with a marked improvement in the extent to which [the] environment became amenable to control". He lists better communications and fire-fighting devices as well as insurance, technical improvements in agriculture and industry and the concept of statistical probability. We may add the greater political stability, the reduction of arbitrariness at least for the propertied classes, which followed Parliament's victory over personal monarchy, the common law's victory over the prerogative; suppression of the radicals after 1649. The political activities (and successes) of ordinary people during the interregnum contributed to a greater belief in the possibilities of human action and initiative to control society and nature, linking up here with the triumphs of science itself, with the discovery of the New World and the new heavens. Add too better and more widespread medical knowledge, thanks in part to publication during the revolutionary decades of Nicholas Culpeper's and many other English translations of medical classics. 1665 saw the last great plague in England. Death was beginning to strike with less obvious arbitrariness. All these things combined to do the cunning man out of a job, for all but the very simple and credulous.[48]

We should not underestimate the transformation in men's thinking which came — ultimately — with the new geography and the new cosmology. Trade widened intellectual horizons. Hobbes compared the American Indians to the Anglo-Saxon inhabitants of England: a new historical relativism. India and China offered examples of non-Christian civilizations. Samuel Fisher and Bunyan asked themselves whether the Koran — published in English translations in 1649 — might not have as good traditional authority in Moslem countries as the Bible in Christendom.[49]

Nor should we forget protestant scepticism of miracles not attested by Scripture, and humanist and protestant canons of textual criticism, which enabled Casaubon to show in 1614 that the allegedly very ancient Hermetic writings dated from the second or third century A.D. — though this did not stop Newton supposing that they incorporated very ancient traditions. Earlier, men had tended to take any evidence in print at its face value, without testing it critically: miraculous stories in a Latin poet were treated no less seriously than miraculous stories in the Bible.[50] In the sixteen-fifties scepticism even of Biblical miracles was expressed in print, and the sanctity of the text of the Bible itself was questioned. The work of the Quaker Samuel Fisher on this subject was to influence Spinoza.[51]

The mid century saw the last attempts at an overall synthesis of knowledge — the wide social vision of Baconian and Comenian reformers, the communist world-view of Gerrard Winstanley, the great synthesis of *Paradise Lost*. As these faded we get a departmentalization of specialized sciences, including the sciences of politics and economics, now separated from theology as Bacon had separated natural science from theology. Divison of labour in the arts intensified professionalism. The development of the market led to the emergence of new professions — writers, architects, virtuoso concert performers, painters, actresses, G.Ps.

Everything worked against the old ways of thought. The Hermeticist doctrine of a primitive wisdom was part of a general assumption that the Ancients were wiser than the Moderns, that the most we could hope for was to recapture some of their knowledge. Yet in the great ideological battle of the seventeenth century, the Moderns inevitably overcame the Ancients. The discovery of America and the Antipodes proved the Ancients to have been wrong; the telescope revealed that they were mistaken in thinking the universe above the moon different in kind from the sublunary world; and so on, and so on. Many of the radical scientists themselves held an optimistic Baconian belief in the power of experiment, the possibilities of using science for the relief of man's estate, and this too cut across the idea of a secret traditional wisdom as well as going counter to the universities' naïve belief in the superiority of classical authorities. The experimental philosophy went better with a belief in progress than in decay.

The decline of magic was a surprising outcome, which could not have been predicted at the beginning of the seventeenth century. Down to that period magic and science had advanced hand in hand. But now magical science, by its association with political radicalism, had become — or was thought to have become — socially dangerous. The mechanical philosophy saved experiment from magic, excluded magic from science, as Calvinists had already excluded it from religion. This is one of the social and ideological reasons for the triumph of the mechanical philosophy (over and above, of course, the technical scientific reasons with which I have neither time nor competence to deal). But there was loss as well as gain. The *magi* had aspired to see the universe as a whole, to have a total grasp of reality. Now specialization set in, with all its limitations. Knowledge was no longer shut up in Latin, to be interpreted for ordinary people by priestly scholars; but it came to be no less securely shut up in the technical vocabulary of the sciences, which the new specialists had to interpret. Newton was as incomprehensible to the common man as Aquinas had been. The wide vision, especially the social vision, of the radical Baconians, was totally lost. Bacon's own millenarianism was hushed up.[52] There was some pure gain — e.g. in technology, in medicine, in the cessation of witch persecutions. As God became a more remote "Supreme Being", so questions were asked about a personal devil working through witches. But there was also the dehumanization of nature, the alienation of man in an unfriendly universe, once he ceased to be linked to nature by the micro/macro-cosm correspondence, once chemical processes ceased to be seen as analogies of sexual reproduction, or of death, burial and resurrection.

Some twentieth-century scientists consider that the mechanical philosophers threw a number of promising babies out with the animistic bathwater. I quote J. Z. Young: "All of us, animals, plants and bacteria, form one closely interlocked network.... It is easy to elevate these facts into a portentous scheme of the whole living world as one 'organism'. Yet there is a sense in which this is true.... The whole mass [of life upon earth] constitutes one single self-maintaining system". That reminds me of ideas which prevailed before the triumph of the mechanical philosophy. Chemistry and physics, a historian of science tells us, have become united in the present century only after physics renounced the view that matter consists of indivisible and impermeable atoms, and chemistry renounced its doctrine of ultimate immutable elements — doctrine evolved originally in opposition to the alchemists. Take Newton's problem of the nature of the "force" of gravity — "it is inconceivable that mere brute matter should without the mediation of something else, which is not material, operate upon and affect other matter without mutual contact" — but the inconceivable was smuggled in by phrases like "universal gravity", "electromagnetic field". We can see all this in better perspective today when "the concepts of matter and causality as understood both by classical physics and by common sense experience have been abandoned by modern physics".[53] Perhaps even the dualism of mind and matter, which has bedevilled philosophy since Descartes, originated in an obsessive rejection of animism.

Religion changed too.

The religion which survived the decline of magic was not the religion of Tudor England. When the devil was banished to hell, God himself was confined to working through natural causes. 'Special providences' and private revelations gave way to the notion of a Providence which itself obeyed natural laws accessible to human study.... It was a religion with a difference.... At the end of our period we can draw a distinction between religion and magic which would not have been possible at the beginning.[54]

So to summarize:

(1) There was a revival of intellectual magic in the fifteenth-sixteenth centuries, which acted as a stimulus to experiment, to the scientific imagination.

(2) This magical revival was opposed by Calvinists, but was received more sympathetically by popular radical sects linked with millenarian revolutionary politics. In the upsurge of 1640-60 both radical sectarian and magical ideas could be published. Yet, paradoxically, the events of the Revolution — freedom of publication and discussion, decline of the power of the clergy — led ultimately to a greater rationalism, a greater scepticism about witches, fairies and magic generally; the Moderns triumphed over the Ancients.

(3) The defeat of the radical revolutionaries, plus a lingering fear that their influence might revive, created social conditions which favoured the victory of the mechanical philosophy — acceptable of course on scientific grounds too. The Royal Society cashed in.

(4) But maybe the circumstances of the acceptance of the mechanical philosophy allowed ideological elements to be incorporated into it from the start; total rejection of the ways of thinking of the *magi* may have closed some doors which might with advantage to science have been left open. Science, in Bernal's striking phrase, is not only "ordered technique"; it is also "rationalized mythology".[55]

I end by quoting Mr Thomas again, at his most disturbing: "The role of magic in modern society may be more extensive than we yet appreciate.... Anthropologists today are unsympathetic to the view that magic is simply bad science.... If magic is to be defined as the employment of ineffective techniques to allay anxiety when effective ones are not available, then we must recognize that no society will ever be free from it".[56] No society ever? Well, not ours anyway.

NOTES

1. A lecture given at the J.D. Bernal Peace Library, 19 October 1976. Published in *Culture, Ideology and Politics: Essays for Eric Hobsbawm* (ed. Raphael Samuel and Gareth Stedman Jones, 1983).
2. J.D. Bernal, *Science in History* (3rd. edn., 1965), p.46.
3. Laslett, *The World We Have Lost*, p.71.
4. K. Dewhurst, *John Locke (1632-1704), Physician and Philosopher*, (1963), p.31.
5. A.L. Rowse, *Simon Forman* (1974), p.8; N. Culpeper, *Works* (1802), I. pp.33-9.
6. See my *Antichrist in Seventeenth-Century England* (Oxford U.P., 1971), *passim*; C. Webster, *The Great Instauration; Science, Medicine & Reform, 1626-1660*, p.549. I have benefited greatly by reading Dr P.A. Trout's unpublished D. Phil. Thesis, *Magic and the Millennium: Motifs in the Occult Milieu of Puritan England, 1640-1660* (University of British Columbia, 1974).
7. B.S. Capp, *The Fifth Monarchy Men*, pp. 187-8.
8. D.P. Walker, *Spiritual and Demonic Magic from Ficino to Campanella* (1958), pp. 204-9; W. Shumaker, *The Occult Sciences in the Renaissance* (California U.P., 1972), p.54.
9. Quoted by M. McKeon, *Politics and Poetry in Restoration England* (Harvard U.P., 1975), p.231.
10. K.V. Thomas, *Religion and the Decline of Magic*, pp.327-35, 361.
11. I. Ehrenpreis, "Jonathan Swift", *Proceedings of the British Academy* (1968), p.153.
12. Quoted in *I.O.E.R.*, p.147.
13. S. Hutin, *Robert Fludd (1574-1637)* (Paris, 1971), pp.83-4, 99.
14. P.J. French, *John Dee* (1972), p.161.
15. A.G. Debus, "Robert Fludd and the Circulation of the Blood", *Journal of the History of Medicine*, 16 (1961), pp.374-93.
16. Thomas, *op. cit.*, p.271; Hutin, *op. cit.*, pp.98, 113, 150; Shumaker, *op. cit.*, pp.193-8.
17. Ed. G. Saintsbury, *Minor Poets of the Caroline Period* (Oxford U.P., 1905-21), III, p.413; R.T. Petersson, *Sir Kenelm Digby* (1952), pp.267, 272-4, 278, 342.
18. Dewhurst, *op. cit.*, p.204.
19. F.A. Yates, *Giordano Bruno and the Hermetic Tradition* (1964), pp.

244-5, 380-1, 451; A. Koestler, *The Sleepwalkers* (1959), pp. 259, 396.

20. Ed. A.R. and M.B. Hall, *The Correspondence of Henry Oldenburg,* X (1975), p. 555; ed. E.G. Forbes, *The Gresham Lectures of John Flamsteed* (1975), p. 322.
21. Debus, *Science and Education in the Seventeenth Century: the Webster-Ward Debate* (1970), pp. 24, 28-9, 42-3, 60-63.
22. French, *op. cit.,* p. 109.
23. Thomas, *op. cit.,* pp. 229, 109, 643-4.
24. Bernal, *op. cit.,* pp. 913, 966.
25. *I.O.E.R.* pp. 25, 49, 69, 147-9; *Mercurius Politicus,* No. 33, 16-23 January 1651, p. 545.
26. Thomas, *op. cit.,* pp. 236-7, 313; Ehrenpreis, *op. cit.,* p. 152; M. 'Espinasse, *Robert Hooke* (1956), p. 113. See now J. Kent Clark, *Goodwin Wharton* (Oxford U.P., 1984), for a fascinating account of the magical beliefs of many respectable Whig politicians in William III's reign.
27. Thomas, *op. cit.,* pp. 369-70; Yates, *op. cit.,* Chapter 7.
28. Ed. A. Peel and L. Carlson, *The Writings of Robert Harrison and Robert Browne* (1953), p. 9.
29. Thomas, *op. cit.,* pp. 498-503, 543, 638-9.
30. G.B. Harrison, *A Second Jacobean Journal* (1958), p. 102.
31. W. Perkins, *Works* (1609-13), I, p. 40, II, p. 333, III, pp. 607-46: I. Mather, *Remarkable Providences* (1890), pp. 189-94.
32. D.H. Pennington, *Seventeenth Century Europe* (1970), p. 126.
33. Hobbes, *op. cit.* (ed. J. Cropsey, Chicago U.P., 1971), p. 122; Browne, *Works* (1852), I, p. 84; *I.O.E.R.* p. 118, and references there cited. Cf. Jeremiah Whitaker, *The Christians Hope Triumphing* (1645), pp. 28-9, a sermon preached before the House of Lords; H. More, *An Antidote to Atheism* (1653), in *A Collection of Several Philosophical Writings* (1712), p. 142.
34. J. Aubrey, *Natural History of Wiltshire* (1847), p. 5; cf. p. 93; *Remaines of Gentilisme and Judaisme* (1881), pp. 21, 205, 241; *Brief Lives* (ed. A. Clark, Oxford U.P., 1898), I, p. 27.
35. Thomas, *op. cit.,* p. 638; C.M. Andrews, *The Colonial Period of American History* (Yale U.P., 1964), I, p. 469.
36. F.A. Yates, *The Rosicrucian Enlightenment* (1972), pp. 111-113.
37. Thomas, *op. cit.,* pp. 304, 376; Debus, *Science and Education,* p. 33. The combination of reason and astrology is interesting.
38. See W. Lilly, *The Last of the Astrologers* (ed. K.M. Briggs, Folklore Soc., 1974), pp. 63, 68, 78, for use of astrologers as propagandists by the Parliamentarians.
39. *W.T.U.D.,* p. 290; L. Clarkson, *The Lost Sheep Found* (1660), p. 32.
40. See Postscript, pp. 297-8 below.
41. Glanvill, *Scepsis Scientifica* (1664), Dedication to the Royal Society.
42. *I.O.E.R.* p. 126. The astrologer is said to have spotted three successive losers.
43. *Ibid.,* p. 19.
44. Pascal, *Pensées* (ed. E. Boultroux, Collection Gallia, n.d.), pp. 85-8, 94; Marvell, *To his coy mistress.* Marvell wrote at almost exactly the same

time as Pascal. See now my *Religion and Politics in 17th-century England*, Chapter 13.

45. Pascal, *op. cit.*, p. 232.
46. Ed. A.R. and M.B. Hall, *The Correspondence of Henry Oldenburg*, I, p. 277.
47. Shumaker, *op. cit.*, p. 198.
48. Thomas, *op. cit.*, pp. 650-52.
49. S. Fisher, *The Rusticks Alarum to the Rabbies* (1660), in *The Testimony of Truth Exalted* (1679), p. 384; Bunyan, *Grace Abounding to the Chief of Sinners* (1666), in *Works*, I, p. 17.
50. F.E. Manuel, *The Religion of Isaac Newton* (Oxford U.P., 1974), p. 44; Shumaker, *op. cit.*, p. 254.
51. R.H. Popkin, "Spinoza, the Quakers and the Millenarians, 1656-1658", *Manuscrito*, VI (Brazil, 1982), p. 132; "Spinoza and the Conversion of the Jews", in *Spinoza's Political and Theological Thought* (ed. C. De Deugd, Amsterdam, 1984), p. 174.
52. Thomas, *op. cit.*, p. 643; *W.T.U.D.*, p. 293, 304-5; Webster, *op. cit.*, p. 24.
53. J.Z. Young, *An Introduction to the Study of Man* (1971), pp. 115, 640; Koestler, *op. cit.*, pp. 501, 518, 536. See Postscript.
54. Thomas, *op. cit.*, pp. 649-40.
55. Bernal, *op. cit.*, p. 9.
56. Thomas, *op. cit.*, pp. 667-8.

POSTSCRIPT

I leave this essay substantially as I wrote it in 1976. Today it would need to be totally rewritten to take account of a series of books which have transformed our understanding of the subject.

Charles Webster's *The Great Instauration* had demonstrated in 1975 "a marked elevation of science and medicine in the public esteem" during the English Revolution, "and an acceleration in the pace of scientific development".[1] In *From Paracelsus to Newton: Magic and the Making of Modern Science* (Cambridge U.P., 1982) he succeeds in reuniting the Paracelsan tradition, through Bacon and Boyle, with Newton, Keynes's last of the magicians. In doing so Webster had to combat "deep prejudices imposed by modern scientific ideology". "The world-view of the Scientific Revolution" was "a diverse phenomenon, the result of a dynamic interplay of forces which emanated from many different directions".[2]

Margaret Jacob, *The Newtonians and the English Revolution* (Cornell U.P., 1976) argues that "the supposed correspondence of the new mechanical philosophy with the actual behaviour of the natural order is not the primary reason for its early success". Sprat saw "the political function of science" as being "the maintenance of order and stability". She shows the social uses to which Newtonianism was put in the eighteenth century: "the Newtonian vision of the natural world provided irrefutable justification for the public order and controlled self-interest sanctioned and maintained by church and state".[3]

J.R. Jacob's *Robert Boyle and the English Revolution* (New York, 1977) illuminates the importance of the social context at the earlier stage in which Boyle's ideas evolved. Boyle had approved of the English Commonwealth, in which careers were opened to the talents. But he abhorred the social radicalism and "enthusiasm" of the sectaries, and evolved his corpuscular philosophy partly in order to refute their ideas. "The leadership of the Royal Society", J.R. Jacob writes, "shared Boyle's social vision in which science, trade and empire were seen to work together to produce the reformation". Their "ideology of science was neither apolitical nor unrelated to religion. Instead, it was an aggressive, acquisitive materialistic ideology".[4] His work complements Margaret Jacob's *The Newtonians*.

Carolyn Merchant's *The Death of Nature: Women, Ecology and the Scientific Revolution* (San Francisco, 1980) reminds us that in the traditional animistic universe the words for "earth" and "nature" were nearly always feminine; and that this corresponded to a real feeling of kinship, of co-operation between mankind and Mother Nature, Mother Earth, which imposed limits on the exploitation of natural resources. But for the mechanical philosophers matter was dead, inert, unrelated to humanity: it was something to be made use of for the good of man. Bacon "fashioned a new ethic sanctioning the exploitation of nature". Nature must be "bound into service", made a "slave", put "in constraint" and "molded" by the mechanical arts.[5] Merchant shows natural magic as a half-way house to the mechanical philosophy: the magus aspired to manipulate nature in the interests of human progress. The mechanical philosophy imposed order on the apparent disorder of nature, insisted on the inertness of matter, and stressed moderation, reasonable judgment, consensus and sovereign law as against the rampant individualism of the radical sects and the magi. For Descartes and Hobbes mechanism meant order and power, dominion over nature. "In 1500 the parts of the cosmos were bound together as a living organism; by 1700 the dominant metaphor had become the machine".[6] This new mode of thought facilitated the tremendous technical achievements of European civilization; it also justified the ruthless exploitation and devastation of natural resources, all over the world; and the subjugation and exploitation of women, slaves and later the working class. Merchant agrees with J.R. and M.C. Jacob that Newtonianism could be used to justify the domination of nature, though Newton himself had secret doubts about the passivity of matter.[7]

Brian Easlea's *Witch-Hunting, Magic and the New Philosophy: An Introduction to Debates of the Scientific Revolution, 1450-1750* (Brighton, 1980), complements Merchant's book in many ways. Arguing, like J.R. Jacob, that the victory of the mechanical philosophy was the consequence of social forces as well as of intellectual conviction, he produces further evidence to illustrate contemporary views that it was a "masculine philosophy", designed to ravish female Nature.[8] Descartes wanted men to be "masters and possessors" of nature. Boyle though that veneration of nature was an obstacle to progress. There were changes of emphasis from Bacon's rape of nature to Sprat's "courtship to nature", but the consequences are the same: "the beautiful bosom of Nature will be exposed to our view; we shall enter into its garden, and taste of its fruits and satisfy ourselves with its plenty". Easlea, like Merchant, notes that Newton was too much of a Hermeticist to have been a Newtonian; and he shares her concern about the social consequences for women and others of the subjugation of nature.[9]

NOTES

1. *Op. cit.*, p. 84. The elevation was perhaps because the esteem was that of a new public.
2. *Op. cit.*, p. 12, and *passim.*
3. *Op. cit.*, pp. 17-18, 38-9, 51, 68, 269.
4. *Op. cit.*, pp. 157-9, and *passim.*
5. *Op. cit.*, pp. vi, 3, 5, 25-30, 42-3, 48, 77-8, 105, 128, 164-6, 169, 187, 227-35, 288.
6. *Ibid.*, pp. 109-11, 117, 125, 192-5, 215-27, 288. Cf. p. 292 above.
7. *Ibid.*, pp. 279, 284-7; cf. A. Koyré, *Newtonian Studies* (1965), p. 91.
8. *Op. cit.*, Chapters 3 and 5 *passim.*
9. *Ibid.*, pp. 111-12, 139, 170-1, 213, *Afterword.*

14. Covenant Theology and the Concept of "A Public Person"

*"I am now no private person. I am a public, and a counsellor to the whole state."**

My subject is the theological concept, which we encounter in England during the sixteenth and seventeenth centuries, of the representative person, or public person, or common person: the phrases seem to be used interchangeably. Adam was a representative of the whole of mankind; it was in consequence of his sin that all Adam's descendants were condemned to eternal death. From this predicament some men were rescued by the second principal representative person, Jesus Christ, who paid the penalty due from all mankind for Adam's sin. The idea that Adam and Christ were in this sense representative persons was shared by a large number of protestants from Luther onwards, though the phrase is not Biblical in any of its variants. Luther criticized the view, which he attributed to "the Schoolmen and almost all the Fathers", that Christ was "innocent and, as a private person, ... holy and righteous for himself only". Christ, Luther thought, was a high priest as well as a suffering servant, "taking thy sinful person upon him".[2]

This theory was held especially by exponents of the covenant theology, a theology which seems to derive in England from William Tyndale. It was also developed by Calvin and at Heidelberg in the fifteen-eighties by Ursinus and others.[3] Its origin coincides in time with a new emphasis on contract in political theory and with new attitudes towards contract among business men and lawyers. We cannot be precise about causal links, since the feudal contract, with its very different social context (the oath of loyalty and the coronation oath), had been familiar long before the rise of protestantism.

* Peter Wentworth in the House of Commons, 1575 (S. D'Ewes, *The Journal of All the Parliaments during the Reign of Queen Elizabeth*, 1682, p. 241).

The *Vindiciae contra tyrannos,* for instance, drew upon this body of ideas perhaps more than upon protestant theories of the covenant, and this tradition had its influence in England. Nevertheless, the actual content of the covenant theology suggests that it was influenced by the growing significance of contracts, and of the debtor-creditor relationship, in the economic life of society as capitalism developed. The Swedes, Bulstrode Whitelocke observed during his embassy of 1653-4, "have but few contracts, because they have but little trade".[4]

At about the same time, too, was developing the sectarian church covenant by which men voluntarily associated with other members of the elect to form gathered congregations. There is an analogy here with the Leveller Agreement of the People. Just as baptism is the symbol of entry into church covenant, of access to the means of grace, so acceptance of the Agreement of the People was the means by which men (or some men) would have contracted into the refounded English state if the Leveller programme had been accepted.[5]

Medieval sacramental theory was rooted in the symbolism which accompanies, and seals, economic or political transactions in primitive society. Livery of seisin is accompanied by (or rather is) the transfer of a piece of earth; homage is symbolically "done"; the Lord Treasurer is appointed by handing him the white staff of office. So the ring in matrimony, water in baptism, laying on of hands in confirmation, the elements in the mass, are all means whereby grace is bestowed. Richard Hooker quoted St. Bernard with approval: "God by sacraments giveth grace ... even as honours and dignities are given, an abbot made by receiving a staff, a doctor by a book, a bishop by a ring".[6]

Protestant sacramental theory evolved in a much more sophisticated social atmosphere. Livery of seisin was already a trifle old-fashioned. Not only were written contracts long established, but verbal agreements were becoming legally more binding; and credit in various forms, by written or verbal bond, was also familiar. Slade's Case in 1602, extended by Warbrook *v.* Griffin in 1610, meant that "the law was now ready to enforce promises other than those formally recorded", provided there was "some evidence that a contract really existed .... The consideration or inducement must be shown, in return for which the unfulfilled promise was made." This important new development of the law of contract gave the individual much more freedom of manoeuvre in regulating his business affairs.[7] Similarly the relationship of serf and lord, mesne lord and overlord, was being replaced by new relationships between king and subject, employer and labourer, debtor and creditor. Voluntary associations, gilds, companies, and partnerships already had their place in the towns.

Now the protestant emphasis on faith as against works, its denial that sacraments are the vehicles of grace, spiritualizes worship and strips it of its symbolical-magical-materialist character. Protestant sacramental doctrine bears the same relation to medieval Catholic doctrine as credit does to a metal currency, Marx long ago pointed out.[8] Faith becomes the more important as external material aids to grace (the counters of salvation) lose their usefulness. The relationship between God and man is direct, and emphasis is placed upon promises, mutual covenants between the two parties. That is why the inner state of mind of the Christian was so significant. God is not mocked: in entering into or renewing a covenant it was essential that the intention should be sincere. In feudal law, by contrast, it was precisely the external forms that counted: livery of seisin was livery of seisin, and its proper performance was all that mattered. A good deal of this attitude entered into popular conceptions of the efficacity of sacraments, whatever the more sophisticated theologians might say. Failure to distinguish between symbol and thing symbolized explains much in the Reformation controversy over indulgences.

"Without a promise there can be no faith", declared Tyndale. "The devil hath no promises: he is therefore excluded from Paul's faith.... If when thou seest the sacrament, or eatest his body or drinkest his blood, thou have this promise fast in thine heart, that his body was slain and his blood shed for thy sins and believest it, so art thou saved and justified thereby".[9] "The sacraments", wrote Calvin, "are a kind of mutual contract, by which the Lord conveys his mercy to us, and by it eternal life, while we in our turn promise him obedience".[10] That Calvin's attitude to justification is remarkably legal has often been noticed; it has been attributed to his training as a lawyer, but he is a lawyer dealing with property and economic relationships. Many shared Calvin's emphases. "Even infants may contract and covenant with God", wrote the judicious Hooker.[11] "God deals with men", declared Richard Sibbes," as we do by way of commerce one with another, propounding mercy by covenant and condition".[12] *The Whole Duty of Man* speaks in terms of a bargain with God.[13]

The direct covenant with God does away with the need for mediating saints: "the master is bound to be just to [his servants] in performing those conditions on which they were hired. By covenant God bindeth himself to fulfil that mercy unto thee only if thou wilt endeavour thyself to keep his laws".[14] The employer in a family workshop deals directly with his employees: serfs had approached their lord through his bailiff or steward. But the relationship to God is conceived not only as a hiring contract: it is also thought of as debtor-creditor relationship — a relationship perhaps even more frequent in sixteenth-century England than the wage relationship. This is the classical form of the covenant as elaborated by the Puritan preachers, Perkins, Ames, Preston and Sibbes. The covenant of works has been replaced by the covenant of grace, under which God enters into obligations to his elect. The covenant of works is with Adam as representative of all mankind; the covenant of grace is with Christ as representative of the elect only, those who have credit. As Perry Miller pointed out, the covenant theology postulates a law-abiding universe. After the Fall and the Flood, God bound himself to an orderly and perpetual succession of the seasons of the year: he also accepts law in his relations with his elect. This is the world of Bacon and Descartes, looking forward to the mechanical philosophy and the mechanistic universe.[15] The fact that God bound himself to the elect by an explicit bond was a means of overcoming the absolute decrees of high Calvinism, and of smuggling free will back into theology. Since God had limited his arbitrary power by covenant, his operations became predictable, comprehensible to human reason. The elect could appeal to his promise if they kept their part of the bargain. "All the evidence we have to show for our inheritance . . . is our faith".[16]

The effect was to re-establish moral obligation on a clearer, more rational basis, to free men under normal circumstances from the incomprehensible decrees of an unknowable God. The transition was from the ineluctable inheritance of sin, and with it impotence to comply with God's law, to a definable contractual relationship. Men are born owing God a debt, but depraved sinners can now claim their rights under the contract which their representative has entered into on their behalf. The element of choice, of freedom of the will, is restored.[17] Milton hoped by education to repair the ruins of the

Fall.[18] As Bulkeley put it, "the covenant which passeth between God and us is like that which passeth between a king and his people; the king promiseth to rule and govern in mercy and righteousness, and they again promise to obey in loyalty and faithfulness".[19] Hence the activism which is such an apparently paradoxical feature of Puritanism. Sibbes expressed this again in economic terms:

Thou hast a title in the common.... How do men strive with their landlord for their commons? They will raise a mutiny, do anything, keep somewhat on it for possession's sake, rather than lose it, if it were but to keep one poor cow upon it.... In Christianity, if we be entered as freemen, where is our scot and lot? Where are our prayers offered up for king, our country, for religion?[20]

It is against this background that we must see the idea that Adam and Christ were representative persons. The covenant of works between God and Adam was replaced by a covenant of grace between God and Christ, "made anon after the former covenant was broken".[21] The covenant of grace was revealed to Adam, promised to Abraham, and renewed to Moses (all public persons).[22] But the formal covenant between God and his elect was entered into on behalf of the latter by Jesus Christ in his capacity as representative person.

This doctrine was elaborated by William Perkins, the greatest English Puritan theologian, and was developed by the covenant theologians who were his followers — Preston, Sibbes, Ames, William Gouge, Thomas Goodwin, William Bridge, John Owen.[23] Preston's contribution was especially to emphasize the legal aspects of Adam's breach of contract, his role as a representative person rather than as a father from whom we inherit physically. Man is born in debt to God: Christ has obtained easier terms for his clients.[24] The covenant theology was summarized succinctly in the Larger Catechism (1648) of the Westminster Assembly of Divines: "the covenant being made with Adam as a public person not for himself only but for his posterity" was replaced by a new covenant made by Christ "as a public person".[25]

What exactly was understood by a public person in the seventeenth century? The king was a public person. John Davies of Hereford assumed that "a great lord" was a public person, who "can scarce a moment spare for heaven".

> And public persons (if they mighty be)
> The public state, and theirs, they still must eye.

Magistrates were public persons.[26] So were even the two men who "in the rights of the inhabitants" of Horncastle Soke impounded the sheep of "divers great rich men" accused of abusing the right of common in the fifteen-nineties. But physicians, because they were not public persons, had no obligation to remain in London in time of plague. Samuel Morland, writing to Secretary Thurloe in December 1655, took it for granted that an ambassador was a public person, who could not travel incognito.[27] But those who spoke of Adam and Jesus as public persons used as their most frequent analogy a member of the House of Commons. Perkins said that all Adam's posterity sinned with him "as in a Parliament whatsoever is done by the burgess of the shire is done by every person in the shire".[28] "As the king, his nobles, knights and burgesses do represent the whole realm in Parliament", declared Thomas Tuke in 1609, "even so did Adam represent the persons of his whole posterity".[29] Thomas Hooker echoed Perkins: "Adam in innocency represented all mankind; he stood (as a Parliament man doth for the whole country) for all that should be born of him".[30]

We note in passing that for Tuke the concept of representation does not necessarily imply election in the modern sense. Nor indeed does the word election. "The word election intendeth the taking out of the best not of the worst out of things", wrote George Wyatt in the fifteen-nineties.[31] Election means selection. So the Western Circuit Assizes in February 1640 could order that "John Spenser, ... yeoman, is to be elected constable of Barton Stacey Hundred".[32] We must beware of carrying modern conceptions back into the seventeenth century.

More important for our purposes is the legal fact that the public person is accepted as representing his clients. Speaking of Christ as a common person, Goodwin observed that "the notion of a public representative to do acts that in law are counted as theirs whom he represents, is common among all nations".[33] "A common person ... is one who represents, personates and acts the part of another, by the allowance and warrant of the law, so as what he doth as such a common person and in the name of the other, that other whom he pesonates is by the law reckoned to do." Christ is like an attorney at law, who has the power to act in our stead. Goodwin instanced receiving money, giving possession of an estate, acting as an ambassador. Christ is also a surety, who binds himself to pay our debts, something that Adam could not be.[34] As the Shorter Catechism of

1647 put it, God must punish "all sin, either in the sinner or in Christ the surety".[35]

The legal consequences of this analogy were drawn with unpleasant thoroughness: "God having once arrested Christ, and cast him into prison and begun a trial against him and had him to judgment, he could not come forth till he had paid the very uttermost farthing".[36] But "by the law, if the surety hath discharged the debt, the debtor is then free." Christ's "death was but the satisfaction and payment"; but "in that he rose again as a common person this assures us yet further that there is a formal, legal and irrevocable act of justification of us passed and enrolled in that court of heaven between Christ and God". "For he hath engaged, and if he should fail [he] might even lose that honour which he hath now in heaven".[37] "When Christ arose, he rose as our head, and as a common person ... God accounts that we rose also with him." "In Christ as a common person, and as a pattern of us, we may be said to have done what Jesus Christ did or doth, or what befalleth him; and we are reckoned by God to have done it.... This is one of the greatest hinges of the gospel." "'I will', saith Christ, 'represent them; they are all virtually in me; and do thou, O Father, reckon them as having a subsistence in me.'... So a covenant was truly struck, through Christ's representing us, as the covenant of works was between God and Adam." The gift of the Holy Ghost was an earnest of this bargain.[38]

The doctrine of the public person, like the whole covenant theology, was often expressed in terms that drew on economic realities familiar to seventeenth-century congregations. Christ, Thomas Goodwin told his readers, "was truly and indeed God's hired servant in his work [of satisfaction], and God covenanted to give him the salvation of those he died for as his wages and reward.... So that, if God be just, he must give forth salvation, otherwise Christ's obedience would cry as the work of an hireling doth for wages".[39] Goodwin speaks much of sureties, earnest money, pawns, and pledges. Gerrard Winstanley in his early pamphlets refers to Christ as the pledge and earnest-penny.[40] The covenant, said Jeremiah Burroughs, is "God's insurance office", at which we have to pay no premium.[41] "You may sue him of his bond written and sealed, and he cannot deny it".[42] God is "willing to indent with us, to make himself a debtor to us". We must "extort, ... oppress the promises, that as a rich man oppresseth a poor man, and gets out of him all that he is worth, he leaves him worth nothing; ... after that manner deal thou with the promises, for they are rich".[43] Johnston of Wariston demanded of Christ: "show then thy satisfaction applied to me before thy Father, and tell him he cannot take twice payment for one debt ... Thy credit is now engaged, let me know that thy Father denieth thee nothing".[44]

"The act of a common person", wrote the Wiltshire antinomian William Eyre in 1654,

is the act of those whom he represents, which in law is accounted as if it had been done by them. Parents and superiors are examples to their children and inferiors, [but] they are not common persons, as Adam was to all his posterity.... We did not choose Adam to be our common person, and yet his sin was imputed to us; so though we did not choose the Lord Jesus to stand in our stead, that is no reason why his righteousness and satisfaction should not be accounted enough.[45]

But when Henry Dunster, President of Harvard, refused to baptize his new-born child since it was not yet a visible believer, he was told that "an infant makes his covenant in his public person"; "an immediate parent is a public person in regard to his children". "There is no further person but Christ for us to stand in", Dunster retorted. He was publicly censored, and soon left Harvard.[46]

The most recent historian of representation in seventeenth-century England tells us that in Elizabethan Parliaments assertions that M.Ps. were "public men" in a special relationship to their electors were "unconsidered and relatively infrequent". But under James I there developed a "stridently assertive, if incoherent, emphasis on the fact of representation".[47] It was at this time that John Preston called on electors "to keep their minds single and free from all respects, so that when they come to choose they might choose him whom in their consciences and the sight of God they think fittest for the place.... Do nothing for fear or favour of men, or for any sinister respect".[48] Such an attitude — and it was supported from overseas by the much more radical Thomas Scott — would strengthen the resistance of freeholders and burgesses faced with pressure from landlords and courtiers; it would contribute to the electorate's growing independence which Dr Hirst traces. The covenant theology made man a partner with God and God a debtor to man, so creating "a kind of equality between us". A point of faith is "when the will of a man claims God's statutes".[49]

But even under Elizabeth M.Ps. had drawn attention to their claim to be public persons and therefore in a special relation to the government. It was argued that an arrested member of Parliament should not be held in custody, "forasmuch as he was not now a private man, but to supply the room, person and place of a multitude specially chosen".[50] In 1626 Robert Mason, attacking Eliot's commitment to prison at the command of the King, insisted that "we sit not here as private men but as public vested for the commonwealth's service, and therefore ought not to be questioned for anything but wherein the commonwealth hath an interest, and for offences done against the commonwealth".[51]

In 1628 Sir Dudley Digges wanted to give no "occasion as though we distrusted him [the King] as public persons".[52] Sir John Eliot in the Tower refused to answer charges relating to words spoken in the House of Commons. "Whatsoever was said or done by him in that place and at that time was performed by him as a public man". He would always be ready to answer for his sayings and doings to the House, "but being now but a private man, he would not trouble himself to remember what he had either spoken or done in that place as a public man".[53] And in 1641 Sir John Wray said "let us remember what now we are, not only Parliament-men but public men and Englishmen.... As public men, forget not whom we here represent, and by how many chosen and trusted".[54] In a Fast Sermon of March 1642 Cornelius Burges pressed home the analogy with Adam and Christ, telling members of the House of Commons to look upon themselves "as public persons, that must both bear the sins of others whom you represent, and purge out the sins of others, or be guilty of them yourselves".[55] In later Fast Sermons Obadiah Sedgwick, Daniel Cawdrey and Thomas Hall addressed M.Ps. as public persons.[56] Peter Sterry distinguished between the two capacities of his audience, "as private Christians" and as "public persons and magistrates",[57] glancing no doubt at the Calvinist doctrine that revolt might be justified if led by the magistrate.

In Adam all men died; in Christ the elect were free. Christ died for all men, but for some more than for others. When the covenant theologians are careful they speak, as Goodwin and Eyre did in the passages just quoted, of "those he died for", those "whom he represents". But very often they speak ambiguously of "us"; "we" were condemned because of Adam's sin, "we" were saved by Christ. This ambiguity at the heart of the covenant theology, and indeed of Calvinism generally, has its political parallels.

"The church" for a Calvinist sometimes means the whole people, sometimes the elect only. Adam represents all men, Christ the elect only; but both are public persons. When Christ is considered in his representative character, the reprobate slip out of sight. Exactly the same slide occurs in seventeenth-century uses of "the people". Ireton defined them, precisely, as "the persons in whom all land lies, and those in corporations in whom all trading lies". Some, even among the Levellers, would have excluded servants and paupers from the franchise (compare the analogy between entry into a gathered congregation and acceptance of the Agreement of the People).[58] Yet Parliament represented "the people", and of course its decisions were binding on the poor as well as on the electors. The state exists for all Englishmen, but for some more than others. The theory of the representative person must have assisted this slide, of which we appear today to be so much more conscious than our seventeenth-century predecessors.

Emphasis on the representative character of the "public men" in the House of Commons came just about the time that questions were being asked about the precise way in which Adam and Jesus Christ "represented" humanity, questions which no doubt arose from the legal analogies we have been considering. For Perkins "Christ, because he is the head of the faithful, is to be considered as a public man sustaining the persons of all the elect".[59] Anthony Burges supposed that Adam "knew himself to be a common parent, and that he received a common stock for all mankind". His sin may be said to be ours "by way of delegation, as if we had chosen him to be our common parent, and had translated our wills over to him, as amongst men it is usual in arbitrations".[60] But that was written in 1659, after men had had a good deal of experience of representation. "As if we had chosen him" betrays uneasiness, since of course we hadn't. Goodwin tried to face this difficulty. There are three ways in which you may come to be a common person, he tells us: either (1) "by choice of the parties themselves, as you choose the burgesses in Parliament"; or (2) they are chosen by another – we did not choose Christ; or (3) "by God's appointment founded upon a law of nature". "Adam was by the law of nature a common parent, and therefore we come to be guilty of that first act by which our nature was defiled." "Generation is but the channel."[61]

By the time Burges and Goodwin were writing, the mere inheritance of sin was being challenged: it must be shown that Adam's posterity were more directly involved in his actions than by physical inheritance of his tainted blood. "A sinful man must beget a sinful man", wrote Thomas Goodwin. But "Adam was a public person ... which no other parent is."[62] The covenant theology had endeavoured to meet this difficulty. Burges wrote that Adam "as our head being in covenant with God, when he became a covenant breaker then we all forfeited all in and by him. So that it's the covenant of God that is the foundation of communicating original sin, as far as sin can be communicated to all mankind, yet natural generation is the medium or way of conveying it".[63]

This is precisely what was being challenged. The Quaker, Edward Burrough, in 1654 answered the question: "Whether did not the man Christ suffer as a public person in the elect's stead?" by saying

Thou makest it manifest that thou does not know the man Christ at all; ... for a public person Christ is not to thee, but a mystery which thou knowest nothing of, and for the redeeming of the elect from under such mouths as thine did and doth Christ suffer.[64]

The covenant theology had striven to replace Adam as our common parent by Adam as our representative, our attorney, just at the time that election to the House of Commons was being stressed, when constituencies were refusing to accept M.Ps. nominated by their betters, whether peers or town oligarchies, when contractual theorists were challenging Filmer's patriarchalism.

Perry Miller pointed out that the developed covenant theology, by postulating a "conditional covenant" into which men could enter freely, achieved almost all that Arminians sought to achieve by the heresy of conditional election. Both are safeguards against the antinomian possibilities latent in revolutionary Calvinism. The conditions attached to the covenant are like those imposed on "a free man of a corporation" by apprenticeship, Cotton suggested: there is no admission to the corporation of the godly by purchase.[65] Bulkeley in 1646 declared that "the Apostle saith *The promise is made unto Abraham* ... He stands as a public person, as the common parent of all the faithful to the world's end ... receiving the promise of faith not only for himself but for all that should *imitate* him in his faith."[66] Imitation implies voluntary action. That was the activism which the covenant theology insinuated into traditional Calvinism.

But in the course of the Revolution political activism came to be expressed in the radical Arminianism which Milton and others were to adopt in the name of human freedom. God could not be just if man were not free.[67] Even the elective principle did not satisfy the extremer wing; there must be a closer link between Christ and his elect than mere representation. Thomas Goodwin denied that Christ was a common person in his incarnation and intercession. Like Milton, he had little interest in the Atonement.[68] "We are said to be risen in Christ as in a common person, and to sit in heavenly places in him ... because we are one with him ... When a man is thus quickened and turned to God, the state of that man is altered; ... he doth now actually sit with Christ in heaven." Christ is "a common person, ... the first fruits of a company of members that are raised with him as a common head".[69] The patriarchs, Goodwin told the House of Commons in February 1646, "may be understood as common persons, representing indeed the nation of the Jews. All the saints are their successors."[70]

All the saints then are common persons? The elect represent the nation? Here in explicit form is the slide from "the people of England" to "the good people". The good people represent the rest, as Christ represented the good people. "The Son and the saints make one perfect man", declared William Erbery, who took over many of Thomas Goodwin's theological ideas. "Though there shall be but one king in all the earth, yet all the saints shall reign on earth also." The Second Coming is when God "appears in glory in us ... God appearing in the saints shall punish kings of the earth upon the earth."[71]

But if Adam represented humanity, Christ should do so too. The scales of justice would not be held even if Christ represented only the elect. A century earlier the radical sectary Henry Hart had rejected absolute predestination on the ground that "it putteth away the covenant between God and man ... in that Christ is denied to be a general Saviour to all men." Salvation depends on actively putting oneself under "the covenant of God".[72] Such ideas no doubt survived underground, to be picked up by the radicals of the revolutionary decades. Thus Henry Denne: "The Lord Christ being a common person, taking our nature upon him, we are said to do that which he did, and to have that done upon us which was done upon him".[73]

Winstanley as usual produced the most radical version of this doctrine.

As the body of the first man was a representation of the whole creation, and did corrupt it, so the body of Christ was a representation of the whole creation, and restores it from corruption and brings all into the unity of the Father again. In this particular lies the mystery of the Fall and the restoration of all things again.

All mankind is "but the one first Adam", the mighty power of flesh. "*The whole bulk of mankind*, when they shall be drawn up to live in the unity of the one spirit, is the second man [i.e. Christ] and every son and daughter of this spirit is of the lineage of the second man". "Mankind ... shall be the mystical body of Christ". Hitherto the second man did never rule in earth, being held down and kept as a servant by the first man. But now things are changing.[74] The oligarchy of grace which the covenant theology still assumed is being explicitly democratized. Christ no longer represents the elect only: he incorporates — indeed he is — all mankind.

Lords were public persons; M.Ps. were public persons; the House of Commons in April 1643 "took the Lord General to be a public person", who might have lands voted to him as an individual.[75] George Wither in 1652 described how he had served the commonwealth "otherwise as a private, and sometimes as a public person".[76] He had been a Justice of the Peace in the sixteen-forties, but he more probably refers to his service as captain and colonel, first in Charles I's army against the Scots in 1639 and then in the Parliamentary army during the civil war. In 1649 the officers of the New Model Army were drawn from a lower social class than when the Earl of Essex had been Lord General, but it was claimed that they too "are public persons", and that the Presbyterian ministers who aspersed them "(though presumed public) are in civil things private".[77] The theory of the public person thus made possible an extension of the Calvinist doctrine that revolt might be justified if led by the magistrate.

The preachers had called on M.Ps. to act as public persons. When after the summer of 1647 the Army effectively took over power from Parliament, it was natural that it, or its leaders, should succeed to the claim to be public persons representing the people. We may see such a claim in the New Model Army's declaration of June 1647: "We were not a mere mercenary army, hired to serve any arbitrary power of a state, but called forth and conjured by the several declarations of Parliament to the defence of our own and the people's just rights and liberties ... against all particular parties or interests whatsoever."[78]

God, Milton wrote in the first *Defence of the People of England*, has "handed over to the state and with it all its officers not patience but laws and arms to avenge wrong and violence". When *Ecclesiastes* asks, Who may say to the King "what doest thou?" he is "instructing neither the Great Sanhedrin nor the Senate, but private persons"; and Milton draws the appropriate conclusions for England. David would not slay Saul "being a private citizen". But public persons are liable to no such limitations: "shall a senate therefore fear to touch a tyrant?"[79] A century earlier Christopher Goodman argued that kings were public persons, but that they might lose this public capacity and "be taken of all men as private persons" if they became tyrants or murderers.[80]

"What makes a public person above a private", William Sedgwick asked in 1649, "but that he hath the civil sword in his hand to administer justice?" This led him to reflect that the Army was superior to Parliament because it had a sharper sword: Parliament lost its authority when it turned England into an armed camp. The Army was composed of "men of the common and ordinary rank of people, most of them of trades and husbandry (with a small mixture of the gentry) which are the body and strength of the kingdom, in which the common interest most lies". "This Army is truly the people of the kingdom", not "in a gross heap" but by the ordinance of God.[81] Just as the elect might be public persons representing the rest, so the New Model was "the Army of God, as public persons and not for a particular interest". As early as 1646 Thomas Edwards reported that John Hitch, former soldier turned preacher, told the incumbent of a Buckinghamshire parish that he, Hitch, "was as public a person as himself".[82]

We see the culmination of this process in Milton's *Samson Agonistes*. Adam and Eve were public persons in *Paradise Lost*: so was the Son of God in *Paradise Regained;* so was Samson. In *Areopagitica* the poet had seen the people of England as a Samson, "shaking his invincible locks"; in the *Defence of the People of England* Samson was a rebel who "thought it not impious but pious to kill those masters who were tyrants over his country".[83] In *Samson Agonistes* Milton carefully prepared the identification of Samson with the New Model Army. In his first speech Manoa referred to his son as "himself an army", and later he spoke of

> those locks
> That of a nation armed the strength contained ...

> Garrisoned round about him like a camp
> Of faithful soldiery.[84]

Harapha denounced Samson as "a murderer, revolter and a rob-
ber", since his nation was

> subject to our lords.
> Their magistrates confessed it when they took thee
> As a league-breaker and delivered bound
> Into our hands.

The regicides and Army leaders were subject to similar accusations
after 1660, when they too had been "delivered bound" to "unjust
tribunals under change of times". Samson's reply was

> I was no private but a person raised
> With strength sufficient and command from heaven
> To free my country.[85]

This echoes the New Model Army's declaration of June 1647,
quoted on p. 312 above. That Army, like Samson, was representative
not so much "as you choose the burgesses in Parliament", but "by
God's appointment founded upon a law of nature": justice and force
well met. Milton endorsed the argument which John Cook had
intended to use against Charles I in his trial: that the High Court of
Justice "was a resemblance and representation of the great day of
judgment, when the saints shall judge all worldly powers".[86] The
godly were public persons because Christ was a public person, and
they were part of Christ. So they could not only oppose but even
judge their sovereign, now a public person no longer.

But when the doctrine of the public person could be extended to
justify a revolution of which the men of property had lost control,
the covenant theology itself became less attractive – in old England if
not in New England. Part of the original point of seeing Adam as a
public person was to substitute the representative for the hereditary
principle. "Adam's offence in eating the forbidden fruit is not to be
reputed as a personal offence, but he being a public person it was a
public sin, even the sin of all mankind." So Samuel Hieron, who died
in 1617. Sin is inherited: heaven is an inheritance, owing nothing to
merit.[87] "Adam, the parent and head of all men, either stood or fell as
a representative of the whole human race." So Milton tells us in the

De Doctrina Christiana: he repeated it in *Paradise Lost*.[88] By this
time Milton was aware that the justice of visiting the sins of the
fathers upon the children was being challenged, by Socinians and
others, and he himself disliked the hereditary principle in politics.
But the Bible is clear on this matter, as Milton abundantly showed,
adding examples of "a very ancient law among all races and all
religions", and quoting Thucydides, Virgil, and the English law of
treason.[89] He clearly felt a little uneasy on the subject. Bunyan had no
doubts. "All had transgressed in the first Adam, as he stood a
common person representing both himself and us in his standing and
falling." Adam and Christ were "the two great public persons or
representators of the whole world, as to the first and second
covenants".[90]

But others were even more uneasy than Milton, and some of them
put the inner light before the letter of the Bible. I quoted Edward
Burrough. Another Quaker, Robert Barclay, flatly rejected the
hereditary implications of the theory. "That Adam is a public person
is not denied," but it does not follow from this that all infants share
Adam's guilt.[91] When we get to Locke the covenant has become
totally Arminian: repentance was an absolute condition of the new
covenant. For Locke, as for Bulkeley,[92] as for Milton in *Paradise Lost*
and *Paradise Regained*, what Christ gives us is a clearer perception of
the reality of God, of the *reasons* for behaving morally. We are no
longer bound by traditional ceremonies. But once we have reached
that stage the covenant theology itself becomes superfluous.[93]
Morality is self-validating.

In its secular form the doctrine of the original contract was not
always liberating. In 1628 Sir Robert Phelips declared that "it is well-
known that the people of this state are under no other subjection
than what they did voluntarily assent unto by their original contract
between king and people".[94] He was arguing against the great anti-
Puritan, Roger Mainwaring. Here the appeal to the past set men free
in the present: the contract was used to call existing authority in
question. But when in New England John Winthrop said that men
were not to be brought under any rule otherwise "than according to
their will and covenant; ... the foundation of the people's power is
their liberty",[95] his intention was to restrict some men's freedom by
means of a contract known or alleged to be known. The Levellers
were soon to hear Ireton at Putney telling them in Hobbist terms
that they must keep their covenants made. The appeal to the past

could be used to impose new chains. Uncertainty concerning what the original contract had said meant that it could be twisted either way.

Consequently many radicals became dissatisfied less with the ambiguities of the conception of the public person than with the whole idea of the dependence of the present on the past. When the Levellers proclaimed that "whatever our forefathers were, or whatever they did or suffered or were enforced to yield unto, we are the men of the present age, and ought to be absolutely free from all kinds of exorbitancies, molestations or arbitrary power",[96] they were no doubt thinking primarily of liberation from the Norman Yoke. But the principle that men were bound only by agreements into which they themselves had freely entered was to undermine the whole idea of a covenant made once for all in remote antiquity by representative persons. It is another example of the dissidence of dissent: puritan individualism dissolved its own central doctrine of the covenant.[97] By 1738 John Taylor could reject the idea of inheritance of original sin as expressed in the covenant theology's picture of Adam as a public person. It is unreasonable, he declared, for any man "without my knowledge and consent" so to represent me that I become guilty of his sin.[98] This line of argument would undermine any theory which based political obligation on a supposedly historical social contract.

So the theory of the public, common, or representative person helped to liberate from the constraints of a traditional status society those who believed themselves to be the elect. If such men could demand their rights from God, could extort the promises from him, they would hardly be more deferential to princes. The theory helped, perhaps, to dissociate the idea of representation from the idea of election (in the political sense, election from below). The slide from Adam representing all men to Christ representing the elect reinforced mental attitudes which saw the church as the whole of society and yet more particularly as the elect members of it, which saw the people as the whole populace and yet more particularly as the men of some substance in that society. The elect were chosen by God; M.Ps. were not elected by the headless multitude. During the Revolution the idea of the public person helped both the godly and the Army to see themselves as in the truest sense representatives of the people, even though not elected by them.

The doctrine faded out after the revolutionary decades, as Arminianism replaced Calvinism, as secular contract theory replaced religious theories, as "natural" rights replaced pseudo-historical rights, as a morality of internal conviction replaced a morality of external observance.

When we ask ourselves what influence the idea of the public person had on the evolution of political thinking in seventeenth-century England, it does not appear to be very great. I find no significant trace of the idea in the writings of Filmer, Hunton, Henry Parker, the Levellers, Winstanley, Milton, Harrington or Baxter. Its direct influence on modern theories of representation, which assume the election of representatives, seems to be nil. But it is worth perhaps pausing for a moment over the greatest seventeenth-century political thinker of all – Thomas Hobbes.

The sovereign in *Leviathan* is a public person – the only public person.

A person is he whose words or actions are considered either as his own or as representing the words or actions of another man, or of any other thing to whom they are attributed, whether truly or by fiction. When they are considered as his own, then is he called a natural person; and when they are considered as representing the words and actions of another, then is he a feigned or artificial person.[99]

Hobbes steers very carefully round the covenant theology's doctrine of the public person. "The true God may be personated", as he was first by Moses and secondly by Jesus Christ. But "to make covenant with God is impossible but by mediation of such as God speaketh to, either by revelation supernatural or by his lieutenants that govern under him and in his name". Hobbes' object here is to substitute Leviathan for Jesus Christ. None represents God's person "but God's lieutenant, who hath the sovereignty under God." Any other "pretence of covenant with God is so evident a lie, even in the pretenders' own consciences, that it is not only an act of an unjust but also of a vile and unmanly disposition". Moses was a political sovereign.[100]

In *Leviathan* Hobbes repeatedly emphasizes that "a common-wealth is but one person", and that the sovereign, whether a man or a body of men, "is the absolute representative of all the subjects". "And therefore no other can be representative of any part of them, but so far forth as he shall give leave."[101] Parliament in a monarchy like England cannot be considered the representative of the people. The sovereign is called "the representative person of a common-wealth".[102] Private men have no political authority "without permission from the representative of the commonwealth". Those who are employed by the sovereign "in any affairs, with authority to represent in that employment the person of the commonwealth" – viceroys, treasurers, generals, authorized preachers, judges, J.Ps., ambassadors – are very carefully called "public ministers".[103]

In *The Elements of Law* (published 1650, but written in 1640) and in the *De Cive* (1642) there is no elaborate description of the sovereign as a representative person such as is fundamental to *Leviathan*.[104] In both the earlier works Hobbes stresses the impossibility of covenanting with God "further than it hath pleased him to declare who shall receive and accept of the covenant in his name", and describes the sovereign in passing as "a person civil". But that is all. What had happened between 1640-2 and 1651 to cause this change of emphasis? It seems to me possible that Hobbes' insistence that the sovereign is the only true representative of the people may owe something to the popularity of the covenant theology, and in particular of the claims made in the sixteen-forties that Parliament and the Army were public persons. Hobbes naturally wished to refute those who "have pretended for their disobedience to their sovereign a new covenant made not with men but with God." But the violence of his language against covenant theologians in general ("so evident a lie", "a vile and unmanly disposition") suggests that he regarded them as significant enemies even though he failed to name them.[105] The covenant theologians had argued that the elected should also be the elect.[106] But the Long Parliament had proved disappointing in this respect, at least to the radicals. Theories of Fifth Monarchism or of the dictatorship of the godly were a natural consequence, as we have seen. The more activist version of the elect as public persons, the version of Thomas Goodwin, John Cook, John Milton and Fifth Monarchists, was sufficiently prevalent in 1651 for Hobbes to wish to refute it.

The frontispiece to *Leviathan* shows the public person of the sovereign incorporating all individual subjects. This may have been inspired by the contemporary concept of the composite Christ: for radical theologians Christ was a representative person compounded of all the faithful.[107] The doctrine that the godly were part of Christ and therefore entitled to act for him in earthly affairs was as dangerous for Hobbes as the claims to inspiration which he so fiercely lampooned.[108] It was characteristic of him to twist his opponents' arguments to suit his own purposes.

The time indeed was propitious. As the godly discredited themselves in the sixteen-fifties, as they fragmented into a welter of competing sects, so the ungodly rule of Leviathan came to seem more and more attractive to men who had property to lose.[109] It mattered less who the sovereign was – the Long Parliament, the Lord Protector, Charles II – or how he had acquired his office, than that he should maintain law, order, property and social security, and be accepted by the bulk of his subjects. For Hobbes the best way to get him accepted seemed to be to say that he represented them: he and no one else.[110] If I am right, then the doctrine of the public person may have had at least a negative influence on Hobbes, making him think out more carefully his own theory of representation. And from there modern political thinking begins.

NOTES

1. First published in *Powers, Possessions and Freedom: Essays in honour of C. B. Macpherson* (ed. A. Kontos, Toronto U.P., 1979).
2. *Commentary on Galatians* (Eng. trans., 1807), I, p. 304. This translation was approved by Edwin Sandys, Bishop of London when it was published in 1575.
3. Tyndale, *Expositions and Notes on Sundry Portions of the Holy Scriptures* (Parker Soc., 1849), p. 9, 76, 87, 96, and *passim*; L. J. Trinterud, "The Origins of Puritanism", *Church History*, 20 (1951), p. 48. I am indebted to David Zaret for help with the covenant theology.
4. B. Whitelocke, *Journal of the Swedish Embassy* (1855), II, p. 438; cf. Alan Everitt, "The Development of Private Marketing", in *The Agrarian History of England and Wales*, IV, *1500-1640*, esp. pp. 543-63.
5. Perry Miller, "The Marrow of Puritan Divinity", *Publications of the Colonial Society of Massachusetts*, XXXII (1935), pp. 292-3. See p. 250 above for the significance of "or some men".
6. *Of the Laws of Ecclesiastical Polity* (Everyman edn.), II, p. 506.
7. A. Harding, *A Social History of English Law* (Penguin edn.), pp. 104-6; D. Little, *Religion, Order and Law* (Oxford 1970), pp. 204-5.
8. *Capital*, III (Chicago, 1909), p. 696.
9. *Doctrinal Treatises* (Parker Soc., 1848), pp. 224, 252-3.
10. *The Institutes of the Christian Religion*, trans. H. Beveridge (1949), II, p. 477; cf. p. 39.
11. *Ecclesiastical Polity*, II, p. 287. Contrast Hobbes, quoted p. 317 above.
12. *Works* (Edinburgh, 1862-4), IV, p. 122; cf. III, p. 394.
13. *Op. cit.* (1704; first published in the sixteen fifties), p. 1; cf. pp. 12-23.
14. *Ibid.*, p. 314; Tyndale, *Doctrinal Treatises*, p. 403; cf. p. 470.

15. W. Gouge, *A Commentary on the Whole Epistle to the Hebrews* (Edinburgh, 1866-7), II, p. 187; G. Hakewill, *An Apologie or Declaration of the Power and Providence of God in the Government of the World* (3rd edn., 1635), II, p. 147; Miller, "The Marrow of Puritan Divinity", pp. 292-7.

16. S. Hieron, *Sermons* (1624), pp. 221, 293, 352, 356.

17. Cf. Perry Miller, *The New England Mind: The Seventeenth Century* (New York, 1939), pp. 401-8; P. Miller and T. H. Johnston, *The Puritans* (New York, 1938), pp. 188-91; my *Puritanism and Revolution*, pp. 240-3.

18. *M.C.P.W.* II, pp. 366-7.

19. P. Bulkeley, *The Gospel-Covenant: Or The Covenant of Grace Opened* (1646), pp. 435-6.

20. *Works*, VII, p. 249.

21. Gouge, *Commentary*, II, p. 185; T. Goodwin, *Works* (Edinburgh, 1861-3), I, pp. 70-1, 74-6; cf. p. 123, 330, 435; Sibbes, *Works*, VI, p. 350.

22. Z. Ursinus, *The Summe of Christian Religion* (1645), p. 124-7; J. Owen, *Works* (1850-3), VI, pp. 76-9; Sibbes, *Works*, VI, pp. 1-25; Bulkeley, *The Gospel-Covenant*, p. 38.

23. See esp. J. Preston, *The Breastplate of Faith and Love* (5th edn., 1634), p. 4 (sermons preached 1625); Sibbes, *Works*, III, p. 571, IV, p. 462, VII, p. 192; K. L. Sprunger, *The Learned Dr. William Ames* (Urbana, 1972), pp. 148-52; Bridge, *A Lifting up for the Downcast* (1648), pp. 136, 182 (I cite from the 1961 reprint); Owen, *Works*, II, p. 179, X, p. 358.

24. *The Saints Qualification* (2nd. edn., 1634), p. 38; Miller, "The Marrow of Puritan Divinity", pp. 281-3; cf. my *Puritanism and Revolution*, pp. 240-2 for Preston and the covenant theology.

25. *The Larger Catechism* (Edinburgh, 1865), pp. 110, 122.

26. Davies, *The Complete Works* (ed. A. B. Grosart, 1878), II, *The Scourge of Folly*, p. 81; Penry Williams, *The Tudor Regime* (Oxford U.P., 1979), p. 391.

27. C. Holmes, "Drainers and Fenmen: the Problem of Popular Political Consciousness in the Seventeenth Century", in Fletcher and Stevenson, *op. cit.*, p. 191; P. Slack, *The Impact of Plague in Tudor and Stuart England* (1985), p. 43; *Thurloe State Papers*, IV, p. 281.

28. Perkins, *Works*, I, p. 161; II, pp. 214-15.

29. L. Brown, "Ideas of Representation, Elizabeth to Charles I", *Journal of Modern History*, II (1939), pp. 26-7. Cf. Corrigan and Sayer, *The Great Arch*, p. 29.

30. Quoted by Miller, *The New England Mind: The Seventeenth Century*, p. 401; cf. pp. 307-8 above.

31. The Papers of George Wyatt (ed. D. M. Loades, Camden fourth series, 5, 1968), p. 71.

32. Cockburn, *Western Circuit Assize Orders, 1629-1648*, p. 186; cf. p. 209 (J.Ps. to elect a constable), 235, 286 (the Assize Court "electing" a constable).

33. *Works*, II, p. 239; cf. Bunyan, *Works*, I, p. 304.

34. Goodwin, *Works*, IV, p. 27. For Christ as surety as well as public

person, cf. Paul Bayne, *An Entire Commentary upon the Whole Epistle of St. Paul to the Ephesians* (Edinburgh, 1866), p. 82 (first published in 1643; Bayne died in 1617); Owen, *Works*, X, p. 358; Sibbes, *Works*, V, p. 326-7, 345; VI, p. 245; Bunyan, *Works*, I, pp. 525, 564.

35. *The Shorter Catechism* (1897), p. 22.
36. Goodwin, *Works*, IV, p. 30; cf. pp. 31-41, *passim.*
37. *Ibid.*, IV, p. 30, 39, 71, 87-8; cf. pp. 32-5.
38. *Ibid.*, I, pp. 254-5, IV, p. 33, 244; cf. p. 265; I, p. 75; and Bunyan, *Works*, I, pp. 525-6, 564.
39. Goodwin, *Works*, IV, p. 215.
40. *The Mysterie of God, Concerning the Whole Creation, Mankind* (1649; first published 1648), p. 28; *The Saints Paradise* (n.d.?1649), p. 53, 119.
41. *The Rare Jewel of Christian Contentment* (1964; first published 1648), pp. 79-80, 201.
42. Quoted in Miller, *The New England Mind: the Seventeenth Century,* pp. 289-90.
43. Preston, *The New Covenant* (5th edn., 1630), p. 331, 477-8.
44. Sir A. Johnston of Wariston, *Diary* (Scottish History Soc., xvi, 1917-40), I.
45. Eyre, *Vindiciae Justificationis Gratuitae, Justification without Conditions* (1654), p. 151. This was an attack on Benjamin Woodbridge of Newbury, who replied at length in *The Method of Grace in the Justification of Sinners* (1656). Pp. 283-99 deal with the concept of a common person. See esp. p. 287.
46. P.F. Gura, *A Glimpse of Sion's Glory: Puritan Radicalism in New England, 1620-1660* (Wesleyan U.P., 1984), pp. 121-2.
47. Derek Hirst, *The Representative of the People?*, p. 8.
48. Preston, *Life Eternall* (4th. edn., 1634), Sermon XII, p. 67; cf. my *Puritanism and Revolution*, pp. 240-1, 255-6.
49. T. Hooker, *The Soules Vocation* (1638), p. 460. I owe this reference to David Zaret.
50. Sir S. D'Ewes, *The Journals of All the Parliaments during the Reign of Queen Elizabeth* (1682), pp. 175, 241; L.F. Brown, "Ideas of Representation from Elizabeth to Charles I", *Journal of Modern History*, 2 (1939), pp. 26-7. Cf. the epigraph to this chapter.
51. M.A. Judson, *The Crisis of the Constitution*, p. 302.
52. *Commons Debates, 1628*, III, p. 221.
53. Crewe, *The Proceedings and Debates of the House of Commons*, p. 163.
54. J. Nalson, *An Impartial Collection of the Great Affairs of State* (1682), I, p. 786.
55. *Two Sermons Preached to the Honourable House of Commons* (1645), p. 37.
56. Sedgwick, *England's Preservation* (1642), p. 25; Cawdrey, *The Good Man* (1643), p. 36; Hill, *The Season for Englands Selfe-Reflection* (1644), p. 22.
57. *The Spirits Conviction of Sinne* (1645), pp. 29-30; cf. Richard Overton, *An Appeale From the degenerate Representative Body the Commons ... to the People Represented* (1647), p. 23.

58. Macpherson, *The Political Theory of Possessive Individualism,* Chapter 3; K.V. Thomas, "The Levellers and the Franchise", in *The Interregnum: The Quest for Settlement,* ed. G.E. Aylmer (1972), pp. 57-78. Cf. Chapter 12 above.

59. *Works,* I, p. 78.

60. *Of Original Sin* (1659), pp. 38-9; cf. 2, 46.

61. *Works,* II, pp. 126-33.

62. *Loc. cit.*

63. *Of Original Sin,* p. 165.

64. "Answer to several Queries put forward by Philip Bennett, who calls himself minister of Christ but is found a deceiver", in *The Memorable Works* (1672), p. 31.

65. J. Cotton, *The Covenant of Gods Free Grace* (1645), quoted by Miller, "The Marrow of Puritan Divinity", pp. 285-6.

66. *The Gospel-Covenant,* p. 38. I have italicized the word "imitate".

67. *M.C.P.W.,* VI, pp. 160-6, 397.

68. *Works,* IV, pp. 70-1, 1, 98-9.

69. *Ibid.,* I, p. 462, II, pp. 241-2, 244.

70. *The Great Interest of States & Kingdoms* (1646), p. 4. Goodwin meant something very different from Richard Montagu when he provocatively described St. Peter as a public person in *A New Gagg for an Old Goose* (1624), p. 64.

71. *The Testimony of William Erbery* (1658), pp. 8, 40; cf. pp. 3-4, 10-11, 15, 18, 23. Cf. Chapter 12 above.

72. *The Writings of John Bradford* (Parker Soc., 1848), pp. 322-3, where Bradford quotes Hart in order to refute him; J.W. Martin, "English Protestant Separatism at Its Beginnings: Henry Hart and the Free-Will Men", *Sixteenth Century Journal,* 7 (1976), esp. pp. 70-2.

73. H. Denne, *Grace, Mercy and Peace* (1645), in *Records of the Churches of Christ gathered at Fenstanton, Warboys and Hexham, 1644-1720* (ed. E.B. Underhill, Hanserd Knollys Soc., 1854), pp. 412-13.

74. Sabine, *Works of Gerrard Winstanley,* pp. 116-17, 120-1, 162-3, 225, 486. My italics. Cf. *Paradise Lost,* V, lines 609-10, and Paul Hobson, *Christ the Effect, not the Cause, of the Love of God* (1820), p. 15. First published 1646.

75. *Mercurius Aulicus,* 30 April 1643.

76. *Parallelogrammaton* (1652), p. 8.

77. [Anon.], *The True Primitive State of Civil and Ecclesiasticall Government* (March 1648-9), p. 15.

78. Haller and Davies, *The Leveller Tracts,* p. 55.

79. *M.C.P.W. IV,* pp. 346-7, 398, 402; cf. *Ecclesiastes VIII: 4.*

80. *How Superior Powers Ought to be Obeyed of Their Subjects* (Geneva, 1558), pp. 187-8, quoted by Q. Skinner, *The Foundations of Modern Political Thought* (Cambridge U.P. 1978), II, p. 223. Goodman may be relying on John Major, *History of Greater Britain* (1521), quoted by Skinner in *ibid.,* II, p. 121.

81. *A Second View of the Army Remonstrance* (1649), pp. 6, 11-13.

82. *The Testimony of William Erbery,* p. 25; *Gangraena* (1646), I, p. 70.

83. *M.C.P.W.*, II, pp. 558, IV, p. 402.

84. Lines 346 and 1493-8. For other similar comparisons, see M.E.R., pp. 429-30, 435.

85. Lines 1178-85, 1211-13. "Subject to our lords" refers to the radical theory of the Norman Yoke, to which the free English people had been subjected. See my *Puritanism and Revolution*, pp. 58-125.

86. Cook, *King Charls his Case* (1649), in *Somers Tracts* (1748-51), IV, p. 196; cf. *M.C.P.W.*, III, p. 597, VI, pp. 499-501, and John Canne, *A Voice From the Temple to the Higher Powers* (1653), p. 14.

87. Hieron, *Sermons*, pp. 373, 420; cf. Hakewill, *An Apologie*, p. 601.

88. *M.C.P.W.*; VI, p. 384. Cf. Addison: "the principal actors" in *Paradise Lost* "are not only our progenitors but our representatives. We have an actual interest in everything they do" (*The Spectator*, No. 273, 12 January 1712).

89. *M.C.P.W.*, IV, pp. 385-8. Cf. Preston: "It is true Adam ran in debt, but do not we pay many debts of our grandfathers and fathers, which we never drunk for?" (*The Saints Qualification*, p. 38).

90. John Bunyan, *Law and Grace* (Oxford U.P., 1976; first published 1659), pp. 28, 55, 94; cf. p. 166. Bunyan cites I John III. 4; Romans V. 12; I Corinthians XV. 22.

91. *Apology*, Proposition Fourth, para, 5. For Burrough see p. 306 above.

92. See p. 310 above.

93. G.R. Cragg, *From Puritanism to the Age of Reason* (Cambridge U.P. 1950), pp. 127-9.

94. Quoted by Gardiner, *The History of England, 1603-1642*, VI, p. 237.

95. Quoted by Miller, *The New England Mind: the Seventeenth Century*, p. 408.

96. Wolfe, *Leveller Manifestoes of the Puritan Revolution*, p. 114; cf. pp. 157-8.

97. Trinterud, "The Origins of Puritanism", p. 53.

98. Quoted in Perry Miller, *Jonathan Edwards* (Toronto, 1949), pp. 277-8.

99. *Leviathan* (Penguin edn.), p. 217.

100. *Ibid.*, pp. 197, 220, 230, 503.

101. *Ibid.*, pp. 405, 220-1, 228, 275-6; cf. pp. 381, 524.

102. *Ibid.*, pp. 241, 307, 317; cf. Chapter 30, *passim.*

103. *Ibid.*, pp. 700, 289-94. Hobbes uses the words "public person" only once and in the negative: councillors without executive authority are not public persons.

104. *The Elements of Law*, ed. F. Tönnies (Cambridge U.P., 1928), pp. 60-1, 97; cf. pp. 84, 133, 138. See also Hobbes, *English Works* (ed. Sir William Molesworth 1839-45), II, pp. 20-2, 69-73 — the *De Cive*; and F.C. Hood, *The Divine Politics of Thomas Hobbes* (Oxford U.P. 1964), pp. 146-9. Cf. p. 251 above.

105. *Leviathan*, p. 230.

106. Cf. Preston, quoted on p. 307 above.

107. Cf. *M.E.R.*, pp. 303-5.

108. *Leviathan*, pp. 440-2, 691-2; cf. pp. 205-6. "To speak by inspiration, like a bagpipe", wrote Hobbes in his *Answer* to Davenant's *Preface*

before Gondibert, in *Sir William Davenant's Gondibert* (ed. D. Gladish Oxford U.P., 1972), p.49. Cf. also Hobbes, *English Works*, II, pp.277-9: the mystical body of the church, of which Christ is the head, is not one person.

109. Cf. W.Lamont, *Godly Rule: Politics and Religion, 1603-1660* (1969), esp. pp.125-9, 175-6.
110. *Leviathan*, pp.227-8.

Index

Abbott, George, Archbishop of Canterbury, 50
Abbott, W.C., 69-70
Abramsky, Chimen, 240
Absolute monarchy, absolutism, 5, 32, 40, 50, 52-3, 97, 104, 132
Addison, Joseph, 323
Admiralty, Court of, 27, 229-30
Aeschylus, 241
Africa, Africans, 127, 130, 171, 288
Agitators, the, 81, 262
Agreement of the People, the, 81-3, 181, 301, 309
Agrippa, Cornelius, 282
Alchemy, chapter 13 *passim*
Ale-houses, 50
Alfred, King of England, 13
Almanacs, 281
Amboyna, massacre of, 109
America, 14, 88-9, 102, 110, 129-30, 162, 165-6, 179, 188, 237, 242, 253, 255, 288, 290-1
Ames, William, 168, 303-4
Amsterdam, 129-32, 136, 139, 171, 285
Amussen, Susan, 217
Anabaptists, 79, 99, 167, 170, 180, 201, 216, 219, 255, 267
Andrewes, Lancelot, Bishop of Winchester, 117, 256
Anne, Queen of England, Queen Anne's Bounty, 115
Anglo-Saxons, the, Anglo-Saxon Chronicle, the, 13, 290
Antal, Frederick, 4
Antigua, 167, 169, 176
Antinomians, antinomianism, 201
Antichrist, 96, 174
Antwerp, 129, 139
Appleby, Joyce, 46, 66

Aquinas, Thomas, 292
Aretino, Pietro, 229
Ariès, Philippe, 188
Aristotle, Aristotelianism, 280, 286
Armada, the Spanish, 87, 109
Arminianism, Arminians, 49-50, 311, 315-17
Army, the New Model, chapter 4 *passim*, 96, 106, 108, 161, 174, 231, 248-9, 261-4, 267, 312-14, 316, 318
Arundel, Thomas Howard, Earl of, 176
Ashley, Maurice, 70
Ashley-Cooper, Sir Anthony, later Earl of Shaftesbury, 92, 253, 280
Ashton, Robert, 111
Asia, 243, 288
Asiento, the, 139
Assada, 166, 177
Astell, Mary, 203
Aston, Sir Thomas, 249
Astrology, chapter 13 *passim*
Atlantic Ocean, the, 110, 134, 140
Aubrey, John, 115-16, 284
Auden, W.H., 65
Austria, 73
Avery, Captain John, 177-8
Aztecs, the, 126

Babbage, Charles, 240
Bacon, Sir Francis, Lord Verulam, Baconianism, 135, 241, 259, 265, 277-82, 286, 291-2, 297-8, 303
Bahamas, the, 174
Baillie, Robert, 70
Bale, John, 227
Bank of England, the, 104-5, 139

Bankes, Sir John, Attorney-General, 108
Baptism, chapter 9 and postscript *passim*, 301
Baptists, 15
Barbados, chapter 8 *passim*
Barclay, Robert, 315
Barg, M.A., 123
Barnes, T.G., 33, 48
Barrington, Sir Thomas, 27
Barton Stacey Hundred, 305
Basset, Anne, chapter 7 *passim*
Basset, Frances, 159
Basset, James and John, chapter 7 *passim*
Bate's Case, 30, 49
Baxter, Richard, 254, 317
Baynes, Captain Adam, 249, 251
Beard, Thomas, 90
Beaulieu, John, 41
Beaumont, Francis, 117
Becker, Carl, 14
Bedford, William Russell, Earl of, 28, 36, 76-7
Bedfordshire, 36
Bedlam Hospital, 191
Behn, Aphra, 167, 201-2
Bekynshaw, John, 150
Bell, Clive, 4
Bellamy, Captain, 165
Bellers, John, 241
Bentham, Jeremy, 240
Berkeley, George, Bishop of Cloyne, 241
Berkshire, 23
Bermuda, 167-70, 181
Bernal, J.D., 275, 281, 293
Bernard, St., 301
Bethel, Slingsby, 88
Bible, the, 3, 106, 162-3, 248, 265, 276, 278-9, 282, 284, 290-1, 300, 315
Birth control, 197, 200, 228
Bishops, 54, 114-15, 253
Blackburn, David, 123
Blackstone, Sir William, 102
Blackwood, B.G., 23
Blake, Admiral Robert, 109, 138

Blake, William, 11-12, 17, 68, 115
Blasphemy Act, 1650, 231
Bodin, Jean, 277
Bohemia, 285
Bolshevik party, Bolsheviks, 25, 152
Bond, Samson, 170
Bonny, Anne, 181
Booth, Sir George, later Lord Delamere, 252
Boothby, Robert, 177
Bordeaux, 134, 181
Boswell, James, 201
Botolph, Gregory, 159-60
Bowden, Peter, 41, 261
Boyle, the Hon. Robert, 114, 276-7, 286, 297-8
Bradford, William, 12
Brahe, Tycho, 276-7
Brazil, 152
Braudel, Fernand, 4, 16-17, chapter 6 *passim*
Breda, Declaration of, 45
Brereton, Sir William, 78-9, 99
Bridge, William, 304
Bright, John, 240
Bristol, 91
Broghil, Roger Boyle, Lord, later Earl of Orrery, 89, 92
Brontë, Charlotte, 69, 242
Brooke, Fulke Greville, Lord, 23
Browne, Sir Thomas, 229, 276, 282, 284
Bruno, Giordano, 7, 280, 282
Buckatzsch, John, 188
Buckingham, George Villiers, first Duke of, 27-9, 36, 38, 43-5, 53, 226, 277
Buckingham, George Villiers, second Duke of, 226
Buckinghamshire, 313
Bulkeley, Peter, 304, 315
Bulmer, John, 229
Bunting, Jabez, 74
Bunyan, John, 6, 15-16, 90, 118, 201, 290, 315
Burges, Cornelius, 308-10

Burials, chapter 9 and postscript
passim
Burke, Edmund, 241
Burns, Robert, 242
Burrough, Edward, 310, 315
Burroughs, Jeremiah, 306
Butler, Martin, 66
Butler, Samuel, 228, 241
Byrne, M. St. Clare, chapter 7
passim
Byron, George Gordon, Lord, 68,
242

Caesar, Julius, 16-17
Caesar, Sir Julius, 24-5
Calais, chapter 7 *passim*
Calves Head Club, the, 162
Calvin, Jean, Calvinists, 49, 74-5,
89, 91, 163, 202, 256, 259, 276,
282-4, 286-7, 292-3, 300-1,
chapter 14 *passim*
Cambridge University, 4, 286
Cambridgeshire, 211, 214
Campanella, Tommaso, 280, 282
Campbell, Mildred, 24
Campeachy, 173
Capp, Bernard, 66, 220
Caribbean Sea, the, 169, 171, 174
Carisbrooke Castle, 81
Carlyle, Thomas, 69-70, 148, 241
Cartesianism, Cartesians, 285, 287;
see also Descartes, Réné
Cartwright, Major John, 68
Cartwright, Thomas, 254
Casaubon, Isaac, 290
Castlehaven, Mervyn Touchet,
Earl of, 227-8
Catholicism, Roman, Catholics,
14, 34, 47, 50, 72, 74, 87, 110,
174, 178-9, 198-9, 214, 219, 227,
243, 274-5, 282-3, 302
Cawdrey, Daniel, 308
Censorship, 29-30, 116, 218-20,
225
Ceylon, 129
Chaloner family, the, 31
Chamberlain, John, 25
Chamberlen, Peter, 265-6, 276

Chambers, J.D., 190, 210
Charenton, 114
Charles I, King of England, 16, 23,
25, 27, 30, 32-4, 36, 38, 41, 44,
46, 49-50, 53, 61, 66, 70-1, 73,
77, 81, 85, 92, 96, 98-101, 104,
108-11, 114, 117, 134-5, 138,
166, 176-7, 193, 247-8, 261, 265,
267, 284, 308, 312, 314
Charles II, King of England, 5, 8,
16, 88, 104, 106, 114, 120, 135,
160, 170, 173, 226, 262, 268,
277, 287, 319
Charles X, King of Sweden, 73
Charlton, Kenneth, 9
Chartism, Chartists, 69, 116,
238-9, 244
Chaucer, Geoffrey, 11, 203
Chaytor, Miranda, 215
Chemical Physicians, the Society
of, 281
Cheshire, 214
Chidley, Mrs Katherine, 191
Child, Sir Josiah, 111
China, 4, 126, 139-41, 243, 281,
290
Christianson, P., 26
Church of England, the, 8, 50, 88,
106-7, 114, 168, 170, 216-17,
239, 287
Clarendon, Edward Hyde, Earl of,
68-9, 77, 98-9, 277
Clarendon Code, the, 169
Clark, Kenneth, Lord, 4
Clark, Peter, 23, 191, 212-15
Clarkson, Lawrence, 231, 264-5,
286
Clerk of the Parliament, the, 30
Clerkenwell, London, 237
Clubmen, 23
Cobbett, William, 68
Cobham, Surrey, 265
Cockburn, J.S., 66
Cokayne Project, the, 38, 102
Coke, Sir Edward, 34, 36, 39, 49,
102, 105, 226, 229
Colbert, Jean Baptiste, 134, 137
Colchester, 222

Cole, G.D.H., 14
Coleman St., London, 167
Collingwood, R.G., 16
Collinson, Patrick, 7, 15, 66, 114, 247
Colyton, 211, 216
Comenius, Jan Amos, 67, 203, 286, 291
Commonwealth, the English, 102, 109-10, 122, 171-3, 297
Condent, Captain Edward, 178
Connaught, 87
Contraception; see Birth control
Cook, John, 264, 314, 318
Cooper, Fenimore, 240
Copernicus, Nicholas, 280-1, 287-9
Cornwall, 150
Corresponding Society, the, 68, 115
Corrigan, Philip, 123
"County community", the, chapter 3 *passim*
Courteen, Sir William, 176-7
Cowell, Dr John, 30
Crabbe, George, 68
Cranbrook, Kent, 213
Cranfield, Lionel, Earl of Middlesex, 38-9
Cranmer, Thomas, Archbishop of Canterbury, 158
Croke, Sir George, 49
Cromwell, Oliver, Lord Protector, 16, 46, chapter 4 *passim*, 99, 101, 104, 109-11, 113-14, 117-18, 122, 138, 148, 166, 172-3, 203, 243, 259, 261, 264, 275, 287, 319
Cromwell, Richard, Lord Protector, 85
Cromwell, Richard, nephew of Thomas, 151
Cromwell, Thomas, Earl of Essex, chapter 7 *passim*
Culpeper, Nicholas, 276, 286, 290
Cumberland, 162

Darwin, Charles, 16, 240
Davenant, Sir William, 176-7, 251, 323-4

Davies, John, of Hereford, 304
Davies, Kathleen, 199
Davis, R.R., 111, 139
Davis, Captain, 178
Dean St., Soho, 236
Dee, John, 110, 276, 278, 281-2
Defoe, Daniel, 103, 117-18, chapter 8 *passim*, 203, 213, 241, 253
Dekker, Thomas, 127
Delamaine, Thomas, 175
Demographers, demography, 5-6, chapter 9 and postscript *passim*
Denne, Henry, 311
Derbyshire, 59-60, 211, 213
Dering, Sir Edward, 44, 99
Dering, Sir Edward the younger, 103
Descartes, Réné, 293, 298, 303; see *also* Cartesianism
Deutscher, Isaac, 4, 95
Devon, 23, 51, 117, 201
D'Ewes, Sir Simonds, 34, 42, 53, 254
Dickens, A.G., 15
Dickens, Charles, 242
Digby, Sir Kenelm, 279
Diggers, the, True Levellers, 15, 100, 115, 162, 180, 257, 262, 265-8, 286
Digges, Sir Dudley, 33, 308
Digges, Thomas, 281, 288
Dissenters, chapter 9 and post-script *passim*, 264
Divine Right, 50, 75, 115-16, 248
Divorce, 181, 189, 224-5
Dobb, Maurice, 113
Dollimore, Jonathan, 66
Donne, John, 201
Dorset, 63, 65
Drake, William, 36
Drogheda, 72, 87, 169
Drury, Robert, 178-9
Dryden, John, 282
Duffy, Maureen, 212
Dunkirk, 88, 111, 138
Dunster, Henry, 307
Dury, John, 67

Dutch, the; *see* Netherlands
Dutton, John, 77

Eachard, John, 115
Earle, P., 211
Earls Colne, Essex, 214
Easlea, Brian, 66, 298-9
East Anglia, 23
East India Company, 128, 139, 177, 186
Eccleshall, Robert, 66, 113
Eden, Sir F.M., 240
Edinburgh, 72
Edward I, King of England, 13
Edward IV, King of England, 145
Edwards, Thomas, 166-7, 254, 313
Egypt, 14, 278
Elections, parliamentary, 24-5, 28, 98, 112, 254, 261, 307
Eleutheria, 168
Eley, Geoff, 123
Eliot, Sir John, 26-8, 36, 50, 308
Eliot, T.S., 65, 145
Elizabeth I, Queen of England, 29, 31, 34-5, 45, 66, 87-8, 140, 201, 204, 208, 213, 216-17, 232, 248, 254, 277, 305
Elizabeth, Electress Palatine, Queen of Bohemia, 176
Ellesmere, Sir Thomas Egerton, Lord, Lord Chancellor, 33-4, 36, 40
Elton, Sir G.R., 6, 12, 29-30, 67, 148, 269
Engels, Friedrich, 97, 105, chapter 11 *passim*
Enlightenment, the European, 135, 162
Erbery, William, 286, 311
Eton College, 228
Essex, 36, 47-8, 51, 98, 191, 212-13, 228
Essex, Robert Devereux, Earl of, 312
Everitt, Alan, 7, 22-3, 136
Everlasting Gospel, the, 171
Excise, the, 37, 79, 120
Exeter, 221

Eyam, Derbyshire, 211
Eyre, William, 307-8

Fairfax, Sir Thomas, Lord, 78, 80, 89
Falkland, Lucius Cary, Viscount, 99
Familists, 99, 167, 283, 286
Farnell, J.E., 26-7, 45, 56-7
Fawkes, Guy, 49
Feake, Christopher, 263
Felton, John, 43-4
Fens, the, 46, 48, 76, 79, 101, 111, 259
Ferguson, Adam, 117, 241
Feudal tenures, abolition of, 45-6, 100, 117, 120, 133, 204, 243
Ficino, Marsilio, 282
Fielding, Henry, 118, 242
Fifth Monarchists, 83, 110, 167, 276, 318
Filmer, Sir Robert, 248, 310, 317
Finch, Sir John, 52
Finley, Sir Moses, 194
Firth, Sir C.H., 73
Fischer, Ernst, 5
Fisher, H.A.L., 148
Fisher, Samuel, 290-1
Flamsteed, John, 280
Flanders, 134
Flatman, Thomas, 279
Fleet marriages, 219
Fleetwood, Major-General Charles, 74, 90
Fletcher, John, 23, 117
Flinn, M.W., 190, 212
Fludd, Robert, 7, 278-9
Forests, 46, 98, 101, 259
Forman, Simon, 201, 276
Foster, E.R., 44
Fox, Charles James, 253
Fox, George, 15-16, 71, 74-5, 167, 176, 184
Fox, Henry, 253
Foxe, John, 49, 158
France, the French, 4, 8, 12, 14, 34, 37-9, 50, 73, 75, 88-9, 97, 101, 104, 106, 113, 118-19,

chapter 6 *passim*, 169, 173, 176, 179, 181, 190, 200, 213-14, 238-40, 242, 285-6
French, P.J., 278, 281
Freud, Sigmund, 194
Fronde, the, 8
Fuggers, the, 128

Gainsford, Captain Thomas, 41, 166
Galileo Galilei, 276, 278, 288-9
Gardiner, S.R., 22, 26, 35, 38-9, 53, 67, 69-70, 91, 172
Gardiner, Stephen, Bishop of Winchester, 158-60
Garfield, John, 229
Gaskell, Elizabeth, 69, 242
Geneva, 285
Genoa, 129, 138
Genovese, Eugene, 13
Gentry, the, chapter 3 *passim*, 98, 105, 112, 138, 204, 265-6
Germany, 38, 123, 132, 137, 180, 190, 236-8, 242, 244, 282, 285
Gilbert, William, 281
Gill, Eric, 5
Gladstone, W.E., 69, 240
Glanvill, Joseph, 276, 287
Glanville, John, 43-4, 61
Glass, D.V., 212
Glossop, Derbyshire, 213
Gloucestershire, 77, 98, 211
Godwin, William, 115
Goethe, Johann Wolfgang von, 241
Goldsmith, Oliver, 68
Gondomar, Diego Sarmiento de Acuña, Count of, 41
Goodman, Christopher, 313
Goodwin, Thomas, 304-6, 308-11, 318, 322
Gouge, William, 255, 304
Gough, Richard, 214
Grand Remonstrance, the, 44, 99
Great Contract, the, 36-7
Great Marlow, 108
Great Tey, Essex, 228
Greece, 4, 11

Greene, Robert, 198
Greene, the feltmaker, 167
Guatemala, 167
Guiana, 166, 173
Guizot, François, 242
Gunpowder Plot, 87
Gustavus Adolphus, King of Sweden, 38, 88

Haak, Theodore, 287
Habsburgs, the, 45, 87
Hair, P.E.M., 216
Hakewill, William, 44
Hakluyt, Richard, 45, 88, 110, 165-6
Hall, Francis, 149
Hall, John, 286
Hall, Thomas, 308
Hallam, Henry, 69
Haller, William, 70
Hammond, J.L. and Barbara, 14
Hammond, Colonel Robert, 82, 90
Hamond, Walter, 177
Hampden, John, 37, 49, 68, 166
Hampshire, 23, 230
Hampstead Heath, 236
Harbage, A., 5
Harley, Robert, later Earl of Oxford, 175
Harold, King of England, 13
Harrington, James, 52, 54, 65, 113, 115, 118, 162, 177, 204, 251-3, 259, 265, 317
Harris, G.L., 45
Harris, V.T., 5
Harrison, Major-General Thomas, 71, 75-6, 89
Harrison, William, 241
Hart, Henry, 311
Hartlib, Samuel, 67, 168, 259, 286-7
Harvard University, 307
Harvey, William, 280
Hassell-Smith, A., 37
Hastings, Battle of, 13
Hatton, Sir Christopher, Lord Chancellor, 44
Heidelberg, 300

Heinemann, Margot, 66
Helmont, John Baptist van, 277, 287
Henry VIII, King of England, 88, chapter 7 *passim*, 248
Henry of Navarre, Henry IV, King of France, 12
Henry, Prince of Wales, 166
Herbert family, the, 31
Hermes Trismegistus, Hermeticists, 278-82, 285-6, 290-1, 299
Hertford, Edward Seymour, first Earl of, later Duke of Somerset, 147, 154
Hertford, Edward Seymour, second Earl of, 37
Hewitt, Robert, 230
Hexter, J.H., 22, 26, 56, 65-7
Hey, D.G., 215
Hibbard, Caroline, 46, 66
Hicks, Sir John, 4
Hieron, Samuel, 314
High Commission, Court of, 50-1, 99, 104, 117
Highland, Samuel, 167
Hills, Thomas, 283
Hilton, Rodney, 15
Hirst, Derek, 22, 24-8, 31, 35, 39, 45-6, 49, 54, 107, 191, 261, 307
Hitler, Adolf, 40, 52, 69
Hobbes, Thomas, 66, 115-6, 135, 241, 251, 284, 287-8, 290, 298, 315, 317-19, 323-5
Hobsbawm, Eric, 4, 15, 139, 179-80
Hogarth, William, 117
Holinshed, Raphael, 13
Holland; *see* Netherlands, the
Holles, Sir John, 36
Hollingsworth, T.H., 211, 216
Holmby House, 73
Holmes, Clive, 22-3
Homosexuality, male, chapter 10 *passim*
Hood, Robin, 175; *see also* Robin Hood Society, the
Hooke, Robert, 282
Hooker, Richard, 255, 301-2
Hooker, Thomas, 305

Horncastle Soke, 305
Hoskins, W.G., 24, 35
Hotham, Charles, 168
Household economy, the, 195-6, 199-200, 256-7, 268-9
Hoyle, John, 231
Hudson, Henry, 283
Hughes, Ann, 23, 48, 51, 116
Hughes, Lewis, 168
Huguenots, the, 89, 114, 133, 169
Hume, David, 68, 116, 118, 242
Hungary, 190
Hunt, Robert, 177
Hunt, William, 15, 46-7, 50-1, 98, 114, 212
Huntingdon, 76, 275
Huntingdonshire, 59
Hunton, Philip, 317
Hussee, John, chapter 7 *passim*
Hyde, Sir Edward; *see* Clarendon, Earl of
Hyde Park, 236
Hyndman, H.M., 244

Iconoclasm, 7
Illegitimacy, chapter 9 and postscript *passim*, 228
Independents, 78, 81-2, 86, 164, 262-4
India, 129, 138, 243, 290
Indians (American), 88, 130, 290
Indonesia, 129
Infanticide, 198, 203, 207-8, 213, 218, 222
Ingram, Martin, 216-17
Instrument of Government, the, 84
International Working Men's Association, the, 239, 241
Ireland, the Irish, 45, 72, 74, 87-8, 98, 110, 169, 172, 180, 200, 242-3
Ireton, Commissary-General Henry, 81, 89, 96, 250, 315
Islam, 129-30, 290
Italy, Italians, 118, 129, 134-5, 190, 229, 282

Jackson, Captain William, 166

Jacob, J.R., 66, 162, 297-8
Jacob, M.C., 66, 162, 297-8
Jacobins, the, 86, 113
Jamaica, 111, chapter 8 *passim*
James I, King of England, 30, 34, 38, 49, 51, 53, 105, 109, 226, 232-3, 275, 307, 312, 318
James II, King of England, 104, 106, 114, 138
Jansenism, 286
Japan, 123, 127
Jesuits, 47
Jews, 167, 172, 311
Johnson, Captain Charles, 181, 186-7
Johnson, Samuel, 231
Jones, Ernest, 238
Jones, J.R., 105
Jones, R.E., 212
Jonson, Ben, 277
Jordan, W.K., 9
Josselin, Ralph, 204
Joyce, Cornet George, 73, 80
Judson, M.A., 29, 53
Justices of the Peace (J.Ps.), 24, 32, 36-7, 39, 47-51, 84, 138, 193, 202, 217, 258

Kennedy, Mark, 48
Kennington Common, London, 238
Kent, 23, 79, 212-13
Kepler, Johann, 276-8, 288
Keynes, John Maynard, Lord, 5, 297
Kirk of Scotland, General Assembly of the, 72
Kishlansky, M., 26
Knafla, Louis, 66
Koran, the, 290
Kuhn, T.S., 4

Labour Party, the British, 244
Ladurie, Emmanuel Leroy, 100
Lambert, Major-General John, 71, 89, 277
Lancashire, 23, 191, 200, 214

La Rochelle, 50, 163, 285
Laslett, Peter, 4, 17, 23-4, 139, chapter 9 and postscript *passim*, 275
Latimer, Hugh, Bishop of Worcester, 149
Latitudinarians, 114, 178, 287
Laud, William, Archbishop of Canterbury, Laudians, 45, 49-51, 53-4, 84, 88, 92, 98, 103, 114, 117, 167-8, 227, 261-2, 275, 282
Law, the common, lawyers, law reform, 37, 63, 105-7, 124, 140, 290
Leader, George, 167
Leader, Richard, 167
Leavis, F.R., 65
Lee, Nathaniel, 230
Leeds, 221
Leeward Islands, 167-8, 170
Leicester, Robert Dudley, Earl of, 277
Lenin, V.I., 86, 91, 95, 97, 112, 140
Levellers, 15, 72-3, 76, 81-3, 86, 88, 99-102, 115-16, 162, 164, 166, 180-1, 197, 233, 248, 250, 253, 255, 257, 259, 261-3, 266-8, 281, 286, 288, 301, 309, 315-17
Lever, Charles, 242
Levine, David, 46-7, 50-1, 212, 215
Lewis, C.S., 288
Libertalia, chapter 8 *passim*
Liebknecht, Wilhelm, 236-7
Lilburne, John, 71, 74, 76, 82, 91, 166, 257, 267, 277
Lilburne, Robert, Governor of the Bahamas, 174
Lilly, William, 286
Lincoln's Inn, 146, 148, 152
Lindsay, Jack, 4
Lisbon, 129
Lisle, Arthur Plantagenet, Lord, chapter 7 *passim*
Lisle, Honor Grenville, formerly Bassett, Lady, chapter 7 *passim*
Littleton, Edward, 33
Liverpool, 169

Locke, John, 75, 114, 116, 135,
164, 195, 253, 276, 278, 315
Lollards, 99, 216, 224
London, 41, 51, 56, 76-8, 81,
98-100, 110-11, 127, 129-33, 140,
146, 155-7, 162, 166, 168, 172,
191, 197, 201, 212-13, 219, 221,
224, 231, 236-7, 250, 264, 267-8,
277, 281, 285, 305
Londonderry, 110
Long Acre, London, 237
Lords, House of, 25-6, 28, 42-3,
53, 82, 85, 114, 149, 262
Louis XIV, King of France, 6, 88,
104, 127, 131, 133
Love, 195-6, 203, 209, 220
Luddism, Luddites, 210
Ludlow, Edmund, 68, 74, 162
Luther, Martin, 163, 300
Lyly, John, 150
Lyme Regis, 211
Lyons, 134

Macaulay, Mrs Catherine, 68, 115
Macaulay, Thomas Babington,
Lord, 69, 240
MacCaffrey, Wallace, 31, 66
Machiavelli, Niccolo, Machiavel-
lian, 77, 248
Madagascar, chapter 8 *passim*
Madrid, 109
Magdalen Hall, Oxford, 167
Magic, 6-8, 13-14, 116, chapter 13
and postscript *passim*
Mainwaring, Roger, later Bishop
of St. David's, 50, 53, 315
Major-Generals, the, 71, 84
Makyn, Bathsua, 258
Malcolm, Joyce, 66
Malthus, T.R., 240-1
Manchester, 78, 236
Manchester, Edward Montagu,
Earl of, 79
Mandeville, Bernard de, 201-2,
241, 260
Manning, Brian, 15, 23-4, 42, 46,
99, 101, 107

Marlowe, Christopher, 66, 227,
230-1, 278
Marriage, chapter 9 and postscript
passim, 285
Marryat, Captain Frederick, 242
Marseilles, 149
Marshall, William, 248, 251
Marsiglio of Padua, 248, 251
Marston Moor, Battle of, 79
Marten, George, 167, 183
Marten, Henry, son of
the above, 33, 167, 183
Marten, Sir Henry, 43-4, 61
Marvell, Andrew, 90, 115, 118,
168, 289, 295
Marx, Karl, Marxists, 4-5, 24, 65,
chapter 5 *passim*, 127-8, 131,
chapter 11 *passim*, 302
Mary I, Queen of England, 13, 198
Mason, Robert, 308
Massachusetts, Massachusetts Bay
Company, 45, 167, 285
Mather, Increase, 284
Mayas, the, 126
Mechanic preachers, 8, 106, 262
Mechanical philosophy, the, 8,
chapter 13 and postscript *passim*
Mediterranean Sea, the, 51, 109,
129, 138, 148
Mercer, Eric, 4
Merchant, Carolyn, 15-16, 46, 66,
298-9
Merriman, R.W., 148
Mersenne, Marin, 285
Meyer, Ernst, 4-5
Microscope, the, 280, 289
Middleton, Thomas, 66
Militia, the, 37, 40, 52, 138, 258-9,
262
Militia Ordinance, the, 71, 99
Mill, J.S., 241
Millenarianism, 115, 276
Miller, Perry, 303, 310
Milton, John, 6, 68, 90, 92, 99,
115-16, 162-4, 179, 201-2, 218,
263, 278, 282, 284, 288, 291,
303-4, 311, 313-15, 317-18
Milward, R.J., 214

Misselden, Edward, 241
Misson, Captain, 163-4, 173, 178, 180
Mitchell, Sir Francis, 48
Modyford, Sir Thomas, 173
"Molly houses", 230-2
Mompesson, Sir Giles, 48
Monck, Major-General George, later Duke of Albemarle, 85, 92, 103, 160, 173, 175, 249
Monmouth, James Scott, Duke of, Monmouth's rebellion, 106, 169, 172, 174, 178, 211
Monopolies, 39, 102, 111
Montagu, Richard, later Bishop of Chichester, 50, 322
Montaigne, Michel de, 257
Montespan, Mme de, 127
Montserrat, 169
Moore, Adam, 259
Moore, D.C., 210
Moorfields, London, 233
More, Sir Thomas, 241
Morgan, Edward, 260
Morgan, Sir Henry, 173-5
Morland, Sir Samuel, 305
Morrice, Roger, 264
Morrill, John, 22-3, 26, 46-7, 65, 117, 260-1
Morris, William, 244
Morton, Thomas, Bishop of Coventry and Lichfield, 177
Mozambique, 127
Mun, Thomas, 45, 241
Muggleton, Lodowick, Muggletonians, the, 75, 167, 176
Myddle, 214

Namier, Sir Lewis, the Namier method, 24, 28
Napier, John, of Merchiston, 276
Napoleon I, Emperor of the French, 13, 86, 113, 136
Naseby, Battle of, 79, 90
Nashe, Thomas, 150
Navigation Act, the, of 1651, 45, 89, 102, 104, 109, 111, 117, 137, 139, 166, 171-2

Navy, the, 88, 138
Nayler, James, 74, 167
Neale, Sir John, 21
Nedham, Marchamont, 251
Needham, Joseph, 4
Nef, J.U., 70
Neile, Richard, Archbishop of York, 30, 53
Netherlands, the United Provinces, Holland, the Dutch, 36, 38, 75, 89, 97, 102, 104, 109-10, 116, 121, chapter 6 *passim*, 168, 171, 174, 176, 190, 201, 219, 238, 256, 284
Nevile family, the, 31
Neville, Henry, 177
Nevis, 167, 169-70
New Draperies, the, 51, 109
New England, 45, 96, 168, 200, 234, 255, 285, 314-15
New York, 129
Newbury, 286, 321
Newcastle, 214
Newcome, Henry, 172
Newmarket, 287
Newton, Sir Isaac, Newtonianism, 3, 114, 116, 135, 276-8, 287, 291-2, 297-9
Nippel, W., 36
Noell, Martin, 89
Nonconformists; *see* Dissenters
Norbrook, David, 66
Norfolk, Thomas Howard, Duke of, 158-60
Normans, the, Norman Conquest, the, Norman Yoke, the, 13, 316, 323
North, Dudley, 241
North, Captain, 178
North, Council in the, 215
Norwood, Richard, 167-8
Norwood, Robert, 251
Notestein, Wallace, 22, 26, 62, 64, 67
Nottingham, 221
Nottinghamshire, 79
Noy, Edward, 32

O'Day, Rosemary, 191
Oldenburg, Henry, 280, 289
Orange, House of, the, 136
Orwell, George, 65
Orwell, Cambridgeshire, 211
Other House, the, 85
Ottoman Empire; *see* Turkey
Overton, Richard, 233, 257, 264, 281
Owen, John, 304
Oxenbridge, John, 167-8
Oxford University, 4, 6, 64, 240, 286

Page, Damaris, 231
Paine, Thomas, 91, 115
Palatinate, the, 35
Palatine, Frederick, Elector, and King of Bohemia, 285
Palliser, D.M., 210
Panama, 173
Paracelsus, Theophrastus, Para-celsans, 277, 280, 285-7, 297
Paris, 114, 132, 134, 146, 152
Paris, Commune of, 240
Parish élites, 46-7, 50-1, 258-9, 261-2
Parish registers, chapter 9 and postscript *passim*, 234
Parker, Henry, 317
Parker, Matthew, Archbishop of Canterbury, 254
Parliament, chapter 3 and post-script *passim*
Parliament of 1614, the, 30
Parliament of 1621, the, 31-2
Parliament of 1628, the, 30
Parliament, the Short, 1640, 177
Parliament, the Long, 1640, 27, 49, 52, 73, 95-6, 99, 102, 107-8, 115-16, 177, 193, 247-8, 318-19
Parliament, the Rump, 82-3, 231, 248
Parliament, Barebone's, 73, 83, 217
Parliament of 1654, the, 259
Parliament of 1656, the, 74
Parliament of 1659, the, 249
Parrington, Vernon, 14

Pascal, Blaise, 287-9
Paul, R.S., 70, 87
Paul, St., 302
Pembroke, William Herbert, Earl of, 27-8
Pennington, Donald, 193, 284
Penruddock's rising, 1655, 169
Penry, John, 41
Pepys, Samuel, 68, 103, 127, 212
Perkin, H.J., 100-101
Perkins, William, 255, 259, 284, chapter 14 *passim*
Perrot, John, 167, 176
Peter, Hugh, 83, 166, 264
Peterhouse, Cambridge, 168
Petition and Advice, the, 85
Petition of Right, the, 32, 42-3, 53, 61
Petty, Maximilian, 250
Petty, Sir William, 110, 116, 240-1, 260, 286
Phelips, Sir Robert, 30, 33, 49, 315
Philip II, King of Spain, 132
Philips, Edward, 162, 202
Philips, John, 162, 202
Physicians, College of, 286-7
Pico della Mirandola, 282
Pilgrim Fathers, the, 12, 255
Pinchbeck, Ivy, 216
Piracy, pirates, 148, chapter 8 *passim*
Place, Francis, 203
Plague, 212, 290
Plantin, James, 178
Plattes, Gabriel, 286
Pocock, J.G.A., 117
Poland, 73
Pole, Reginald, Cardinal, 159-60
Polygamy, 178, 201, 218
Pontefract, 73
Ponting, Clive, 13
Poor, the, chapter 12 *passim*
Poor law, the, 258-9
Pope, Alexander, 117
Popley, William, 153
Portugal, 131-2, 139, 177
Poulett, John, Lord, 49
Poulton, Diana, 4

Prague, 282
Presbyterians, Presbyterianism, 75, 78, 83, 193, 254-6, 264, 312
Prest, W.R., 5, 59, 66
Preston, John, 303-4, 307
Pride's Purge, 73, 83, 248
Prince, Thomas, Leveller, 88
Prince, Thomas, American, 255
Privy Council, the, 25-6, 33, 37, 102, 262
Proctor, Sir Stephen, 39
Protestantism, protestants, 7, 47, 49, 179, 274, 283-4, chapter 14 *passim*
Providence Island, Providence Island Company, the, 62, 88, 110, 164, 166, 173, 177
Prynne, William, 68
Puckrein, Gary, 176
Puritanism, Puritans, 5, 7, 12, 14, 34, 47-8, 51, 69-70, 73, 76, 89-90, 92, 98, 113-14, 161, 168, 173, 193-4, 199, 202, 207, 249, 254-5, 259, 261-2, 268, 282, 285, 287, chapter 14 *passim*
Putney Debates, the, 75, 81, 174, 249-50, 266, 315
Pym, John, 27-8, 30, 34, 36-7, 41, 50, 68, 110, 166

Quaife, G.R., 214
Quakers, 15-16, 90, 100, 115, 167-8, 170-2, 176, 212, 227, 262, 268, 285, 310
Quincey, Thomas de, 241

Rainborough, Colonel Thomas, 250
Rainborough, Major William, 277
Ralegh, Sir Walter, 30, 34, 41, 45, 88, 166, 173, 278
Randall, Giles, 59
Ranters, 15, 100, 162, 167, 176, 178, 187, 201-2, 218, 231, 257, 262, 264, 286
Rattansi, P.M., 7
Rayner, Robert, 283

Razzell, P.E., 192, 214
Read, Mary, 165
Reform Bill of 1832, the, 84
Reformation, the protestant, 49, 87, 94, 140, 195, 199, 215-16, 240, 275, 283-4, 302
Reformation of Manners, Society for the, 231
Rembrandt, Harmensz van Rijn, 6
Restoration of 1660, the, 8, 85, 90, 114, 161, 202, 204, 287
"Revisionists", chapter 3 and postscript *passim*
Revolution, the American, 14-16, 115, 139
Revolution, the Chinese, 14
Revolution, the Commercial, 111, 139
Revolution, the English, 12, 14-15, Part II *passim*, 180, 231, 242-3, 263, 266, 293, 297, 310, 316
Revolution, the French, 14, 25-6, 69, 77, 97, 107, 112, 121, 200, 242, 261
Revolution, the Industrial, 4, 102, 104, 107, 111, 126, 129-31, 133, 139-40, 199, 202, 268, 290
Revolution, the Russian, 14, 25-6, 112, 121
Ricardo, David, 240
Rich family, the, 110
Rich, Sir Nathaniel, 33, 36
Rich, Colonel Nathaniel, 250
Rich, Richard, Lord, 146
Rich, Robert, 167, 176
Richard II, King of England, 13
Richardson, R.C., 191
Richardson, Samuel, 118, 201
Richardson, W.C., 148
Rightson, William, 167
Roberts, Captain, 164-5
Roberts, S.K., 23, 51, 117
Robespierre, Maximilien, 86, 91
Robin Hood Society, 162, 180
Rochester, John Wilmot, Earl of, 227
Roe, Sir Thomas, 176
Rogers, John, Puritan minister, 35

Rogers, John, Fifth Monarchist, 74

Rogers, J.E. Thorold, 240

Rogers, Woodes, 174

Rome, Roman Empire, 11, 17, 89, 140, 159, 201

Rosicrucians, the, 285

Rous, John, 98

Rousseau, Jean Jacques, 264

Rowse, A.L., 8-9

Royal Society, the, 8, 103, 108, 116, 168, 277, 279-80, 287, 289, 293

Rubens, Peter Paul, 6

Rubicon, the, 16-17

Rude, George, 15

Rudolf II, Holy Roman Emperor, 276

Ruff, G.M., 5

Rumbold, William, 162

Rupert, Prince, 176

Russell, Conrad, chapter 3 *passim*

Russia, 51, 95, 130, 139-40, 190

Rye House Plot, 184

Sabbatarianism, 47-8, 114-15, 163, 181, 236-7, 262

Sadler, Ralph, 152-3,

St. Christopher, 169-70, 184

St. John, 230

Saint-Malo, 140

St. Olave's parish, London, 212

Salisbury, Margaret Pole, Countess of, 159

Salisbury, 212

Sallee, 51

Salmon, Joseph, 167

Samson, 313-14

Sandys, Sir Edwin, 27, 30, 32, 110

Savile, Sir John, 33

Sayer, Derek, 123

Schofield, R.S., 210

Science, history of, 3-4, 6, 8, chapter 13 and postscript *passim*

Scotland, the Scots, 13, 39, 52, 54, 72, 75, 77-8, 98-9, 101, 109, 133-4, 162, 169, 180, 219, 275-6, 312

Scott, Thomas, Puritan pamphleteer, 166, 307

Scott, Thomas, regicide, 264

Scott, Sir Walter, 69, 242

Scott, William, 167

Scrooby, Nottinghamshire, 12

Sedgwick, Obadiah, 308

Sedgwick, William, 262-3, 313

Seekers, 286

Selden, John, 26-7, 34, 54, 277

Self-Denying Ordinance, the, 71, 79-80, 99

Serbia, 190

Settlement Act of 1662, the, 107, 259

Seymour, Sir Francis, 39

Seymour, Jane, Queen of England, 147, 152, 154, 157

Shakespeare, William, 7, 11, 13, 65-6, 150, 203, 241, 278, 285

Sharp, Buchanan, 24

Sharpe, J.A., 66

Shaxton, Nicholas, Bishop of Salisbury, 149

Shelley, P.B., 68, 116, 242, 264

Shepard, Thomas, 213

Shepherd, Simon, 66

Sherland, Christopher, 42

Ship Money, 22, 37, 39, 49, 59-60, 109, 166

Shropshire, 212

Sibbes, Richard, 260, 302-4

Sibthorpe, Robert, 50

Sidney family, the, 31

Sidney, Algernon, 162, 253

Sidney, Sir Henry, 213

Simon, Joan, 9

Sixtus V, Pope, 276

Skinner, Quentin, 66

Skipp, Victor, 211

Slack, Paul, 212

Slavery, slaves, 130, 163, 169-75, 260

Smith, Adam, 5, 12, 103, 118, 240-1

Smith, Preserved, 4

Smith, Sir Thomas, 249-50

Smyth, Leonard, 154

Socinians, 314

Sombart, Werner, 131

Somerset, 23, 33, 48-9, 63, 65

Southwark, 141

Spain, Spaniards, 36, 38-9, 41, 49, 87-9, 97, 102, 110, 118, 129, 132, 134-5, 165-6, 169, 173-5, 240

Spence, Thomas, 115

Spenser, John, 305

Spinoza, Benedict, 291

Spittlehouse, John, 276

Sports, Book of, the, 50, 262

Sprat, Thomas, 287, 298

Spufford, Margaret, 15, 66, 191, 211, 215

Stafford, 78

Staffordshire, 78-9, 99

Stalin, J.V., 86

Star Chamber, 84, 99, 117

Staves, Susan, 121

Steele, Sir Richard, 277

Sterry, Peter, 308

Stone, Lawrence, 8-9, 67, 70, 105, 135, chapter 9 and postscript *passim*, 230-1, 242, 257

Stoughton, William, 255-6

Strict Settlement, the, 105, 204, 209

Stubbe, Henry, 252-3

Suckling, Sir John, 176

Suffolk, 98

Sully, Maximilien de Béthune, Duke of, 134

Surinam, 167-8

Surrey, 265, 268

Sussex, 23

Sutcliffe, Matthew, 254

Sweden, Swedes, 73, 301

Swift, Jonathan, 242, 260

Swinburne, Henry, 216

Tangier, 109

Taunton, 211

Tawney, R.H., 10, 14, 22, 24, 26, 38, 44, 65, 67, 70

Taxation, 34-41, 50-3, 77, 79, 85

Taylor, John, 316

Telescope, the, 289, 291

Temple, the Inner, 108

Temple, Sir William, 284

Terling, Essex, 212

Tetbury, Gloucestershire, 211, 216

Tew, Captain Thomas, 178

Thackeray, W.M., 242

Thames, the river, 141

Thaxted, Essex, 212-13

Thirsk, Joan, 7, 15, 23, 35, 46, 136, 188

Thirty-Nine Articles, the, 239

Thirty Years War, the, 49

Thomas, Dalby, 260

Thomas, Keith, 6-7, 13, 15, 191, 198, 274, 277, 281, 283, 285-6, 290, 293-4

Thomas, P.W., 8

Thompson, E.A., 4

Thompson, E.P., 4, 13, 15, 105, 210

Thompson, Maurice, 166

Thomson, George, 4

Thorpe, Serjeant, 251

Thurloe, John, 72, 89, 92, 305

Thucydides, 315

Tithes, 106, 115, 262

Toland, John, 162

Toleration, religious, 78, 98-9

Tories, 68, 106, 264

Tourneur, Cyril, 66

Toynbee, Arnold, 4, 131

Traherne, Thomas, 203

Trevelyan, G.M., 26, 123

Trevor-Roper, H.R., Lord Dacre, 67, 70, 83, 105

Trilling, Lionel, 8

Trinidad, 167

Trotsky, L.D., 86, 264

Tuck, Richard, 66

Tuke, Thomas, 305

Turkey, Turks, the Ottoman Empire, 127, 229, 262

Tyndale, William, 300, 302

Tyrell, James, 253

Udall, Nicholas, 228

Underdown, David, 23, 46, 65

U.S.S.R., 4, 243, 264

U.S.A., 4, 11, 13-14, 16, 132, 137, 238-9, 243
Urban VIII, Pope, 276
Ursinus, Zacharias, 300
Ussher, James, Archbishop of Armagh, 254
Uxbridge, Treaty of, 52

Vagabonds, vagrants, 200-1, 212, 217, 253, 255, 257-9
Valencia, 149
Vallière, Mlle de la, 127
Van Dyck, Sir Anthony, 5-6, 117, 176
Vane, Sir Henry, 27, 75-6, 89
Vaudois, the, 73
Vaughan, the Rev. Henry, 185
Veall, Donald, 193
Venables, General Herbert, 172-3
Venice, Venetian Ambassador, 25, 109, 125, 129, 133, 229
Verrio, Antonio, 5
Victoria, Queen of England, 14, 69, 124, 194, 237
Vindiciae Contra Tyrannos, the, 301
Virgil, 315
Voltaire, François-Marie Arouet, 125, 253

Waldegrave, Powle, 186
Wales, the Welsh, 149, 200, 215
Wales, Council in the Marches of, 215
Walker, D.P., 7
Wallenstein, Albrecht von, 277
Waller, Edmund, 86, 168
Waller, Sir William, 80
Wallington, Nehemiah, 203
Walsall, 78
Walter, J.D., 117
Walwyn, William, 88, 257
Warburg and Courtauld Institute, the, 7
Ward, Seth, later Bishop of Salisbury, 280
Wards, Court of, 100, 117, 204
Wariston, Johnston of, 307

Warwick, Robert Rich, Earl of, 27-8, 88
Warwickshire, 23, 48, 51, 212
Washington, George, President of the United States, 91
Waterford and Lismore, Bishop of, 227
Waterloo, Battle of, 13
Weber, Max, 131
Webster, Charles, 4, 7, 66, 274, 297
Webster, John, 280, 286
Welsers, the, 128
Wentworth, Sir Thomas, Earl of Strafford, 24, 27, 32-3, 37, 44, 84, 98, 117
Western Design, Cromwell's, 166, 171, 173
West Indies, the, 45, 87, 130, chapter 8 *passim*, 216
Westminster, 77-8, 80
Westminster Assembly of Divines, the, 166, 304
Weston, Lancashire, 191
Wexford, 87
Whigs, 239, 243, 253, 293
White, John, 227
White, Captain, 115
Whitehall, 12, 84
Whitelocke, Bulstrode, 73, 99, 108, 277, 301
Wife-sale, 198, 218
Wildman, John, 75, 175, 281-2
Wilkes, Wilkesites, the, 115
Wilkins, John, later Bishop of Chester, 280, 282, 287-8
William I, King of England (the Conqueror), 124
William III, King of England, 68, 117, 138, 175, 293
William the Silent, Prince of Orange, 91
Williams, Gwyn, 180
Willingham, Cambridgeshire, 211
Willoughby, Francis, Lord, of Parham, Governor of Barbados, 170
Wilson, Charles, 139

Wilson, D. A., 5
Wiltshire, 63, 65, 214, 307
Wimbledon, 211, 214
Windsor Castle, 5
Winslow, Edward, 171
Winstanley, Gerrard, 96, 164, 203-4, 257, 259, 265-8, 286, 291, 306, 311-12, 317
Winthrop, Henry, 169
Winthrop, John, father of the above, 169, 315
Witchcraft, witches, 11, 116, chapter 13 *passim*
Wither, George, 118, 168, 312
Women, chapter 9 and postscript *passim*, 256, 258, 268
Woodbridge, Benjamin, 321
Woolrych, Austin, 22
Wordsworth, William, 68, 116
Worsley, Benjamin, 110

Wray, Sir John, 308
Wright, L.B., 6, 14, 67, 186
Wrightson, Keith, 15, 46-7, 50-1, 212-15
Wrigley, E.A., 210
Wriothesley, Henry, later Earl of Southampton, 147, 151
Wyatt, George, 305

Yates, Dame Frances, 7, 274, 285
Yeomen, 46-7, 77, 260-1, 264
York, 201, 251
Yorkshire, 24, 33, 68-9, 78, 80, 99, 165, 249
Young, Alfred, 13
Young, Arthur, 203, 241
Young, J.Z., 292

Zurich, 216